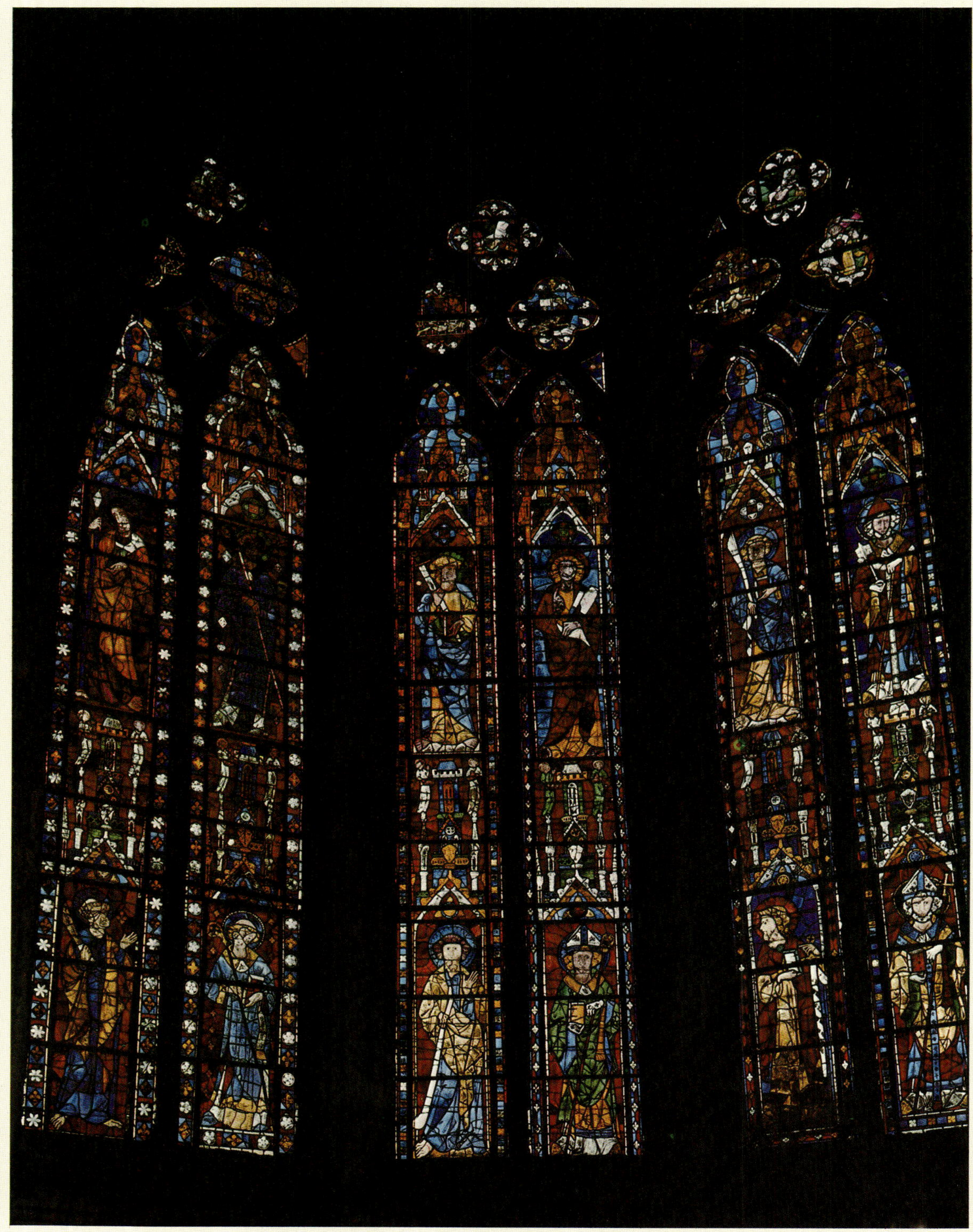

PLATE I Hemicycle. *(Edouard Fièvet)*

The STAINED GLASS *of Saint-Père de Chartres*

By MEREDITH PARSONS LILLICH

WESLEYAN UNIVERSITY PRESS

Middletown, Connecticut

Publication of this book has been aided by a grant from
The Millard Meiss Publication Fund of the College Art Association of America.

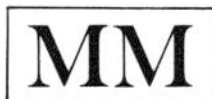

The publisher also gratefully acknowledges the support of the publication of this book by Syracuse University and the Andrew W. Mellon Foundation.

Library of Congress Cataloging in Publication Data

Lillich, Meredith P 1932–
The stained glass of Saint-Père de Chartres.

Bibliography: p.
Includes index.
1. Glass painting and staining, Gothic—France—Chartres. 2. Glass painting and staining, French—France—Chartres. 3. Chartres, France, Saint Pierre (Church) I. Title.
NK5349.C5L54 748.5′945′1 77–13926
ISBN 0–8195–5023–X

Manufactured in the United States of America
First Edition

For Jean Lafond (1888–1975)

Contents

List of Figures & Plates

Bay numbers of the Saint-Père windows are shown on the fold-out plan at the end of this volume. They conform to the bay numbers of the Archives photographiques, as do those of all other monuments discussed except Chartres Cathedral. For Chartres Cathedral windows, the numbering of the Delaporte monograph has been followed.

FIGURES

COLOR PLATES

MONOCHROME PLATES

THE STAINED GLASS OF SAINT-PÈRE DE CHARTRES

Introduction

AFTER Chartres, what? After the windows of Chartres, and of Bourges, Sens, and Notre-Dame — the beautiful color-saturated glass of the years around 1200, an aesthetic culminating in a final burst of glory at the Sainte-Chapelle — what took place? This question has preoccupied scholars during the last half-century, for, from the mid-twelfth century the activity of the stained glass workshops of Gothic France was scarcely interrupted for a span of two hundred years. Through troubled times — the Angevin struggle, the Tunisian crusade, the Flemish wars of Philippe-le-Bel — the manufacture of the *vitrearum novarum praeclara varietas* beloved by Abbot Suger was suspended only by the plague of 1348. Indeed, after a quarter-century hiatus, beautiful windows again were produced in quantity before 1400. It is the pre-plague period, however, which concerns us here. Perhaps unfairly, the landscape is dominated by such towering achievements as Chartres Cathedral and the Sainte-Chapelle. Once scholars began to sense the inadequacy of the first theories of the development and decadence of the art based almost exclusively on these monuments, some interesting regional research began to emerge. Lafond thoroughly charted his native Normandy for us, Jane Hayward has investigated early Angevin work, Grodecki's writings have touched here, there, and everywhere. Work is now underway and will continue for many years on the little-publicized regional schools, for the French volumes of the *Corpus Vitrearum Medii Aevi*.

I would like to contribute to these scholarly projects the barest outline of a school of glass painting heretofore vaguely suggested by Grodecki, a "school of the West."[1] This school was active for perhaps a century (ca. 1225–1325) in an area generally southwest of Paris. Its major remaining monument is Saint-Père de Chartres. The stained glass of the abbey church of Saint-Père, which has not heretofore been critically examined, will be the subject of the body of this study. In the fifth chapter the silhouette of the Western school will be briefly sketched, relating Saint-Père in more detail to other recognizable monuments of the school. Most of these monuments are ripe for research. Evron is an unknown at the present time; Sées was barely mapped in a brilliant exploratory essay by Lafond; recently published documentation dictates a new analysis of Vendôme; Le Mans was published in the 1860's; the basic works on Tours, not so difficult a puzzle as most of the other monuments, were products of interested amateurs and are incomplete and largely descriptive. Scholarly study and evaluation of other provincial schools is also needed. Burgundy is the example which leaps to mind. There also is no work of detail and substance on the north of France in the thirteenth century, and nothing up to date on the Lyonnais. It is to be hoped that this monograph on Saint-Père and the brief sketch of Western achievements will aid in the eventual illumination of a period of stained glass rich and varied beyond expectation.[2]

What is the particular importance of the stained glass ensemble of Saint-Père? Why should it be the subject of monographic study? Justification for such research is not difficult to provide. The clerestory windows of Saint-Père comprise an ensemble, a full set — in itself something rare. Not a single window is missing without trace. The glass is, moreover, in good condition, not marred by drastic restoration. Beyond the simple fact of its rarity, such a set provides a unique opportunity for the study of the principles of design and arrangement of a total glazing from a period from which very few such opportunities remain. Moreover, the relatively short glazing campaign gives the principles more validity. They can be assumed to represent the method of near contemporaries.

Not only is the Saint-Père ensemble interesting in itself; it also represents a pivotal period in the history of glassmaking as well as the best work of a regional school hitherto unexplored. The period of the last quarter of the thirteenth century was a turbulent one in the development of the stained glass medium. Problems of design, of color, even of the actual manufacture of glass, were reworked during the decades in question, the ultimate solutions of which stood as standard formulae for window-making for the next century and more. *"Rien ne ressemble moins à un vitrail du XIIIe siècle qu'un vitrail du XIVe,"* says Emile Mâle.[3] When such a turning point occurs in an art form, the moment of transition always bears examination. What formulae were tested and discarded? Why did a particular color harmony win popularity while others fell into disuse? Were economic pressures or the discovery of new technical methods, such as silver stain, the overriding instigators of change, or did they merely intensify a tendency already present? The vast series of windows at Saint-Père is bursting with answers to such queries.

The only solid work specifically dealing with the transitional period is Jean-Jacques Gruber's pioneer essay *"Quelques aspects de l'art et de la technique du vitrail en France (Dernier tiers du XIIIe siècle, premier tiers du XIVe).*[4] Discussions of the silver stain technique rarely refer to the artistic climate which heralded its invention. The soaring canopies of the fourteenth century and the "band window" design have received more attention, but the transitional experiments are not so well known. Grisaille of the transitional period, and for that matter, inscription style, are still uncharted in print. A monograph on an important monument like Saint-Père should mine considerable data for such investigations. Why should one study Saint-Père? The subject is not only rich in historical and stylistic materials, the exemplar of an interesting regional style; it is also a beautiful work of art.

NOTES

1. Grodecki's phrase is not to be confused with the twelfth-century school of Aquitaine (Anjou-Poitou) first proposed by Lucien Magne, *Décor du verre* (Paris, 1913), p. 122ff.

2. Sections of this monograph have been presented previously at the Kalamazoo Sixth Conference on Medieval Studies, 1971; and in the *Bulletin des Sociétés archéologiques d'Eure-et-Loir,* 1971 and 1972.

3. Emile Mâle, "La peinture sur verre en France," in André Michel, *Histoire de l'art,* II (Paris, 1906), p. 392.

4. Université de Paris, Faculté des lettres, *Travaux des étudiants du Groupe d'Histoire de l'art* (Paris, 1927–1928), pp. 71–94 (available in this country at Yale). See also several recent essays written in conjunction with multi-media exhibitions, cited in my Selected Bibliography (Verdier, Gillerman).

{ CHAPTER I }

History and Documentation

THE BUILDING

THE church of Saint Pierre, the lovely Gothic structure which graces the banks of the Eure in the lower town of Chartres and which since the Revolution has served it as parish church, had a long and distinguished history as church of the Benedictine abbey of Saint-Père-en-Vallée. This ancient monastery, founded in the sixth or seventh century and situated at that time beyond the walls of the city,[1] was touched to some degree by the well-publicized disasters in the cathedral's history: Norman invasions and city fires. The great Chartrain fire of 1134 destroyed the abbey's roof timbers, and Abbot Foucher (reigned 1150–1171) mobilized a campaign of construction which was to continue intermittently for the next century and a half. Saint-Père still retains a primitive west tower-porch[2] which predates that disaster, and an ambulatory of the resultant construction campaign.

Foucher's architect, the monk Hilduard, began work at the east end and by ca. 1165 had finished the new chevet, of which the present ambulatory is the sole remainder.[3] Funds were lacking to commence work on the nave, and an enclosing wall was constructed across the west side of Hilduard's new choir.

It is possible but not likely that the new choir was glazed throughout. The point is worth raising only because, according to the account in *Gallia christiana*

(VIII, col. 1226E), Etienne I (Abbot 1172–1193) "ecclesiam vitreis fenestris ornavit, eique supremam manum imposuit." This fancy was based most probably on the history of the abbey written in 1672 by Dom Bernard Aubert,[4] whose section on Abbot Etienne is full of errors and unproven hypotheses. Unfortunately this has been the basis for assuming there was a complete lost twelfth-century glazing, which throughout the nineteenth century was even identified with the present windows.[5] Evidence of such a large-scale campaign is minimal. A single medallion panel of twelfth-century manufacture, representing the Ascension of Christ, and two scraps of border, were found used as stopgaps in the later windows during the restorations of 1906–1908. Popesco has suggested the south radiating chapel as their place of origin.[6]

During excavations for the temporary wall of Hilduard's choir, the body of St. Gilduin was discovered in a small vaulted chamber, and on May 9, 1165 it was moved with great pomp to the chapel of St. Nicholas (northwesternmost radiating chapel of the choir).[7] Gilduin was of a noble Breton family related to the Chartrain family of Puiset. He died about the age of twenty-three at Saint-Père on January 27, 1077 (n.s.) on his return from a trip made to Rome to refuse the honor of a bishopric. The chronicles maintain that it was solely as a result of the miraculous discovery of his body[8] and the costly gifts thereafter brought by pilgrims to the tomb that the abbey, impoverished by the construction of the choir, finally was able to begin work on the new nave.

The remainder of the fabric of the present church — nave and new upper structure of the choir — was built and glazed from the late twelfth century through the early fourteenth century. Although no archival documents remain covering the construction, many documents do exist which make it clear that the abbey during these years was enormously wealthy and powerful[9] and enjoyed a privileged relationship with the Capetian crown.[10] The piers of the north aisle of the nave, Romanesque in form, may date ca. 1190–1195, slightly before those of the cathedral nave. Those of the south aisle, on the other hand, are inspired by the pier style of the cathedral rebuilt after the 1194 fire, and were probably erected after an interval during which the primitive nave structure was razed.[11]

The nave of Saint-Père is a three-story chartrain elevation. The triforium has no balustrade and is formed of four trefoil arches per bay, decorated with quatrefoils in the spandrels (alternately pierced and blind). The clerestory windows are doublet-and-rose (large lancets and very small oculus); they include a *meneau en délit.* This nave upper structure probably reached completion just before mid-century.[12]

Thus before ca. 1250 the church of Saint-Père stood complete, with a mid-twelfth-century chevet and a newly-finished nave. The decision must have been made shortly thereafter to modernize the chevet. For reasons of economy and also perhaps from a sense of urgency, the monks chose to tear down the upper stories only, leaving the main arcading and aisle vaulting of Hilduard's construction to form the foundation for a new rayonnant upper structure. Their decision and the subsequent demolition probably occupied the years ca. 1245–1255/60.

The dating of the rayonnant construction, of some importance for dating the stained glass, is unfortunately problematical. The exquisite upper stories of the hemicycle and choir, full-blown rayonnant in the manner of Tours Cathedral, constitute a campaign occupying, possibly, the years between ca. 1250 and 1270. The new construction undoubtedly began at the west where it joined the existing nave. The campaign was probably completed without interruption. Details of the hemicycle differ only to a very slight degree from those of the choir.[13]

It is difficult to date many of the features of the rayonnant style with precision, since once introduced they appeared again and again in the architecture of the entire second half of the thirteenth century and even thereafter. In general features — dimensions and general design of clerestory, triforium with passage and quatrefoiled balustrade — the choir of Saint-Père greatly resembles that of Tours, probably finished ca. 1260.[14] The tracery design in the clerestory and the openwork "screening" of the triforium at Saint-Père appear to be only slightly scaled-down versions of those at Tours, which is, after all, a small cathedral.

The attractively uncomplicated theory that the Saint-Père choir architecture, and by implication the glazing, are merely an immediate local copy of Tours must be disallowed as far too simple, however. Many architectural details differ strikingly. Among the special features of Saint-Père are the recessed spandrels of the triforium, mentioned earlier; the colonnette which runs up the center of each triforium bay but does not link with the clerestory; the isolated épi without matching crockets, at the top of each triforium lancet; and the "straight-line" arches of the exterior of the apse clerestory windows. Tours accounts for the basic architectural flavor of Saint-Père, but not the spice.

The picture of Tours as the model for the stained glass is an even more distorted one. Tours and Saint-Père are not parent and child but kinsmen; their similarity derives from the relationship of both monuments to the Western French school of glass, a kinship which will be charted in Chapter V.

THE GLASS

The upper part of the church of Saint-Père contains stained glass from glazing campaigns of ca. 1245, ca. 1270, and ca. 1295–1315. This body of glass is now found in the clerestory of the nave (architecture ca. 1240's) and the pierced

Saint-Père: Construction of architecture and stained glass

Church rebuilt under Abbot Aganon in mid-tenth century. Present western tower, dating ca. 990?

Fire in 1077.

Church rebuilt in late-eleventh century.

Fire of 1134 (roof timbers destroyed).

ca. 1151–1165: construction of choir by monk Hilduard. Discovery of St. Gilduin's body in 1165 at end of construction.

ca. 1190: north aisle of nave erected (to one side of Romanesque nave).

——— old nave (on site of present south aisle) torn down.

[ca. 1195–1225; dates of Chartres Cathedral nave]

ca. 1210–1240's: south aisle built copying cathedral pier design; nave elevation completed; old cloister torn down and rebuilt. Nave at clerestory level after ca. 1240.

Church was complete at mid-thirteenth century (twelfth century choir and thirteenth century nave and cloister).

ca. 1240–1250: stained glass made, both grisaille and color (now found in choir). Probably intended for the nave.

Not before 1250 but closer to 1260–1265?: upper choir and hemicycle torn down to ambulatory vaults and rebuilt west to east (choir clerestory mullions earlier than hemicycle).

The church was again complete, as it stands today, with early thirteenth-century nave and new chevet.

ca. 1270: earlier glass re-used in new choir. Bays 14–15 glazed with new designs (too narrow for older panels). Choir triforium glazed with grisaille contemporary with Bays 14–15 but of mediocre quality. Several panels now in Bay 22 (original location unknown).

ca. 1295–1300: hemicycle glazed (finished after 1297).

——— hemicycle triforium glazed (naturalistic foliage grisaille, now largely missing).

ca. 1300–1315: nave glazed (standing figure group first, narrative group added?).

triforium and the clerestory of the chevet (architecture ca. 1270). A surface comparison of dates of the glass and its architectural framework is grossly misleading, however, for the earlier part of the building (the nave) now contains the latest glazing (ca. 1305). Conversely, the latest part of the architectural construction (the chevet) includes among its windows examples of all the glazing campaigns, including that of ca. 1245 (redesigned for its present setting).

The glazing campaign of ca. 1245 probably provided windows for the newly-erected nave, although this hypothesis cannot be proven. Remnants of this campaign are now located in the clerestory of the choir. The campaign of ca. 1270 was inaugurated to provide windows for that choir, and its product consists largely of grisailles for tracery lights (Pls. 40, 41) and for the pierced triforium. Only two windows containing colored and figured glass (Bays 14 and 15, Pls. 31–33) can be assigned to the campaign of ca. 1270, and these two are "facing windows" occupying an architectural bay too narrow to accommodate the earlier glass which was placed in its neighbors. The impressive final campaign of the church produced, first of all, the masterwork of the Western school — the seven blazing windows of the hemicycle[15] of Saint-Père (Pl. I)—and then, after ca. 1305, proceeded in some haste to provide for the twelve vast, emptied clerestories of the early thirteenth-century nave.

Each group of glass — that in the choir, the hemicycle, and the nave — has its special characteristics and problems. The choir presents re-used glass of ca. 1245 and a small amount of work from the date of the "re-use" (ca. 1270), in an alloy which is difficult to analyze. Indeed, in dealing with medieval glass reworked within a quarter-century, fools rush in where angels fear to tread. The hemicycle presents a totally different picture — a consummate masterpiece. The nave, finally, offers for perusal a wealth and variety of glass design which delights the eye, uneven in quality but never dull, full to bursting with ideas and energy, evidence of a decade's bustling activity in a humming workshop.

Excepting the lone Romanesque scene published by Popesco, there is no firm evidence that the lower windows ever contained medieval glass. It seems odd that a church would be glazed only at the top.[16] It was, however, the new "top" of which the monks were most proud at the moment when the fabric was finished and their attention turned to its embellishment. It may be that the wars and plagues of the fourteenth century cut short a glazing campaign before it progressed to the windows at aisle level.

The series of windows in the choir is the earliest in the church (Pls. II, III, 17–30, 35–39). Excepting only Bays 14–15 (Pls. IV, 31–34, 42) and the tracery and triforium grisailles (Pls. 40–41, 43), the group gives stylistic evidence of dating perhaps a quarter-century earlier than the architecture in which it is found. It is composed of designs, both color and grisaille, which probably were intended for the nave clerestory at its completion in the 1240's and which were re-used for the new choir ca. 1270. The triforium grisaille and the glass of Bays 14–15 were designed about that time to complete the choir ensemble, as the two bays in question were too narrow to accommodate the earlier panels.[17]

The window groups of the hemicycle and nave belong to the era of the last Capetians, around and after the year 1300. Those of the hemicycle (Pls. I, V, 3–14), presumably dated after 1297 by the figure of St. Louis, logically would come first to complete the chevet ensemble. Of consistently high quality, they were probably in planning and process of fabrication almost from the completion of the upper choir structure. The St. Louis is more likely a final addition than an initial subject choice. The nave series (Pls. VI-XII, 48–63, 67–84) is of uneven quality, some fine and some quite mediocre, and evidently hastily done. The group can be dated by donations of the first decade of the fourteenth century, by which time the nave's doublet-and-rose architecture was considerably out of date. There is evidence of some tampering with the buttresses of the nave about the same time,[18] which may have been triggered by the presence of new scaffolding for the glass and by the desire to embellish the then slightly old-fashioned nave to match the newer eastern end of the building. It is fairly safe to assume that most of the construction and glazing had been undertaken by the first decade of the century, because thereafter documents mention donations for accessories of lesser importance.[19]

The nave groups maintain as strong a design plan as do those of the choir and hemicycle, but give evidence of having been executed in some haste and by artists of varying degrees of skill. These are the windows for which outside funds were sought and obtained, and which offer concrete evidence for dating. The nave donors form a touchstone by which to measure the stylistic evidence for dating the rest of the church and at the same time a *terminus ante quem.* Of the half-dozen benefactors, four are identifiable.[20] The first is Jehan I de Mantes, abbot from 1306–1310, whose kneeling figure appears in the lower row of Bay 22 (Pl. 63).

This bay, the Peter window (Pl. 59), is the earliest and most confused of the narrative group in the nave. It is formed of earlier pairs of panels vastly augmented to fill the expanse of the broad clerestory space. It seems likely that the abbot gave it upon the occasion of his election to office, or shortly after that event. He emerges as possibly the guiding personality in the planning and execution of the nave narrative series.

Another donor is Béatrix de Montfort-l'Amaury, widow of Robert IV, Count of Dreux. Her escutcheons can be seen in the roundel above Bay 19 (Pl.

51, Fig. 12), a narrative window which ranks stylistically later than Abbot Jehan's bay but before the others in the group. The Countess died March 9, 1312 (n.s.) and had begun dispersing her estate before that date.

Bay 21 (Pl. 57), a window of colored figures originally framed by diaper, contains a large kneeling figure of another donor, Laurent Voisin. Laurent was dean of the cathedral from at least 1293 until his death late in 1314 or very early in 1315.

While figures or escutcheons of the above-mentioned benefactors remain in the church, and hence are discussed more fully in later chapters, the most generous donor to the nave glazing is traceable only through documents. Nicolas de Maison-Maugis, a canon of the cathedral during the first decade of the fourteenth century and thus a confrère of Laurent Voisin, gave the abbey the sizeable sum of £300 carn. for windows in the nave:[21]

> trois cens livres Chartrains pour estre mis et employéz es vittres de la nef . . . . Ce fut fait l'an de grace mil trois cens et onze, le jeudi seiziesme jour d'Aoust [1311, Thurs. Aug. 16].

Unfortunately the date is in error, as August 16 fell on a Monday in 1311.[22] The terminal dates for this important donation would be after 1292, when Nicolas acquired properties which he cedes in this gift, and before May 21, 1308, when he died.

The sum he gave to the abbey for nave windows — £300 carn. — undoubtedly would have paid for several bays even in the wildly unstable and periodically inflationary economy of the early fourteenth century.[23]

The striking feature of the glass ensemble of Saint-Père is the overall coherence of its plan, a layout of considerable intricacy and refinement. Notwithstanding the differences of style and execution among three series of glass whose production probably ranged over sixty years, the overall glazing of the church seems to have been conceived and carried to completion as a single vision. The hemicycle clerestory was planned quite naturally as the focus of light and color. It contains no grisaille at all and no diaper filler. The choir windows re-use older glass, but their redesign was by no means haphazard. The older panels of standing prophets in medallions and of grisaille were carefully adapted to the new choir lights. The narrow Bays 14–15 of the choir were filled with designs matching them. More important, the decision to alternate color and grisaille in vertical patterns — a unique concept — was taken in the choir. The nave windows of standing saints adapt the same procedure to broader areas and a different window format, presenting strips of color sandwiched vertically between grisaille rather than in one-to-one alternation. The final decision to alternate the standing figure bays in the nave with color-saturated narrative windows picking out the themes of the tracery medallions of the hemicycle may have been a final refinement, a coda of lavish variation worked on the main themes in the church.

RESTORATION AND REPAIR

The abbey's fortunes declined during the universal troubles of the fourteenth century, when the church suffered from floods in 1342 and 1366, and occasional damage during the Hundred Years War.[24] The only alteration to the glazing was the walling up of the southwesternmost bay of the hemicycle (Bay 7) to strengthen the spiral staircase added to the exterior at that time, running from triforium level to the roof. Bay 7 had been glazed, without much doubt, with the other hemicycle windows at the beginning of the century, and its glass has largely been lost. Only one fragmentary and mutilated panel (Pl. 15) remains which can be ascribed to it.[25]

The fifteenth and sixteenth centuries saw few repairs of major consequence affecting the glazing.[26] During these years the abbey fell into a period of decline and lost lands and privileges, including, in 1491, that of electing residing abbots. It was not until the seventeenth century that the abbey began glass restorations and repairs in earnest. In 1631, when general repairs of the entire upper structure of the church were undertaken, a contract was signed with the mason Pierre Dallonne and the master-glazier Pierre Dubois to

> . . . descendre et refaire le pied droit de la vistre appellée la vistre de Saint-Vincent, restablir les pierres, asseoir le dicte vistre en plomb et gougeonnée de fer.[27]

In 1650 the abbey fell under the authority of the Benedictine reform congregation of Saint Maur. From 1654 to 1659 the Congregation undertook extensive repairs, especially of the roof, buttresses, and glass. In 1663 two new windows were pierced into the north aisle of the choir to provide more light. Sometime within the last quarter of the century, the monks wanted even more light in their church and stripped several of the clerestory bays of some of their colored panels. The extent of this dismemberment is conjectural, but its date is controlled by Dom Aubert's 1672 chronicle, listing scenes "before," and a drawing of the monastery predating the eighteenth-century additions, indicating the south clerestories "after" (Pl. 1)[28].

As part of the late seventeenth-century dismemberment, choir Bays 8–9 and 16–17 (see Pls. 17–19, 35–37) lost their thirteenth-century grisailles[29] as well, which, to judge from the state of those panels still in existence in other choir bays, may have become heavily calcified and darkened. Bays 20–21 of the nave lost the framing lancets of blue and dark red lozenge diaper, the pattern of which can still be seen in the tympana of each window (Pls. 55–57).

Happily, not all of the dismemberments were to be final. Bays 22–23 of the nave, both of which contain saints' legends, each lost all the panels of the framing lancets (see Pl. 60), leaving only a central vertical strip of color in each window.[30] Some of the panels have disappeared, but many of them were glazed in a con-

---

Major Losses to Medieval Glass

hemicycle: Bay 7 (blinded ca. 1350)

choir: Bays 8–9 — grisaille lancets (removed ca. 1700?)

Bay 13 — tracery grisaille and figure lancets (destroyed in World War II)

Bays 16–17 — grisaille lancets (removed ca. 1700?)

nave: Bays 20–21 — colored diaper (removed ca. 1700)

Bay 23 — 12 narrative panels and arches (removed ca. 1700)

Minor Losses to Medieval Glass
(limited to whole panels)*

hemicycle: Bay 5 — right tracery quatrefoil
— lower right figure, middle panel

choir: Bay 9 — upper right figure, head panel
— upper left figure, middle panel

Bay 11 — upper right figure, middle panel

Bay 17 — lower right figure, middle panel

nave: Bay 19 — 2 narrative panels

Bay 21 — St. Gregory, two lower panels

Bay 22 — 2 narrative panels and arches

Bay 27 — 2 narrative panels (center, lower row, left lancet)
— 2 angels in arches

All north bays and 23, 27, 29 on south — roses

* The purpose of this list is to highlight losses of medieval designs, especially figure or narrative. Grisaille and canopy panels vary widely in degree of restoration but the original design can usually be defined.

---

fused and meaningless fashion and at an unknown date into two lower windows opening onto the ambulatory (Pl. 71). They were rescued from such indignity by the restorers in 1905–1908 and returned to the nave bays in as near the original order as it was possible to ascertain.

So much for documented major alterations before the Revolution. Additions to the glass were meager, comprising a pair of panels inserted for some mysterious reason into the Peter window, Bay 22; a window of unknown location (now lost) given by Jehan II Pinart, Abbot 1464–ca. 1480; and various escutcheons added to several clerestories. The panels added to the Peter window show two standing prophets against *damasquiné* ground (Pls. 62–63). Judging by the *damasquin* and the light use of silver stain they are late-fourteenth-century, and they were obviously designed (or altered) in a scale and with canopies to match those in the bay.

The lost window of Abbot Jehan II (Pl. 66), preserved in a Gaignières drawing,[31] included the kneeling abbot and his coat of arms, a seated St. James as pilgrim, and the inscription:

> VIe daoust Jour certain mil quatre cens octante et hui(t) Jehan pinart Abbé de ceans, cet ymage cy metre fi(t).[32]

It was placed, according to a note on the drawing, in a "Vitre a gauche dans la nef . . ." which, judging from the broad and untraceried format, must have been in the lower aisle.

Of the various escutcheons added from time to time to the stained glass[33] the earliest was a fifteenth-century emblem formerly in the rose over Bay 25 of the nave.[34] It was probably the coat of arms of Etienne II le Baillif (27th abbot of Saint-Père, 1394–1416), a great restorer and benefactor of the monastery. Four other escutcheons, of two donors of the fifteenth and sixteenth centuries, are still to be found in the grisaille panels of the same bay (Pl. 75). In the right lancet are two coats of arms of Hélie de Bourdeilles (1423–1484), archbishop of Tours and later cardinal;[35] in the left are those of François de Brilhac (34th abbot, 1522–1540).[36] Five seventeenth-century escutcheons formerly were in the clerestory windows. One, unidentified, was in the south choir (Bay 17) (Pl. 37).[37] The other four were in Bay 24 of the north nave. Two of these were the arms of Louis I Barbier de la Rivière (abbot 1635–1670); the others belonged to one of his three predecessors in the office, either Philippe III (1595–1599); Henri (1620–1624), or Philippe IV (1624–1635), all of the family of Hurault de Cheverny (Pl. 73).[38]

The damage to Saint-Père during the Revolution presumably included the destruction of any lower windows and all church furniture within reach, but the clerestory glass and the grisaille of the choir triforium escaped without notable mutilation. Saint-Père, having served briefly as a saltpeter factory, became the parish church of the *ville-basse* in 1801. The adjoining cloister buildings, built ca. 1700, were occupied by cavalry, and the former parish church, Saint-Hilaire, situated directly to the north, was razed to "faciliter l'accès des fidèles à l'église Saint Pierre." Debris saved from the sixteenth-century windows of Saint-Hilaire was used in two windows of the ambulatory of Saint-Père and presumably as stopgaps in the clerestories where needed. All was removed in the 1951–1954 restorations.

Still remaining, however, is a *belle salade* of Renaissance fragments put into the triforium of the hemicycle,[39] replacing the original fourteenth-century grisailles whose traces also remain in the lancet tops there. This stunning sixteenth-century patchwork, a haphazard and meaningless jumble of largely unidentifiable scraps, traditionally has been connected with Saint-Hilaire and the glasspainter Robert Pinaigrier. The celebrated name of Pinaigrier was first connected with Chartrain windows by André Felibien in the late-seventeenth century,[40] and it was Pierre Le Vieil[41] who specified the church as Saint-Hilaire, the artist as "Robert Pinaigrier," and the date of execution as 1527–1530. The tradition has died hard, being recorded most recently by Emile Mâle and the Chartrain archivist Maurice Jusselin.[42] Jean Lafond, however, in his thorough study of the Pinaigriers, doubts not only their connection with the glass now in the Saint-Père triforium but even the existence of the legendary Robert Ier, "le bon Pinaigrier."[43] Moreover, Loïc Martine[44] recently has found a document of ca. 1803 in the Chartres library attributing the triforium debris not to Saint-Hilaire but to another unspecified church. No matter. The Renaissance debris given a home in Saint-Père after the Revolution varies widely in quality. Some fragments of it could stand as models of the best of the French sixteenth-century school of glass painting.

From 1820–1840 several perfunctory attempts were made to repair the stained glass in Saint-Père.[45] In 1841 the church was classed a "monument historique." In 1854, despite reports by M. Lassus on the ruinous condition of the windows, the Commission des Monuments historiques refused a request for funds for restoration,[46] and for the remainder of the century those meager repairs which were undertaken were financed by the impoverished parish.[47]

The first thorough restoration of the Saint-Père glass was undertaken by the architect Etienne Brunet in 1905–1908. The restorers were Charles Lorin of Chartres (north side and fifth window of south nave) and Edmond Socard and Henri du Basty of Paris (remainder of south side). In addition to general releading, restoration of missing pieces, and repainting of old glass,[48] it was Brunet's expressed intention to (a) remove all nonconforming fragments from

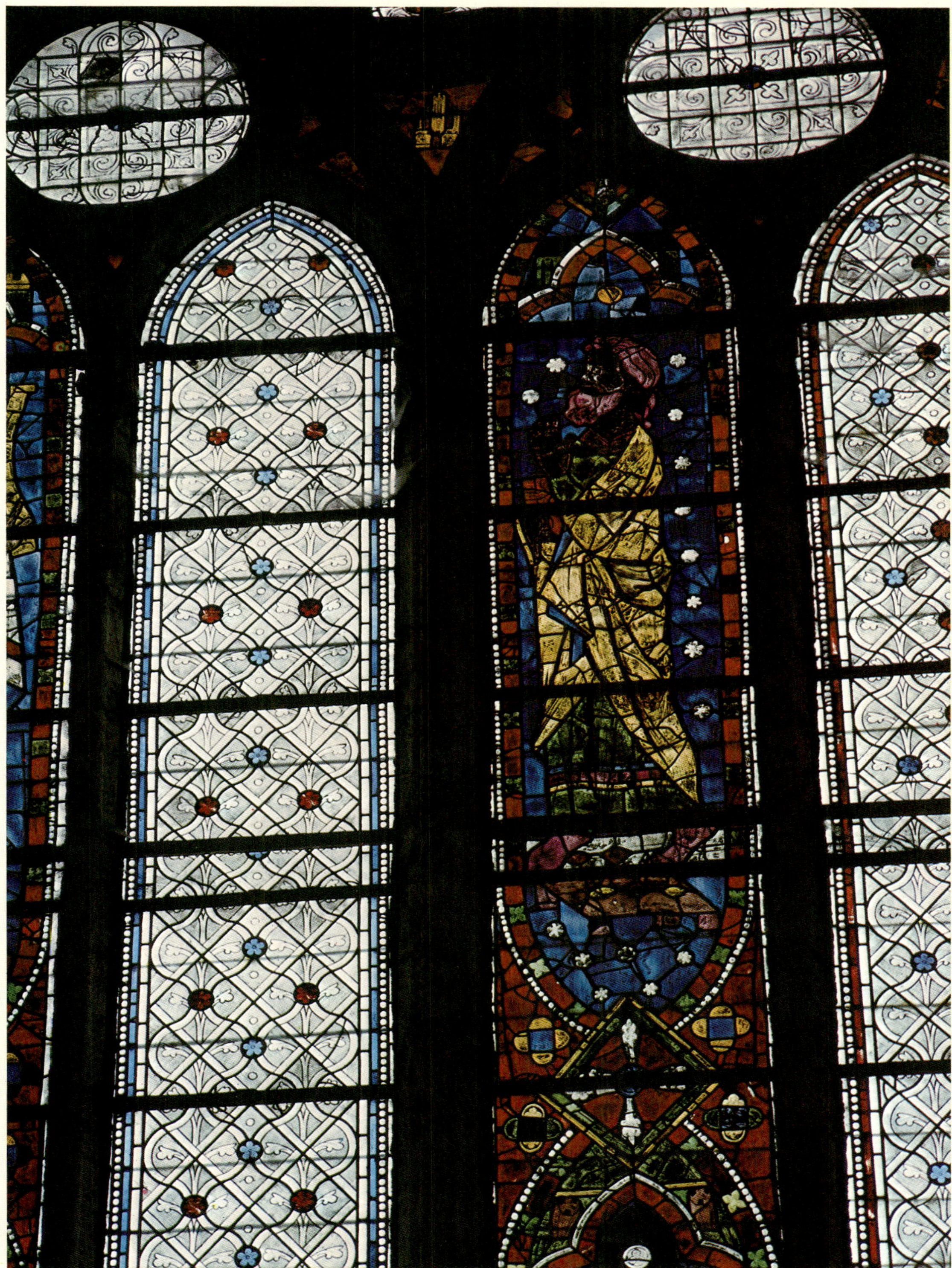

PLATE II Choir: Bay 8. Patriarch (right lancet, top). *(Edouard Fièvet)*

the clerestory windows,[49] and to place them in windows of the ambulatory, and to (b) replace in Bays 22–23 of the nave the panels which had been removed from them after the seventeenth century, which he had discovered glazed into several lower apsidal windows (see Pl. 2).[50] By 1918 when Chartres was bombed and the glass taken down and stored in the cathedral crypt, the entire clerestory had been repaired and restored.

In 1936 attention was finally turned to the triforium. A restoration was undertaken by Charles Lorin and Delange. The sixteenth-century debris from the triforium apse was taken to the Cluny Museum, and two panels of it were included in the 1937 stained glass exhibition in Paris. It was replaced in the church after the war.

From 1939–1946 the glass of Saint-Père was again removed to the cathedral crypt and the Tour-Blanche in Dordogne. It survived the war intact save for the tracery panels and colored glass of Bay 13 in the south choir (Pl. 30), hit by a grenade while in the packing case. The fenestration of the church, damaged by bombardment in 1944, was repaired in 1948, and in 1951–1954 a complete restoration and photographing of all the glass was undertaken prior to its re-installation in the church.[51]

New designs now fill the missing lights of Bays 23 (south nave) and 13 (south choir), as well as other isolated locations, some of the formerly blank tympana, and the oculi of the nave bays. With the exception of the choir figures, which adapt medieval cartoons,[52] the new glass, by the late François Lorin, is intended to harmonize in color with the medieval designs but to be easily recognizable as modern work. The church, since the mid-60's served by a community of Franciscans, was fortunate to be in the competent hands of a skilled and tasteful artist.

NOTES

1. The city walls were enlarged to enclose Saint-Père in 1369.

2. Louis Grodecki (*L'architecture ottonienne* [Paris, 1958], pp. 208, 241 fn. 139, 284) dates the tower ca. 990.

3. The upper stories were replaced in the thirteenth century. The north bays of the ambulatory as well as the last bay of the south aisle retain their twelfth-century groined vaults. For further traces of the mid-twelfth-century construction, see André Mussat, *Le style gothique de l'ouest de la France (XIIe-XIIIe siècles),* (Paris, 1963), pp. 57–58; Pierre Héliot and Georges Jouven, "L'Eglise Saint-Pierre de Chartres et l'architecture du moyen âge," *Bulletin archéologique du Comité des travaux historiques et scientifiques,* nouv. sér., VI (1970), pp. 134ff.

4. Dom Bernard Aubert, "Veritable inventaire de l'histoire de la royalle abbaye de Sainct-Pere-en-Vallee de Chartres," Bibl. Chartres ms. 1151; a legible eighteenth-century copy was made for Gaignières, Bibl. Nat. ms. fr. 22474.

5. See Benjamin Guérard, *Cartulaire de l'abbaye de Saint-Père de Chartres* (Paris, 1840), I, p. cclj; Ferdinand de Lasteyrie, *Histoire de la peinture sur verre* (Paris, 1857), I, p. 40, fn. 3; also A. J. Bushnell, *Storied Windows* (New York, 1914), p. 116.

6. See the intriguing reconstruction by Paul Popesco, "Les panneaux de vitrail du XIIe siècle de l'église Saint-Pierre de Chartres, ancienne abbatiale," *Revue de l'art,* X (December, 1970), pp. 47–56; Louis Grodecki, in *Bulletin monumental,* CXXI (1963), pp. 78–79; *Vitraux de France,* catalogue by Françoise Perrot (Amsterdam, Rijksmuseum, 1973), pp. 40–42.

Evidence for and against a complete glazing in the twelfth century is equally circumstantial. Dom Aubert in 1672 describes nave clerestories which, at an unknown later period, were partially dismantled and placed in the choir aisles (Pl. 71). Since the motive was to obtain more light, one can assume it was an act of the eighteenth-century mentality. Clearly, the choir aisles were not filled with twelfth-century glass when they received these émigré panels. A complex explanation could of course obtain: that the panels were stored somewhere; that the hypothetical Romanesque glass in the aisles was ravaged during the Revolution; and that the émigrés were housed there after the Concordat. Ca. 1905 they were replaced in the nave clerestories. For other evidence of non-twelfth-century glazing in the lower windows, see Pl. 66.

7. The body remained there until 1666, when it was moved to the chapel of St. Stephen, the Maurists confusing Gilduin with the better-known deacon St. Stephen (see discussion in Chapter VIII). In the nineteenth century, the body was in the little church of Champhol (see Abbé Bulteau, *Description de la cathédrale de Chartres* [Chartres, 1850], p. 280, fn. 3 and p. 281). In 1948 it was returned to Saint-Père.

8. For reports of the saint's life and of the discovery of the body, see "Vita S. Gilduini," *Acta Sanctorum,* III (27 January), 408; *Gallia christiana,* VIII, col. 1226; "Historia inventionis et miraculorum S. Gilduini," *Analecta Bollandiana,* I (Brussels, 1882), pp. 152–157; parts of this text are reprinted in V. Mortet-P. Deschamps, *Recueil de textes relatifs à l'histoire de l'architecture* (Paris, 1929), pp. 88, 90; Dom Charles du Jardin, Bibl. Nat. ms. lat. 12689, fol. 303; Dom Aubert, especially chs. 52, 89.

9. See Eugène Berger, "Etude historique et archéologique sur l'abbaye de Saint-Père de Chartres," thesis, Ecole des Chartes, I (1913), pt. III; summarized in *Positions des thèses* (1913), pp. 12–15.

10. Philippe-le-Hardi, in 1284, exempted the abbey from taxes (Arch. d'Eure-et-Loir, H.6, no. 10). Philippe-le-Bel, in 1296, addressed the monks on the subject of his unpopular cinquantième war-tax in an equivocal letter which bears interpretation as a royal bequest (see Chapter VI at footnote 10). Cf. a similar donation by Philippe-le-Bel to Bourges: "En 1313, les chanoines obtinrent de Philippe le Bel la remise d'un subside de 400 livres qui leur était demandé à l'occasion des guerres de Flandre, avec permission d'employer cette somme aux réparations importantes de l'église. . . ." (Amédée Boinet, *La cathédrale de Bourges* [Paris, 1952], p. 10; see also p. 35 fn. 2). One of the earliest images of Saint Louis, canonized in 1297, fills the axial clerestory window; see M. Lillich, "An Early Image of Saint Louis," *Gazette des beaux-arts,* LXXV (1970), pp. 251–256.

11. See Héliot-Jouven, pp. 160–161; Louis-Marie Michon, "L'abbaye de Saint-Père de Chartres, étude archéologique sur l'église abbatiale et les bâtiments monastiques," thesis, Ecole nationale des Chartes (1922); Paule Bienvenüe, "Les bâtiments conventuels de l'ancienne abbaye Saint-Père de Chartres," *Bulletin monumental,* CXVI (1958), p. 7; Ad. Lecocq, "Dissertation historique et archéologique sur la question: Où est l'emplacement du tombeau de Fulbert, évêque de Chartres, au XIe siècle?", *Société archéologique d'Eure-et-Loir, Mémoires,* V (1877), p. 319.

12. Cf. Beauvais triforium of ambulatory, trefoil arches, ca. 1225–1235; pierced quatrefoils of Saint-Quentin (Aisne), ca. 1245–1250; Saint-Nicaise de Reims, the last major building to use doublets in clerestory, begun 1231 and probably in construction at clerestory level about 1240;

Notre-Dame, Paris, where the *meneau en délit* was introduced between 1225–1240; Gallardon, a similar but more advanced chartrain elevation dating ca. 1245. I am indebted to the late Professor Robert Branner for advice on the architectural study of Saint-Père.

13. In the straight choir the capitals of the vault springers, those of the triforium, and those of the exterior and interior clerestory mullions have no imposts; those of the exterior of the hemicycle do. The spandrels of the triforium in the straight choir have a rather unusual recessed panel such as is found in the eastern bays of Strasbourg; those of the hemicycle do not. See Robert Branner, *Saint Louis and the Court Style in Gothic Architecture* (London, 1965), pp. 19, 95. The buttresses are of slightly different design, those of the hemicycle having an engaged vertical strip added to the sides. The tracery of the hemicycle clerestory seems slightly more articulated, the lancets being trefoiled at the top and the upper lights of the tracery quatrefoiled to bring it more closely in line with the tracery patterns of the triforium screen. Hemicycles, however, generally vary in tracery from the straight bays of a choir.

14. Branner believed that the upper stories of Tours were planned and begun about 1245, slowed down during crusade (1248–1254) and finished before 1260. The glazing is dated ca. 1257–1270. See Francis Salet, "La cathédrale de Tours," *Congrès archéologique,* CVI (1949), p. 36; Marcel Aubert *et al., Le vitrail français* (Paris, 1958), pp. 156 and 163. This work will be referred to hereafter as *VF.* Mussat (p. 165) states that construction began ca. 1240 and was finished ca. 1270–1275 (wood purchased for the roof in 1279). The relationship between Tours and Saint-Père is discussed by Héliot-Jouven, p. 177.

15. Bay 7, now blind, was originally glazed. See fn. 25 infra. The few grisaille fragments left in the hemicycle triforium can also be dated with the clerestory ensemble ca. 1295–1300, as they exhibit a lovely naturalistic foliage. Almost all of this beautiful grisaille was removed after 1801 to provide space for the Renaissance fragments; see fn. 39. Remaining bits occupy lancet arches (see also Bay 6 [Pls. 44, 45], and Bays 16 and 17 of the triforium, where naturalistic grisaille debris has been placed).

16. Jean Lafond, "Le vitrail en Normandie de 1250 à 1300," *Bulletin monumental,* III (1953), fn. 1, cites Sées, Saint-Ouen de Rouen, and Cologne as monuments where the clerestory was glazed at the same time or earlier than the lower windows.

17. The mid-twelfth-century lower story of the choir has an irregular alternation of weak and strong piers.

18. Jouven formerly suggested that the lower flyer, which exhibits a now useless rut for water drainage, must have been the original design, the upper flyer and monolithic colonnettes being added at "l'extrême fin du XIIIième siècle." But see Héliot-Jouven, pp. 159–160.

19. Abbot Jehan de Mantes, donor of the glass of Bay 22, gave a bourdon named "Saint Pierre" for the belfry in 1308. (See *Gallia christiana,* VIII, col. 1229 [p. 219, fn. 2] and Dom Aubert, ch. 108.) In 1325, according to Dom Aubert, a new reliquary was provided for one of the abbey's venerated relics, the bones of the virgin Ste. Soline, martyred at Chartres in early Christian times. The new reliquary is mentioned in inventories of 1399, 1665, and 1790. (See F. de Mély, "Les Inventaires de l'abbaye de Saint-Père-en-Vallée," *Revue de l'art chrétien,* sér. 4, especially V [XXXVII] [January, 1887], pp. 63, 71, 72.)

20. An anonymous lay couple and an unidentified abbot complete the group. See Pls. 78 and 53.

21. There are several copy-sources for the document, the original of which is lost: a) the most complete copy, Dom Muley, II, 133–134; b) Dom Aubert, ch. 109; c) Archives d'Eure-et-Loir, H200; d) Archives d'Eure-et-Loir, H1, I, 484.

22. The error was probably in the original, as it occurs in all known copies. See Maurice Jusselin, "Un donateur pour les verrières de Saint-Père de Chartres au debut du XIVe siècle," *Bulletin monumental,* LXXXIX (1930), pp. 540–541.

23. On the fluctuation of the Chartrain baronial coinage between 1292 and its suppression by Philippe-le-Long in 1319, see Eugène de Buchère de Lépinois, *Histoire de Chartres* (Chartres, 1854), I, pp. 413–419 and 560ff. For a discussion of glaziers' wages in 1317, see Yves Delaporte, *Les vitraux de la cathédrale de Chartres* (Chartres, 1926), p. 20 and fn. 1.

24. See Dom Aubert, ch. 110. Jean II of France marshalled his forces in Chartres in 1356; peace talks concerning his ransom were held near Chartres in the hamlet of Brétigny in 1360.

25. M. Lillich, "Découverte d'un vitrail perdu de Saint-Père de Chartres," *Bulletin de la Société archéologique d'Eure-et-Loir, Mémoires,* année 108, no. 13 (1964), pp. 264–268. On the *tourelle,* see Héliot-Jouven, pp. 167, 169.

26. Lucien Merlet and E. Bellier de la Chavignerie, "Documents sur des travaux exécutés à Notre-Dame de Chartres et dans d'autres églises du pays chartrain pendant le seizième siècle," *Archives de l'art français,* VII (1855–1856), esp. pp. 384–390).

27. See Michon, pt. I, ch. IV, pp. 29ff. citing "registres des tabellions" of the abbey 1527–1631 (Archives d'Eure-et-Loir E 2184). My gratitude is due to Mme. Katrine Grodecki for arranging with M. Michon's widow to consult the thesis. See also Maurice Jusselin, "Les peintres-verriers à Chartres au XVIe siècle," *Société archéologique d'Eure-et-Loir, Mémoires,* XVI (1931), p. 218. There is no clue as to which window was then called the window of St. Vincent; perhaps it is totally lost.

28. Dom Aubert, chs. 136–138. The drawing is Arch. Nat. NIII Eure-et-Loir 3^1. It shows the medieval cloister buildings; Pl. 1 shows a very small detail of the monastic ensemble. The Congregation tore down and replaced the medieval cloister with eighteenth-century structures (razed in the mid-1960's).

29. The panels, as well as those referred to below in Bays 20–21, are lost. The lancets are now filled with clear glass or twentieth-century copies.

30. Twenty-eight panels remain, plus the tympana, in Bay 22; forty panels plus tympana in Bay 23, which has a differently proportioned format. A photograph found in the files of the Lorin glass studio shows Bay 22 before or during the 1905–1908 restorations (Pl. 60). Another photograph (Pl. 71) found in the Michon thesis shows one of the ambulatory windows filled with a jumble of panels from Bay 23.

31. The original is in the Bodleian Library, Oxford (Ms. Gough Drawings — Gaignières 9, fol. 57). A mid-nineteenth-century copy of the original is in the Bibliothèque Nationale, Paris (Dept. des Estampes, Gaignières no. 3569, fol. 57). The Oxford drawing has not been published previously. For the Bibl. Nat. copy see: Joseph Guibert, *Les dessins d'archéologie de Roger de Gaignières,* Series II, Vitraux, Planches 1 à 100 (Ambroise-Etival) (Paris, n.d.), pl. 92. Two other Gaignières drawings of fifteenth-century windows are listed erroneously as from Saint-Père in Ad. Lecocq, "Monuments chartrains de la collection Gaignières," *Société archéologique d'Eure-et-Loir, Procès-verbaux,* III (1868), pp. 238–243. These drawings were made in reality from glass in the crypt of the cathedral.

32. Both original and copy show the date as "mil quatre cens octante et hui(t)," although the date customarily given for Pinart's death is January 13, 1480 (*Gallia christiana,* VIII, col. 1232A, but see col. 1283E which states he died in 1502). The Bibl. Nat. copy has "fin" for "fit" in the second line of the inscription.

33. These are described in detail as they existed in the nineteenth-century by the Comte d'Armancourt, "Chartres. Notes héraldiques et généalogiques," *Société archéologique d'Eure-et-Loir, Le Cinquantenaire,* I (1960), pp. 126–416. Nothing is added to this in Gaudeffroy-Penelle, Charles Métais and Albéric du Temple de Rougemont, *Armorial chartrain* (Paris, 1974).

34. Armancourt, no. 302, p. 388 and fn. 1. It has since been lost.

35. Armancourt, no. 48, p. 185.

36. Or his uncle Christophe de Brilhac, 32nd abbot (1491–1514). More probably it was

François, as his tomb stood in the south aisle of the church. Armancourt, no. 56, pp. 191–192.

37. This panel was used in Bay 17 only as a stopgap, occupying the middle light of the figure of a patriarch, lower right. Armancourt, no. 285, p. 380.

38. Willemin's plate of 1806 shows them still in the window: N. X. Willemin, *Monuments français inédits, pour servir à l'histoire des arts* (Paris, 1806), v.1, pl. 55. See also Armancourt, no. 16, pp. 163–164 and no. 141A, pp. 268–269. All seventeenth-century escutcheons have been removed from the church. The workmanship is typical seventeenth-century enamel painting on glass, of very poor quality.

39. The original grisailles, Dom Aubert tells us, had colored borders and traceries of gold *fleurs de lys* on blue. For nineteenth-century descriptions of the fragments after their placement in the triforium, see Bulteau, p. 298; Abbé Jean-Charles-Benjamin Poisson, *Chroniques de l'abbaye royale de Saint-Père-en-Vallée* (Chartres, 1857), pp. 418–419, 428; and François de Guilhermy, Bibl. Nat. nouv. acq. fr. 6098 (1856–1858), fol. 197v. The Renaissance debris is also mentioned by the restorer who removed it, Charles Lorin, "Les vitraux de moyen âge, ceux de Chartres en particulier," *Société archéologique d'Eure-et-Loir, Le Cinquantenaire,* I (1906), p. 465.

40. André Félibien, *Entretiens sur les vies et sur les ouvrages de plus excellens peintres anciens et modernes,* 2d ed., I (Paris, 1685), p. 711: "Mais Vous pouvez avoir veu en plusieurs églises de Chartres des vitres peintes depuis l'an 1520. . . . Plusieurs estoient peintes par un nommé Pinaigrier Vitrier. . . ."

41. Pierre Le Vieil, *Art de la peinture sur verre* (Paris, 1774), p. 42.

42. Mâle, *L'art religieux de la fin du moyen âge en France,* 4th ed. (Paris, 1931), p. 119, fn. 4, refers to the artist as "Jean Pinaigrier." Jusselin surprisingly repeats the tradition without having unearthed the slightest proof for it in the monumental archival research undertaken for his "Peintres verriers," pp. 221–223.

43. Jean Lafond, "La famille Pinaigrier et le vitrail parisien au XVIe et au XVIIe siècles," *Bulletin de la Société de l'histoire de l'art français* (1957), esp. pp. 72–73; see also Lafond in *VF,* p. 324b, fn. 9.

44. Martine's research on the triforium fragments is unpublished. His authority is a local historian of the early nineteenth century, Hérisson (text with Bibl. Chartres ms. 1509).

45. Michon, ch. 7.

46. Dossier, *Monuments historiques* (Eure-et-Loir, Chartres, Eglise St. Pierre, 453) (documentation of restorations since 1842).

47. Funds were found somewhere for an incredibly bad series of windows for the axial chapel. The designer was Paul Durand, who published the program in "Eglise de Saint-Père à Chartres: Explication de la nouvelle décoration exécutée dans la chapelle de la Sainte-Vierge," *Société archéologique d'Eure-et-Loir, Mémoires,* III (1863), pp. 298–320. In 1872 Abbot Vassard donated five more new windows (nave aisle). The nineteenth-century glass remained in the church during World War II; remains of it may still be seen there.

48. I have published two examples of heads of old glass repainted with modern features: Lillich, "Saint Louis," p. 252, fig. 1; M. Lillich, "Les vitraux de Saint-Pierre de Chartres," "*Les monuments historiques de la France,* no. 1 (1977), ill. p. 55.

49. We are indebted to the restorers for several publications of the "nonconforming debris": a) Charles Lorin, "Médaillon du XIIe siècle dans l'église Saint-Pierre de Chartres," *Société archéologique d'Eure-et-Loir, Le Cinquantenaire,* I (1906), pp. 508–514 (see fn. 6 supra); b) Comte Paul Biver and Edmond Socard, "Le vitrail civil au XIVe siècle," *Bulletin monumental,* LXXVII (1913), pp. 258–264.

50. See fn. 30 supra. The plan in Pl. 2 is marked with locations of the panels then in the ambulatory.

51. Jean Trouvelot was the *architecte-en-chef* and François Lorin of Chartres the glass

restorer. Photographs taken while the glass was down are now available as montages in the *Archives photographiques.* See also Trouvelot's 1939 drawings in the Archives: J. Trouvelot, "Eglise Saint-Pierre de Chartres, dépose des vitraux (dessins de repérage des panneaux et mise en caisse. 29 dessins). 1939."

52. The glass of Bay 13, south choir, was destroyed by a grenade. See Chapter II, fn. 1. The restorer François Lorin, made use of the old glass when possible — from the lower portions of the bay, mostly — and of old photographs and the designs of other choir bays. His design does not copy the original one, however, which was not available to him. See old photographs (Pls. 28, 30) and a drawing (Pl. 29) of the lower right figure of Bay 13 in de Lasteyrie, reproduced by Olivier Merson, *Les vitraux* (Paris, 1894), p. 75. It differs from the similar designs in Bay 16 only in the detail above and below the figure.

{ CHAPTER II }

Choir: Style

THE ten windows in the clerestory of the choir at Saint-Père are, from a stylistic point of view, the most challenging in the church. They comprise Bays 8–17, according to the numbering of the *Monuments historiques,* five windows on each side of the straight choir clerestory (see fold-out plan). The glass contained in these five huge bays exhibits a combination of color and grisaille unique in medieval glazing: an equal number of completely colored figure lancets and almost completely uncolored grisaille ones alternate vertically around the choir (Pls. 17, 18, 20, 21, 25, 30, 31, 33, 35, 36). As each window contains four lancets, the combination becomes, left to right: color-grisaille-color-grisaille. The upper tracery lights are glazed in grisaille (Pls. 40, 41). Grisaille also fills the triforium which underlines the clerestory (Pl. 43).

The tracery of each bay is designed as two lancets, each divided by a mullion and surmounted by a roundel with pierced spandrels (see Fig. 1). The space above the two divided lancets is filled by a large, lobed rose, pierced spandrels to either side, and a pierced triangle below.

Much of the choir glazing seems to predate its architecture. Unfortunately, no documentation exists for either the glazing or the building campaigns. The architecture of the choir triforium and clerestory, discussed in Chapter I, can be dated ca. 1260–1270. Most of the glass finds its proper stylistic milieu ca. 1245.

Saint-Père Choir Prophets: Cartoons

Cartoon A	Bay 8: used twice (left figures)
	Bay 9: used once (top left — middle panel now a restoration)
Cartoon B	Bay 8: used once (bottom right)
	Bay 9: used twice (upper right — new head panel)
Cartoon C	Bay 10: twice (*Daniel* and *Enoch*)
Cartoon D	Bay 10: once *(Habbakuk)*
	Bay 11: once *(Ezekiel)*
Cartoon E	Bay 10: once (upper right)
	Bay 11: once (upper right)
Cartoon F	Bay 11: twice (left)
Cartoon G	Bay 12: once (top right)
	Bay 13: once (top right)
Cartoon H	Bay 12: once (top left)
	Bay 13: once (*Balaam,* top left)
	Bay 17: once (bottom left)
Cartoon I	Bay 14: twice (left)
Cartoon J	Bay 14: twice (right)
Cartoon K	Bay 15: twice (left)
Cartoon L	Bay 15: twice (right)
Cartoon M	Bay 13: once (right bottom)
	Bay 16: twice (bottom right, top right)
Cartoon N	Bay 13: once (bottom left)
	Bay 16: once (bottom left)
Cartoon O	Bay 12: once (bottom left)
	Bay 16: once (top left)
	Bay 17: once (top left)
Cartoon P	Bay 12: once (*Noel,* bottom right)
	Bay 17: once (bottom right — middle panel is modern)
Cartoon Q	Bay 17: once (top right)
	This cartoon is a close variant of Cartoon G
Cartoon R	Bay 8: once (top right)
Cartoon S	Bay 9: once (bottom left)

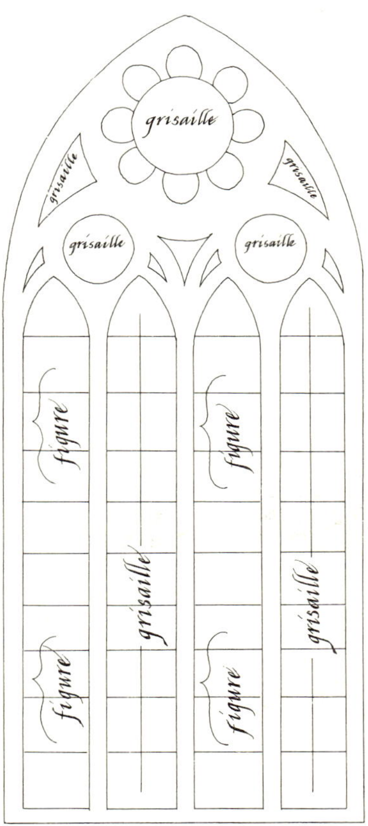

Figure 1 Format of Bays 8–17 (choir). (Drawing by Kevin McIntyre)

This conclusion can be reached by studies of a number of elements of the windows: grisaille design, colors employed and their balance, the combination of color and grisaille, figure-framing devices, and inscription style. A small amount of the choir glass can be distinguished from the early work, and falls contemporary with the achievement of the architecture, ca. 1270. It adapts to the older patterns, however, and it seems to have been made only when the shape or dimensions of the lights made the re-employment of older panels problematical.

The glazing of the choir windows, although of a homogeneous pattern maintained through the entire choir, falls into three stylistic groups. The first and earliest group is the lancet glass — both color and grisaille — of Bays 8–13 and Bays 16–17, comprising eight of the ten choir windows (see fold-out plan). The second is the glass — color and grisaille — of the remaining two windows, i.e., Bays 14 and 15. The last group, more difficult to classify because of its

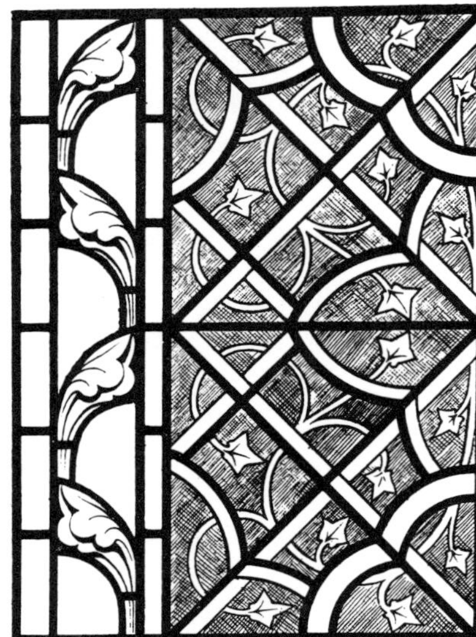

Figure 2 Grisaille patterns from St. Germer-de-Fly, 1260's. *(After Ottin).*

mediocre condition, is the grisaille glazing of most of the choir triforium and large parts of the clerestory tracery lights as well. The date of the last two groups could well be contemporary but the first group falls well before them.

We are attempting, therefore, to compare three groups of glazing from two campaigns: an earlier group comprising a large amount of colored glass and a smaller amount of grisaille;[1] a later group consisting of a very small amount of color and grisaille of a high quality; and another later group of rather mediocre grisaille. Let us deal with the comparison of grisaille styles first.

The function of grisaille glazing was undergoing a fundamental revision in the middle two quarters of the thirteenth century. For various reasons — chiefly economic necessity and the desire for more light in church interiors[2] — glaziers began to experiment with various ways not only of employing grisaille alone and in combination with color but also of lightening the grisaille design itself. From about 1230 to 1300, grisaille changed from crosshatched, idealized and centralized patterns[3] to continuous, naturalistic and clear-grounded ones. The use of bosses was developed to emphasize and give accent to the panel arrangement. Leading became more regular, although the panel division was often strongly maintained by a pattern known as "bulging" the quarries at the corners of the panel and around the boss in the center.[4] A trellis pattern often was painted parallel to such leads. Clear grounds replaced crosshatching. The desire for greater naturalism produced oak leaves and clover to replace the ancient pal-

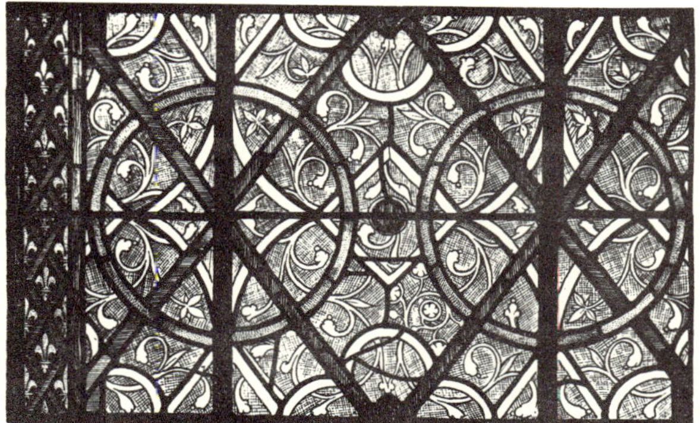
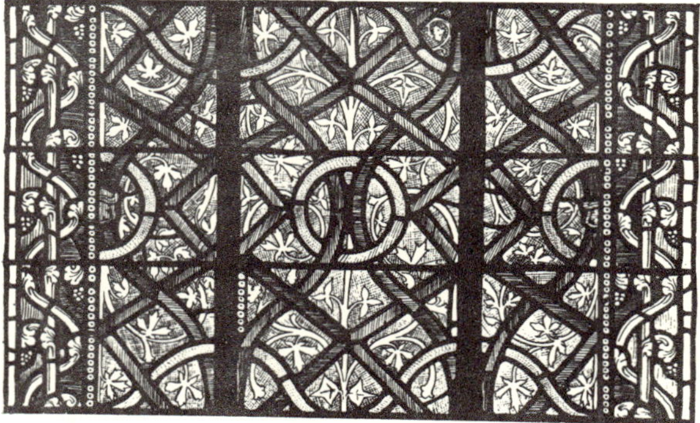

Figure 3 Grisaille patterns from Saint-Urbain, Troyes, ca. 1270. *(After Day).*

mettes. And the device of a central stem running vertically through the panels of a lancet was instigated in place of the older, self-sufficient centripetal panel designs. These features broke into traditional grisaille design one by one during the mid-thirteenth century, and no real order of precedence can be established for their adoption.[5] Examples can be found of almost every possible combination of the old and new (see Figs. 2 and 3). Naturalistic foliage was inserted into the older centripetal panel design, for instance,[6] and the new continuous trellis and central stem systems were employed with idealized palmette leaves[7] and/or with a crosshatched ground. The last-named style, as a matter of fact, is just what occurs in the two later windows (Bays 14–15) of the Saint-Père choir (Pls. 31, 33, 42), and it is precisely the indecision and transitional aura of the design which dates it ca. 1260–1270.[8]

The grisaille in the tracery lights of the Saint-Père choir shows quite different experiments of a similarly transitional nature. Grounds are occasionally clear (Pl. 40). Some of the roses and spandrels are leaded in regular lozenges (Pl. 41). A few spandrels are filled with a continuous, foliated stem. The painting in the tracery lights is much heavier and more pedestrian than that of the lancet grisaille in Bays 14–15, but the temerity with which new features are introduced stamps both groups as contemporary, ca. 1260–1270.

The grisaille of the triforium below[9] sings the same tune, albeit rather weakly. These panels are in appalling condition. Many of them are largely inept, old restorations, and the genuine bits which remain are usually in a state of deterioration.[10] The painting, when old, is dull, tight, and hard. In spite of the

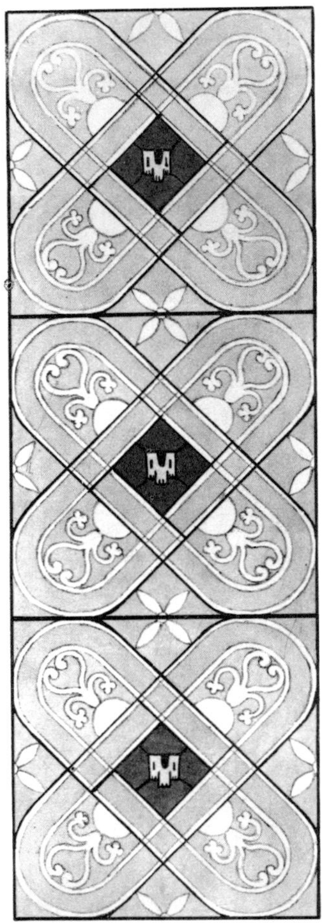

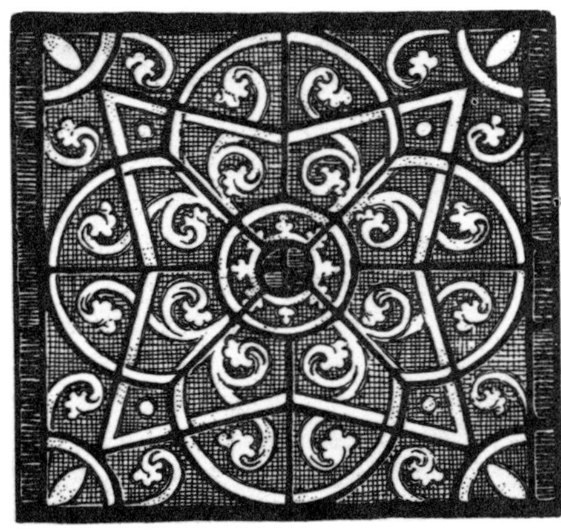

Figure 4 Choir: grisaille pattern of Bays 12, 13. *(After F. de Lasteyrie).*

Figure 5 Choir: grisaille pattern of Bays 10, 11. *(After Day).*

mediocre workmanship, however, the same hesitant search for new formulae which can be seen in the clerestory grisaille of Bays 14 and 15 and in many of the clerestory tracery lights is also evident here (see Pl. 43). The grounds are usually clear. Leading varies from patterns "bulged" to varying extents to absolutely regular quarrying. The foliage, although almost always still of the older idealized type, often sprouts from a new central stem. Most of the roundels in the triforium still maintain a centripetal design — this will begin to relax by ca. 1300 in the apse — but some combine it with more naturalistic foliage than previously. What can one say about such a hodgepodge? Only that the artist, in this case a rather unskilled journeyman, was tempted by the same desire for stylistic experiment as his more talented co-workers in the clerestory. The campaign of glazing dates ca. 1260–1270.

So much for the choir grisaille which is contemporary with its architectural setting. The attractive panels in the grisaille lancets of Bays 10–13[11] predate the period of transition which is evidenced by the grisaille described above. Almost completely uncolored, on a crosshatched ground, with patterned leads and palmettes forming self-contained centripetal patterns repeated panel after panel, the grisailles of Bays 10–13 (Pls. 38, 39 and Figs. 4, 5) are virile examples of a fairly widespread mid-century type such as can be found at Auxerre (Fig. 6) and Troyes cathedrals (Pl. 85).[12] That they date from the mid-1240's, almost exactly contemporary with Auxerre and Troyes, seems very likely.

A comparison of the Saint-Père choir grisailles with those of Tours, a closely related monument of the Western school, underlines these conclusions. The grisaille in the two clerestory windows of the Tours choir (Canons of Loches window and the Eight Bishops window, Bays 5 and 11),[13] dating ca. 1257–1270, falls stylistically between the two Saint-Père grisaille types. It is crosshatched with a centripetal pattern and idealized foliage, like the earlier Saint-Père style of Bays 10–13, but the leading has become a quasi-regular quarry pattern, "bulged" at the center and corners of each panel. It is a logical intermediary to the more regular trellis-work and central stems of Saint-Père Bays 14–15.

On the basis of grisaille analysis, then, two periods can be established for the Saint-Père choir glazing: ca. 1260–1270 for the choir triforium, for Bays 14 and 15, and for all of the choir tracery lights; and ca. 1240–1245 for the lancets of Bays 10–13. An extension of the discussion to aspects of the colored glazing will demonstrate that the lancets of Bays 16–17 join the ca. 1245 group, and that, excepting the two later Bays (14–15), all the choir lancets have been re-used in their present position.

The first piece of evidence for a date in the 1240's for the choir lancets is provided by the infrequent inscriptions found therein. Unfortunately only a very few prophets are singled out for identification. Of the thirty-two figures contained in the eight windows under consideration, only five are named: "Ezekeel" in Bay 11 (Pl. 21); "Abbacuc," Daniel, and "Enop" (?) in Bay 10 (Pl. 20); and "Noel" (?) in Bay 12 (Pl. 24).[14] The letters are broad, blocklike, and widely-spaced, a mixture of capitals (angular majuscules) and uncials (rounded majuscules). The most decorated letters of the few inscriptions included at Saint-Père are the E, which is rounded and occasionally closed on the right, and the A, which is blocklike and sometimes has a V-shaped crossbar and sometimes a more-or-less strongly emphasized horizontal bar at the top. U is rendered as V.

Medieval lettering[15] employed capitals, uncials, and minuscules (small letters derived from majuscules). Uncials appeared ca. 800 and gradually increased in use until the achievement of a complete uncial alphabet, or Gothic majuscule, commonly know as "Lombardic." The Saint-Père nave windows, ca. 1300–1310,

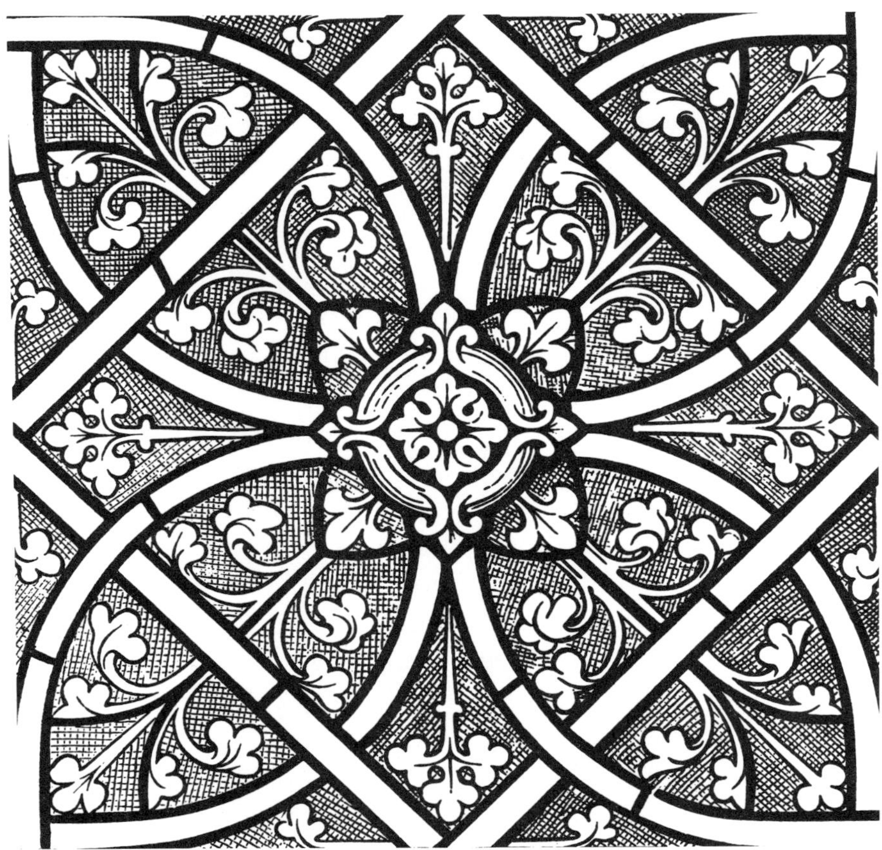

Figure 6 Grisaille pattern from Auxerre, 1240's. *(After Viollet-le-duc).*

contain many beautiful examples of "Lombardic" script. Not in general use until the last quarter of the thirteenth century, "Lombardic" was completely superseded by the middle of the next century in northern Europe by Gothic minuscule or "Black-letter," the alphabet still used occasionally in German printed books. The letters of the Saint-Père choir inscriptions in question are largely capitals, E being the only consistent true uncial.

Equally important are the blocklike proportions and wide spacing. Such well-spaced and undecorated lettering is extremely rare in glazing after 1250. Common in the twelfth century, it can be seen at Saint-Remi[16] at the end of that century; at Chartres and Bourges; at Reims in the Henri de Braine window (1227–1240); and in the choirs of Auxerre and Troyes cathedrals (both in the 1240's).[17] The Le Mans choir inscriptions, which date ca. 1250–1260,[18] are already more cramped by comparison, although similar in some letter forms and in the general proportions of letters. At Amiens the apse window of 1269 has blocklike letters in an irregular, cramped grouping, and the Sts. Edward and Edmund window of ca. 1280 in the same cathedral has an inscription clearly foreshadowing the vertical emphasis of the "Lombardic" and "Black-letter" styles. The inscription in the Canons of Loches window at Tours, ca. 1260–1270, exhibits similarly cramped, elongated, and irregular lettering.[19] Saint-Urbain at Troyes (1266–1277) has many beautiful transitional inscriptions. The letters are beginning to slant and curve, they are longer and narrower in proportion, and they are often thickened on the vertical and thinned on the horizontal. Compare also the "Lombardic" inscriptions of such windows as the panels from the Cluny Museum (château of Rouen?), the window from Saint-Germain-Village (Eure), and the Templar Jaques le Clavier panel from Sainte-Vaubourg, all designs of the 1260's[20] and all closer to the "Lombardic" alphabet than the prophets' inscriptions of Saint-Père.

Most telling, however, is the comparison with the inscriptions of the Sées clerestory.[21] Sées is a monument, like Saint-Père, of the Western school of glasspainting. Its choir windows have been dated with precision by Lafond ca. 1270–1280,[22] or approximately contemporary with the new glass designed for the narrow Bays 14–15 of the Saint-Père choir (which have no inscriptions). Uncials and capitals are combined at Sées, but the balance is clearly tipped in favor of the former. In the "Mestre Osmont" inscription[23] (northwesternmost choir bay), for example, the first T is a capital, but the second is an uncial and so are the M and N. The letters are vertically stressed and compressed in spacing. The Saint-Père choir is unquestionably a considerably earlier form, and a date before 1250, that is to say immediately preceding the inscriptions of another Western school monument, Le Mans, seems undeniable.

A similar conclusion results from a study of color and how it is used in the Saint-Père choir. All of the early colored lancets (see Pls. II, III) are characterized by a heavy predominance of blue. It is the only color in use for the figure grounds. Red is unquestionably a secondary color in these windows. Brown and dark green, as well as a dark mustard yellow and a muted and rather opaque white, are prevalent in the coloration of the figures themselves. Flesh tones are dark. The general effect is rich and glowing, but also rather quiet in the presence of so many receding tones. In contrast, the glazing of Bays 14–15 (Pl. IV) shows a much more even balance of red and blue, clearer flesh tones, less muted yellow and white, and a very light clear green in abundance, a green found nowhere else in the choir. J.-J. Gruber, in his valuable treatise on glass technique during the period 1270–1328, has singled out just such features as coming into importance then: "l'éclaircissement de la gamme," the more frequent use of yellow and green, and the abandonment of neutral figures against a strong blue ground, with the subsequent result of a more equal balance in importance of all colors.[24] If his date of 1270 be taken, then, as a convenient dividing line, the four colored lancets of Bays 14–15 would clearly fall after and the rest of the lancets of the choir well before.

Two other stylistic features at Saint-Père — the framing devices employed for the choir figures and the combination of colored glazing with grisaille — are of particular importance and interest for the progress of clerestory design in the thirteenth century. This relationship is most easily explained in the context of the general development of the Gothic clerestory and its glazing. From at least the late twelfth century the common device for high windows was the large single figure under an abstracted arcade or canopy form, decorated with motifs from the architectural repertoire (pediments, crenellated walls, etc.). The design of one figure to one lancet is a logical one and, moreover, legible from the ground. This formula occurs in both the early single lancets and in the doublet-and-rose window introduced at Chartres. With the enlargement of clerestories in the thirteenth century, the single-figure design was usually retained and adapted to the new dimensions by various means: either two figures were put in the lancet instead of one (like pairs of "disputing philosophers"), or the single figure was framed with two wide borders in place of only one.[25] The doublet-and-rose design was old-fashioned by ca. 1240, however. Clerestory tracery at the mid-century presented the puzzled glazier with an increasing number of awkwardly long, narrow lights to fill. Except for the few clerestories where medallions of the type popularized by the Sainte-Chapelle ca. 1245 were employed, the old idea of one figure to one lancet revived quickly. The result is the band window. This well-known design, formerly mislabeled the "fourteenth-century formula"[26] because of its currency then, consists of a horizontal parade of figures under canopies, one in each light, extending across the vast width of the clerestory bays. The space in the window which sandwiched this band of figure panels above and below was absorbed by grisaille, cheaper and passing more light to the increasingly elegant rayonnant architecture.

As might be expected, the period between the general adoption of the multi-mullioned tracery (1240's) and the crystallization, in the band window ca. 1265, of the solution to the problem such tracery presented to glaziers, saw various experiments in clerestory design.[27] The glass in the Saint-Père choir — both the early series of choir figures and the later glazing of Bays 14–15 — falls within this unsettled period. The solutions at Saint-Père to the problems of the framing of large clerestory figures and of the combination of color with grisaille can be called almost unique. First, let us look at the solutions to the problem of the framing of large figures in the two groups of choir glass.

In all the glass except that in Bays 14–15, the figures stand one above the

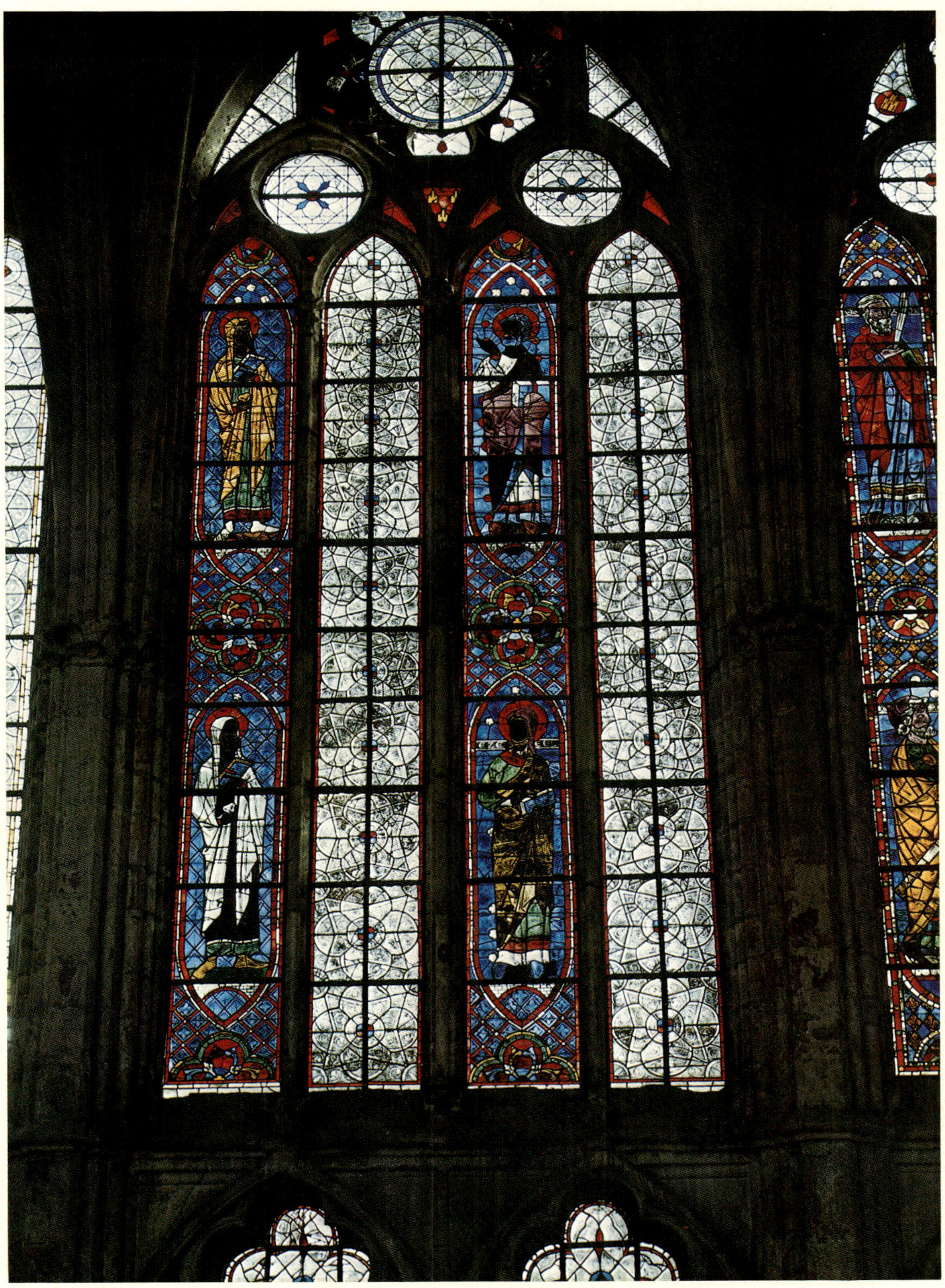

PLATE III South side of the choir: Bay 11. *(Edouard Fièvet)*

other, each in a narrow, greatly elongated medallion frame (see Pl. II). The space between these medallions contains diaperwork, fleurs-de-lis, rosettes and palmettes from the standard repertory of filler designs (see Pls. 17, 21, 25, 36). In Bays 14–15, on the other hand (Pls. 31 and 33), the figures appear in niches, complete with gable and architectural motifs above them and rather large bases beneath their feet. Except for these elaborate bases, which are extremely precocious for the thirteenth century,[28] the canopied figures of Bays 14–15[29] can hardly be distinguished from contemporary dated examples in the Western school, such as the aforementioned two windows at Tours, or the series from Sées Cathedral.

The medallion figures of the rest of the choir are quite another story. Large clerestory figures framed in medallions occur elsewhere, as far as I know, only in two other places: (1) in a few bays of Troyes Cathedral choir, ca. 1240–1250 (Pl. 87);[30] and (2) in a lost panel fragment originally from the choir of Tournai, which was in construction from 1243 and dedicated 1255.[31] Indeed the Tournai saint is framed by both an architectural dais and a medallion, the former inside the latter. In all three cases the solution may have been an original invention by a glazier confronted by the same problem. From the early thirteenth century the length of clerestory lights, as well as their width, had troubled glass designers. The seven long apsidal lancets of Chartres show a confusion of ideas — elongated single figures under canopies (the famous "Big Angel"), enlarged and simplified medallion scenes, "disputing" pairs under individual canopies — the whole repertoire, in fact, now presented in three superimposed rows rather than two.[32] No one solution ever crystallized, however, and the problem of how to fill long lancets plagued glaziers until the band window formula emerged ca. 1265.

Large figures placed one over the other, each under a complete architectural dais, cannot help but disintegrate surface design into a conjunction of rather unrelated areas. This fact eventually helped spark the development of immensely elongated canopies and bases in the last years of the thirteenth century, a development which dominates the entire history of glazing thereafter up to and even including the Renaissance.[33] But before the development of canopies and bases, a few abortive experiments were made to achieve the same end — i.e., to alleviate the awkwardness inherent in individual daises stacked up in rows — by combining the large single figure with the medallion framework and diaper and so to unify the surface of the window without sacrificing clarity. At Saint-Père this experiment is found in its purest form, for no attempt was made to superimpose a connective "story" on the figures such as was done, for example, at Troyes in the Wise and Foolish Virgins window. It must be noted, though, that the Saint-Père figures have been re-used in narrower lancets, and may originally have been side by side in "disputing pairs"[34] like the Troyes Bishops and Kings window (Pl. 87).[35]

It may be asked whether or not it was the influence of the Sainte-Chapelle which prompted these isolated experiments with large figures in medallion frames. On the contrary, I believe the reverse to be true. They very probably predate the strong Parisian influence of the late 1240's and succeeding decades. The combination of large figures and medallion frames is not absolutely unknown in earlier glazing, as can be seen from one window of framed seated prophets in the Chartres clerestory,[36] and seems a logical extension of the enlarged, simplified medallions also found there and later on a more vast scale at Troyes. The windows of Troyes contain diverse and unrelated subjects, ranging through parables, saints' lives, the Passion, and contemporary history. At Troyes the basic problem was to present such narratives legibly in long narrow lancets far from the viewer's eye. Stories are often simplified, therefore, to a single figure or pair of figures, occasionally placed under primitive canopies (e.g. Theophilus legend window, southwest choir) but commonly in enlarged medallions. Therefore, the use of the medallion framework for the Bishops and Kings window and the Wise and Foolish Virgins window at Troyes is a quite understandable extension of its use in the neighboring narrative windows.

Large medallions were not destined for popularity, however. Their place was quickly usurped in the 1250's and later by windows of Parisian influence. At Le Mans, which postdates the Sainte-Chapelle by up to a decade and includes many beautiful windows of the Parisian type, exactly the reverse of the Troyes designs occurs: not only large single figures but also simplified scenes are invariably placed under canopies (see the window of Sts. Gervais and Protais and St. Etienne, apse clerestory, first north). In the Tours choir, with the advent of the band window formula, the dichotomy in clerestory design — Parisian-type medallions and large figures under canopies — was formalized. The Saint-Père choir lancets fit into this picture of stylistic turbulence as rare and original transitional designs predating the influence of the Sainte-Chapelle, i.e., ca. 1240–1245.

The combination of grisaille and color at Saint-Père is even more unique. This combination undoubtedly dates from the placing of glass in the present architecture, ca. 1270, and therefore is virtually contemporary with the first appearance of the horizontal banding formula mentioned above. It is indeed an alternate resolution of the problem.[37]

The combination at Saint-Père comprises strips of color and grisaille, vertical rather than horizontal, which alternate around the choir. Each window of four lancets is thus divided vertically into color-grisaille-color-grisaille (see Fig. 1). Although drastically complicated stylistically by the re-use of so much older glass, the combination invented by the Saint-Père glazier who put the glass in its present position (and who also designed and executed the glass in Bays 14–15) was essentially similar to that of the precocious glazier of the band windows of Tours. Both men combined large blocks of color with uncolored grisaille so as to accentuate their greatest contrast, at Tours horizontally and at Saint-Père, in an isolated example, vertically.

Combinations of color and grisaille in the same window design can be found from all periods of stained glass.[38] After the invention of the band window ca. 1265, the vast majority of such combinations falls into that category. The combination of large contrasting blocks of color (canopied figures) and of grisaille seems to have originated in the Champagne-Burgundy area. Colored figure panels are framed with grisaille panels in the early thirteenth century in the clerestory of Reims Cathedral (ca. 1235–1240, some of the colored glass re-used) and most notably at Auxerre (ca. 1240–1245). Both the Virgin chapel and the choir clerestory of Auxerre include windows filled with a vertical colored strip (figure panels) framed by vertical strips of grisaille. This vertical alternation is adopted at Saint-Père at about the same time the Tours designer is arranging his blocks of color and grisaille horizontally.

The Reims and Auxerre lancets are of broad proportions, however, while those of the Saint-Père rayonnant choir are divided by mullions into four elongated lights with an elaborate tracery corona of roundels and spandrels of various shapes. The glazier, prevented by the stonework from employing the established tripartite arrangement of "figure sandwiched in grisaille," decentralized his design and alternated vertical color and grisaille strips down the choir. A tentative solution, it produces a very pleasant effect at Saint-Père, where it is used for all the clerestories of the straight choir. It is undeniable, however, that this "shutter" effect would be successful only in such a complete series; a single such window could not happily be inserted into the glazing of a monument. The Saint-Père "shutter" design and the Tours "band window" design are equally valid, approximately contemporary efforts to solve the same problem, i.e., the combination of blocks of color and grisaille in immense rayonnant windows. The flexibility and internally controlled balance of the Tours solution assured its triumph.

Observations on the pose and draperies of the Saint-Père patriarchs take the same shape as the remarks on decorative detail. The early group are ferocious and hieratic — the quality of symbol underlined by the pose, mostly full-face or full-profile. The worthies of Bays 14–15 are more lightweight, more courtly, and take a graceful three-quarter stance. The early group includes several styles of drapery painting, the long abundant linework (for example Bay 16, top left) being perhaps the most backward-looking. Similarly heavy drapery painting, actually more archaic, hangs on in a single bay of Le Mans (axial upper ambulatory ca. 1250). The painting of Bay 15 is more spare and spiky, not unlike Sées Cathedral (ca. 1275) in its brevity and angularity. Nor has it any of the rounded definition and grasp of mass of one of the fine early hands of Saint-Père, that of Bay 16, bottom left.

To reconstruct, then, the probable sequence of events in the Saint-Père ateliers during the middle of the thirteenth century: the stylistic evidence seems to indicate an early date (in the 1240's) for the body of the choir glass, both grisaille and figures, and a date somewhat more advanced (closer to 1265–1270) for the glazing of Bays 14–15, the tracery lights of the choir, and the grisaille in the triforium. In the face of a vacuum in documentation for these years one must rely on such differences in style for any hypothesis offered. The possibility exists, of course, that an older and more archaic master could have been responsible for the "earlier" glazing, while his younger contemporary was designing in a somewhat more advanced vein at the same moment. I cannot easily accept such a theory for the following reason. It seems logical to assume, when both grisaille and figure work in some windows stylistically predate the grisaille and figures of other windows, that there is probably a hiatus between their dates of execution. An "older, archaic" master hypothetically responsible for most of the choir glass would more likely have designed all the figures, while his younger contemporary would have been assigned all the grisaille (or responsibility for the designs might have been reversed). When, in both prestige and non-prestige elements, a group of designs (i.e., all choir clerestories excepting 14–15) are stylistically distinct from another group (Bays 14–15), it seems much more likely that the whole shop which produced the "archaic" windows was indeed earlier than the shop which designed the "advanced" ones.

If, then, one accepts the hypothesis that a gap of some twenty years or more intervenes between the design of the two choir groups, and that the later work is contemporary with the architecture in which it is found, the problem presents itself of the original location of the earlier work. It comprises thirty-two figures[39] and, at present, a somewhat lesser number of grisaille panels,[40] a considerable number to "relocate," even hypothetically.

Discounting the possibility of a glazed cloister or a series of lower aisle windows (broad undivided lancets at Saint-Père), the early choir glass must have been intended either for the twelfth-century choir or for the nave, newly completed by the early 1240's. The choir architecture would have had an appearance not unlike that of Saint-Germer-de-Fly (Oise),[41] or the original Saint-Germain-des-Prés choir before the windows were lengthened.[42] With seven single windows in the apse and ten double windows in the choir, the maximum total of twenty-seven lancets might have been available. If their width in relation to the supporting ambulatory arcade was comparable to that in Saint-Germain-des-Prés,[43] the lancets would easily have been wide enough for the present choir figures, but could have accommodated no more than one figure vertically.

The preferred hypothesis is that the early choir glass was intended for the nave. The new nave added to the twelfth-century choir was probably complete by the 1240's.[44] It would be a fair assumption, then, that the main body of glass now in the choir, dating from the early 1240's, was originally planned for the nave. The question of measurements becomes vital here. Each lancet of the huge doublet windows in the nave measures 174–175 cm. across, including the two vertical irons they now possess. The choir bay measurements vary considerably, but 63 cm. can be taken as an approximate measure of the width of the early grisaille.[45] It is evident that a design consisting of narrow borders (say, 10 cm. wide) plus two vertical strips of grisaille framing a central colored block of panels,[46] *à la rémoise,* would be impossibly wide for the lancets of the nave. If indeed the choir glass came from the twelve windows of the nave, the following arrangement is suggested: (a) grisaille — at least four nave windows of grisaille, two panels wide, divided by an iron down the center and enclosed by a wide border of 19–20 cm. Fragments of such borders have been found in the church.[47] Two such borders (40 cm.) plus two grisaille panels (126 cm.) plus irons would fit the nave doublets exactly, in a design similar to those of Bourges and Reims ca. 1235;[48] (b) figures — either eight nave windows containing four figures each (i.e., two figures to each doublet lancet, surrounded by decorative filler and a wide border?), or, a lesser number of windows containing eight figures each in "disputing pairs" like the large medallion figures at Troyes.[49] The latter theory is more attractive and could account for the debris from the church which seems to have formed part of the early standing prophet series.[50]

There is no reason to assume that the ca. 1300–1315 glazing of the nave retained the thirteenth-century irons. Neither is there any reason to assume that the alternating arrangement of light and dark in the nave reflects an older glazing pattern.[51] Hypothesis upon hypothesis; it would seem, therefore, that the glass originally intended for the nave was probably not arranged in any grisaille/color combination. It is more likely that the earlier plan was for windows entirely colored or entirely grisaille (except, perhaps, for borders) and that the idea of combining the two waited upon their redesign ca. 1270.

If the nave, then, had been filled with an abundance of beautiful standing prophets, why were not four of them used to fill Bays 14–15? Measurements provide an answer. The dimensions of the upper stories of the choir were predetermined by the twelfth-century arcading standing below them. The early arcading varies considerably and somewhat irregularly in width, Bays 8–9 being the largest and Bays 14–15 by far the smallest.[52] The lancets of Bays 14–15 are barely 50 cm. wide, whereas the narrowest figure-panel at present in the choir exceeds that width even when it is completely denuded of borders or filets. For the same reason, older grisaille of the type re-used in Bays 10–13 could not have been cut down to 50 cm. width without hopelessly truncating its centripetal pattern.[53] The extra width of Bays 10–11 (Pls. 20, 21) is taken up by inserting an unnecessary vertical iron of 3.5 cm. down the middle of the grisaille.[54]

A somewhat more delicate question is whether or not the medallion frameworks formed part of the original design. As the older grisaille was a uniform width of about 63 cm., it is tempting to assume that the original width of the figure-panels was the same. One has only to glance at the choir to see, however, that in Bays 8–9 (Pls. 17, 18) the border follows the lancet-head rather exactly and that in Bays 12–13 (Pls. 25, 30) and 16–17 (Pls. 35, 36) the "medallions" are sliced at the sides by a thin border which frames the entire light. I believe one may go so far as to advance the hypothesis, then, that the coarser border and the filler (significantly not diaperwork in this case) of the broader Bays 8–9 dates from the redesign ca. 1270, and that the framing of these figures has been largely revamped to suit the great width of the lancets.[55] Furthermore, I would suggest that the dimensions and overall design of the colored glass in Bays 10–11 most closely approximate the original, and therefore by extension that the diapering and the unadorned filet medallion-frameworks of these windows and of most of Bays 12–13 and 16–17 are original, ca. 1240–1245.

Whether or not the choir glass was ever actually installed in the nave windows for which it was probably designed is a question which seems likely to remain moot. What is more certain is that fast upon the nave's erection followed the chapter's decision to raze the twelfth-century choir and rebuild it in a more modern style. An attractive hypothesis would be that the glass ready for installation in the new nave was held and redesigned for immediate installation in the new choir when it was finished at a date close to 1270. Work could have begun, in fact, as soon as the architect provided the masons with templates of the window tracery.

An interesting footnote concerning the installation of the glass in the new choir underlines the probable excitement and improvisation in the Saint-Père workshops during the third quarter of the century. All of the choir windows, even the late Bays 14–15, include an added strip which heightens them slightly. In the north windows the strips are inserted obviously and rather awkwardly about mid-height (often in the arch of the lower figure's medallion frame) (see Pls. 17, 20, 25, 35), while on the south the windows' decorative filler is simply continued at the bottom (Pls. 18, 21, 30, 36). The most logical assumption would be that after the glass was redesigned and ready for the north side, including the new Bay 14, the architect decided to push his audacious clerestory another step toward heaven. The north side would then require patching before installation, while the unfinished southern panels could easily be extended to fill the new dimensions. Bay 15 (Pl. 33), the new bay on the south, has slightly more sophisticated figure bases than those of Bay 14 (Pl. 31).[56] The conclusion seems obvious: the ca. 1270 choir was rising while the glass was in the workshop for reworking.

The Saint-Père choir glazing is of interest not only because of its beauty and its connections with other monuments in the "West"[57] but because its transitional style throws light upon the development of many stylistic formulae during the artistically turbulent years of the second and third quarters of the thirteenth century. The design of grisaille, the combination of grisaille and color, the arrangement of legible figure patterns for the new narrow lancets of the clerestory, the changing style in the framing of large figures — all these issues were current in the Saint-Père atelier. Further complicating their solutions and our understanding of them is the fact that during the course of this rapidly fluctuating period the architecture of the nave was completed and that of the upper choir razed and rebuilt, probably leaving much recent, expensive and beautiful glass to be re-situated. The program most likely went as follows: the glass now in the choir lancets, except Bays 14–15, made around 1240–1245, original placement (if any) unknown but probably intended for the nave; glass of Bays 14–15 made around 1265–1270 for the architecture in which it is found; grisaille of the choir clerestory tracery and triforium approximately contemporary to Bays 14–15 but by an inferior artisan. The unique combination of color and grisaille which the glazier of 1270 produced is probably his alone, and in no way reflects the original design of the nave.

The grisaille/color striping in the choir, although never destined for widespread adoption, is quite successful in such a large series of windows and is very beautiful. Apparently the monks at Saint-Père, so *au courant* with the architectural fashion, were pleased with it too, for in preference to other more popular solutions at the turn of the century they had it adapted for use in the extensive early fourteenth-century glazing of the nave.

NOTES

1. The amount of grisaille is less because only four of the eight early windows retain their antique grisaille lancets. See fn. 11, this chapter. Almost all the colored glass, on the other hand, remains. The only exception is Bay 13; see Chapter I, fn. 52. The modern glass is the work of François Lorin after World War II, and succeeds to an admirable degree in both blending with and distinguishing itself from the medieval glass around it.

2. See M. Lillich, "The Band Window: A Theory of Origin and Development," *Gesta* IX/1 (1970), p. 31, fn. 13. I have analyzed thirteenth century grisaille forms in "A Redating of the Thirteenth-Century Grisaille Windows of Chartres Cathedral," *Gesta* XI/1, (1972), pp. 11–18; and "Three Essays on French Thirteenth-Century Grisaille Glass," *Journal of Glass Studies* XV (1973), pp. 69–78.

3. Arnold's "Herba Benedicta." See Hugh Arnold, *Stained Glass of the Middle Ages in England and France,* 2nd ed. (London, 1939), pp. 165–166.

4. The ultimate development of leading into absolutely regular quarries came into its own with the advent of the silver stain technique in the fourteenth century.

5. It is my feeling that naturalistic foliage first became common in Normandy, but this impression may be caused by the greater number of examples there or, at any rate, of published examples (thanks to the tireless efforts of M. Jean Lafond). The grisaille at Saint-Germer-de-Fly (Oise), dated 1259–1266 (see Fig. 2), and that of Sainte-Vaubourg (Ardennes, near Rouen), consecrated in 1264, as well as the grisailles possibly originating from the château of Rouen, all include some naturalistic foliage in otherwise transitional designs. See Lafond, "Normandie," pp. 328ff.; Viollet-le-duc, *Dictionnaire raisonné de l'architecture française du XIe au XVIe siècle,* IX (Paris, 1868), pp. 453–454. Arnold, p. 166, proposes that naturalistic foliage was used first in England.

6. Sainte-Vaubourg (Ardennes, near Rouen), consecrated 1264. See Lafond, "Normandie," pp. 328ff.; and fn. 5, this chapter.

7. Six panels in the Cluny Museum, possibly from the château at Rouen, ca. 1260 (Lafond, "Normandie," p. 337; illustrated in *La revue des arts,* V [1955], pls. on p. 181 and opp. p. 182). A primitive central stem (which does not yet grow only upwards) is combined with formalized leafage, quite irregularly bulged leading at the corners, all on a clear un-crosshatched ground. A very nice transitional example. A sizeable group of fragments of this "Cluny Museum" grisaille was purchased by the Corning Museum of Glass; see Lillich, "Three Essays," pp. 73–75; *Medieval Art in Upstate New York,* ed. Lillich (Syracuse, New York, Everson Museum of Art, 1974), pp. 20–21.

8. Very similar grisaille can be seen among the tremendous variety of patterns at Saint-Urbain at Troyes (ca. 1266–1272). It occurs in some panels at Saint-Germer-de-Fly (1259–1266) as well. Figs. 2 and 3 give a small selection of such designs.

9. The remains of grisaille in the apse triforium are considerably more advanced — an exquisitely painted naturalistic foliage — and probably date with the glass of the apse clerestory, after 1297 (see Pls. 44, 45).

10. It is difficult to account for the extremely dilapidated state of the choir triforium windows. They are protected on the outside by the aisle roofing and inside by a balustrade and arcading. Presumably none of the marauders who for various reasons did their mischief in the church through the centuries ever gained access to the triforium, which can be reached only from an upper story of the western Romanesque tower. Yet many of the triforium panels are dull copies of uncertain date, and almost all the rest of the glazing is weathering badly, bulging, losing its paint. There is some evidence that even in the fourteenth century the monks wished to

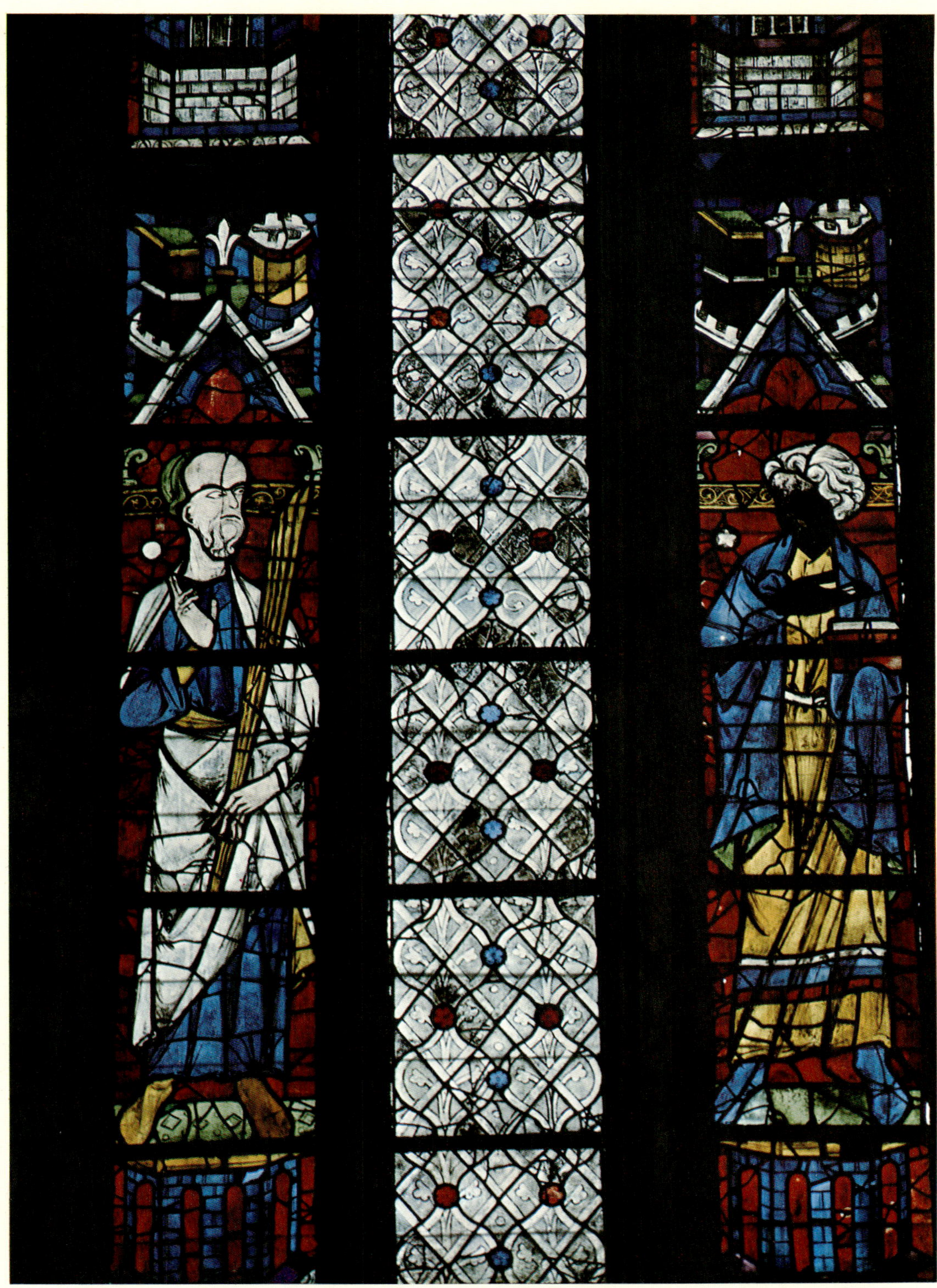

Plate IV Choir: Bay 14. Patriarchs (bottom). *(Edouard Fièvet)*

replace it. Panels in the style of the lovely ca. 1300 grisaille of the apse triforium are found installed in Bay 8 and Bays 16–17 of the choir triforium. These panels have no borders; the apse triforium lancets are sufficiently wider than those of the choir to necessitate the cutting off of the filet borders:

apse Bay 1 — 93 cm.
Bays 2, 3, 4, 5 — 90–91 cm.
Bay 6 — 100 cm.
choir Bays 16–17 — 71–77 cm.
(Choir bays vary — see clerestory measurements, fn. 46, this chapter.)

Bay 8 of the choir, which lies directly adjacent to the apse, may well have received its replacements (the top panels of the two right lancets) when the apse triforium was glazed. The fragments of later grisaille in Bay 16, on the other hand, closely resemble those which remain in the partially blind Bay 7 of the hemicycle, and indeed may be the glass removed from there when it was walled up to accommodate the *tourelle d'escalier* added in the fourteenth century.

11. There are two patterns. One can only presume that all of the choir windows but the narrower Bays 14–15 were originally filled with similar types of early grisaille design. See fn. 1, this chapter. The date of its removal from all but the present four windows is uncertain, but it predates this century and presumably the Revolution as well, since no work of any consequence was carried out on the glass during the nineteenth century. Since some of the remaining old work is now so devitrified as to present a very dark appearance, it is a likely assumption that the other panels were removed to obtain more light, probably at the same time as the replacement of the colored diaper by clear glazing in the nave Bays 20–21 (between 1672-ca. 1700). See Chapter I, fns. 28, 29.

12. The lateral walls of the Virgin chapel of Auxerre have two broad grisaille lancets and two others combining figures with grisaille (the familiar Hubericus Presbiter window is on the north). The clerestory also contains a variety of grisaille patterns, some of them heavily color-spotted. See Charles Cahier-Arthur Martin, *Monographie de la cathédrale de Bourges,* I. (1841–1844), planche de grisailles G, no. 1. The grisaille at Troyes is in the Virgin chapel. See Charles Fichot, *Statistique monumentale du département de l'Aube,* III (Troyes, 1894), figs. 152–153.

13. For illustrations see drawings in Jean-Jacques Bourassé and F. G. M. Manceau, *Verrières du choeur de l'église métropolitaine de Tours* (Paris and Tours, 1849), pls. V and XI.

14. See Chapter VII, fn. 3. A sixth inscription in the same style (Balaam) barely can be discerned in the ca. 1905 photograph of Bay 13 (see Pl. 30), top left figure. The original colored glazing of Bay 13 was largely destroyed in World War II.

15. The following paragraph is paraphrased from: British Museum, *A Guide to the Medieval Room* (Oxford, 1907), pp. 181–183.

16. *VF,* fig. 79, p. 108.

17. For a discussion of the Auxerre dating see Lillich, "Band Window," pp. 28 and 33, fns. 22, 25; for Troyes see fns. 30 and 35, this chapter.

18. See *VF,* pp. 155–156, for Le Mans dating.

19. The C is closed as well as the E. The T and H are now curved and thickened in the middle of the vertical strokes. N is still in blocklike capital, however. See also the Tree of Jesse window, illustrated in Henry Kraus, *The Living Theatre of Medieval Art* (Bloomington, 1967), p. 83.

20. Lafond, "Normandie," illustrations pp. 332, 335, 338. Notice the tremendous variety of transitional patterns in these three grisailles.

21. The inscriptions in the apsidal chapel are true "Lombardic," slightly later, more cramped, and more markedly vertical. See, for example, the "Amicus dei" window (discussed in Lafond, "Les vitraux de la cathédrale de Sées," *Congrès archéologique,* III [1953], pp. 72–73).

22. Lafond, "Sées," esp. p. 61; Lafond, "Normandie," p. 349.

23. For illustration, see *Normandie monumental,* IV, part 1, fig. p. 117 (1893–1899).

24. Jean-Jacques Gruber, "Quelques aspects," p. 73; the quoted phrase comes from the same author, *VF,* p. 66.

25. Both solutions are found in the Chartres transept clerestories, especially on the east side. See Delaporte and Houvet, III, pls. CXCII–IV, CXCVI–II, CXCV, CCV, CCVI, CCVIII.

26. It is now generally recognized that the first band window designs date not from the fourteenth century, but well within the third quarter of the thirteenth century. See Lillich, "Band Window," pp. 26–33.

27. This unsettled situation explains to a great degree, I believe, the quick popularity of the Sainte-Chapelle medallion type, a form clearly *déjà vu* by ca. 1245, and even more clearly inappropriate to the clerestory position. The choir clerestory of Tours (ca. 1260–1270) contains two precocious band windows amid a general preponderance of Parisian medallion windows.

28. The Amiens window in the easternmost chapel of the nave, north aisle, given by Drieu Malherbe in 1296, has four standing figures with no bases at all. (Illustration in Georges Durand, *Monographie de l'église Notre-Dame cathédrale d'Amiens,* II [Paris, 1901–1904], fig. 255.) The elaboration of bases became widespread only during the fourteenth century. The large standing saints in the Saint-Père nave and apse, dating ca. 1300–1315, have no bases.

29. Bay 15 is, to a slight degree, stylistically more advanced than Bay 14. In the latter, the bases of the upper figures have a frontal strip across the bottom, whereas in Bay 15 the piece is no longer frontal but follows the perspective slant of the bases's sides. Compare Pls. 31 and 33. The canopies of Bays 14–15 are mentioned briefly by Rüdiger Becksmann, *Die Architektonische Rahmung des Hochgotischen Bildfensters* (Berlin, 1967), p. 18 and fn. 47.

30. See Jean Lafond, "Les vitraux de la cathédrale Saint-Pierre de Troyes," *Congrès archéologique,* CXIII (1955), pp. 29–62, esp. 46–48; see also Louis Grodecki in *VF,* p. 140.

31. For dating of Tournai choir 1243–1255, see: Jacques Gardelles, "Note sur la construction de la cathédrale de Tournai au XIIe siècle," *Cahiers de civilisation médiévale,* XIIe année, no. 1 (1969), pp. 43–46. For the lost Tournai glass panel, see: Jean Helbig, *Les vitraux médiévaux conservés en Belgique 1200–1500, Corpus Vitrearum Medii Aevi* Belgique I (Brussels, 1961), Annexe 2: "Vitraux détruits, disparus ou exportés au XXe siècle," p. 287 and fig. 167, also pp. 203–204 on dating of Tournai Cathedral choir. Fig. 167 is a reproduction in black and white of a drawing by Capronnier which can be found in the original color in: Edmond Levy, *Histoire de la peinture sur verre en Europe et particulièrement en Belgique* (Brussels, 1860), pl. 8. See also p. 63 of Levy's essay entitled "Histoire de la peinture sur verre" in this book — the pagination of each essay is distinct — where he refers to the panel in pl. 8 as "seul débris des verrières primitives du choeur de la cathédrale de Tournai . . ." The predominant color indicated by Capronnier's drawing is blue, employed both for the grounds behind the figure and inside the medallion. The halo is red, and the architecture above the gable predominantly yellow and red. Green is of very minor significance.

This lost panel may have been among those from the Cathedral of Tournai which formed part of the collection of Baron Houtart of Monceau-sur-Sambre before World War I. It was not, however, one of the four such panels exhibited by him in 1911 in the Exposition de Charleroi, although Helbig's unfortunate phrasing might suggest it. (Helbig, CVMA Belgique I, p. 287). See *Catalogue général* of the Charleroi exposition, published at Brussels, 1911, where the four exhibited panels are listed and described on p. 315, as nos. 238–241. Three of them are illustrated (and all four are reported as having been destroyed in 1940 while in the Musée de la Halle-aux-Draps in Tournai) in Helbig's valuable but difficult-to-use work: *De Glasschilderkunst in Belgïe* (Antwerp, 1943), I, p. 113 (nos. 838–840, 842) and pls. IX and X, nos. 6, 8 and 9. The lost panel with which we are concerned, i.e., the Levy-Capronnier drawing, is listed in the same volume on p. 108 (no. 774) and pl. IX (no. 5).

32. Delaporte and Houvet, III, esp. CCXXV, gives a view of them all. The "Ange thuriféraire" is found in the first window north of the axial one, Delaporte's Bay 121.

33. The idea definitely predated the introduction of the silver stain technique, as can be seen at Evron (Mayenne), where the architectural niches already are seven panels high. See Jean Lafond, "Le vitrail du XIVe siècle en France," in Louise Lefrançois-Pillion, *L'art du XIVe siècle en France* (Paris, 1954), p. 212; and my Chapter V.

34. Cf. fn. 25, this chapter. "Disputing pairs" occur as late as Châlons-sur-Marne (Bay 9, south nave). See Arthur Watson, *The Early Iconography of the Tree of Jesse* (Oxford, 1934), for a discussion of disputing pairs as a particularly Christian invention after classical models in which disputation is not suggested (pp. 56–57).

35. For detailed illustrations of this window see Fichot, figs. 127–129 and 131–132. The window contains four lancets with a large rose over each pair and a third rose above. All the glass is colored. The bishops and kings are placed in large medallions in three horizontal rows, and each pair seems to "dispute" as do the Saint-Père figures (now across a lancet of grisaille). Fichot (pp. 309–311 and p. 309, fn. 1) claims that the inscriptions refer to Hervé, bishop of Troyes (1206–1223), Pierre de Corbeil, archbishop of Sens (1200–1222), Philippe Augustus (ruled 1180–1223), and Henri I, brother of Baudouin, Count of Flanders and Hainault, crowned in 1206 as Latin emperor of Constantinople. The drapery style, however, could not predate ca. 1235 at the earliest. The choir clerestories of Troyes are customarily assigned to the reign of Bishop Nicolas de Brie (1233–1269) whose arms appear in several of them. If, indeed, the brother of the Count of Hainault is intended, here is a tenuous link with the lost Tournai panel (see fn. 31, this chapter). See Lafond, "Troyes," p. 48 where he dates them in the 1240's, and p. 47, where he endorses the identifications of Fichot, remarking in p. 47, fn. 2 that it is also the opinion of Hans Reinhardt of Bâle. The "young" emperor in the window, therefore, would be the young Frederick II, emperor of Germany. See also Louis Grodecki in *VF,* pp. 140ff.

36. Arnold, pl. XI, and Delaporte and Houvet, III, pls. CCXXIII and CCXXV. See also the earlier and smaller examples at Canterbury (Bernard Rackham, *The Ancient Glass of Canterbury Cathedral* [London, 1949] pls. 6, 8 and 63).

37. The Saint-Père resolution found few adherents and remained a cul-de-sac in contrast to the general acceptance of the horizontal band design. I have discussed this phenomenon briefly in "Band Window," p. 29.

38. The types of combinations are analyzed and their development discussed briefly in Lillich, "Band Window," p. 28. See also Lucy Freeman Sandler, "A Follower of Jean Pucelle in England," *Art Bulletin,* LII (1970), p. 372. See Chapter IV, fn. 7.

39. Two fragments taken from the church in the restorations of the early 1950's (now in storage) may augment the number. Each shows the feet and robe hem of a similar standing prophet. The measurements, necessarily approximate because of the fragmentary nature of the debris, seem to coincide with those of the choir prophets. One of the fragmentary figures (Pl. 16) holds a phylactery with letters in a comparable block script: DAVI.

40. See fns. 1 and 11, this chapter.

41. Paul Frankl, *Gothic Architecture* (Baltimore, Md., 1962), pl. 7A. Saint-Germer-de-Fly was begun ca. 1132.

42. Frankl, p. 41.

43. This arcading remains at Saint-Père. The rayonnant reconstruction was begun at triforium level.

44. See discussion Chapter I.

45. The grisaille panels, discounting the framing filets, are square in design and uniformly 63 cm. in height. Measurements of width are as follows:

Bay 11 — 68 cm. including central iron of about 3.5 cm.
60.3 cm. without iron and without filet borders.
Bay 13 — 64.25 cm. total width.
59 cm. without filet borders.

Bays 10 and 12 across the choir mirror these measurements, of course, and the other bays contain no old grisaille (except for Bays 14–15, 50 cm. wide, in the later style). The slight discrepancy between height and width can be explained by the fact that the vertical filet borders slice slightly into the design. The filet borders were probably added when the glass was redesigned ca. 1270.

46. Measurements of the figure panels are more difficult to deal with than those of the grisaille because it is uncertain how much of the present medallion frameworks was originally designed for them and how much added ca. 1270.

Bay 9 — 56 cm., figure alone.
75.5 cm., total width of figure lancet (the left and right lancets vary slightly).
Bay 11 — 53.25 cm., figure alone.
58.5 cm., figure and framing medallion.
67.75 cm., total width of figure lancet.
Bay 13 — 50.5 cm., figure alone.
65 cm., total width of figure panel.
Bay 17 — 51 cm., figure alone.
64.5 cm., total width of figure lancet.

Bays 8, 10, 12 and 16, opposite, accord. The total width of the later figure panels in Bays 14–15 is 50–51 cm.

47. Scraps of three different border designs measuring between 18–20 cm. are among the debris removed from the church during the restorations of the early 1950's. The debris is now in storage. These are not to be confused with the handsome twelfth-century border published by Popesco, p. 51.

48. I have discussed the Bourges grisailles briefly in "Three Essays"; fragments of the series were purchased recently by the Corning Museum of Glass. On Reims, see reference in Lillich, "Chartres Cathedral," p. 12.

49. See fns. 30 and 35, this chapter.

50. See fn. 39, this chapter.

51. The alternating effect, in its present form, is false to a degree, as the modern grisaille in nave Bays 20–21 replaces colored diaper which was there until the late seventeenth century and is still visible in the lancet arches (Pl. 56).

52. A glance at the triforium balustrade easily confirms this statement. The balustrade quatrefoils in Bays 14–15 are squeezed almost out of recognition.

53. See measurements in fn. 45.

54. The uncut form can be seen in the lancet arches and in the lower left grisaille panel of Bay 10 (Pl. 20). Bays 8–9, which are even wider, no longer retain their medieval grisailles.

55. The arcaded houses and the bases beneath the feet of the prophets in Bays 8–9 differ radically from anything found elsewhere in the choir. They are, in fact, much closer to the rough-and-ready style evident in some of the Le Mans clerestories. See Chapter V.

56. See fn. 28, this chapter.

57. The place of Saint-Père in the Western school and the "Westernness" of its style will be discussed in Chapter V.

{ CHAPTER III }

Hemicycle: Style

THE six glittering windows of the hemicycle of Saint-Père[1] function as a visual lodestone, concentrating attention on the sanctuary of the church (Pl. I). The series of the hemicycle is the only completely colored ensemble in a monument where — in the choir and again in the nave — important experiments in the combination of grisaille and colored panels took place. The coloring of the ensemble is not only unrelieved but also the most brilliant in the church, an equal balance of red, clear blue, and strong yellow.[2] It is probably the gaiety and intensity of the color harmony of the hemicycle, more than any other single factor, which successfully focus the diverse elements of the church's comprehensive glazing plan.

Each of the windows contains two long, narrow lancets surmounted by tracery formed of three quatrefoils (see Fig. 7). In each lancet are two standing male saints, placed one over the other, each under an elaborate canopy. There are four such figures to a bay, making twenty-two in all, plus the Madonna and Child and the Crucified Christ in the axial window. Below the Madonna and Crucifixion in this window are figures of St. Louis and the abbey's patron St. Gilduin; in all other cases, however, the saints are apostles or anonymous bishops or abbots. The uppermost quatrefoil in the tracery contains, in each window, an identical upside-down angel bearing two crowns of martyrdom. The two quat-

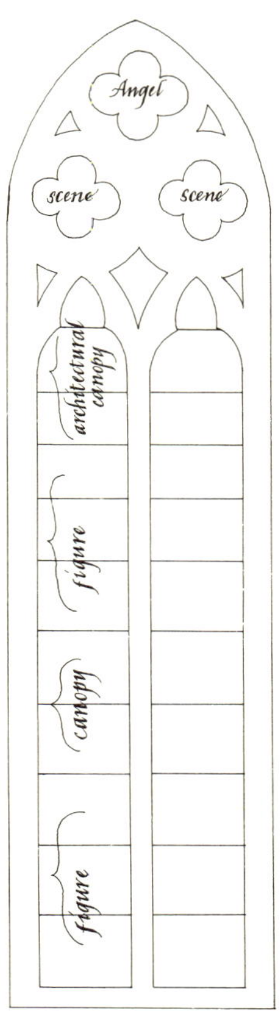

Figure 7 Format of Bays 1–6 (hemicycle). (Drawing by Kevin McIntyre)

refoils beneath this angel present a series of saints' martyrdoms, forming a secondary plot-line to the main theme of the lancets below. Both the main series of saints and the counterpoint of martyrdom scenes depict apostles and other saints intermingled.

Any critique of the hemicycle should commence with an appreciation of the designer's achievement in "ensemble," in the musical sense of the term. No less than his predecessors who designed Bays 14–15 to augment the early patriarchs of the choir, the hemicycle master planned his holy men to conform. They line up in two rows, as do those of the choir; and he provided them with canopies, developed versions of those of Bays 14–15. The full-face and profile poses of many of them are a more subtle mimicry, a leit-motif recalling the archetypal seers of the choir's first group.

The problems of interest in the hemicycle are, however, of totally different significance from those of the choir. The general date is not seriously in question, nor with it, the importance or influence of the ensemble. Although no documentation corroborates my *a priori* assumptions, it seems likely that the hemicycle glass was designed and installed in a brief period of time, with expense not spared, under the guidance of a single skilled artist and therefore largely his personal product. The total absence of a donor's shadow, the painstaking planning and execution, the iconography and the quality of the workmanship lead to the supposition that the abbey itself ordered and paid for the group as the chief jewel in its sanctuary's crown. The dating is not elusive. Aside from the *terminus post quem* offered by the presence of the image of St. Louis,[3] who was canonized on August 6, 1297, however, it is based only on internal and stylistic evidence. The church building was probably finished no later than the early 1280's. The choir glass, in the process of redesign while the architecture was rising, could have been installed almost immediately. Although there are few indications in the nave windows to date them measurably later than those of the hemicycle,[4] the importance of the sanctuary and the fact that the choir was already glazed would suggest that the hemicycle came after the choir in time. Furthermore, the apse group denotes careful, painstaking work, while the nave saints and some of the historiated bays (notably Bay 22, the Peter window) evidence an air of haste.[5] The donations for the nave fall within the years ca. 1302–1312;[6] it seems a fair assumption, therefore, that the ensemble of the hemicycle was complete shortly after the turn of the fourteenth century. Because this date falls so quickly after that of St. Louis's canonization, it is more than likely that the hemicycle windows were begun well before that historic event, and that their roster was altered to include him.[7] I would suggest as a date for the hemicycle ca. 1295–1300.

The twenty-four standing figures of the ensemble all bear the signature of a single style, and form an example of Western glazing of the first quality. By "Western" is meant a style rather than a geographical area, although in fact this style occurs in monuments which are in the "West" — Maine, Touraine, and as far as the fringes of Normandy. The general characteristic of this style, the development of which will be outlined in Chapter V, is boldness, or, perhaps one could say, freedom. It is an art of extremes. Draughtsmanship is crude, imprecise, expressionistic, and economical. Forms are exaggerated. The broadness of handling produces a sense of drama and of force.

The color harmony mentioned earlier, a gaudy tripartition of primaries, is one of the most characteristic trademarks of Western glazing.[8] In some cases, notably at Vendôme and Sées, it became reduced to a formula — red ground, alternating yellow and blue robes. In the Saint-Père apse the harmony is employed with considerably more variation and sophistication. Simple apostles are garbed as in the following examples:

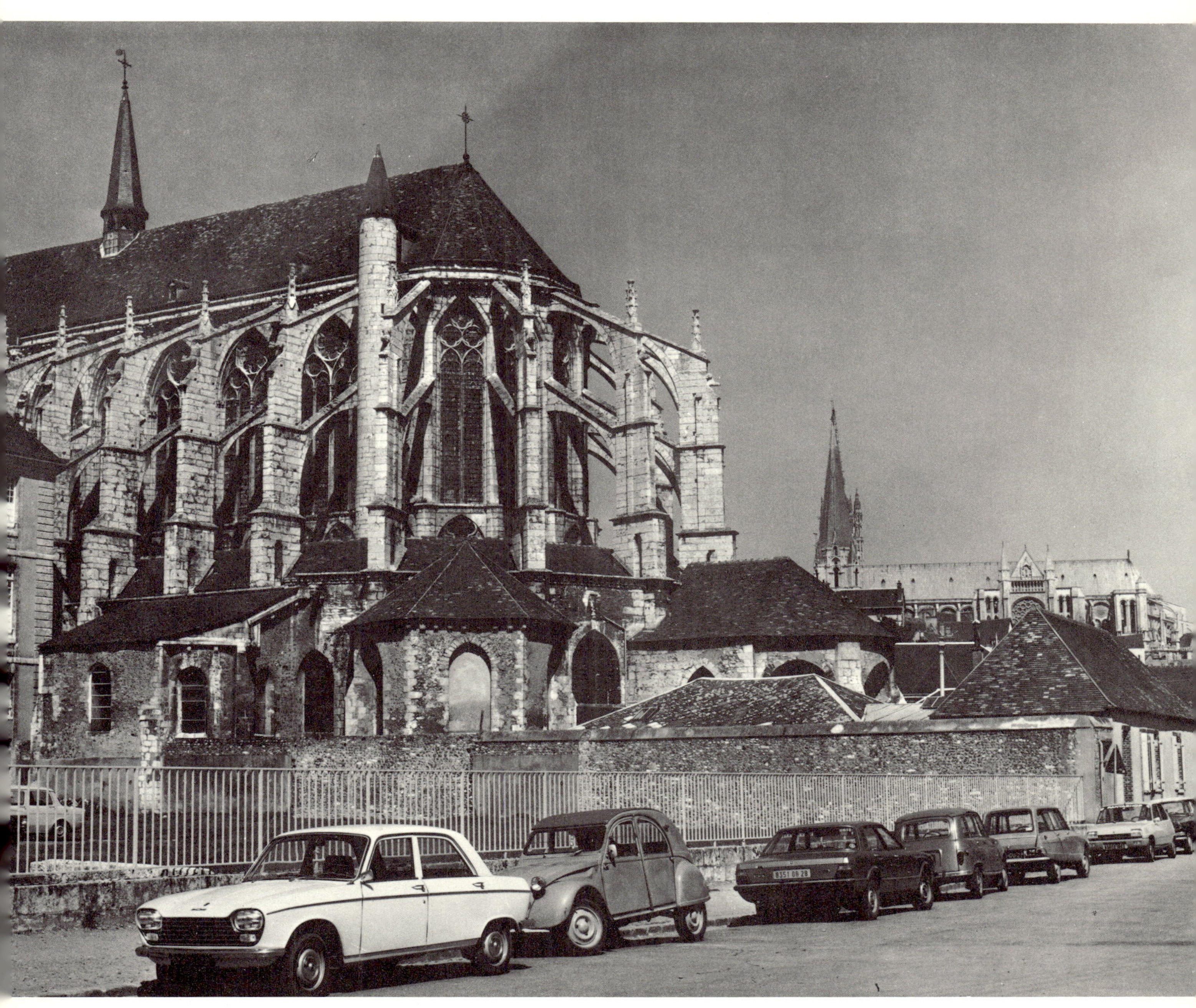

Saint-Père de Chartres *(Edouard Fièvet)*

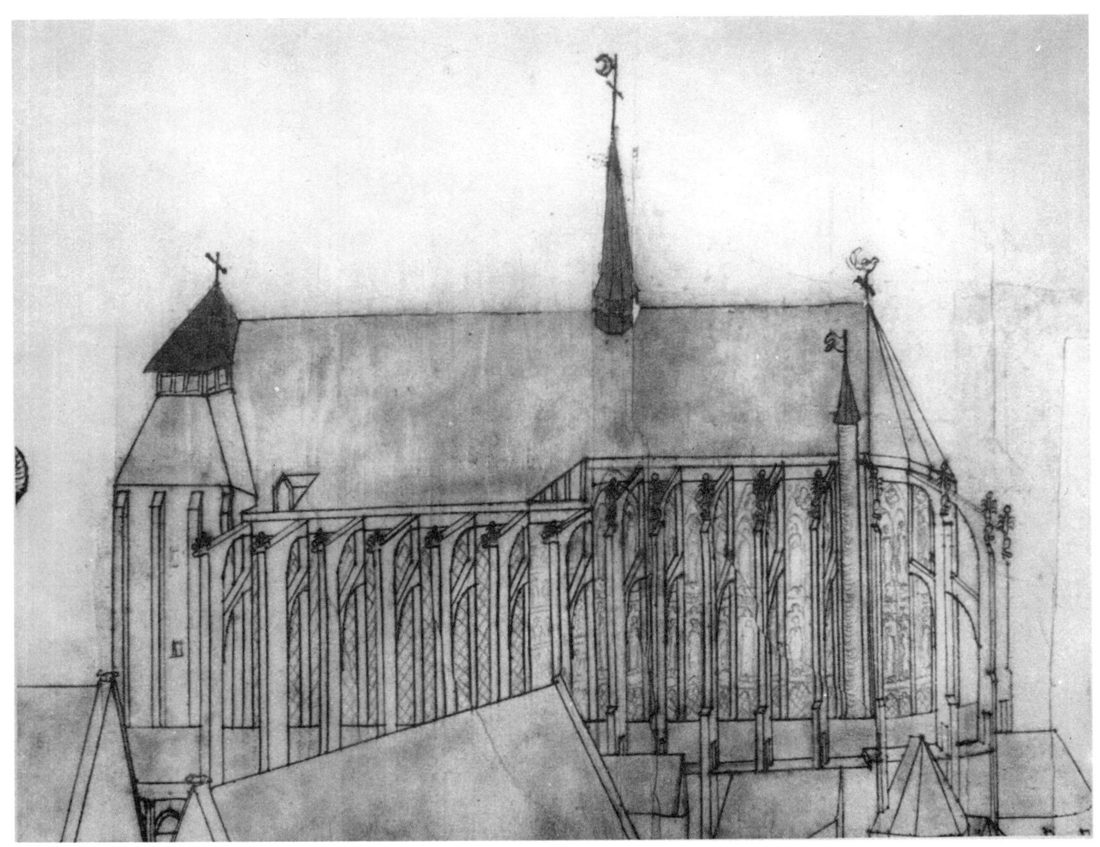

PLATE 1 South flank of Saint-Père de Chartres. Late 17th century. *(Paris, Archives nationales N III, Eure-et-Loir 3.[1] Detail.)*

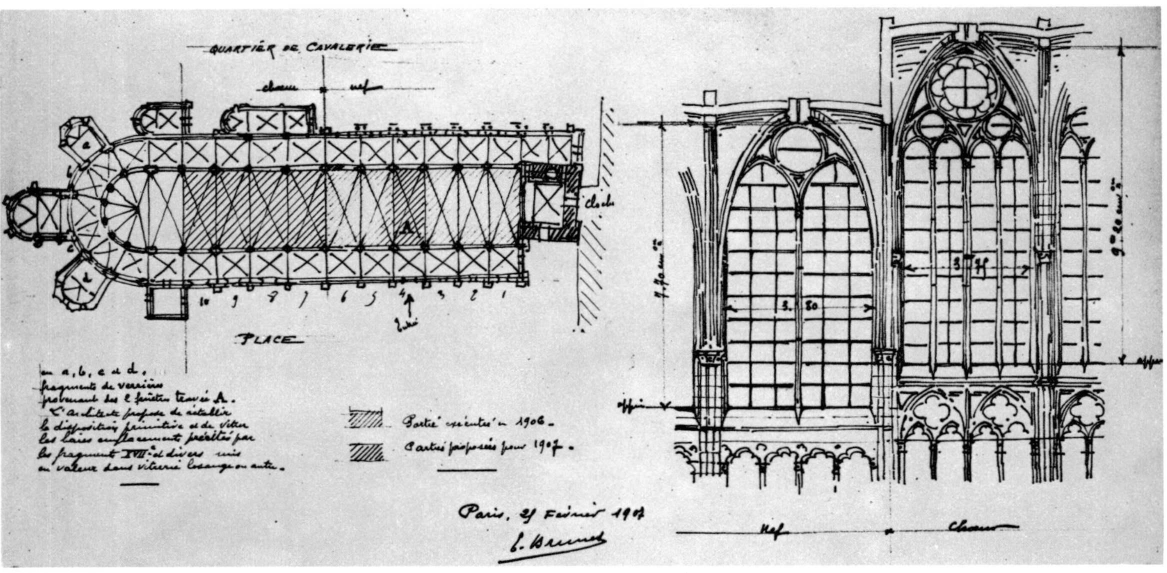

PLATE 2 Saint-Père de Chartres. Plan and drawings submitted during restorations 1907. *(After E. Brunet)*

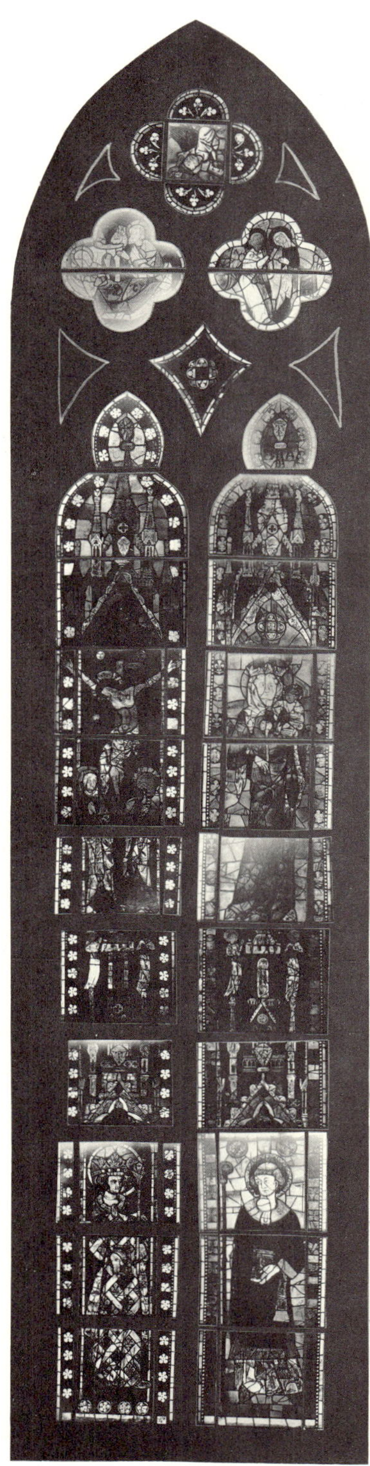

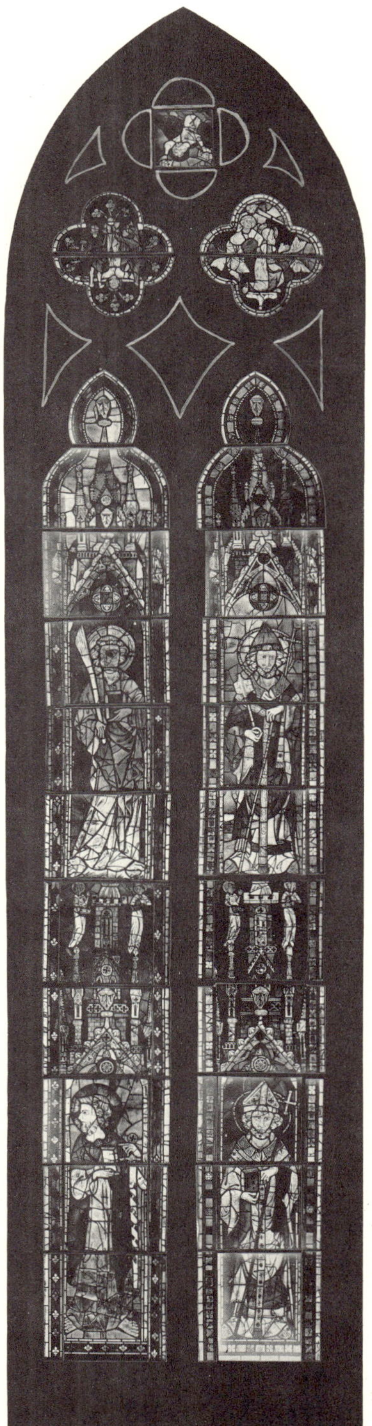

Plate 3 Hemicycle: Bay 1. *(Paris, Archives photographiques)*

Plate 4 Hemicycle: Bay 2. *(Paris, Archives photographiques)*

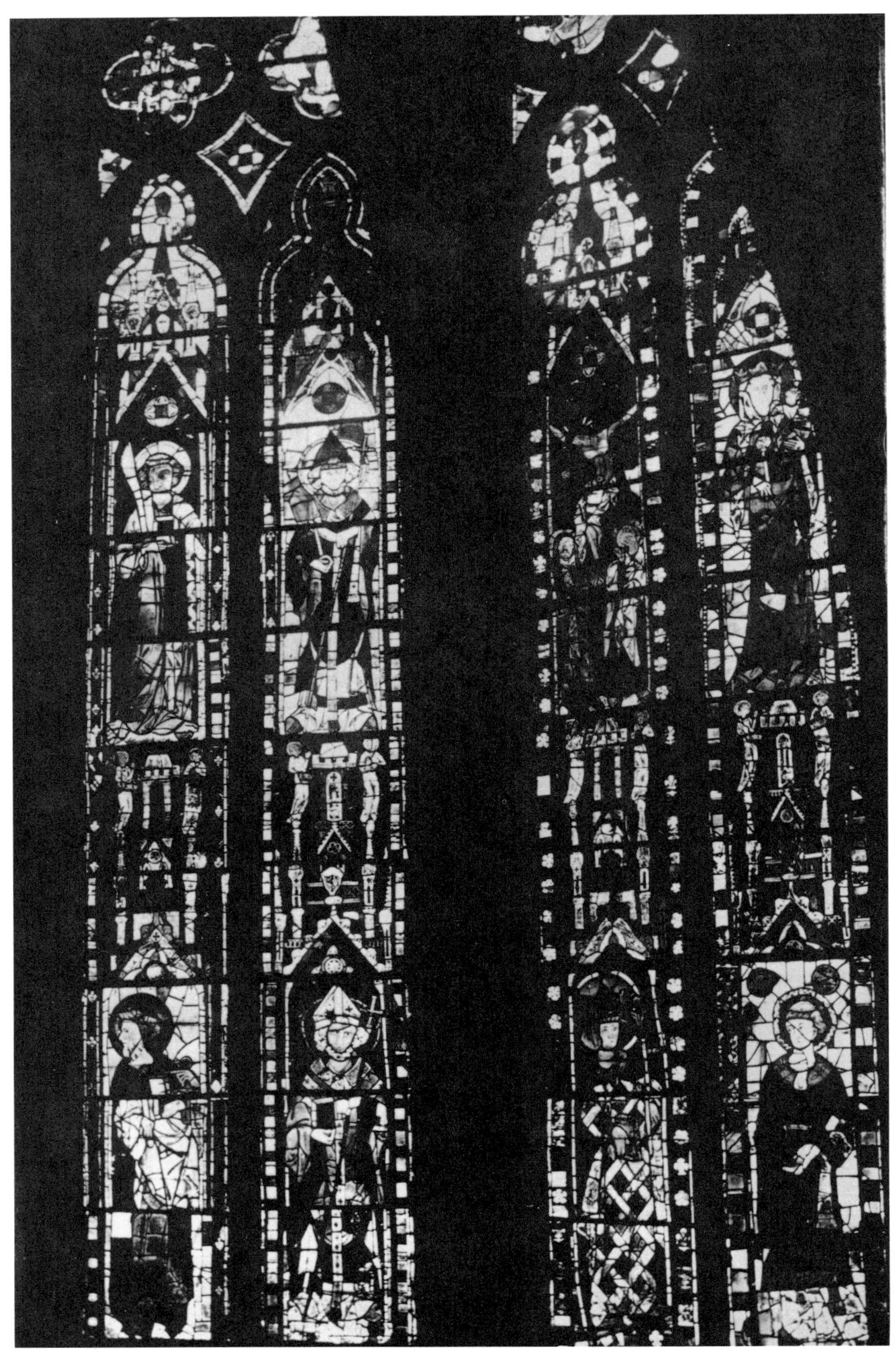

PLATE 5 Hemicycle: Bays 1, 2. Before 1905 restorations. *(Photo from Jean Lafond collection) (Paris, Archives photographiques)*

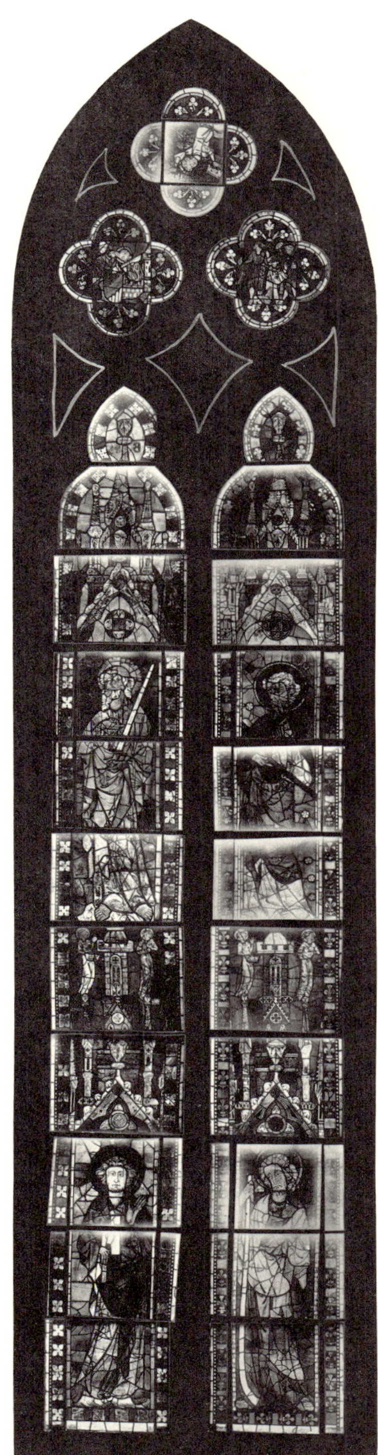

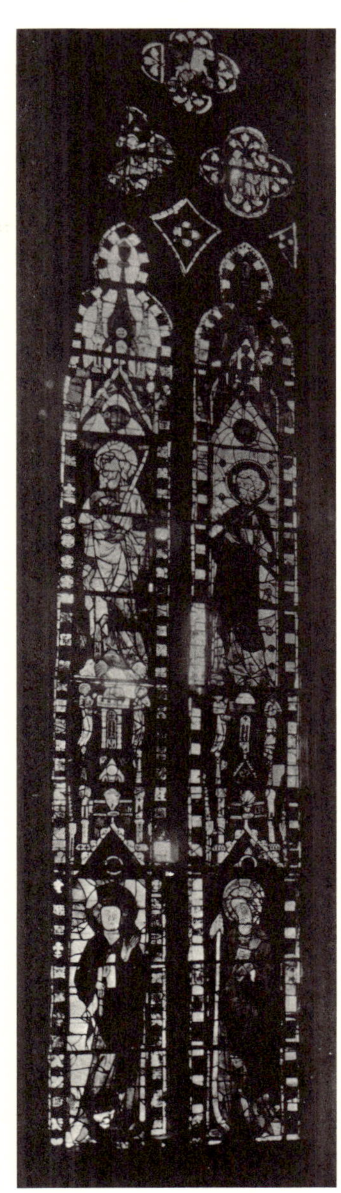

PLATE 6 Hemicycle: Bay 3. *(Paris, Archives photographiques)*

PLATE 7 Hemicycle: Bay 3. Before 1905 restorations. *(Photo from François Lorin studio) (Paris, Archives photographiques)*

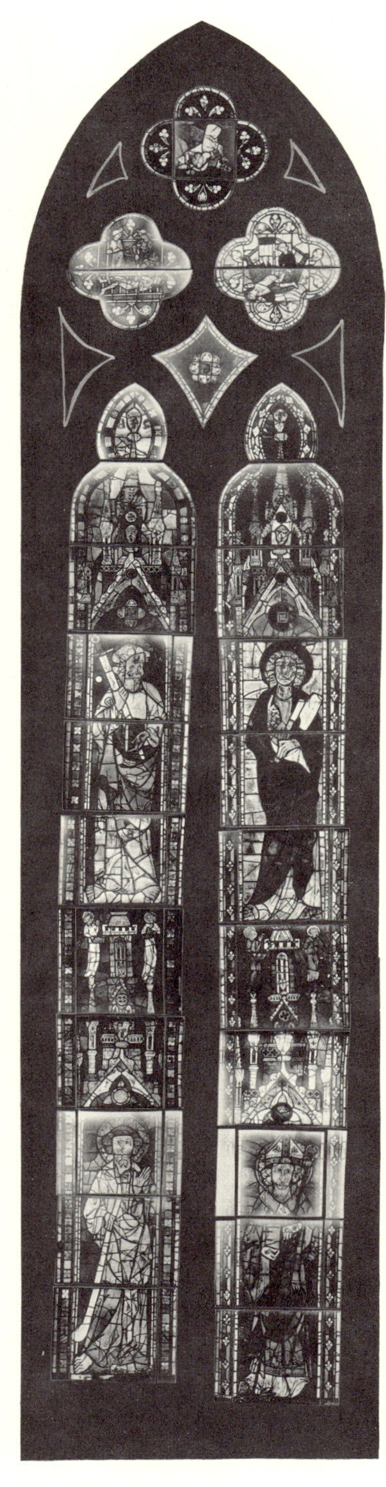

PLATE 8 Hemicycle: Bay 4. *(Paris, Archives photographiques)*

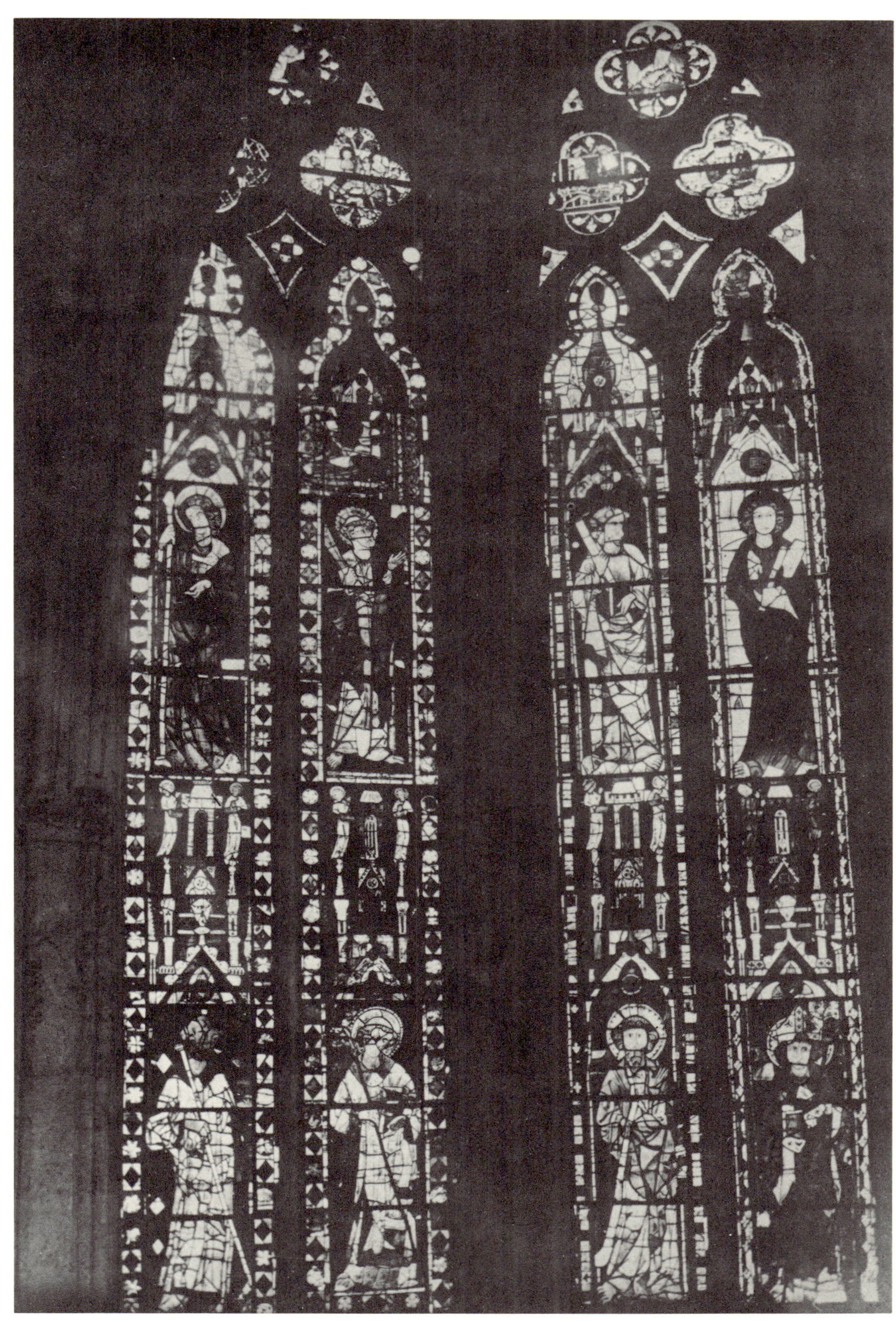

PLATE 9 Hemicycle: Bays 6, 4. Before 1905 restorations. *(Photo from Michon) (Paris, Archives photographiques)*

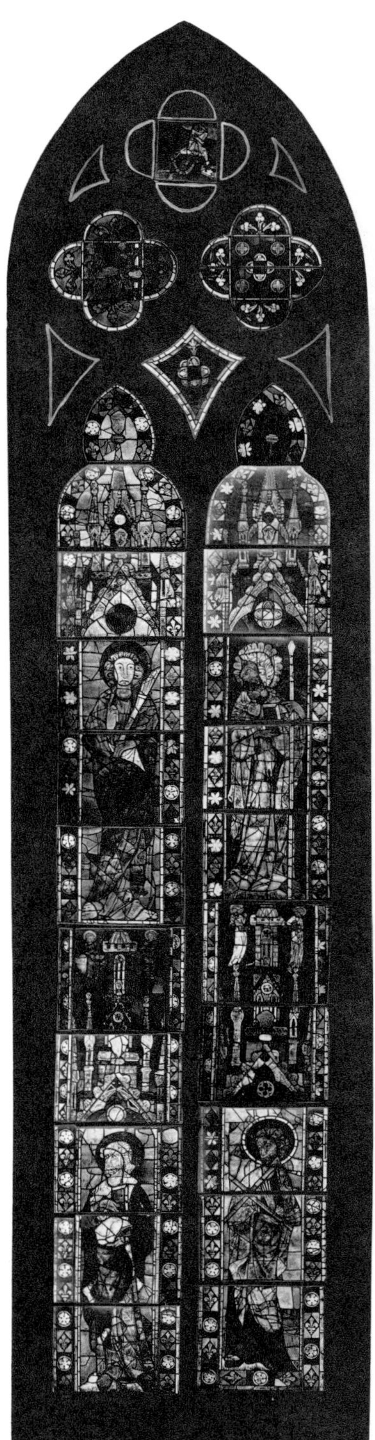

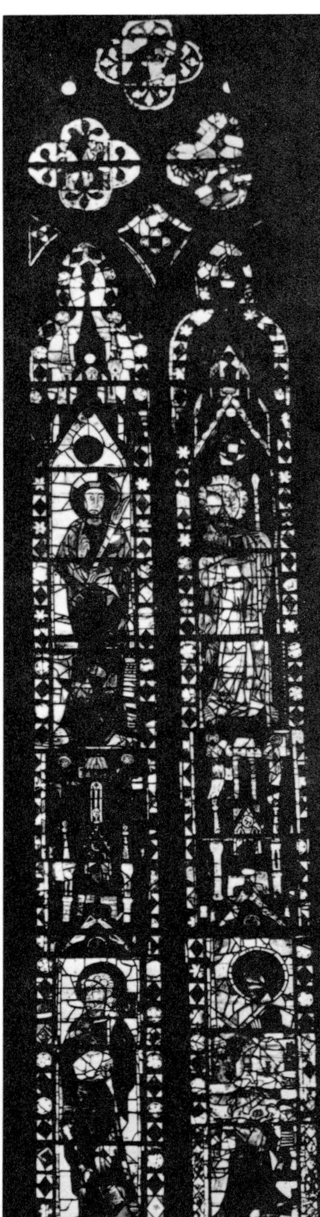

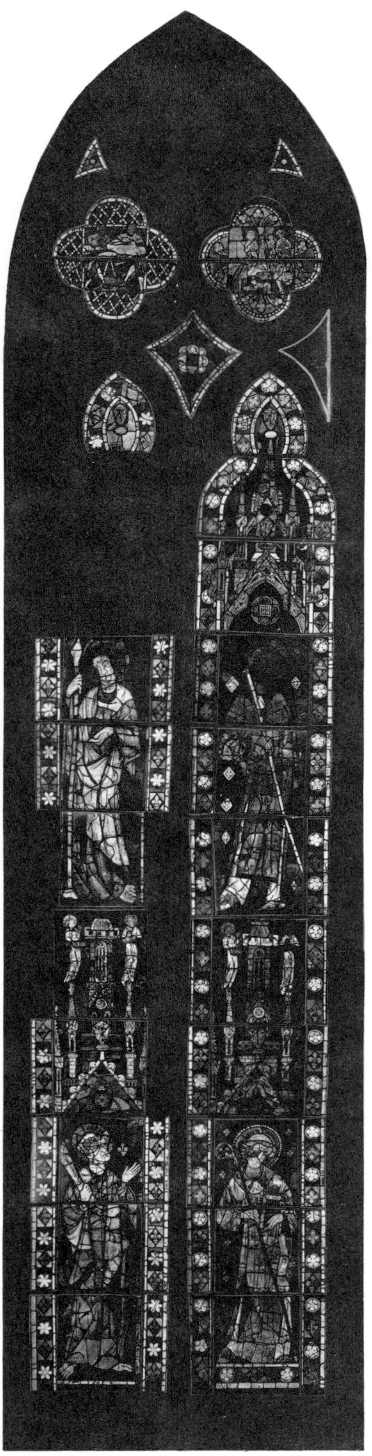

PLATE 10 Hemicycle: Bay 5. *(Paris, Archives photographiques)*

PLATE 11 Hemicycle: Bay 5. Before 1905 restorations. *(Photo from Jean Lafond collection) (Paris, Archives photographiques)*

PLATE 12 Hemicycle: Bay 6. *(Paris, Archives photographiques)*

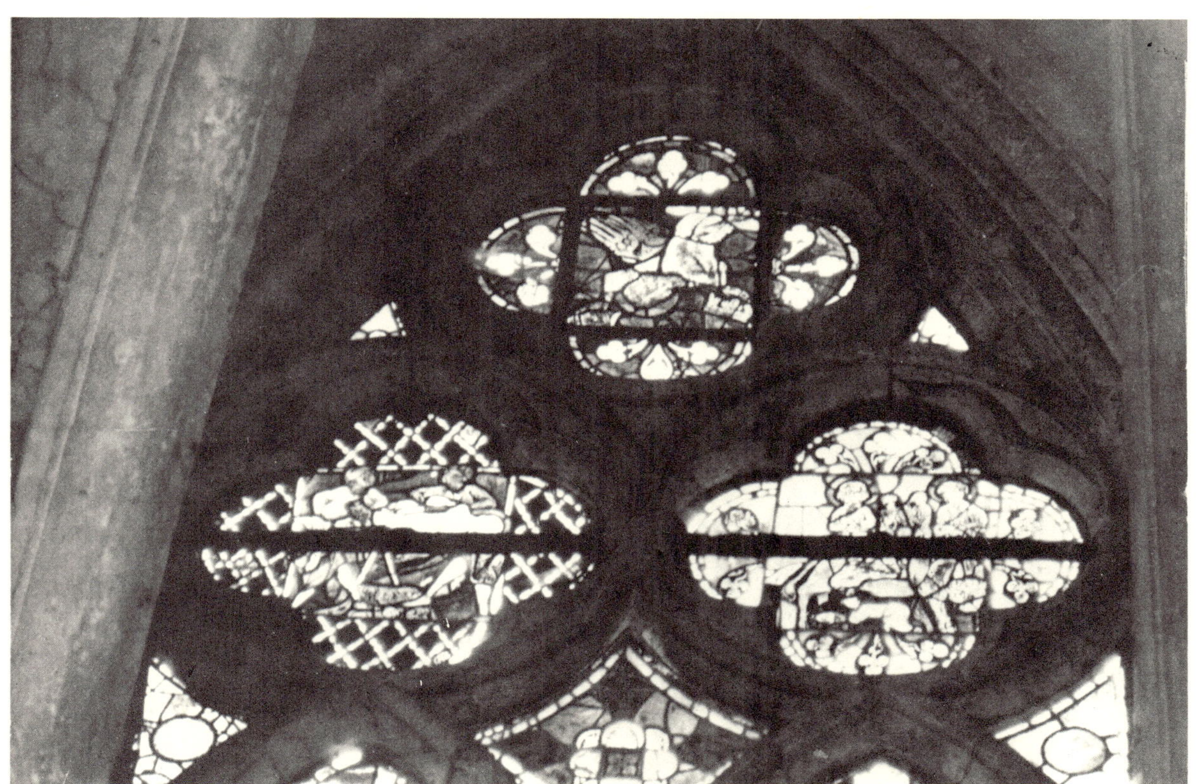

PLATE 13 Hemicycle: Bay 6 tracery. *(Paris, Archives photographiques)*

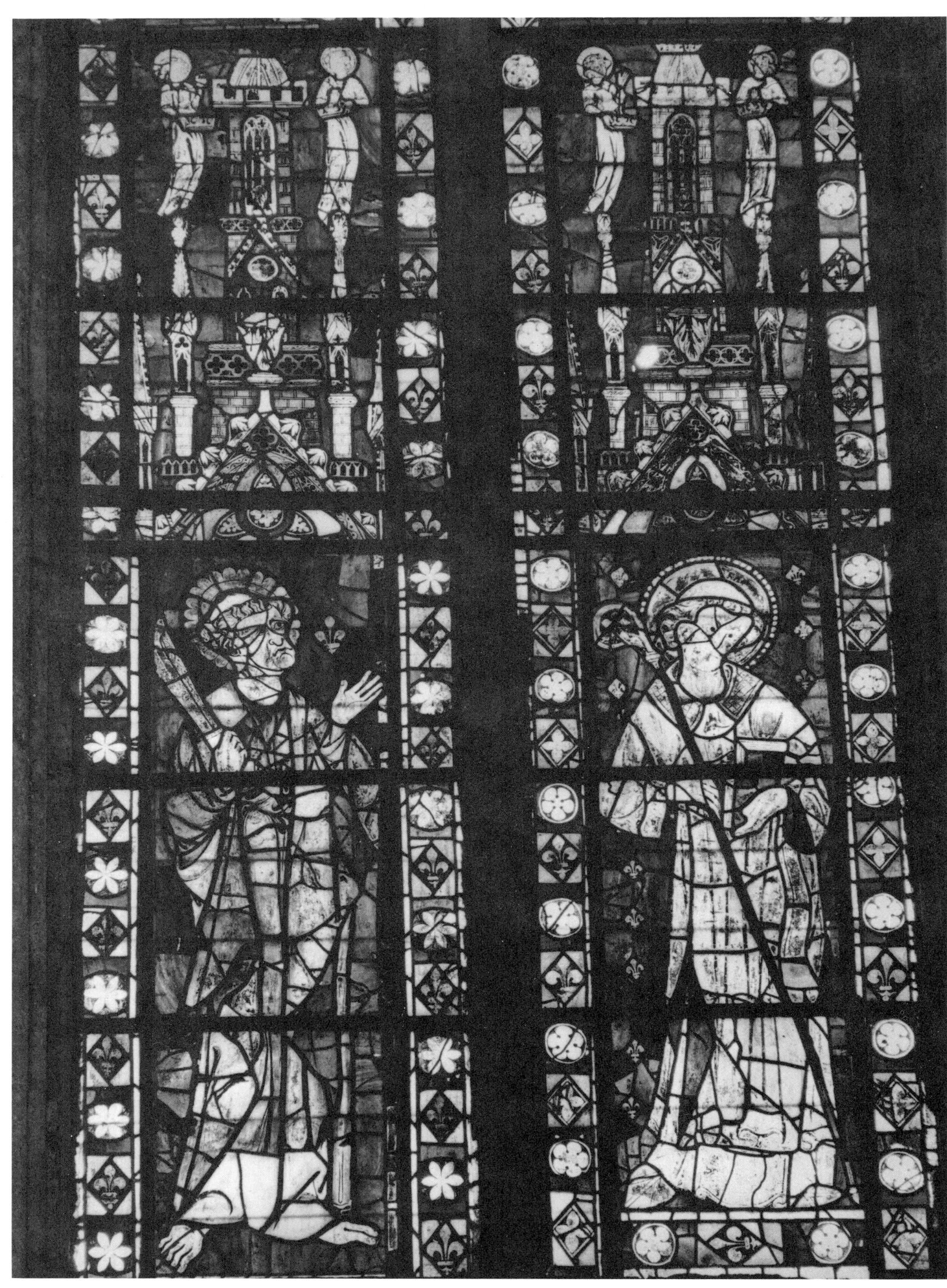

PLATE 14 Hemicycle: Bay 6 canopywork. *(Photo: Edouard Fièvet)*

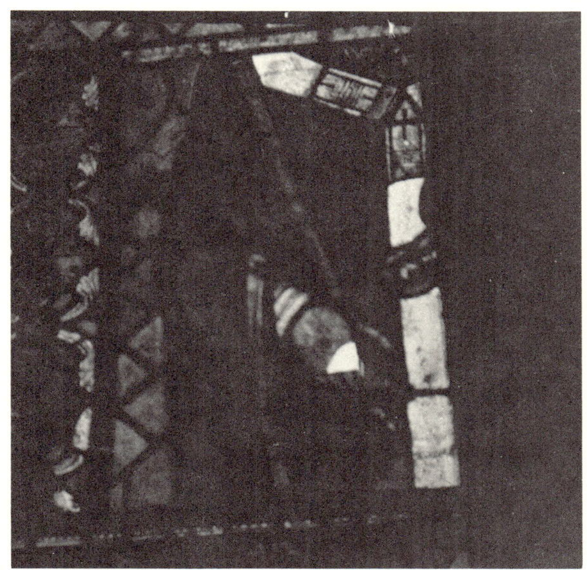

PLATE 15 Fragment probably from hemicycle Bay 7. *(Photo: Meredith Lillich)*

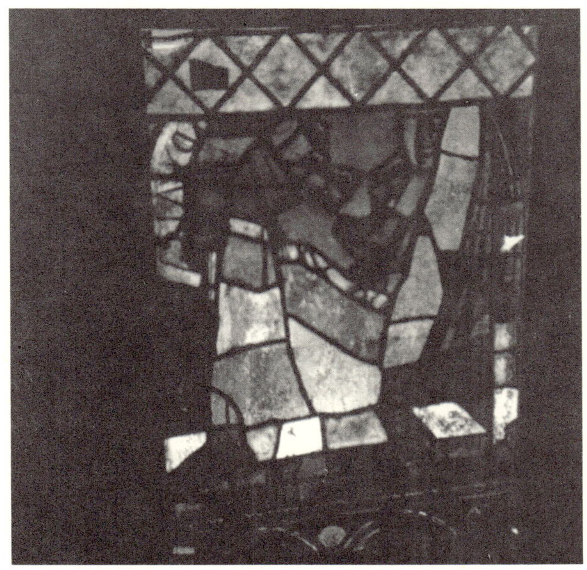

PLATE 16 Fragment probably from choir series. *(Photo: Meredith Lillich)*

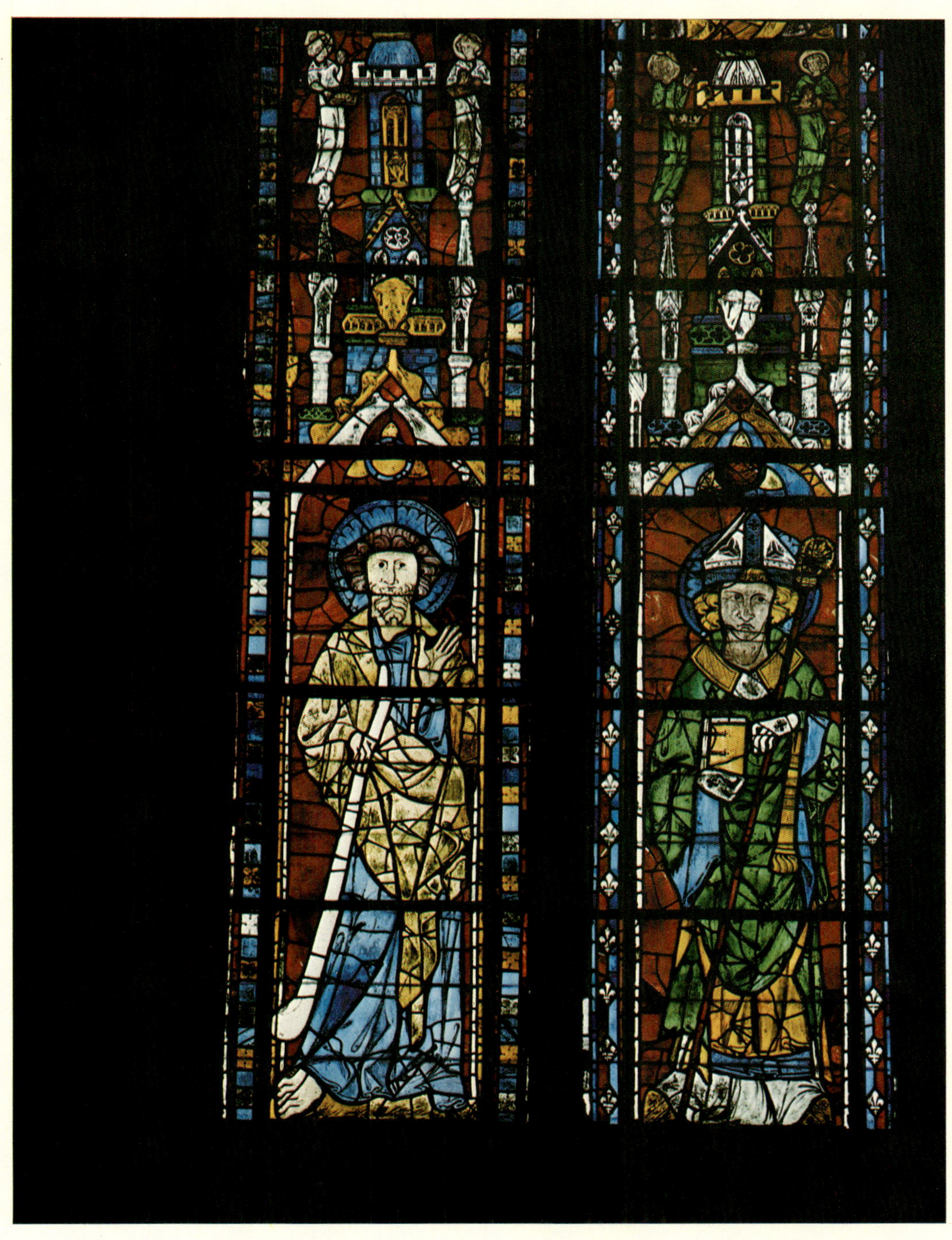

PLATE V Hemicycle: Bay 4. Apostle and Bishop or abbot saint (bottom). *(Edouard Fièvet)*

Bay 3, top right: The ground is blue. The saint has white hair and a red halo with a white pearled border, and wears a yellow robe and a red mantle lined in green. He carries as an attribute a green cross. (Pl. 6).

Bay 4, top right: The ground is red. The figure has yellow hair and a green halo, and carries a white sword with a green and yellow handle, and a red book. His robe is yellow and his mantle blue with a green lining, and he stands on a white base. (Pl. 8).

Ecclesiastical figures become much more complex, for example the Saint Peter as Pope:

Bay 2, top right: The ground is blue. The hair is white, the tiara red, and the halo blue bordered in white pearls. He carries white keys and a gold cross-staff. He wears white gloves, a yellow amice, a red chasuble with sleeves lined in yellow, a white pallium, a blue maniple, a white alb under a blue dalmatic and red tunicle, and yellow caligae. Of the complete vestment only the stole is lacking. (Pl. 4).

Compare the prelate of Bay 4 (Pl. V). The grounds of figures and canopywork panels are blue or red, in no regular pattern of alternation, the artist apparently guarding the option to maintain better control of his color balance.

The master planner intended the hemicycle group to be the fulcrum of the Saint-Père glazing design, not only a brilliant core but artistically his "best work." Thus it is that the work most characteristic of the Western school of glazing, in color and in spirit and at the same time the most varied and richly drawn, is found here. The clerestory ensembles of the West rely for impact on force of color and expressionistic drawing rather than precision, or elegance of draughtsmanship, or complexity of design. It is not a subtle art. Within this framework and from this perspective, care and imagination were cultivated in the Saint-Père hemicycle. In a group of windows depicting an assemblage of somewhat similar saints under identical canopies, no two physiognomies are alike, no two attributes exactly the same. The carefully-plotted variation is surprising when one realizes that many cartoons appear several times, as happens in the earlier glass of the choir,[9] the nearly contemporary work in the Saint-Père nave and in the Western school in general. Unlike the choir or the nave, it is difficult to plot the exact number of cartoons used in the hemicycle. Some, like that used for Saint Peter as Pope, the archbishop below him in Bay 2, and the bishop of Bay 4 (see Pls. 4 and 8), are immediately recognizable. Painstaking mutations make other cartoons considerably more elusive to trace. A partial suggested list follows:[10]

Cartoon A:	Bay 2 bottom left Bay 5 top right	Cartoon E:	Bay 3 bottom right Bay 6 top left
Cartoon B:	Bay 4 top right Bay 5 top left	Cartoon F:	Bay 2 top right (St. Peter) Bay 2 bottom right Bay 4 bottom right
Cartoon C:	Bay 3 top left (St. Paul) Bay 5 bottom left	Cartoon G:	Bay 3 top right Bay 5 bottom right
Cartoon D:	Bay 2 top left Bay 3 bottom left Bay 4 bottom left		

A comparison of any cartoon "family" will show the degree of individuality the artist was able to distill in its members. In groupings such as Cartoons A and B, the basic change is that of attributes, although no color is ever repeated in the same area, and even the flesh differs considerably in tone. In group C, in addition to the change of attributes, the first of the figures has been given St. Paul's bald head and a longer, more pointed beard (Pl. 6). In group G (see Pls. 6 and 10) the heads again vary drastically in type, one being a youth and the other an aged man (the mid-panel of the second figure is a modern restoration). In group D the first figure resembles the other two in the middle and lower panels only, and then with changes in attribute and hand position. There are probably other such affinities of "parts" which have been so well disguised that they elude detection altogether.

The figures are at once massive and dramatic. Head-to-body proportion is usually about 1:5 — there is nothing willowy about this army of saints! — but exaggerations of gesture and posture and intensity of expression imbue them with life. The format adopted, a standard one for clerestory glazing presenting rows of standing, immobile figures under canopies, is a layout which implies the static "presentation" of images to the observer. The Western school, with its aesthetic goal of dramatic expressionism, resisted this implication occasionally by recourse to large simplified "scenes." Those of Le Mans are an example in the school's early period, as are those of Evron at its finale. A less awkward and more stylistically coherent manner of energizing the canopy-row format was that perfected in the hemicycle of Saint-Père, where the figures have intrinsic drama. Their hands are of exaggerated size; their gestures are almost theatrical, the attributes are as much "exhibited" as held. They stare out at us, the audience, in startling full-face, or equally effective profile, their eyes full of messianic zeal.

The draughtsmanship is spare. Modeling is minimal; mass is implied in brief linear strokes rather than spelled out in elaborate gradations of shading. The quality of drawing is uniformly superior in all bays save Bay 6 (Pl. 12), where an assistant's hand is probably evident in the meandering and occasionally illogical drapery folds, less effective hands, and slightly vacuous expressions.

The lower two figures of the axial bay (Pl. 3) — St. Louis and St. Gilduin — exhibit something of the good intentions hastily executed which mark even the best of the large saints of the nave, further evidence to support the suggestion that they were inserted into the program of the apse while it was en route to completion or soon thereafter. Sts. Louis and Gilduin[11] are, in contrast to their companions, more stilted and rigid of posture. The cartoons are more static, gestures more prosaic, the color more mannered (for example Gilduin's robe of "wine dregs" red) and the drawing more mediocre. In all this they resemble the occasionally workaday figures of large scale found in the nave. The resemblance suggests a comparable date in the first years of the fourteenth century, and well before the final designs of the nave which progress toward an emphatically fourteenth-century tonality of white and yellow.

The medallion martyrdoms in the upper tracery of the hemicycle, to which must be added the canopywork with its crown-bearing angels and gargoyles, offer a rather less uniformly "Western" aspect than the large saints. Two distinct styles are evident in the medallions. A fluid, expanding, and somewhat crudely-drawn manner is found in the two quatrefoils of Bay 1 (Annunciation and Nativity) (Pl. 3) and in the right medallion of Bay 2 (Beheading of the Baptist by a contorted, energetic executioner) (Pl. 4). Details are more precise and gestures more anatomically rendered in the second group, consisting of the eight[12] remaining martyrdoms (see Pl. 13), but the life-spark is missing from these spiritless tableaux. The incredibly postured upside-down angels (one cartoon repeated in all six bays) of the upper tracery quatrefoils exhibit the brusqueness of the former, "Western" type. The precise and tightly-drawn gargoyles of the canopywork, on the other hand, appertain to the second group, as do the elongated, sylphlike angels also in the canopywork[13] (Pl. 14).

Inhabited canopywork appears with frequency chiefly in Normandy. The proportions of head to body, "international-style" contraposto and general weightlessness of the canopywork angels, as well as the spare painting within emphasized silhouettes, also relate them to Norman glazing (Fécamp is the contemporary Norman series which leaps to mind). The Norman leaven was certainly at work in the fabric of Western art when the Saint-Père apse windows were made ca. 1300. The intermingling of the two diverse styles[14] — the disparate aesthetics of the two groups of tracery lights, and the canopywork in which occasional Norman figurative motifs grace structures formed of predominantly Western elements — appears in the hemicycle of Saint-Père only in the glazing of secondary importance, however. The important and imposing jury of saints speaks an unaccented Western tongue.

This unaccented Western tongue is at its purest and most characteristic in the Saint-Père hemicycle, a group which sets the key for recognizing "Westernisms" not only in the rest of the church but in other monuments as well. In addition to a notable abstraction and simplification of color, of what does the style consist? Facial features are pronounced and over-simplified, and of purely linear definition. Noses are long, formed customarily in a line extending from the eyebrow. Eyes are black and staring, lidless. A half-round defines the swell of the chin; another the curve of a youthful cheek; a set of undulating waves, a worried brow. Gone are the soft definitions of nature; the artist prefers the simplifications and exaggerations of the cartoonist. Just as simplified line governs the detail, so linear contour characterizes the expressive forms (facial shapes, hands and feet). The hair is allowed to curl and billow only within well-contoured limits. The bodies stand frozen in Gothic immobility, draped in folds which do not so much articulate a body (frequently the arms are unbelievably short, the legs equally inexplicably long) but define the areas of focus: face, hands and attribute, feet. Drapery, like hair, is allowed a rich existence but only within the strongly-defined contours of the silhouette. Fold patterns are achieved by outline, with a minimum of internal definition. Fold lines are short, emphatic, economically placed; shading is sparse or non-existent. The lines of the leading itself are often used to connect areas of focus within the design. The central function, in these windows, of color, line, and contour — elements which, after all, comprise the very essence of the medium of stained glass — qualify the hemicycle at Saint-Père as one of the great achievements in that medium.

What is the relationship between the largely homogeneous ensemble of the hemicycle and the more diverse and tangled stylistic groupings of the Saint-Père nave? It can be said in general that the ensemble of the hemicycle and most of the nave windows exhibit the same expressionistic virility characteristic of the Western school. The difference, at least in the case of the standing saints of the nave, is often one of quality. The abbey was evidently anxious to see the glazing project brought to completion. The nave designs, which will be investigated in Chapter IV, are vigorous but carelessly drawn, and repeated with minimal changes in inscriptions and attributes. The figures of both the hemicycle and nave groups emit the same poise and sense of mass; but the latter embody a dreadful wallpaper sameness in spite of their personal labels. The hemicycle ensemble was to prove, to the nave designer, an ideal unattainable in haste.

The windows of the hemicycle, then, are the central piece of work in Saint-Père. In their row design, strength and flair of draughtsmanship and unabashed color they perfect and concentrate ideas presented by the choir designer. They in their turn form the model for the colored glass of the nave, in particular the less skillfully-executed nave saints, also in rows under canopies, crude and expressionistic in design and highly-colored. The ensemble of the hemicycle is a proud declaratory statement of an art form which would not long withstand the pressures, new goals, and changed techniques[15] of the fourteenth century.

NOTES

1. See Chapter I at fns. 15 and 25.
2. The same color formula appears in a few of the nave windows discussed in Chapter IV.
3. See Lillich, "Saint Louis."
4. The canopywork over the standing saints is more developed in the nave. See Chapter IV, fn. 15. The coloration of the historiated Bay 18, relying heavily on white and yellow, foreshadows developed fourteenth-century practice after the advent of the newly invented silver stain technique (see Pl. XII).
5. See discussion of Bay 22 (Chapter IV and Chapter XI).
6. See Chapter I; see also fuller accounts in the discussions of individual bays, Chapter X and Chapter XI.
7. The only internal evidence of any alteration in plan in the apse is the height of the saints, which varies, in a few cases necessitating the reduction or elimination of the lower border (Bay 4, Bay 5 left, Bay 6 left). Cartoon B is by far the tallest. Most, but not all, of the present lower borders are modern work. There is some evidence at Vendôme, another monument of the Western school, that the St. Louis there may have been inserted into older work. See M. Lillich, "The Choir Clerestory Windows of La Trinité at Vendôme: Dating and Patronage," *Journal of the Society of Architectural Historians,* XXXIV (1975), esp. p. 244.
8. On the pivotal position of Saint-Père in the mature Western school see generally Chapter V.
9. Cartoons were re-used generally. See Auxerre, Lyon, Saint-Urbain de Troyes.
10. The figures of the axial bay, none of them particularly distinguished, were each drawn to a fresh cartoon.
11. The careful choice and identification of Sts. Louis and Gilduin differ just as measurably from the rather haphazardly individualized saints around them. Their programmatic significance and its connection with subjects chosen for the nave will be investigated in Chapters VI and VIII.
12. The right medallion of Bay 5 is lost.
13. Becksmann (p. 16) comments briefly on the "Statuetten" in the Saint-Père hemicycle canopywork.
14. See references to Bay 22 and Bay 28 in Chapter IV. Sées is the monument where the Western and Norman styles form an obvious, uneasy alliance; Vendôme can also be mentioned in this regard.
15. The pressures appear to have been often economic. Among the new goals was the development of perspective; among the changed techniques, perhaps the most obvious was the employment of silver stain.

{ CHAPTER IV }

Nave: Style

THE twelve bays of the nave contain two basic designs in alternation, narratives in canopied rows and monumental standing saints framed in grisaille.[1] The nave windows are a late example of doublet-and-rose built ca. 1240–1245, the two immense lancets surmounted by a small rosace and pierced corner lights (see Figs. 8–10). Their broadness probably posed a source of aesthetic irritation to the early fourteenth-century glazier which he mitigated by adopting a flexible *panneautage* in three parts, as if each lancet contained two vertical mullions.[2] Although the proportions of the grid pattern thus established differ between the narrative and single figure windows, the ironwork of both forms three horizontal panels and in most cases ten vertical ones plus a curved upper row.[3]

The decoration of the nave clerestory was a unified concept in plan and execution, a plan not only sophisticated in its own complexity but carefully related to the rest of the church glazing. The hemicycle ensemble is recalled by the heavy coloration of the historiated panels and by their subjects (in quite a few cases employing scenes already illustrated in the tracery medallions of the hemicycle), as well as by the similarity of the canopied apostles and ecclesiastics of the color/grisaille bays. The latter nave bays reflect, no less intentionally, the vertical alternation of grisaille and standing figures in the choir. Thus despite a span of almost three-quarters of a century the design of the stained glass of Saint-Père, to an unusual degree, presents a coherent whole.

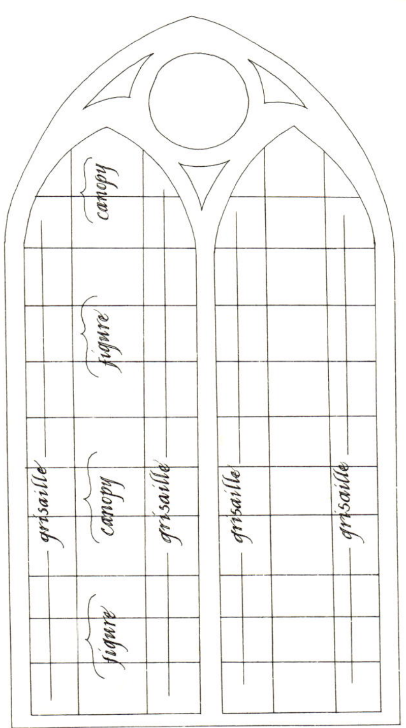

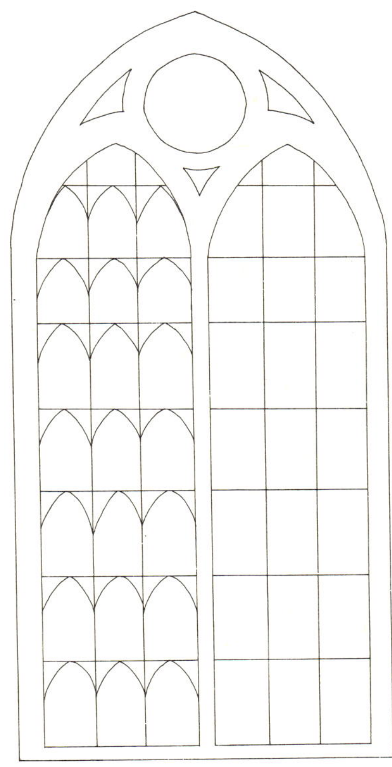

Figure 8 Format of figure bays (nave). (Drawing by Kevin McIntyre)

Figure 9 Format of 7-row narrative bays (nave). (Drawing by Kevin McIntyre)

FIGURE WINDOWS

The six nave windows containing large saints framed in grisaille or diaper (Pls. 55, 57, 72, 75, 83, 84) comprise twelve broad lancets, each with two figures one over the other, a total of twenty-four personae in all. Excepting the Madonna and Child and the donor figure of the left lancet of Bay 21,[4] all are saints, those on the north apostles with name-inscriptions and attributes, and those on the south ecclesiastics — popes (Bay 21), bishops and archbishops (Bay 25), and abbots (Bay 29). A few of the beatified churchmen also retain their original inscriptions.[5]

In the color/grisaille bays the vertical irons are placed to allow the central figured strip greater width than the two framing-strips (see Fig. 8).[6] Part of each framing-strip is taken up by a narrow colored border running around the entire lancet. The vertical grisaille in the nave, therefore, really functions as a frame albeit a conspicuous one, to the colored figure strip, unlike the choir design,

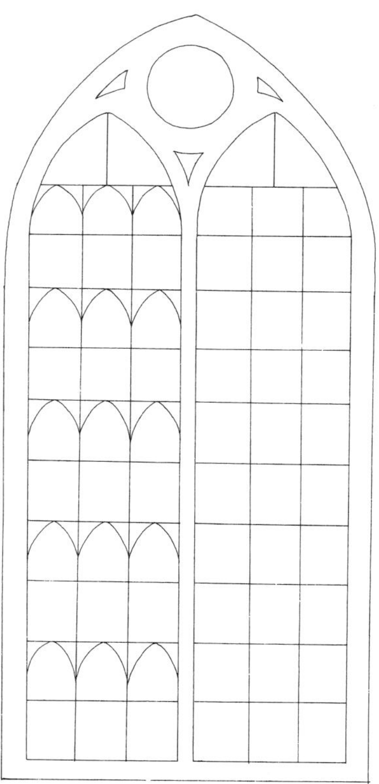

Figure 10 Format of 5-row narrative bays (nave). (Drawing by Kevin McIntyre)

where it functions as an equilibrant. It is a stylistic throwback to the pioneering color/grisaille designs of Reims, Auxerre, and Lyon.[7] Such a reversion is the more curious considering the vogue of the band-window design in the Western school of glazing by the early fourteenth century.[8] I believe it is better understood as a master designer's skilled variation on themes from the hemicycle and the choir than, as has been suggested,[9] purely an attempt to make the proportions of the broad lancets conform to the narrower, more vertical aesthetic of the day.

The original grisaille remains in four of the windows and traces of the original diaper in the other two. While the diaper (see Pls. 55–57) is a simple, archaizing pattern,[10] the grisaille designs offer an interesting and varied group of early fourteenth-century motifs, the only antiquated feature retained being the crosshatched ground.[11] The patterns in the two southern windows (Bays 25 and 29) are, like the colored glass of these bays, works of lesser quality and imagination than those on the north. Regular lozenge leading, in both, encloses glass painted with a vertical stem and rather dull, partially-naturalized foliage. Bay 25 (Pl. 75) has an ordinary central stem; the stem in the Bay 29 grisaille (Pl. 46) rises along the inner side of the panels, a variant also found in the grisaille of another Western monument, Sées Cathedral.[12] Colored lozenges in simple foliate patterns accent the centers and horizontal edges of the panels without so much as rippling the deadly regularity of the lead and filet latticework.

The grisaille of Bay 28 on the north (Pls. X, 47) offers a similar pattern to that of Bay 29, enlivened by imagination. The unusual inner rising stem recurs, but foliated with more varied and naturalized leafage. The quarries and their filet patterns have been "bulged" into graceful curving forms, animated by central bosses and the use of colored filets over the bars. In Bay 24 (Pls. 72, 74), the same basic formula emerges produced by the master himself. The draughtsmanship is exquisite. Elegant maple and clover leaves grow from the inner stem. The bulged leading is of some intricacy, combining interlocked filet patterns in red, in blue, and in delicate painted designs in the English manner.[13]

The colored portions of these windows — the large standing saints under their growing canopies and, of lesser importance, the borders — exhibit a much more muted coloration than the hemicycle ensemble. The primaries still provide the ingredients, but primaries which are, themselves, mutants (see, for example, Pl. VII). The red is darker, a port-wine shade occasionally approximating purple or brown. The blue is clearer and "thinner," the yellow quite mustard-like. Grounds are red or blue, again in no regular alternation, and white plays a slightly augmented role in canopywork. Most of the figure strips in question are heavily colored. In the more skillful productions of the north side of the nave, white, green and brown are introduced more often for variation. Bay 28 (Pl. X) in particular, a window which has been singled out for praise on account of its grisaille, exhibits a varied palette of these secondary colors as well as gold and red, with white occupying a larger proportion of surface in robes, attributes, and canopies. In this single window, which contains more highly-colored grisaille as well, the artist has made a recognizable attempt to match the effects of his colored and colorless glazing. By and large, however, the coloration of the nave saints follows the lead of the hemicycle in intent. The glass "material" used in the hemicycle and that of the nave series, it should be remembered, were different "batches" made under different conditions.[14] In the nave series, with the possible exception of the exemplary Bay 28, the primaries have been sought out and combined in a manner resembling the model in the hemicycle.

Other elements of design are no less dissimilar. The nave iconography is clearly an ordering and patterning of the apsidal chorus, and will be discussed in this light in the iconographic study, Chapter X. Canopy design and draughtsmanship in the nave ensemble are based to no less a degree on the hemicycle.

Canopies are more adventurous but composed of a nearly identical vocabulary of motifs.[15] The figure style exhibits a similar crude broadness of execution and insistence on mass. No one comparing the elongated wiry toes and grasping pawlike hands of, say, Bay 20 (Pl. 55) to those of the hemicycle ensemble could doubt that the source lay there. Quality is a more pertinent issue, for the nave saints seem to have been drawn and executed in some haste. In almost all but the superior Bay 24, cartoons were repeated exactly, two to a bay.[16] This was a familiar economy in Western glazing, but in the Saint-Père nave, figures of the same cartoon appear next to one another with little or no variation except their attributes.[17] The relaxation of care in decoration is even more evident. While it can be noted in almost any motif or element common to the two ensembles (haloes, decoration on swords and pikes, etc.), the difference is clearest in a comparison of papal or episcopal vestments. The painstaking and rich decoration of the hemicycle ecclesiastics has evaporated without a trace.

Nevertheless, the nave windows are certainly attractive. Delicacy of drawing was in any case never the strong suit of Western glazing. Rated by quality and "hand," the southern Bays 25 and 29 (Pl. 75 and Pls. 46 and 84) contain work of a pedestrian level; the once-diapered Bays 20 and 21 (Pls. 55–57, VII), both possibly commissioned by the same patron,[18] rate slightly higher; and the northern Bays 24 and 28 (Pls. 72, 74 and Pls. 47, 83, X) qualify as the skillful and inventive designs of the series. Of the latter two, Bay 28 could, judging from the varied anti-Western color scheme and the small heads and longer body proportions, be the work of the Norman master who designed most of the apse medallions.[19] It is curious, however, how little the variation in quality and style affects the group's total effectiveness in the glazing scheme of the church.

NARRATIVE WINDOWS

The six nave windows alternating with the figure series (Pls. 48, 51, 59, 69, 76, 79) contain lives of the saints and of the Virgin and the Passion of Christ in a format of canopied rows, heavily colored throughout. Variation in style, layout, color, and general quality is quite as wide as in the nave series of standing saints, with which they are contemporary. As in the case of the figure group, however, the overall plan of church glazing does not suffer thereby.

Small narrative panels were an anomaly in Western school glazing.[20] Furthermore, the over-broad doublet windows of the nave must have taxed the ingenuity of an artist accustomed to the slender, soaring lights of early fourteenth-century architecture. Although the narrative windows are products of a single decade, they evidence definite progressions in the use of artistic means for legible dramatic presentation in the clerestory. The artist (or artists) reworked and refined each solution. With the ultimate goal of suggesting a relative chronology for the series, I will discuss the stylistic elements in turn.

The most easily recognizable progression is in the row format. The broadness of the early thirteenth-century windows was ignored at the beginning. Bay 22 in the north nave (Peter and Paul) (Pl. 59) and the right lancet of Bay 19 on the south (Joachim and Anne) (Pl. 51) are divided into seven rows of three scenes each, a strongly horizontal pattern allowing only for figures too small to be deciphered at the distance (see Fig. 9).

The confused potpourri of primitive canopy and figure styles among the panels of Bay 22 leads to the hypothesis that the window was put together out of older glass, augmented by new work where necessary. The older panels were probably designed in pairs instead of sets of three (see Fig. 11), and from their size it seems most likely that they were intended for a window on the ground floor of the church or other abbey building.[21] As Bay 22 was the donation of the abbey's new leader ca. 1305, Abbot Jehan de Mantes, the hypothesis can be extended to suggest that it was the first nave window glazed, a sort of hastily-mounted "priming" for donations the new abbot sought — and obtained — for the remaining narrative bays. Its awkward seven-row design would, under such circumstances, result from the re-use of the older panels.

In any case, the seven-row format was short-lived. The right lancet of Bay 19 (Joachim and Anne) is the only other example. The new format comprising five rows of scenes (Fig. 10), each formed of six panels (two rows of three), appears in the left lancet of the same bay, continuing the narrative of the Virgin with the Infancy scenes.[22] It is used in the remaining four windows. The effect is at once more vertical and more legible, and allows for more developed canopies as well.[23]

Although the custom of framing small narrative scenes in rows of canopied panels never remotely approached the medallion device in popularity, it probably was invented at about the same time. A few examples occur in Chartres Cathedral, most notably the Saint-Chéron window (Bay XLII) in the north apsidal chapel.[24] In the chapels and clerestories of Saint-Urbain at Troyes, a monument of the second half of the thirteenth century with indubitable connections with Saint-Père, medallions, borderless scenes and canopied ones are combined in a transitional stew.[25] Medallions began to fall into disuse at the end of the century, and canopies were the major device to usurp their function in the late Gothic era.[26] The adoption of the canopied-scene design for a full-scale campaign of clerestory glazing at Saint-Père in the first decade of the fourteenth century was a progressive and experimental artistic decision.

The development of canopies at Saint-Père progressed as follows:

Bay 22 (north), early panels — primitive canopies with little or no decoration (Pls. VI, 59, 62, 63, Figs. 11, 14).

Bay 22, later panels } — simple canopies with more elaborate
Bay 19 (south), right lancet } decoration (Fig. 14; Pls. 59, 62, and 51).

Bay 26 (north) — the same type of canopy in a new five-row format (Pls. IX, 77, 78).

Bay 23 (south) — the same type of canopy with blocklike architectural motifs added from the vocabulary of the Western school (Pl. 69).

Bay 27 (south) — similar forms, with crockets added to the arches of the canopies (Pls. 81, 82).

Bay 19 (south), left lancet — crocketed gables also are added (Pls. 53, 54).

Bay 18 (north) — the same forms, but with the greatest variation and elaboration of architectural vocabulary (Pls. XI, XII, 49, 50).

A comparison of the first and last bays shows in a nutshell the direction and velocity of change in Gothic design at an important transitional moment.

The study of color in the series proves equally telling. Red and blue predominate in the early Peter window (Bay 22) (Pl. VI, two left panels), the highlights being a strong gold. There is little white. The right lancet of Bay 19 follows the same heavily-colored pattern, as does Bay 26 (Baptist) (Pl. IX), where large areas of brown are introduced and the blue/red pattern is splintered in a diaper ground. Strong gold and also white become increasingly important in the succeeding bays, as the more elaborate architectural frames present the opportunity for their use. Bay 18 (Pl. XII) is a color composition in which the base has finally shifted from red and blue to yellow and white. The color of this window, like the canopywork, is not in transit; it is, in fact, the only bay in the church which has arrived stylistically in the fourteenth century. The aerial luminosity so long attributed to the introduction of the *jaune d'argent* technique has been sought in Bay 18 with pot-metal glass.[27] Silver stain, although certainly the ideal device for the lightened windows of the new century, was by no means the harbinger of the new aesthetic.

It remains to investigate the drawing styles in the narrative series. How many artists were at work? Had they participated in the apse campaign and/or the nave figure series? Is the best work of the various ensembles connected by any stylistic relationships? And did the whole shop work on a given window or was each the product of a single artisan?

The study of the hemicycle style suggested that the master was the strong guiding hand there, responsible for the overall plan, probably for the cartoons and their variations, and the execution of most of the figures. Some of the architectural motifs show Norman influence, as do most of the tracery medallion

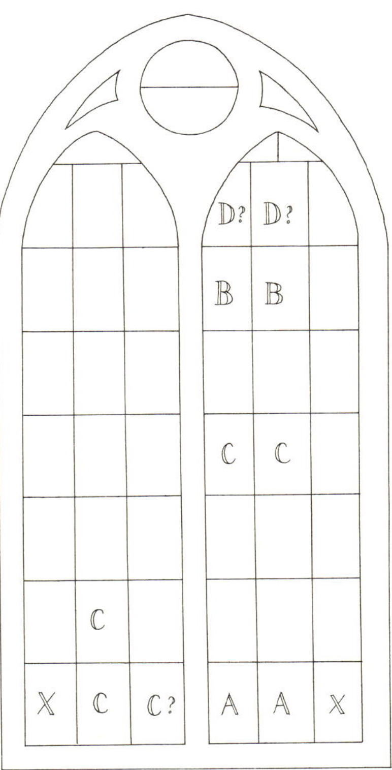

Figure 11 Bay 22: re-used panels. (Drawing by Kevin McIntyre)

scenes. In the nave saints series, on the other hand, the best grisaille and figure work appear together in a bay; those of the north side are of consistently higher quality than their opposites.

The earliest of the narrative windows, Bay 22 on the north, presents a most complex stylistic puzzle. The window, so crucial to the dating and relationship of the various hands of the hemicycle and nave, unfortunately offers only a jigsaw puzzle of stylistic and iconographic problems. Central among these is the donor's panel dating by inscription no earlier than ca. 1305 (Pl. 63) and yet among the stylistically early core of the panels of the window (although by no means so primitive as the standing Peter and Paul, Pl. 62). As even the small early group is not stylistically coherent, the intended form or source of them defies solution. The present clerestory form is clearly an afterthought, an augmentation, and just as clearly, from stylistic evidence, at the vanguard of the immense glazing project donated to the nave ca. 1305–1315.

The more primitive re-used panels of the ensemble amount to about a quarter of the total.[28] The elapsed time between their design and their use in

Bay 22 cannot have been much more than several decades, judging from the canopy forms employed. They were designed in pairs and, excepting only the earliest two (A in Fig. 11), show detailed draughtsmanship and a tight, confined arrangement, a liking for profile and full-face, comparatively small heads and elongated bodies, delicately drawn hands and gracefully positioned feet, and a tableau-like quality. In a word, they resemble the hemicycle tracery medallions.

The re-used panels of Bay 22 can be grouped as follows (compare Fig. 11 and Pl. 59):

A — Panels of standing figures of Peter and Paul (Pl. 62). The most primitive canopy design in the window occurs in these panels. Figure proportion, canopy development and architectural motifs, as well as the draughtsmanship itself, are similar to the glazing of Sées Cathedral (1270–1280).

B — The martyrdoms of Peter and Paul. The figure style here is similar to that of the apse medallions, which also show martydoms. The architectural motifs of these panels are also found in the apse, in a more complex stage of development.

C — Two panels of the Fall of Simon Magus (Pl. VI). One panel of the Calling of Peter, and one panel of the Giving of the Keys (Pl. 63). These four panels, to which can be added the donor panel of the kneeling Jehan de Mantes (marked "C?" in the diagram), exhibit a common canopy and figure style, which is graceful, static, and slightly naive in appearance.

D? — Panels of the Christ Judge and the angel receiving the martyr's soul (Pl. 68). These panels are the only other ones in the window which show any evidence of the style of the medallions in the hemicycle tracery; note especially the faces, and the hands of the "soul" and of the angel. Their proportions and arrangement, however, are in keeping with those of the later panels of Bay 22. (Note especially the angel's expressively exaggerated embrace.)

X — Two standing prophets (Pls. 62, 63). Panels of a much later date, employing silver stain, perspective columns, and a *damasquiné* ground. The date and circumstances of their insertion into the ensemble of Bay 22 are unknown.

While it is unfortunate that the earliest nave narrative window should present such stylistic disorder, the deviant panels fill a gap in the history of the abbey glazing, falling as they do between the latest choirwork of Bays 14–15 (ca. 1270–1280) and the hemicycle ensemble (ca. 1295–1300) and exhibiting obvious stylistic connections with both the Western and Norman strains at Sées.

The typical Saint-Père narrative style takes wing in the remaining panels of Bay 22, and its course of refinement can be charted through the succeeding ensembles. Loose and sketchy draughtsmanship is combined with exaggerated gesture and a sense of mass and of movement, as in the large figures of the church. In the small scale of Bay 22 and the right lancet of Bay 19 (Pl. 51) the result is usually overcrowded chaos. At their best the figures emit a rustic charm (Annunciation to Joachim principals, Anne presenting her daughter at the steps of the temple); a sense of movement (the revived sick man carrying his bed in Bay 22, Pl. 62); or of drama (the successful Simon Magus/ram story of Bay 22, Pl. 62).

Necessary breathing space was afforded by the five-row format of the succeeding ensembles. Only Bay 26 on the north (Baptist) (Pls. IX, 76–78), the masterpiece of the series, takes full advantage of the increased space to enlarge proportions and spotlight movement.[29] It is not only size which makes the difference in Bay 26, however. The artist has reduced his personae to a workable minimum, given full rein to his bent for expressionism in movement and gesture, and enriched his creation with the comforting regularity and pleasing scintillation of a latticed ground. Bay 26 is a chef d'oeuvre of dramatic narration.

While the accomplishment of the Baptist window was not sustained, features of the style appear to advantage in the remaining bays. The same dramatic simplicity which renders the scenes so clear and recognizable at the great distance appears again in the left lancet of Bay 19 on the south nave (Virgin) (Pls. 53, 54). The artist of the Virgin story, who perhaps lacks the verve of the Baptist master, has learned from him the value of a minimal set of characters and the use of the whole row of three panels as a stage. The comparison of the left Virgin lancet of Bay 19 with the older format in the right lancet pinpoints the progression from "narration" to "drama."

Perhaps the artist of the Virgin lancet painted a cartoon made by the Baptist master, with whom he seems to have served his apprenticeship. A few draperies in Bay 26 (for example, the women presenting the infant John to his father) have the abundant loop-folds of the Virgin painter. They are more traditional in French Gothic art than the style of his master.

The expressionistic exaggeration of movement and gesture which enlivens the Baptist window — note, for example, the visual pattern of the seated Herod, upper right lancet, and the two execution scenes of the left lancet — becomes the most attractive feature of Bay 23 on the south (Sts. Clement and Denis) (Pl. 69). An iconographically complex ensemble, the right lancet of which is a visual amalgam of several famous Saint-Denis manuscripts,[30] Bay 23 is saved from utter confusion by the expressive energy of its design. The spidery saint on his trestle, the colorful mad dogs and the angular duet of the saint and his executioner at the fiery furnace are noteworthy.[31] It is interesting to note that a single scene of the early Peter window, that of the Simon Magus/ram episode (Pl. 62) unmistakably radiates the same vigorous spirit.

By comparison, the south Bay 27 (Sts. Agnes and Catherine) (Pls. VIII, 81, 82) is a disappointing and confused narrative resembling the seven-row ensembles of Bays 22 and 19. Only one lesson has been learned, that of spreading a scene across all three panels. The same judgment applies to the Passion of the north Bay 18 (Pls. XI, XII, 49, 50) marked by its use of color and the intricacy of its canopywork as the final product of the nave series. The blame in this case falls to some degree on the model, which, from iconographic evidence, was probably an art object of the twelfth century or before.[32] The layout is confused, the drawing naive, the struggles with scale occasionally pathetic. The effect is a childlike charm. But what a difference, had the St. Denis expressionist, who proved what could be done with an assigned model, been put to work on the Passion.

While the achievements of the Saint-Père atelier vary in the narrative series, it was unquestionably the same shop which produced the contemporary standing saints of the church. The awkward abbots and stolid bishops of the south side of the nave resemble the less artful designs of the Passion window and the Agnes-Catherine bay just as the energetic and dramatic figures of the hemicycle compare with those of the Baptist story and Bay 23. In dealing with an art form as technically complex as stained glass, it is bold to attempt to isolate artistic personalities. Between the extremes — i.e., the superior grasp of materials and design of the Baptist window and the naiveté of a bay like the Agnes-Catherine ensemble — lie traces of how many individuals? It is impossible to say. The Virgin lancet of Bay 19, for example, could be a separate artistic product, or the cartoons could have been prepared by the Baptist master for execution by a less spirited assistant.[33] The Norman influence in the hemicycle and in the handful of early panels incorporated into the Peter window dies out completely. Either the responsible artist produced no more or his style absorbed characteristics of the Western atelier in which he found himself. The latter is the more attractive theory, since the large standing apostles of Bay 28 (north) have a more varied color scheme and longer proportions with smaller heads than the other standing saints of the nave. Aside from this abortive Norman influence three stylistic types are found in the narrative group: a simplified dramatic manner (Bay 26 and left lancet of Bay 19); a style based on distortion and exaggeration (brief traces in Bay 22, particularly the Simon Magus/ram scene, and Bay 23); and a more untutored group in which exaggerated gestures and awkward design appear in compositions which are often touched with charm but overcrowded and indistinct (most of Bay 22, right lancet of Bay 19, Bay 27, Bay 18).

The twelve narrative lancets in the nave are products of varying quality, of several markedly personal styles, probably done in a comparatively short space

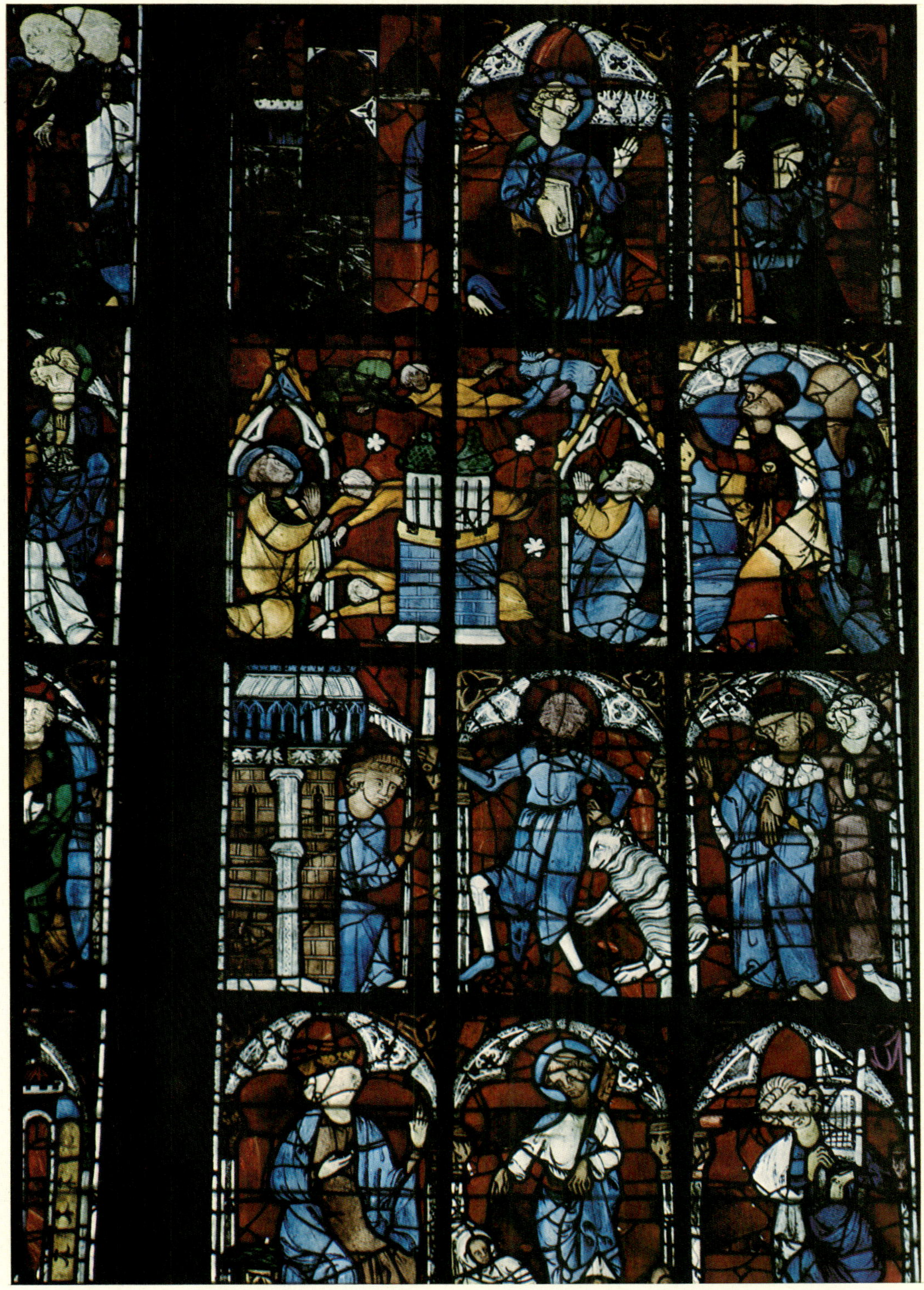

PLATE VI Nave: Bay 22. St. Peter window, Simon Magus. *(Edouard Fièvet)*

of time. These are the windows for which the abbey, possibly impoverished by the hemicycle project, solicited donors. Some of the calligraphy is recognizable from that earlier atelier, however. The artist who could render the cutting of Malchus' ear (north Bay 18, Pl. 50) with such matter-of-fact unconcern very possibly placed his apprentice piece among the hemicycle martyrdoms. The tragic stories of Sts. Agnes and Catherine (Bay 27 on the south, Pls. 81, 82), hardly less ingenuous in rendition, contain figures of the willowy insubstantiality found in the hemicycle's canopywork angels (Pl. 14). The master was occupied, most likely, during these years with Bay 23 in the south nave (Clement and Denis), a window which exhibits in sophistication of thought, design, and handling of source materials the excellence one would expect of the hemicycle designer. Bay 26, the Baptist window, is more puzzling (Pls. IX, 77, 78). The most successful narrative group in the church, it resembles the other storied bays hardly at all.[34] Its figures, fully as sculptural as those of the hemicycle, are lightly touched by a mannerist influence. The draughtsmanship is closer to Bay 23 and to the better-quality nave saints (generally speaking those on the north) than to the hemicycle, and its archaic ground resembles the diaper which originally framed the standing saints of Bays 20 and 21 (Pl. 56). The force of a free spirit emerges within the old framework.

In general, each of the narrative windows of the nave speaks a consistent tongue in all its composite scenes.[35] The fact that the traceable progression in the elaboration of canopywork and in color harmony does not closely parallel the styles of scene design, however, would indicate that a master planner exerted some control throughout the campaign. The narrative windows of Saint-Père form a unified artistic expression in spite of variations of execution. The strength of the Western style is the more noteworthy considering these variations. It is a vigorous style, relying on exaggerated features and gestures, simplified harmonies of color, and sketchy, loose drawing — a style in which grace and elegance surrender unconditionally to power and energy.

NOTES

1. Bays 20 and 21, closest to the sanctuary, were originally framed in colored diaper, remnants of which are still visible at the top of the windows. See Pl. 56.

2. Louis Grodecki, describing panels from Bay 26 included in the 1953 Paris exhibition at the Musée des Arts Décoratifs, assumed in error that the windows did contain mullions. (Louis Grodecki, *Vitraux de France du XIe au XVIe siècle* [Paris, 1953], p. 20.)

3. The exceptions are Bay 22 (Peter window) and the right lancet of Bay 19 (Virgin), both divided into seven rows. See discussion infra.

4. See Chapter X, Bay 21, Laurent de Voisin.

5. See Chapter X, Bays 21, 25, 29.

6. The width of the sections of Bay 25, for example: 50 cm./68/50 (excluding irons); 175 cm. across lancet including irons. Compare the measurements of a narrative bay of comparable size in fn. 23, this chapter. The nave bays vary slightly in width.

7. See Lillich, "Band Window," p. 28 and fns. To add to my remarks in that article: Linas (Essonne) belongs with this group (see Lafond, "Normandie," p. 357, fn. 3); on the Angers Virgin see also Jane Hayward, "The Choir Windows of Saint-Serge and their Glazing Atelier," *Gesta* XV (1976), pp. 259–260; on the Saint-Remi tribune, Grodecki now believes the combination of color and grisaille to be a modern restoration.

8. Its use at Tours, Sées, and Vendôme is sketched in Chapter V.

9. See Lewis Day, *Windows*, 2d ed. (London, 1902), p. 160. Compare Arnold, pp. 187–188, who says simply that the artist adapted the choir design to the broad doublet-and-rose tracery of the nave.

10. It may have been specified by the donor, the Canon Laurent de Voisin, Dean of the cathedral. Lafond traces the use of archaistic diaper ground in Chartres as late as the Chapelle Saint-Piat (Lafond, "XIVe siècle," p. 212).

11. Was the hatched ground retained to harmonize the nave glass with the early grisaille of the choir? Clear-ground grisaille of an intervening date (and inferior workmanship) appears in the choir triforium, and traces of clear-ground grisaille of a date contemporary with the later hatched work are found in the rosaces of Bay 19 (largely restored) and Bay 21 (only debris). By the end of the thirteenth century the cathedral contained grisaille with clear grounds (Bays 29 and 36 near the entrance of Chapelle Saint-Piat and Bays 146–148 in north transept clerestory; see Lillich, "Chartres Cathedral," pp. 15–17). On the other hand, the hatched ground appears in grisaille of the hemicycle triforium of Saint-Père, which is virtually contemporary with the nave (scraps remaining above inserted sixteenth-century panels).

12. Axial clerestory. On Sées, see Chapter V.

13. For example, the mid-thirteenth-century grisaille of Lincoln. See also an illustration of early thirteenth-century grisaille from Stanton Harcourt (Oxon.) in Christopher Woodforde, *English Stained and Painted Glass* (Oxford, 1954), pl. 3. It is a very rare design in France.

14. A re-reading of Theophilus' "De diversis artibus" serves as a reminder of how little control the medieval glazier actually maintained anteriorly over the shades in his palette. Another consideration would be the centuries of weathering, which attacks and alters some shades more than others, contrary to the extraordinary opinion of Robert Sowers, "On the Blues in Chartres," *Art Bulletin*, XLVIII, no. 2 (June, 1966), pp. 220ff. Cf. in particular Vendôme, Bay G, which is now too dark for photographing; similarly, the axial clerestory of Sées; the south choir clerestories of Le Mans.

15. See Chapter V, fn. 11. A significant advance in the nave canopywork has been analyzed by Becksmann (p. 19), that is, the substitution of framing architecture (brickwork here) for the columns used previously. This type of architectural framework is typical of the mature Western monuments, namely Vendôme, where it seems to be introduced, and Evron. See: M. Lillich, "Vendôme," pp. 238ff., figs. 3 and 5.

16. Bay 21, of necessity, contains different cartoons for the Virgin and Child and for the kneeling donor. Bay 29, mediocre work heavily restored, contains three cartoons for its four figures (Pl. 84).

17. The most forced case is that of St. Judas and St. Barnabas in Bay 28, both based on the same cartoon but carrying vastly different attributes in different positions (Pl. 83).

18. See Chapter X, Bay 21.

19. See concluding remarks of this chapter.

20. See Chapter V. Examples are the "Evron" window in the upper ambulatory of Le Mans; perhaps the St. Julien window of Angers, a very polished work; the Sainte-Radegonde glazing?

21. Such a surmise is based on the projected size of a two-panel format window. Small single windows are found in ground-floor locations in both the Saint-Père chevet (mid-twelfth century) and nave (early thirteenth). Small scenes were far from rare in upper windows during the second half of the thirteenth century, as the fame of the Sainte-Chapelle spread. Such windows were almost always medallion designs, however. The canopy-row design, found in a few narrative windows of Chartres Cathedral, may have appealed more to the late-Western school. There is too little remaining evidence to make a judgment. (See Chartres Bay 42, north choir chapel, Saint Chéron window, illustrated in Delaporte and Houvet, II, pl. CXXIII–CXXVI; occasional isolated scenes in the clerestory have canopy frames, e.g., Bays 71 and 72, illustrated in Delaporte and Houvet, III, pl. CLXXXVI.)

22. The Infancy lancet not only serves in this capacity iconographically but also to balance the Passion bay (Bay 18) directly opposite, on the north.

23. Bay 19 has the following measurements of width: right lancet (seven-row): 55 cm./56/55; left lancet (five-row): 57+/52.5/57; 174 cm. across lancet including irons. The five-row panels are narrower (the outer two include borders) and taller (two layers of panels form each row of design).

24. Delaporte and Houvet II, pl. CXXIII and text vol. p. 344; also illustrated in *VF,* p. 65. Small donor figures and angels are not infrequently presented under canopies (the transept rose lancets, the thirteenth-century angels surrounding Notre-Dame de la Belle Verrière, etc.) and occasionally donor panels showing guild scenes.

25. Bays B, C, and E of the choir clerestory include scenes under single and double primitive canopies; the scenes in Bay A have no frame of any kind; Bay D has medallions (one illustrated in *VF,* pl. VIII). Some of the Saint-Urbain glass has been heavily reworked and restored. Bay letters are those of the *Monuments historiques.*

26. Another design almost as venerable as the others, that of figures placed directly against grisaille, also enjoyed a period of popularity in the early fourteenth century.

27. Cf. Evron, an example of another typical fourteenth-century feature usually attributed to *jaune d'argent,* that of soaring canopywork, there achieved without the use of silver stain. Silver stain was probably introduced to the Chartrain area in 1328, when the Canon Guillaume Thierry was allowed to insert a horizontal strip into the foot of one of the great thirteenth-century windows of the south cathedral transept to light an altar he had founded (*VF,* p. 165). The strip is very advanced for its date, entirely composed of white and *jaune d'argent.* Lafond sets the "invention" of silver stain at ca. 1310 and its earliest appearance in the Ile-de-France and Normandy 1310–1330 (Lafond, "XIVe siècle," pp. 211; 234, fn. 41; and 236; Lafond, *Trois études sur la technique du vitrail* [Essai historique sur le jaune d'argent] [Rouen, 1943], pp. 55–57; Lafond, "Un vitrail du Mesnil-Villeman [1313]," *Bulletin de la Société nationale des antiquaires de France* [Séance du 8 décembre 1954], pp. 94–95).

28. Bay 22 was drastically dismantled in the late seventeenth century and re-assembled by Charles Lorin in the restorations of ca. 1905. As some of the more primitive panels remained in the window during the interval, according to the notes of de Lasteyrie and Guilhermy in the mid-nineteenth century, and as a Gaignières drawing (Pl. 65) done before the dismantling shows parts of some of them, it can be assumed that the earlier panels were undoubtedly an original part of the ensemble. See Chapter XI, Bay 22; Chapter I, fn. 30.

29. The craze for canopywork quickly absorbed the new space, especially in the hands of an inferior artist (see Bay 27 on the south, Agnes/Catherine window, Pls. 81, 82).

30. See Chapter XI, Bay 23.

31. The left lancet (St. Clement) suffers from the loss of most of the left-hand panels, but

the top scene of the saint with the anchor around his neck and the middle episode of the spring struck from the rock can be mentioned.

32. See Chapter XI, Bay 18.

33. The Virgin lancet differs markedly from the Baptist bay in color harmony. The former employs clear, balanced primaries; the latter aligns itself with the mannered color palette of the Laurent Voisin bay (port-wine red, clear thin blue, mustard yellow, etc.) (Pl. IX). The color harmonies employed by the school of the West are discussed in Chapter V.

34. Its only predecessor could be the left lancet of the Virgin window (Bay 19), which shows a similar talent for dramatic simplicity. Whether this lancet is an earlier project by the Baptist master or the work of an assistant under his control is an open question. I prefer the latter hypothesis, since the painting style varies.

35. The obvious exception is Bay 22 (Peter window). Each lancet of the Virgin bay (Bay 19) is stylistically homogeneous within itself.

{ CHAPTER V }

The Western School of Stained Glass

SAINT-PÈRE is the chief monument in a school of regional glass painting in France which can be called the school of the West.[1] Possibly an offshoot of the latest work in the north transept of Chartres Cathedral, ca. 1235, the school developed and flourished for almost a century to follow. It was represented to a greater or lesser degree in most of the monuments of importance to be glazed during that period in Maine and Touraine, in a geographical area situated to the southwest of Paris between the fringes of Normandy on the north and the territory of the old Angevin dynasty to the west and south. An occasional detail typical of the more elegant glass style of Normandy appears in this body of Western windows, the most unequivocal being the use of small gargoyles and of figures in canopywork.[2] A more consequential source of inspiration, however, was probably to the East, in particular Auxerre and Troyes Cathedrals at the formative stages, and possibly Saint-Urbain de Troyes later on. Many germinal ideas,[3] either originating there or transferred by that path from the late-twelfth-century Rémois glass painting — the list ranges from basic issues of scale, layout, and subject program to minor details such as the popularity of the profile figure — were to find their greatest field of experimentation not in Burgundy or Champagne but in the Western school.

The influence of the Sainte-Chapelle at mid-century may explain this phenomenon. Parisian windows appeared in both East and West in the third quarter of the thirteenth century.[4] No Eastern school emerged from the art of Semur-en-Auxois and Auxerre, however, to challenge the preeminence of Parisian ideas[5] as the Western school succeeded in doing. It resisted the intrusion of the precise and elegant Norman style with the same vigor. The Western school is one of the rare strongly individual regional styles of glass painting to emerge before the next century.

Definable by about 1240 — which is to say, roughly contemporary with the prestigious archaisms of the Sainte-Chapelle — Western expressionism manifests itself with vitality for several generations. It is submerged in the 1320's through a combination of arteriosclerosis from within and the broader stylistic impact of the new technique of silver-staining.[6] We define the great glass painting style of the fourteenth century as Norman: the Cathedral of Rouen's Lady Chapel, Saint-Ouen, Evreux and so on. It is a fairly safe assumption that things would have taken a different turn without the new *jaune d'argent.*

A definitive inquiry into the foundations of the Norman style is too vast a task to be essayed here. One must hazard some guesses, however. A tightly-drawn, heavily contoured, stable type of design crops up here and there in Western ensembles, and eventually dominates them. Silhouettes are emphasized and painting within them is spare. Small-headed figures hold quiet tableau-like postures, framed by canopies, in a color harmony of rich, deep saturation sparked by a generous sprinkling of scintillants — tiny broken areas of white. One must assume that this art is not Parisian in origin; the whites of the Sainte-Chapelle are few and unbroken, the figure style at its best is more free and unshackled, and of course the medallion format more emphatically traditional. Is this, then, the Norman style of the pre-silver-stain era?[7] Some of the late-thirteenth-century debris of the Evreux nave aisles and the early-fourteenth-century series of Sts. Edward and Louis at Fécamp provide food for thought. In Western monuments this tightly drawn style can be noted at Le Mans (ca. 1255, bays adjoining hemicycle), at Sées (the glass of north transept and apsidal chapels dating ca. 1280), and La Trinité de Vendôme (hemicycle clerestories, ca. 1290). Since it is a counter-style to Western expressionism I shall designate it for convenience, in the succeeding discussion, by the label "Norman."

What are the characteristics of Western glass? Chiefly a sometimes crude expressive force and a freer, less precise draughtsmanship. Color and scale also are exploited to communicate an intensity of mood. The typical color gamut — though not the only one — of the developed work of the Western school is a commingling in almost equal parts of the three primary colors. The resultant design is brilliant, occasionally even gaudy. A strange mottled green and shades of brown make another typical combination, not at all gaudy, but not Parisian and certainly not Norman either in its almost mannered effect.

Very thick and irregularly blown glass was used, "d'une sorte de beauté rustique que l'on pourrait comparer à celle de la faïence, pendant que les verres [of Normandy] sont comme de la porcelaine fine."[8] The difficulty in observing this quality in glass — the window should actually be taken down, if a clerestory — has prevented the gathering of conclusive evidence. In the triforium of the apse of Tours, it has been noted,[9] *bosselage du verre* is common in many pieces, the heads and hands often painted on *verres bosselés* to accentuate their physiognomy. The Saint-Père panels included in the 1953 Paris exhibition proved a similar case for that monument; and I have noted such very thick, uneven glass from the exterior clerestory passages of Vendôme and Evron.

An interest in large scale preoccupied the Western glaziers. As all of the remaining windows of the school are at least at triforium level, the typical large single figure would seem a logical choice. Small scenes and medallions, however, were far from banished from upper lights in later thirteenth-century French glazing. In the Tours chevet, for example, beautiful Parisian medallion clerestories far outnumber the two upper band windows, and the series of the hemicycle triforium (Pl. 88) by the glaziers of the school of the West. Le Mans is another site where the two rival styles keep house together. The Western saints and prophets maintain a sense of isolation and mass which is more akin to large-scale portal sculpture than to other schools of glass painting. It is precisely this sculptural quality which begins to disintegrate in the final phases of the Western style, in the second decade of the fourteenth century, in the narrative groups at Evron.

The Western school experimented creatively throughout its course of development with problems of layout. The giant single figure "medallions" of the Saint-Père choir are an interesting example, possibly adapted from designs in Troyes Cathedral (Pl. 87), and ultimately from the handful of large medallions at Chartres.[10] After the early work at Saint-Père the "medallion" idea was discarded entirely and canopies employed, often incorporating Norman gargoyles but otherwise composed of a large and quite distinctive group of decorative motifs, again ultimately derived from Chartres.[11] The late canopywork of the school of the West maintains a sense of solid, almost blocklike structure.

The combination of canopied figures with grisaille was a transitional problem in stained-glass design, fully exploited in the Western school. The band windows of the Tours and Sées clerestories are pioneering examples of a familiar fourteenth-century arrangement, "une formule appelée à un grand avenir."[12] At Saint-Père at almost the same moment (ca. 1275) bands of color and grisaille were being combined in vertical alternation. The vertical pattern lived on in the later work at Saint-Père after 1300, while Western glaziers at Vendôme apparently tried an arrangement of the figure-band across the bottom of the bay.[13] At Evron the latter layout appears, but instead of grisaille the designer has substituted the grotesquely elongated canopies which were to become another commonplace of the glass painting of a later century.[14]

The adventurous spirit and expressive energy of Western glazing throughout an important period of transition in French glass-painting are noteworthy. The cohesion of the school is also manifest in numerous decorative motifs as well as an occasional iconographic oddity. St. Barnabas holding a flame is the most obvious example of a regional iconographic deviation. Rarity that he is, he appears at Vendôme, Saint-Père (twice), and Evron. Architectural and decorative elements which can be found as early as the first Saint-Père panels, ca. 1240–1245, occur at Le Mans a decade later and in succeeding monuments enriched by a developing range of detail. The three late ensembles of the school, Vendôme, Saint-Père, and Evron, exhibit a conjunction of similar motifs as unmistakable as a signature.

The work of the Western school can be charted chronologically as follows:

?Chartres, north transept	ca. 1235
Saint-Père, glass now in choir[15]	ca. 1240–1245
Le Mans, several bays of choir clerestory[16]	ca. 1250–1260
Tours, two bays of clerestory and the apse triforium series (Pl. 88)	ca. 1260–1270
Saint-Père, Bays 14–15 and present choir arrangement (employing older glass)	ca. 1270
Sées, choir clerestory	ca. 1270–1285
Vendôme, La Trinité, choir clerestories (Pl. 89)	ca. 1290–1300
Saint-Père, apse and nave clerestories	ca. 1295–1315
Evron, choir clerestories (Pl. 90)	ca. 1310–1320

The glazing of Saint-Père de Chartres is the largest and most cohesive body of work of the school of the West. Comprising, as it does, some of the earliest identifiable work of the school as well as important examples of design and arrangement from the developing period and more windows in the mature style than the other two late monuments together, it is indeed the school's pivotal monument.

The school of the West apparently did not radiate from a central model[17] but developed in a gradual and more organic manner. The relationship of the prophets of the Saint-Père choir, the early work of the school, to the latest glazing of the north transept of the cathedral is not at all clear. Toward the end of the campaign of Chartres Cathedral, a style of greater expressive power and even brutality appeared, in the south rose (ca. 1220–1230), then the north rose (ca. 1230–1235) and the western clerestories of that transept (ca. 1225–1235).[18] The Saint-Père prophets of ten to fifteen years later are several steps further along the path. Similar decorative elements can be found, but not employed in the same roles, and just how much of a debt the fierce and almost theatrical prophets owe directly to the more hieratic personages of the Chartres transept[19] is difficult to judge. The Saint-Père figures do not occupy their original positions at present. What remains of the first layout, a bizarre attempt to combine huge figures in an elephantine medallion and diaper framework, echoes an older design in the Chartres hemicycle (Delaporte Pl. CXVIII), albeit very faintly. It could have been adopted from more contemporary designs at Troyes (for example Pl. 87) or from further north,[20] or it could have been invented independently.

The parentage of the profile pose used so effectively at Saint-Père (for example, Pls. 17, 24, 30, 35, 36) and again at Tours[21] (Pl. 88) is not typically Chartrain either. The likeliest source would again appear to be Burgundy/Champagne, where strikingly similar dramatic figures emerge later in the more nervous glazing style of Saint-Urbain de Troyes (ca. 1270's) and once in the rather more stolid apostles at Châlons-sur-Marne (ca. 1275).[22] Unfortunately no evidence now remains of the missing link, a common ancestor of Saint-Père and Saint-Urbain.[23]

In the West the logical monument to provide continuity between Chartrain art and the early windows of Saint-Père would be Angers, but a search there for origins of the Western group under discussion in this chapter yields nothing. Only the single later medallion window of St. Julien, dated "après 1240 et jusque vers 1260," shows comparable head-to-body proportions and expressive silhouetting. It is, however, an art much less "brutal" and violent than the group under discussion, as Grodecki and Hayward noted[24] in comparing this exceptional window to the axial clerestory of Le Mans. Auxerre, Troyes, and ultimately the Rémois art seem more likely antecedents.

The choir of Auxerre, in particular, contains large-scale figures of a marked expressionism. Grodecki writes:

> Dans les fenêtres hautes — dont le style revient, pour le principe, à l'art chartrain — on voit une autre modalité de ces exagérations expressives, qui touchent, ici, à la brutalité.[25]

The less well-known triforium of Troyes Cathedral (Pl. 86)[26] contains figures as distorted and expressionistic as the most extreme designs of Le Mans. At the same time the stamp of Saint-Remi upon them is unmistakable.

The conclusion seems unavoidable that if the school of the West derives from a late, "brutal" strain at Chartres, it is through an intermediary, and that intermediary is not Western but from Burgundy-Champagne.

The chronicle of the development of the Western school would be elusive indeed were Saint-Père lost to us. Le Mans, another early site, is a monument of vast riches and vaster puzzles. Among its thirteenth-century treasures are a handsome but scrambled set of Parisian medallion windows in the upper ambulatory, a set invaded only once by the local patois of its "Evron window." The immense clerestories overhead range over an even broader stylistic spectrum, running from a dull, prim drawing to the extremes of caricature. Western characteristics such as the crude expressiveness, unusual coloration, and many of the decorative motifs seen in the early Saint-Père glass are identifiable among this bewildering array of styles, but in no particular sequence.[27]

At Tours, in somewhat similar fashion, the Parisian style permeates the upper ensemble, even of the two precocious band windows.[28] Their experimental format aside, it is not those well-mannered ecclesiastics but the impressive and less well-known apostles of the apse triforium series (Pl. 88) which are truly Western. Indeed, the exaggerated drawing of the later Saint-Père work — most notable in hands and toes — seems to have been introduced at Tours.

Sées (Orne), even less familiar, has been included in the past with Normandy because of its geographical proximity and the pure Norman quality of its architecture. Of the glass, the ambulatory and transept chapels especially have a Norman cast, and it was to those ensembles that Lafond, in his superb pioneer study,[29] devoted the greater part of his attention. Related to the school of the West are most of the great band windows of the choir clerestory, figures whose bodies he called "trapus à l'excès et parfois difformes" and whose faces he labeled "souvent d'une laideur cocasse," at the same time acknowledging a magnificent sonority of color.[30] The art of Sées more closely allies itself with the unpolished primitive force of Le Mans and the Saint-Père nave than with the nervousness found in the Tours triforium and the Saint-Père hemicycle. Its reduced color scheme recurs in certain bays of Vendôme and Evron.

Of the three late monuments of the school of the West, it is Saint-Père where the pure unadulterated tongue is spoken. Vendôme and Evron are both smaller and more dilute ensembles where a greater role is accorded to the "Norman" style,[31] the courtly proportions and greater constraint of which were to conquer all. Vendôme, moreover, was not only a less ambitious program to begin with, but suffered embellishment and revision in the sixteenth century; the present band window formats in the hemicycle can be traced to a comparatively recent restoration. Not the least problem was formerly the traditional date, particularly untenable for the grisaille: "Si un document ne fixait pas à 1306 le début de la reconstruction de la Trinité de Vendôme — et si Saint Louis ne figurait pas dans l'iconographie — on attribuerait sans hésiter au dernier quart du XIIIe siècle . . . les fenêtres hautes du choeur."[32] The date can now be correctly placed ca. 1290, and the color, general compositional spirit, and decorative detail (Pl. 89) compared more favorably with the other two late monuments. The vicissitudes nonetheless have made of Vendôme a most fragile bridge between the crystallization of the Western school and the final vestiges of the style, found at Evron.

Evron, like Sées, has been grouped with the Normandy school by past authorities;[33] and like any number of monuments, it has suffered from modern restoration.[34] The westernmost bay in the north choir (Pl. 90), which differs markedly from the others in style and layout, is of a piece with the standing saints of Vendôme (Pl. 89). Elsewhere a creeping academicism is evident,[35] finding its direction in new and borrowed ideas — the new soaring canopies may have been introduced here. They are not without that dull mechanical quality which so often permeates such compositions for the remainder of the Gothic era. The three bays of this architectural fancy in the hemicycle contain large-scale figures in which can be discerned the final vestiges of the Western style. The remaining two bays have layered scenes of a fresh approach, which is characterized most obviously by an interest in large-scale narrative. The latter had been tried tentatively in the West at Le Mans, ca. 1255,[36] and rejected. At Saint-Père an insistent dichotomy was maintained between small-scale histories and monumental standing figures, the polarized types positioned for strong contrast.

The spirit of the Western school flickers and dies at Evron. The style can be presumed dead before the *coup de grâce* dealt it by the introduction into the West of the technique of silver stain, present at Chartres Cathedral in 1328.[37] Perspective, introduced into the glazing art at about the same time,[38] was no less fatal to the Western aesthetic. Both silver stain and perspective are features of the somewhat workaday glass in the Chapelle Saint-Piat of Chartres, ca. 1330–340, which owes its debt not to the bankrupt school of the West but probably to Normandy.[39]

This brief survey of Western ensembles reveals that Saint-Père is the kingpin of the structure, the essential monument wherein the style finds definition. But such definition is not a simple matter of model and copies. The campaigns of Saint-Père are interwoven into the school's evolutionary tissue, and progress at Saint-Père is gaugeable chiefly by regional comparisons. The Western school occupies a very important position in the development of French stained glass, spanning, as it does, the transitional years between the early-thirteenth-century marvels of Chartres and Bourges and the emergence of the full-blown fourteenth-century mode of glazing. This transition is not as yet well charted.[40] Other regions no doubt had their roles to play. One thing at least is abundantly clear: it was not, as was once thought, a period of decline or "decadence" following the efflorescence of Chartres.

NOTES

1. Grodecki has long suspected the existence of such a school, which he tentatively grouped around Tours (conversation, 1958). Lafond reported in 1954: "M. Louis Grodecki estime que les vitraux de Saint-Père de Chartres et de Vendôme procèdent d'une Ecole de l'Ouest de la France (Poitiers, Tours)." (Lafond, "XIVe siècle," p. 235, fn. 58.) In a letter of April 1967 Grodecki explained that one of his reasons for grouping the Western school around Tours was the commonly held assumption that none of the Saint-Père glass pre-dated the choir architecture.

2. Western examples: Saint-Père hemicycle; Vendôme south choir; Evron. Cf. Evreux, nave aisles; Fécamp. Both features are standard in later Norman ensembles as well.

3. See the discussion of Auxerre and Troyes in Chapter II, and of the Reims iconographic programs in Chapter VI, fn. 1 and the Conclusion.

4. Notable examples in the East are: Saint-Julien-du-Sault, ca. 1250; Troyes Cathedral, lateral chapel windows (see Lafond, "Troyes," p. 29ff.). In the West: Tours, most of the choir clerestory; Le Mans, upper ambulatory lights (excepting only the "Evron window").

5. Grodecki in *VF,* pp. 118 and 115 (discussing Saint-Julien-du-Sault).

6. The basic studies on silver stain, by Jean Lafond, are cited in fn. 27 of Chapter IV.

7. Jean Lafond, whose expertise in Norman glass is universally recognized, was hesitant on the issue, feeling that too little remains to make a judgment.

8. Grodecki, *Vitraux de France,* pp. 24–25.

9. Chanoine H. Boissonnot, *Les verrières de la cathédrale de Tours* (Paris, 1932), pp. 44–46. In contrast, Lafond noted only one *bosse* at Saint-Ouen de Rouen, Normandy: Jean Lafond, *Les vitraux de l'église Saint-Ouen de Rouen, Corpus Vitrearum Medii Aevi,* France IV-2/1 (Paris, 1970) p. 36. Saint-Ouen is fourteenth century, however.

10. See Chapter II, discussion of Chartres medallions at fn. 32.

11. A common vocabulary of decorative motifs can be observed in the canopywork at Vendôme, Saint-Père, and Evron, the three mature ensembles of Western glazing. Although friezes of quatrefoils, brickwork, roof tiling, etc. were common to all Gothic schools of glass painting, in these monuments we are dealing with a characteristic "handwriting" in which workmanship and grouping of motifs are markedly similar. Cf. Chartres Cathedral, Bay 61, the Joseph window; Bay 105; Bay 134.

12. Grodecki in *VF,* p. 156. See Lillich, "Band Window," pp. 26–33.

13. That at least is the present arrangement on the north. The more standard band window arrangements now in the other Vendôme bays are the result of modern restoration. See Lillich, "Vendôme," p. 240.

14. Lafond discusses Evron ("XIVe siècle," p. 212): "On n'a donc pas attendu le XVe siècle pour 'concevoir le dais comme une flèche de cathédrale, avec ses contreforts, ses arcs-boutants, ses fleurons.' Et ce n'est pas l'invention du jaune d'argent — absent ici aussi — qui a provoqué l'essor des tabernacles."

15. Excepting Bays 14–15 and not in present arrangement.

16. Grodecki: "Ce style est peut-être le dernier stade de l'évolution amorcée par les ateliers chartrains des roses du transept, vers 1225–1235; mais nous manquons totalement de preuves pour l'affirmer." (*VF,* p. 320a, fn. 62).

17. The situation Grodecki envisioned (see fn. 1, this chapter) had Tours as inspirational center for Vendôme, Evron, Saint-Père and the last windows of the Le Mans choir clerestory, nearest the north transept.

18. See especially Grodecki in *VF,* pp. 130, 134.

19. Eastern clerestories: Bays 99–100; 102 (St. Denis giving oriflamme to Clement); and 136–137 ("large medallion" windows). Western clerestories: Bays 86–87 and 92–93 have double borders; Bay 89 has disputing pairs (Bay 90 also, now lost); Bays 149–150 and 152–153 are "large medallion" windows. I have left aside those eastern clerestories considered to be probable Renaissance copies by Jan Van der Meulen, "A *Logos Creator* at Chartres and its Copy," *Journal of the Warburg-Courtauld Institutes,* XXIX (1966), esp. p. 96.

20. See discussion of Tournai in Chapter II, fn. 31.

21. Bourassé and Manceau, pl. XVI.

22. The profile was maintained as late as Saint-Ouen de Rouen. See Lafond, CVMA France IV, pls. 51, 58, 62; col. pl. VI.

23. It is disappointing not to find facial profiles in the glass of the triforium of Troyes Cathedral, an ensemble which otherwise has the appearance of the common progenitor of Saint-Père and Saint-Urbain de Troyes. The Troyes triforium glass is, however, so largely restoration that it provides highly suspect evidence at best. See fn. 26.

24. See Jane Hayward and Louis Grodecki, "Les vitraux de la cathédrale d'Angers," *Bulletin monumental,* CXXIV (1966), esp. p. 52 and fn. 2, illustrations pp. 50–51 (N-2 and N-3, nos. 31 and 30).

25. *VF,* p. 140.

26. The Troyes triforium is filled with standing prophets and patriarchs. Almost all of the roundels above the lancets are original (larger percentage of restoration in north bays than in south), as are many heads. The lower panels of all lancets are suspect as are the inscriptions. Generally speaking, the hemicycle windows retain much more old glass than those of the straight choir; the easternmost bays of the choir are on the whole in better shape than the bays near the transepts.

27. Color is more like in the extreme designs of Bays A, F and G; mood coincides more exactly — as does lettering style — in Bay B; and so on. Only Bays C and K, which face each other across the choir, can be discounted from consideration. One is forced to assume that the Le Mans shop comprised artists of several backgrounds working in cooperation. Bay letters are those of the *Monuments historiques.*

28. Lillich, "Band Window," pp. 26ff. Their coloration is more advanced, however. The rich red/blue motley in the medallion windows, a color grouping never popular in the school of the West, is rejected for a gamut which brightens those hues considerably by large areas of strong yellow, white, or green.

29. Lafond, "Sées," pp. 59ff. There is some Norman work in the debris in the transept clerestories as well. See also M. Lillich, "A Stained Glass Apostle from Sées Cathedral (Normandy) in the Victoria and Albert Museum," *Burlington Magazine,* CXIX (1977), pp. 497–500 and opp. p. 471.

30. The Saint Peter from Sées in the Victoria and Albert Museum was described in 1936 by Bernard Rackham in a pithy note which could as easily have been written to characterize the entire Western school: "The powerful effect . . . is enhanced by the simplicity of its colouring. . . . The characteristic economy of the painting should also be noticed. Brushwork is reduced to a minimum. . . ." (*A Guide to the Collections of Stained Glass* [Victoria and Albert Museum, Department of Ceramics, London, 1936], p. 26 and pl. 1).

31. Vendôme Bays H and J, flanking the axial bay, have the tighter, more precise design of the tracery medallions of the Saint-Père hemicycle and some of the chapel windows at Sées, a

style which I have tried to identify as Norman. Cf. the Fécamp windows. The canopywork crockets are of clover or pointed trefoils; the framing colonnettes have truly architectural capitals instead of the non-functional foliate motif typical of Western work; the brickwork is not double-lined in the Western manner; color is dark and blue-oriented, and color areas more fractured.

32. Lafond, "XIVe siècle," p. 212. The glazing at Vendôme was much more extensive than now appears. The campaign probably commenced in the late 1280's, the St. Louis being a late addition to the program. See Lillich, "Vendôme."

33. See for example Marcel Aubert, *VF,* p. 167.

34. Henri Carot restored the windows in the first years of the present century; a heated controversy ensued over his compensation. In 1911 he unsuccessfully tried to sell to the French government three stained-glass "groups" which he said he had reconstituted from debris in the church. See dossier, *Monuments historiques* (Mayenne, Evron, Eglise, 853). Several of the "groups" have recently come to light in the auction of the Acézat collection in 1969.

35. The extremely dull fourteenth-century panel of the Sacrifice of Abraham now in the nave triforium of Tours may be a final work in this academic style, although proof is lacking. (Illustrated in Lafond, "XIVe siècle," pl. XLIII.)

36. Illustrated in *VF,* pl. 117.

37. Earlier examples: 1313, Mesnil-Villeman (Manche); 1327, fragment from Rouen; before 1328, Saint-Alban (Côtes-du-Nord). See Chapter IV, fn. 27.

38. Saint-Ouen de Rouen, 1325ff. (illustrated in Grodecki, *Vitraux de France,* pls. 20 and III); Evreux, 1325ff. (pl. 19 of same catalog); Königsfelden, 1325–1328. English provincial glass first exhibits perspective ca. 1330, according to Dr. Peter Newton (lecture at Courtauld Institute, 1963). Lafond believed that perspective was disseminated from Paris (see especially "XIVe siècle," p. 225).

39. Only the archaic diapered ground recalls Saint-Père, where it is found in the Baptist window, Bay 26 (see Lafond, "XIVe siècle," p. 212). Inhabited canopywork is a popular Norman motif; saints placed directly against grisaille, although not originating in Normandy necessarily, recall contemporary work at Saint-Ouen. (See Lafond, CVMA France IV.)

40. There is an excellent pioneer study: Jean-Jacques Gruber, "Quelques aspects," an essay referred to in my Introduction, fn. 3. Note that the monuments he studied as examples of a new pictorial freedom sound like a list of the school of the West: Maître de Saint Chéron at Chartres, Le Mans, Tours clerestory, Vendôme, Evron, Saint-Père. (See also Gruber's chapter, "Technique," in *VF,* p. 66.)

Subject matter of Saint-Père clerestory

Hemicycle:	Bay 1 — lancets:	Crucifixion, Virgin & Child, Sts. Louis and Gilduin (local saint)
	tracery:	Annunciation, Nativity
	Bays 2–6 — lancets:	Standing apostles and bishop- and abbot-saints (Bay 2 — Peter⟷Bay 3 — Paul)
	tracery:	Martyrdoms
		Bay 2 — Peter, Paul; Bay 3 — Baptist, Stephen
		Bay 4 — Lawrence, Vincent; Bay 5 — Andrew (lost)
		Bay 6 — Eustace, Bartholomew; Bay 7 — (lost)

Choir: Standing Old Testament prophets and patriarchs

*Nave:** Legends

Bay 18 — Passion⟷	Bay 19 — Anne & Joachim (cathedral's relic) — Virgin (= Infancy)
Bay 22 — Peter & Paul⟷	Bay 23 — 2 martyrs who brought Christianity to France (Clement and Denis)
Bay 26 — Baptist⟷	Bay 27 — 2 virgin saints (Agnes and Catherine)

Standing saints

Bay 20 — Philip, Thomas James, Matthew	Bay 21 — Virgin & Child, donor, 2 pope-saints (Gregory, possibly Gregory VII; Silvester)
Bay 24 — John Ev., Andrew, James, Bartholomew	Bay 25 — 4 bishop saints (incl. Martin of Tours and Lubin, bishop of Chartres)
Bay 28 — Matthias, James the Less, Judas, Barnabas	Bay 29 — 4 abbot saints (incl. Maur, Benedictine saint)

* In the nave, the even-numbered bays depict New Testament subjects, and among these, Bays 20, 24, and 28, the Apostles. Odd-numbered bays relate to the history of the Church.

{ CHAPTER VI }

Iconography–Introduction

BECAUSE the glazing of the Saint-Père clerestory is complete and is reasonably homogeneous in date and style, it has great value to the student of medieval iconography. How did a French master glazier get his program, how did he arrange his subject matter? To what extent was he a free agent in design and arrangement? What were his visual sources, his textual sources? Was the choice of saints dictated more by tradition or by a donor's demands? The sheer quantity of preserved contemporary windows at Saint-Père makes possible hypothetical answers to many such inquiries.

The circumstantial evidence in the Saint-Père windows seems to reveal a single strong will at work, or more accurately several agents — perhaps no more than two — guiding to completion a beautifully structured master plan. Donors' individual wishes played almost no role at all. Although the abbey church received a number of traceable and occasionally sizeable donations for glazing the nave, visual credit for them in the windows, if given at all, is extremely discreet. Nicolas de Maison-Maugis, a canon of the cathedral and one of the abbey's most generous donors, is not represented at all. Three anonymous benefactors, an abbot and a secular couple (Bay 19 south and Bay 26 north) (Pls. 53 and 78), are honored in figures so insignificant that they have passed completely unnoticed in

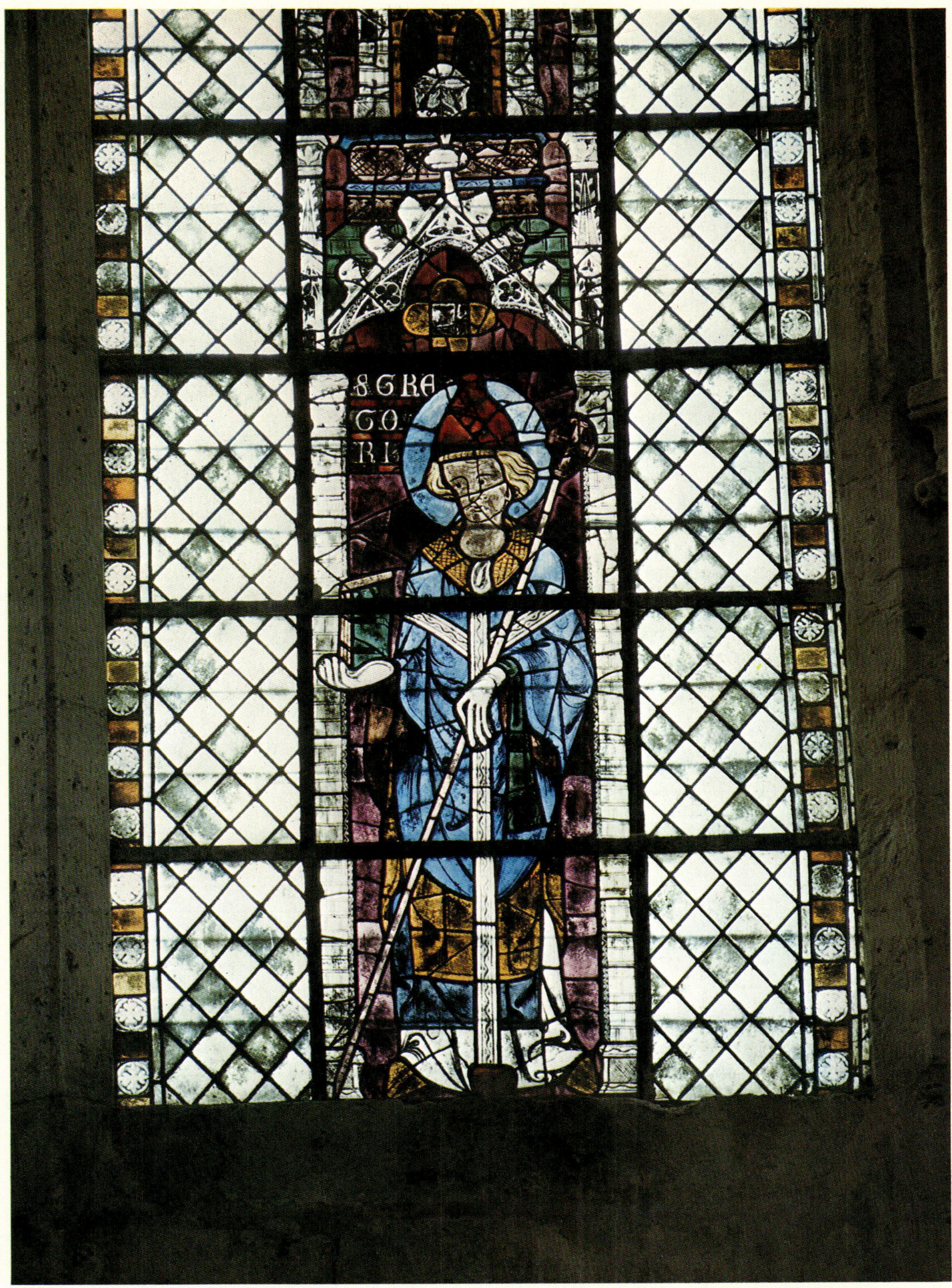

Plate VII Nave: Bay 21. St. Gregory (right lancet, bottom). *(Edouard Fièvet)*

previous descriptive accounts of the glazing. From the visual point of view the Canon Laurent Voisin, another benefactor of the abbey, is quite the most conspicuous donor in the church (Pl. 57). Yet his figure and that of the Virgin to whom he is praying have been inserted into the complex program of the nave bays with almost no disruption of their sequence, either stylistically or iconographically.

The iconographic program of the church was carried out with a rare consistency. The glass of the hemicycle, a brilliant, colored glory undiminished by grisaille, contains devotional saints and apostles standing beneath canopies, surmounted by a series of medallions illustrating martyrdoms in the tracery. The large figures of the hemicycle flank a central axial bay in which are found the Virgin and Child and the Crucifixion (Pls. 3, 5), a particularly Rémois program found possibly in the late-twelfth-century glass of Saint-Remi de Reims and later in both glazing programs of the hemicycle of Reims Cathedral.[1] The choir presents a solemn parade of large, standing prophets and patriarchs. The nave bays contain two alternating window designs. One consists of legends unfolding in canopied rows, while the other presents large canopied saints. The north side of the nave is devoted to the New Testament, presenting large figures of the apostles, the lives of the Baptist and Peter, and scenes from the Passion. On the south, church history is illustrated by standing pope-, bishop- and abbot-saints, the lives of the virgins Agnes and Catherine, and of the saints instrumental in bringing Christianity to France, Clement and Denis, as well as a life of the Virgin in which the apocryphal accounts concerning Sts. Anne and Joachim are given great emphasis.

The iconographic program falls into two phases, although the second was probably no more than an elaboration of the original conception. The choir and hemicycle comprise the original phase of planning, on a simpler level, while the program for the nave glazing marks a fresh and more sophisticated approach to both design and iconography. There seems to be no time lapse between them, and indeed the two phases may have overlapped slightly.

Because the Old Testament prophets in the choir take their place in the general iconographic scheme so naturally, the assumption is fairly sound that the overall plan for the clerestory was devised at the time they were moved to their present home, ca. 1270–1280. Their original position, real or intended, is unimportant to iconographic studies. What is important is that, when the plan was conceived to redesign them for the new choir, the glazing of the hemicycle, the devotional focus of the church, was undoubtedly planned as well. The abbey, which had been building and glazing for over a hundred years, very likely had to pause during the following years for funds. This short hiatus probably occurred between work on the choir (involving little expense as much older grisaille and figured glass were used), and the hemicycle. There is no indication in either series of any private donations. Work was probably resumed on the hemicycle series before the end of the century, and the St. Louis of the axial bay (Pl. 3), possibly inserted when the windows were nearing completion, was among the first devotional figures of the new king-saint, dating perhaps as early as ca. 1300–1305.

The program was completed in the nave with the aid of several large benefactions in the first two decades after 1300. The earliest glazing of the nave legend series is a donation by the Abbot Jehan de Mantes (Bay 22) (Pl. 63). It includes a hodge-podge of panels hastily assembled, some of which must have comprised a shorter series intended for elsewhere. The probable date of their assembly in the nave is 1306. The Abbot Jehan thus takes on pivotal importance as the prime mover behind the marvelous artistic achievement of the nave. In piecing together documentation of donations, stylistic evidence, and clues gleaned from the iconographic program the presence is felt of an erudite and tasteful, strong-willed administrator. It seems altogether probable that this force was the Abbot Jehan.

Jehan de Mantes became abbot in the spring of 1306. He did not face an easy task. The economic and political environment was no doubt precarious. As Pegues has stated, "The first decade of the fourteenth century was represented in France by a nightmare of scandalous affairs of state, prolonged judicial ordeals based often on outrageous charges, confiscations secretly prepared and violently executed, disastrous alterations of money, and a crushing military defeat."[2] But Abbot Jehan was a man of some means and devoted to his church and in the four brief years of his abbacy, he donated not only the glazing of Bay 22 but also a "majorem campanam" for the belfry. The state of the glazing program in the year of his election was probably the following — choir completed, hemicycle in progress and almost completed, and nave either not yet begun or in a preliminary planning stage. The inclusion of St. Louis and St. Gilduin, the abbey's local saint, in prime position under the crucified Christ in the axial bay of the hemicycle may possibly have been one of his first artistic decisions. The pair of specific and supremely appropriate saints differs vastly, from an iconographic point of view, from the mass of vaguely identified holy men which surrounds them.

The nave, however, was the large task of the early fourteenth century. When, a quarter century before, Old Testament figures were programmed for the choir and a radiance of apostles and martyrs for the hemicycle, it is possible that legends were intended for the nave. The nave windows are of the older doublet-and-rose form with no vertical mullions interrupting their broad expanse. Whatever the original proposal, it was probably revised, elaborated, and refined to play upon the stylistic and iconographic ideas already presented in the late-thirteenth-century glazing. The complicated stylistic program of the nave — an alternation of small scene compositions with large figures flanked in grisaille — is related to the earlier groups in the church as variations on a theme. The description applies equally to the iconography.

The confusion of apostles, abbots, and bishops in the hemicycle was ordered in the nave as though a magnet had been dropped among iron filings. The iconographic relationship between the Old Law patriarchs of the choir and the New Law saints of the nave was intentionally underscored by stylistic devices. The panel size and proportion and the vertical color-grisaille format of the older glass was tastefully adapted to the nave windows, broader and squatter in proportion and lacking mullions. Several of the subjects of the martyrdom medallions of the hemicycle tracery were taken over and elaborated as full-scale legends in the nave: The Annunciation and Nativity of Bay 1 in the Virgin lancet (Bay 19), the martyrdoms of the Baptist (Bays 3 and 26), and of Peter and Paul (Bays 2 and 22).[3]

Within the nave itself the pattern is clear. Bays of legends alternate with framed, single, standing saints, the whole presenting a statement of the origins of Christianity and church history, including reference to the abbey of Saint-Père. On the north, apostles are interleaved with the legend of the Precursor, the Passion of Christ, and the life of Peter, the whole forming a sort of visual Gospel. On the south the saints of ecclesiastical history, popes, bishops, and abbots, take their places amid the legends of two virgin saints, the two martyrs (Sts. Clement and Denis) who effected the transfer of Christianity to France, and the Virgin Mary and her mother of particular Chartrain veneration. Reference to the abbey itself is confined largely to its royal and ecclesiastical connections, as in the coupling of Sts. Louis and Gilduin, and the choice of a Benedictine abbot and a Chartrain bishop among the nave saints. With the notable exception of Gilduin, who was buried at Saint-Père, relics owned by the abbey are not honored. The iconography presents a perfectly balanced statement, in art, of the history and meaning of Christianity as exemplified by a specific Christian church.[4]

The choice of the saints which fill in this outline is worthy of study. The confused roster of apostles reflects the general uncertainty of the period concerning their number and precise identity, an uncertainty no less marked in the apse group. Having decided upon twelve apostles, the early-fourteenth-century iconographer and glazier were not yet equipped for the tasks of identifying them "correctly" and of providing them all with distinguishable attributes. In the twelve are three Jameses, the associate Barnabas, and a Matthias; Peter, Paul, and Simon are omitted altogether. The attributes, as will be seen in the discussions to follow, reflect the general state of flux of such identifying symbols at the end of the thirteenth century. The most startling is the rope given to Judas Thaddeus (Pl. X), a symbol probably derived from the legend of the Lord's betrayer.[5]

The single identified figure in the quartet of abbots (Bay 29) is Benedictine, and at least one of the four bishops (Bay 25) is Chartrain, while one of the two beatified popes (Bay 21) is of significance to Saint-Père because of his connection with the local saint, Gilduin.[6] As mentioned above, the importance of the relic of St. Anne in the cathedral probably secured the inclusion of a whole lancet of the Virgin's apocryphal history (right lancet of Bay 19). The two virgin saints, Agnes and Catherine (Bay 27), are more difficult to account for.

Women saints definitely were not popular at Saint-Père. The church contains no others, and a contemporary missal of the usage of Saint-Père includes in its series of saints only Anne, Agnes, and Soline, a local virgin whose relics rested in Saint-Père.[7] Catherine's life, at least, seems to have been fashioned especially for a theologian donor. Even the famous wheel martyrdom was omitted to obtain space for a detailed exposition of her powers in philosophical debate. Perhaps here lies the shadow of Nicolas de Maison-Maugis.

Of the three female saints illuminated in the missal, Anne found accommodation in the Virgin lancet while Soline had a whole chapel — perhaps glazed, who knows? — to herself and her tomb. It was Agnes who was selected to confront the Baptist across the nave. The reason is simple. She is by her name his feminine counterpart, a rebus of his attribute, the *Agnus Dei,* which he holds at the top of his window.[8] And it is certainly not accidental that she and he stand over the west end of the church, traditional location of the baptismal font.

The pairing of Clement and Denis (Bay 23) is the most meaningful grouping in the nave. A priestly iconographer has left an unmistakable mark here in tracing the historical connections of Peter, the patron and name-saint of the abbey, whose legend unfolds directly across the nave in Bay 22, with St. Denis, patron of the royal house of France. Clement, uncommon and otherwise inexplicable, is the link.[9] Consecrated pope by St. Peter, Clement himself was the instigator of St. Denis' mission to the Franks. The pairing of Sts. Louis and Gilduin in Bay 1 of the hemicycle is a parallel idea: a reference to the abbey (Peter, Gilduin) in each case is paired with a reference to the royal house (Denis, Louis). The two examples, nave and hemicycle, are very likely contemporary products of the same iconographer.

Although specific, unequivocal documentation is lacking, the iconography suggests a direct relationship between abbey and crown, perhaps a donation.

While Saint-Père was not under the king's control as one of the "royal abbeys," the Capetians had maintained ties with it even before Philippe-le-Bel purchased the county of Chartres in 1286. A letter from this monarch[10] to his war-tax collectors in 1296 refers to funds to be returned to the abbey:

> Philippus, Dei gratia, Francorum rex, universis collectoribus quinquagesimi ad quos presentes littere pervenerint, salutem. Mandamus vobis quatenus, in colligendo et levando dictum quinquagesimum in terra religiosorum virorum abbatis et conventus sancti Petri Carnotensis, in qua habent altam justiciam, vocetis gentes eorumdem, et, ipsis gentibus presentibus, dictum quinquagesimum colligatis, ipsis religiosis, *juxta ordinationem a nobis factam,* de eodem quinquagesimo porcionem debitam persolvatis. Actum Parisiis, die martis post conversionem sancti Pauli, anno Domini millesimo ducentesimo nonagesimo quinto. [Jan. 30, 1296 n.s.]

A royal donation for windows? A royal gift which the abbey commemorated by the insertion of Sts. Louis and Gilduin into the axial bay of already extant hemicycle windows, and by the incorporation of the legends of Clement and Denis into the nave program[11] then perhaps in the initial planning stages? Although the particulars remain elusive, the royal connection does not: the St. Denis window was most probably designed from two manuscripts in the royal Abbey of Saint-Denis, one of which (Bibl. Nat. ms. fr. 2090–92) was made to the order of the same king.

The probable iconographic sources of the legend windows of the nave provide a fascinating glimpse into the working methods of an early-fourteenth-century stained glass shop. Given the pattern and order of subjects the artist or artists seem to have relied to an almost exclusive degree on manuscripts or portable objects. In the Passion window (Bay 18, north) the primary source — unknown — can even be dated approximately as a work of at least a century earlier. The St. Anne lancet of Bay 19, south, is another strangely *retardataire* example, exhibiting the rambling narrative and proliferation of detail usually marking the work of an earlier age. For the Church and Synagogue figures in the Passion window the artist used an illumination from a known contemporary missal (Pl. 96).[12]

The legends of Agnes, Catherine, and Clement seem to rely heavily on passionals or the Golden Legend rather than on visual sources. Parts of the life of Peter (the later panels) seem to record details from canonical texts not customarily found in art. The St. Denis lancet, however, presents such a clear relationship with two manuscripts of the Abbey of Saint-Denis that a trip by the glazier to the library and scriptorium there is not only possible but likely. The three volumes of the "1317" life of the saint, in preparation for years and probably near completion at the death of Philippe-le-Bel in 1314, remained in the workshop for three more years awaiting an interleaved translation for the new king. Some time during these years, before the book's transfer in 1317 to royal possession, the glazier probably saw it and the "1250" saint's life which was owned by the Abbey of Saint-Denis as well.

The Virgin lancet (Bay 19) and the beautiful Baptist window (Bay 26) are classic works in the mainstream of French Gothic iconographic tradition. Each, however, contains a minute clue to an unusual source. The Nativity in Bay 19 (Pl. 53) includes a midwife undoubtedly copied from a non-French art object of the eleventh century or before. The Virgin in the Baptist's Nativity in Bay 26 (Pl. 77) derives from the Italian Pseudo-Bonaventura Meditations (dating in the latter part of the thirteenth century), and at Saint-Père she makes perhaps her first appearance in the north.

The subject matter of the glazed clerestory of Saint-Père can be studied not only for its intrinsic interest but as a valuable statement of the limitations and possibilities of an age.

NOTES

1. *VF*, pp. 108 and 140; William Hinkle, *The Portal of the Saints of Reims Cathedral, A Study in Mediaeval Iconography* (College Art Association, 1965), Appendix G (Saint-Remi) and Appendix J (Reims Cathedral); Hans Reinhardt, *La cathédrale de Reims* (Paris, 1963), pp. 183, 186, and pls. 42 and 43; Eva Frodl-Kraft, "Kirchenschaubildern in den Hochchorfenstern von Reims, Abbildung und Abstraktion," *Festschrift für Otto Demus und Otto Pächt, Wiener Jahrbuch für Kunstgeschichte,* 25 (Vienna, 1972), pp. 53–86; Louis Grodecki, "Les plus anciens vitraux de Saint-Remi de Reims," *Beiträge zur Kunst des Mittelalters, Festschrift für Hans Wentzel zum 60. Geburtstag* (Berlin, 1975), pp. 65–77.

2. Franklin J. Pegues, *The Lawyers of the Last Capetians* (Princeton, 1962), p. 36. I have discussed Abbot Jehan de Mantes further in Chapters I, IV, and XI.

3. Three of the hemicycle medallions are now missing, one from Bay 5 and the two originally designed for the now blind Bay 7. The hemicycle medallion subjects not found in the nave are Eustace and the three deacon-saints Stephen, Vincent, and Lawrence. It is recorded that a window of St. Vincent existed in 1631; see Chapter 1, fn. 27. Nave legends not now represented in the hemicycle are those of the two virgin-saints Agnes and Catherine. Clement and Denis present a more sophisticated relationship with the hemicycle (see discussion infra).

4. The iconographic pattern, although explicit, in no way resembles Aubert's general program for medieval glazing (available to English-speaking readers in perhaps a more explicit form than was intended by Aubert; see Marcel Aubert, *French Cathedral Windows of the Twelfth and Thirteenth Centuries* [New York, 1939], pp. 7–8) and increases the scepticism with which his theory must be regarded. Nor can the theory be said to apply only to early-thirteenth-century programs. The iconographic ordering of the Chartres Cathedral glazing exhibits much greater freedom than that of Saint-Père. The medieval artist organized his material but apparently not according to any single pre-determined canon.

5. See Chapter X.

6. See Chapters VIII and X.

7. Chartres, Bibl. mun., ms. 519 (first half of the fourteenth century), destroyed in World War II. (Yves Delaporte, *Les manuscrits enluminés de la Bibliothèque de Chartres* [Chartres, 1929], p. 93.) The missal included illuminations of other saints found in the windows: Louis, Clement, Denis, Lubin, and Maur, as well as a Church and Synagogue (fol. 130v.).

8. One is less hesitant to suggest such a possibility since the current research by Professor William R. Cook into sources of monastic sculptural programs in verbal association familiar to monks from their oral scriptural tradition. (Paper at Conference on Cistercian Studies, Kalamazoo, 1977.) Dom Jean Leclerq has traced the same associative patterns in sermons. See Chapter XI, fn. 78.

9. Clement is found next to Denis in the Sainte-Chapelle frescoes, but not in the same bay (Robert Branner, *The Painted Medallions in the Sainte-Chapelle in Paris* [American Philosophical Society, Transactions, no. 58] [Philadelphia, 1968], fig. 1). Since the Saint-Père artist of Bay 23 knew and studied Parisian manuscripts, he may also have known the frescoes. Clement and Denis face each other on the jambs of the south portal of Chartres Cathedral (the Martyrs bay); each is the second figure from the door. See also this chapter, fn. 7.

10. Emphasis added. Arch. d'Eure-et-Loir, H. 25; a late-eighteenth-century copy is Dom Muley, Bibl. Chartres ms. 1136, CLV; Guérard discusses this letter and the *cinquantième* tax briefly in v. 1, p. clv, para. 136, and v. 2, p. 724. See Chapter 1, fn. 10. On the *cinquantième* in general see Joseph R. Strayer and Charles H. Taylor, *Studies in Early French Taxation* (Cambridge, Mass., 1939), pp. 48, 50.

11. These windows are discussed in Chapter VIII (Sts. Louis and Gilduin), and in Chapter XI, Bay 23, St. Denis lancet.

12. See discussion Chapter XI, Bay 18.

{ CHAPTER VII }

Choir: Iconography

choir: Iconography

THE exclusive subject matter of the choir is a solemn procession of forty large, standing figures of Old Testament prophets and patriarchs[1] holding closed books, palms, or phylacteries. With a handful of exceptions, the scrolls and inscription bands carry only decorative floral or pseudo-script motifs; and as the figures have no attributes, specific identification in most cases is impossible. Some of the holy men are veiled, some wear Phrygian pointed caps, some are bearded. All are shod, and eight of them are haloed. The haloes probably function as elements of design rather than of identification, as they are not bestowed upon all of the beatified prophets.[2] Nineteen cartoons were used for the forty figures, most of them appearing twice or more (see chart, Chapter II).

Six of the forty figures are named. These are "DAHIEL," "ABBACVC," and "EHOh" in Bay 10 (Pl. 20), "EZEKEEL" in Bay 11 (Pl. 21), "NOEL" in Bay 12 (Pl. 24), and "BALAAM" in Bay 13 (Pl. 30); Balaam was destroyed in World War II.[3] It is conceivable that some of the phylacteries now filled with a primitive pseudo-script originally held names, but the lovely foliate ornament found in many of the black "inscription bands" behind the figures' heads is original thirteenth-century decoration. Occasional figures have neither scroll nor black band. The series, therefore, in its present location in the choir,[4] has never contained appreciably more identifying labels than it now has.

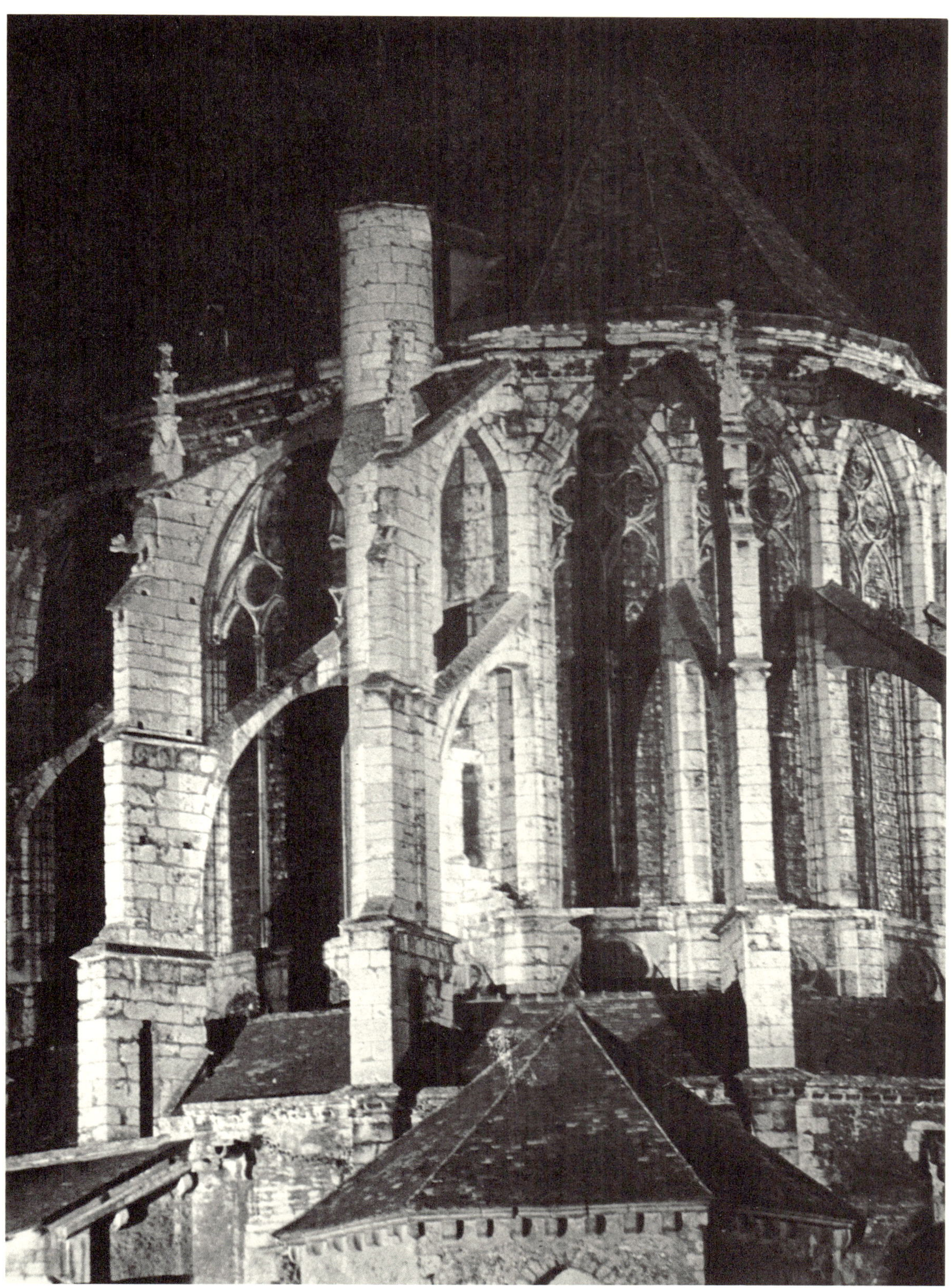

Saint-Père: straight choir *(Edouard Fièvet)*

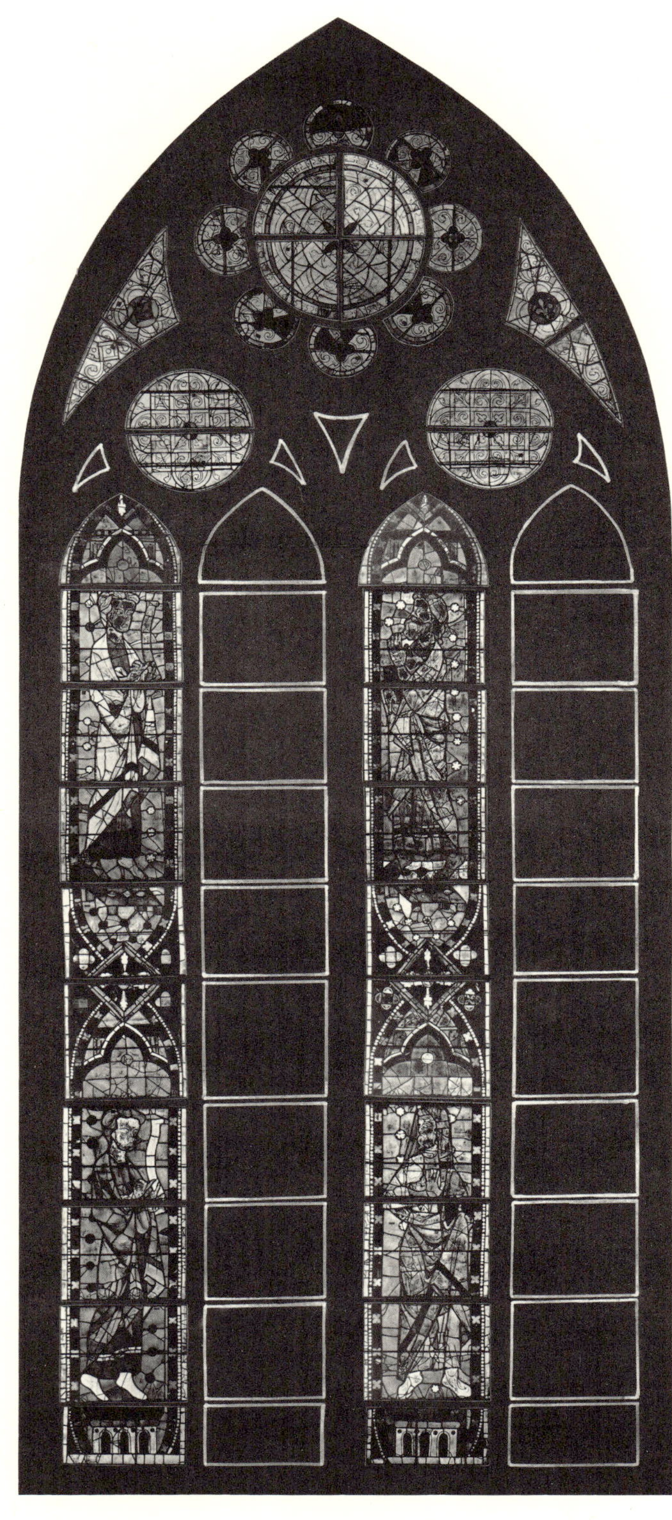

PLATE 17 Choir: Bay 8. *(Paris, Archives photographiques)*

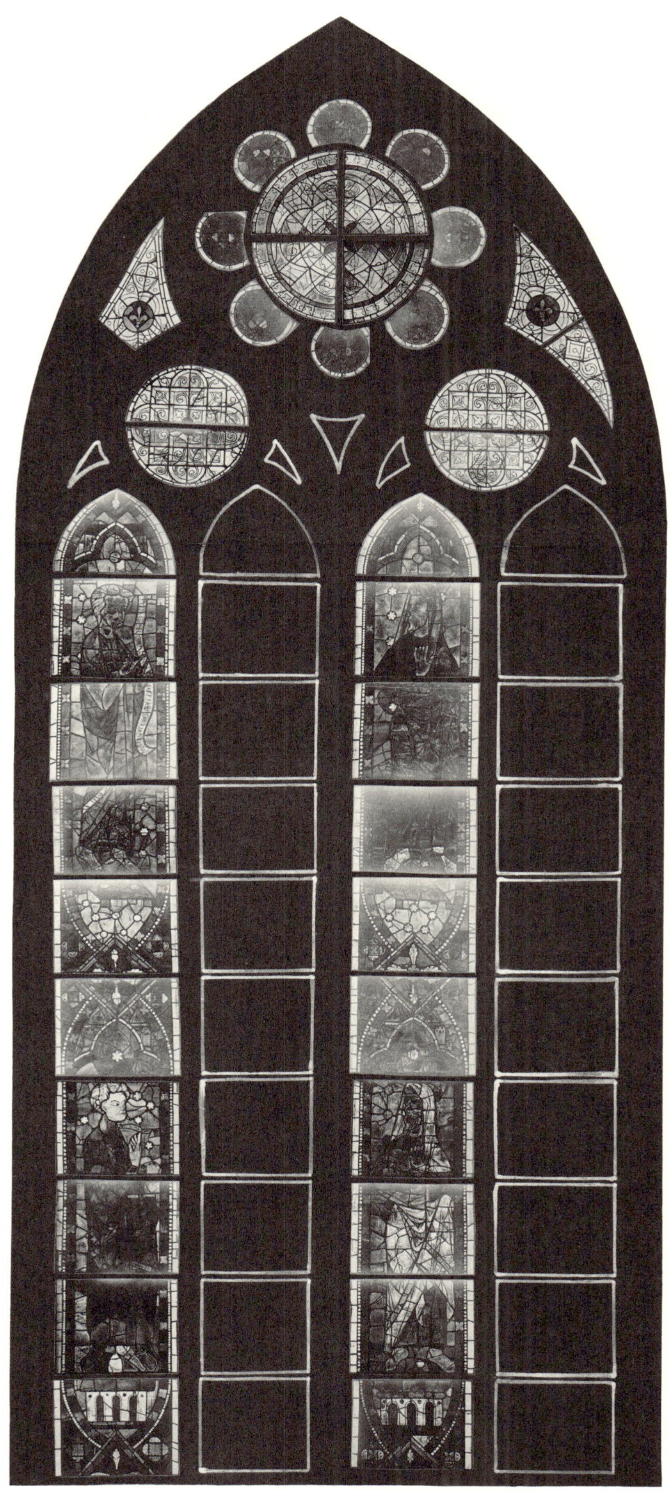

PLATE 18 Choir: Bay 9. *(Paris, Archives photographiques)*

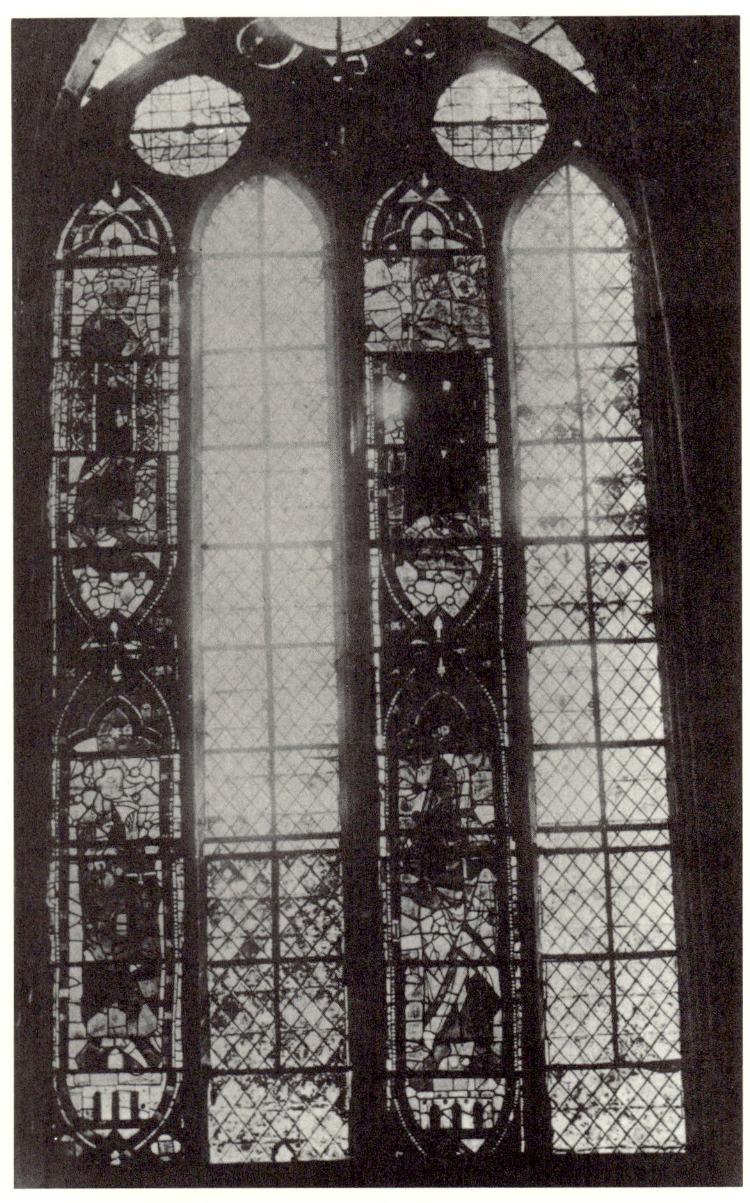

PLATE 19 Choir: Bay 9. Before 1905 restorations. *(Photo from François Lorin studio) (Paris, Archives photographiques)*

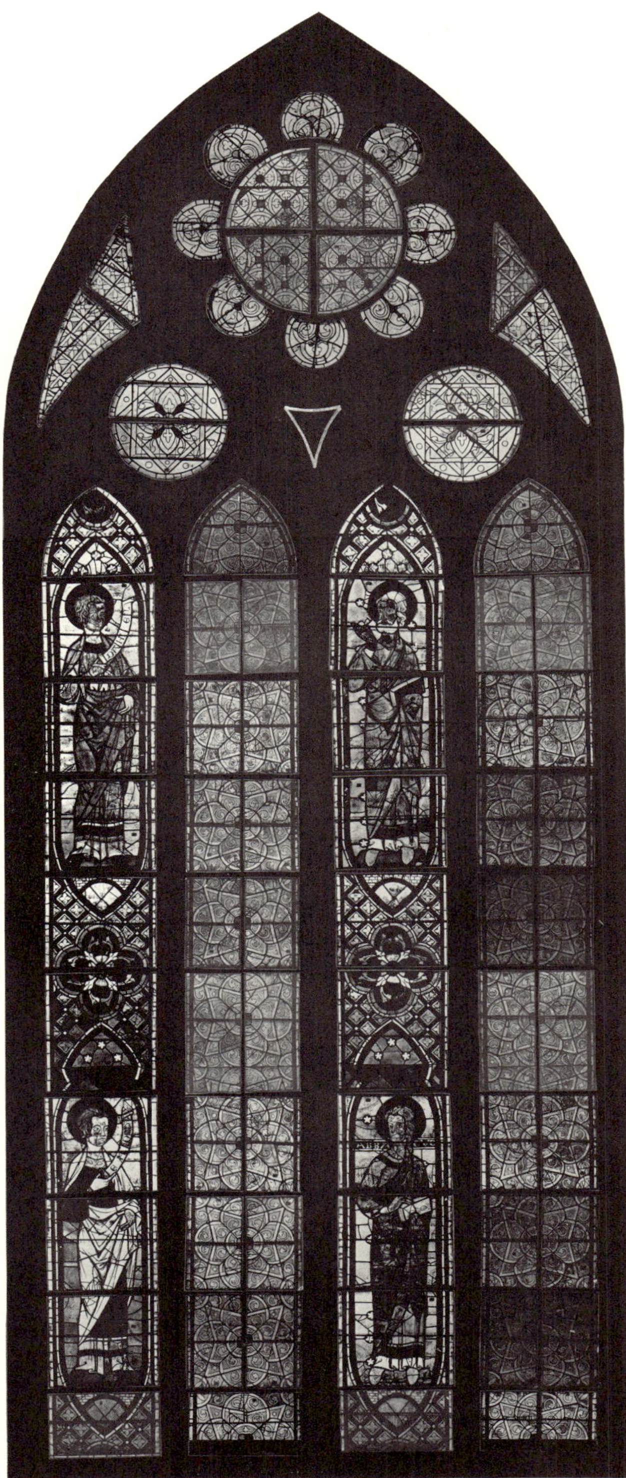

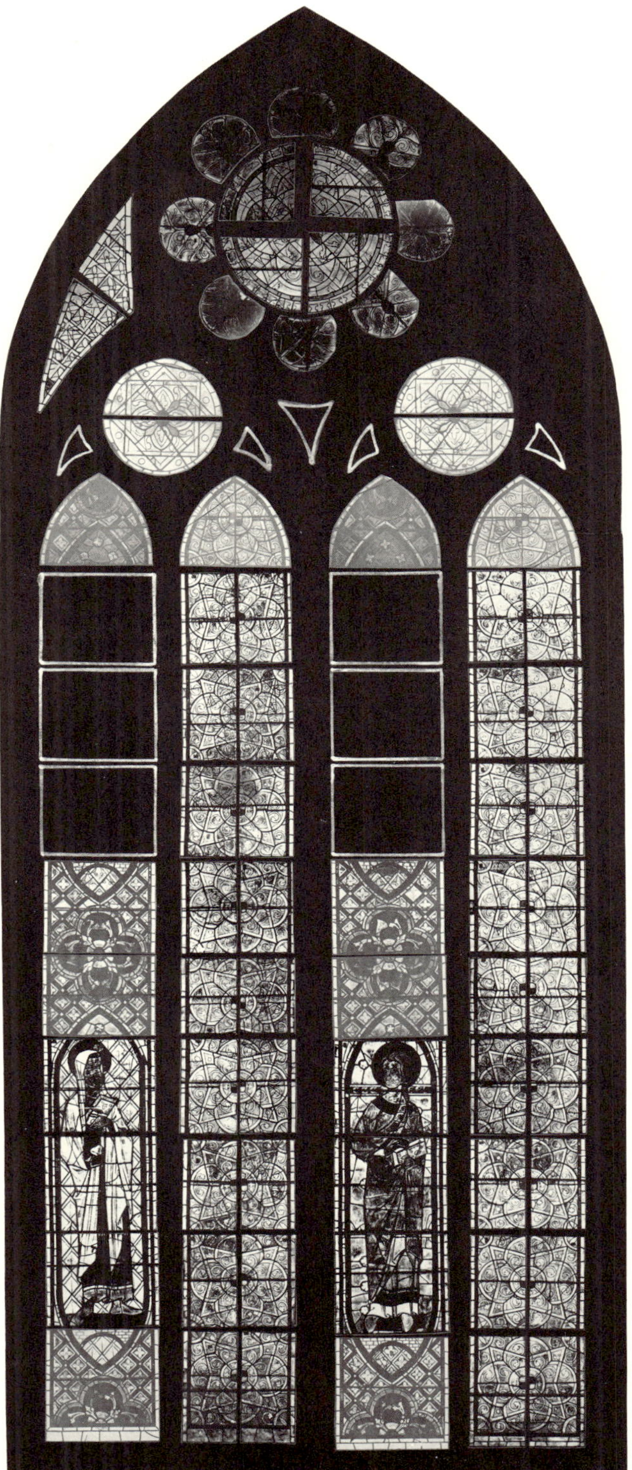

PLATE 20 Choir: Bay 10. *(Paris, Archives photographiques)*

PLATE 21 Choir: Bay 11. (Photos of upper figures missing) *(Paris, Archives photographiques)*

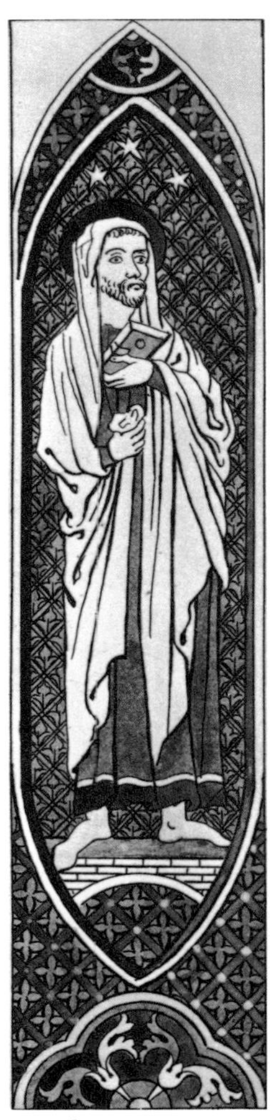

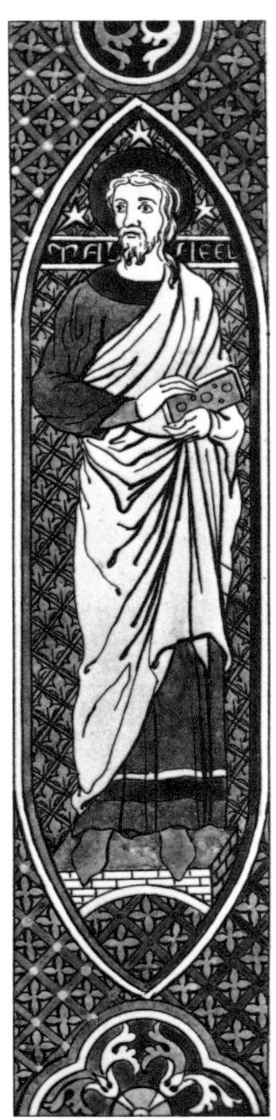

PLATE 22 Choir: Bay 11. *(After Willemin, 1806)*

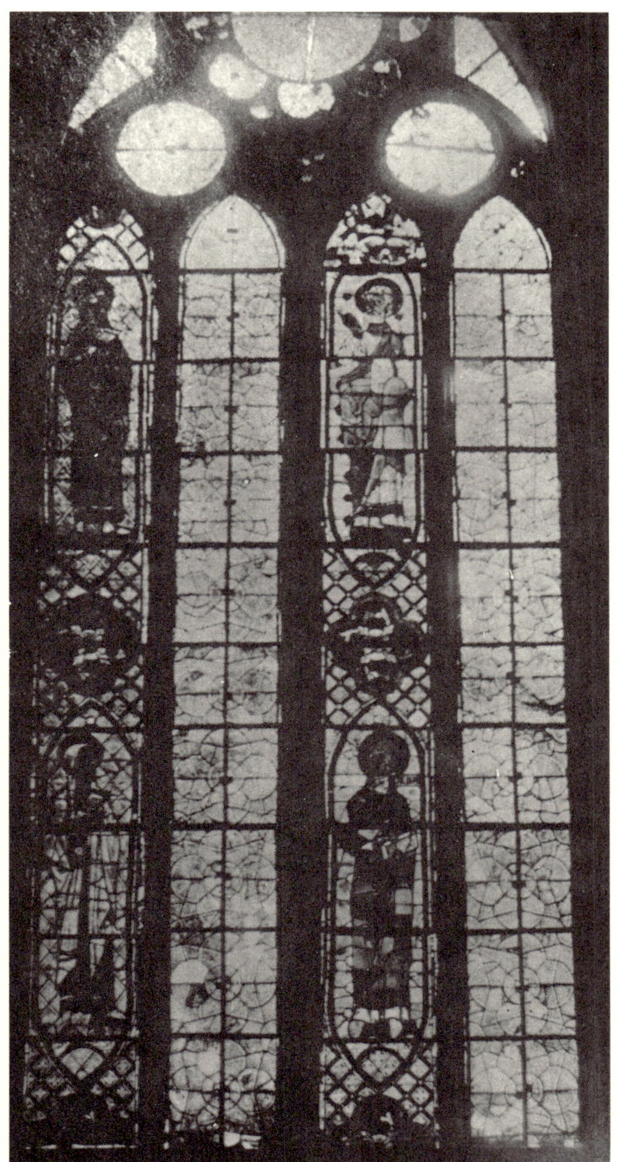

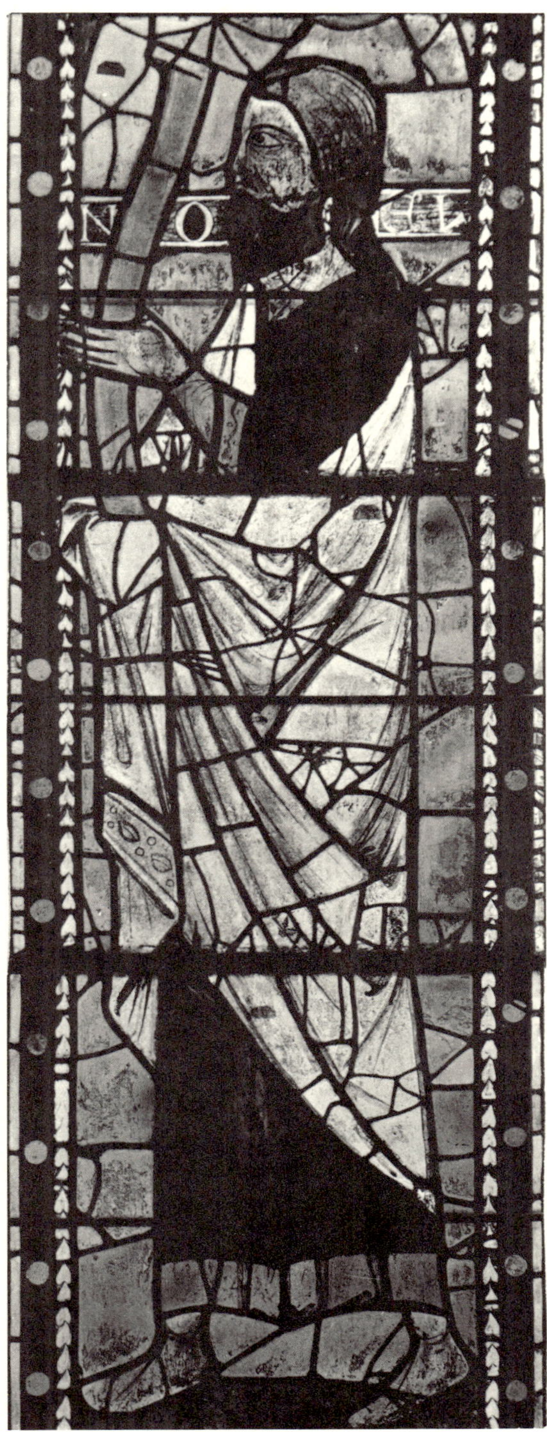

PLATE 23 Choir: Bay 11. Before 1905 restorations. *(Photo from François Lorin studio) (Paris, Archives photographiques)*

PLATE 24 Choir: Bay 12. Patriarch (Noah?). *(Paris, Archives photographiques)*

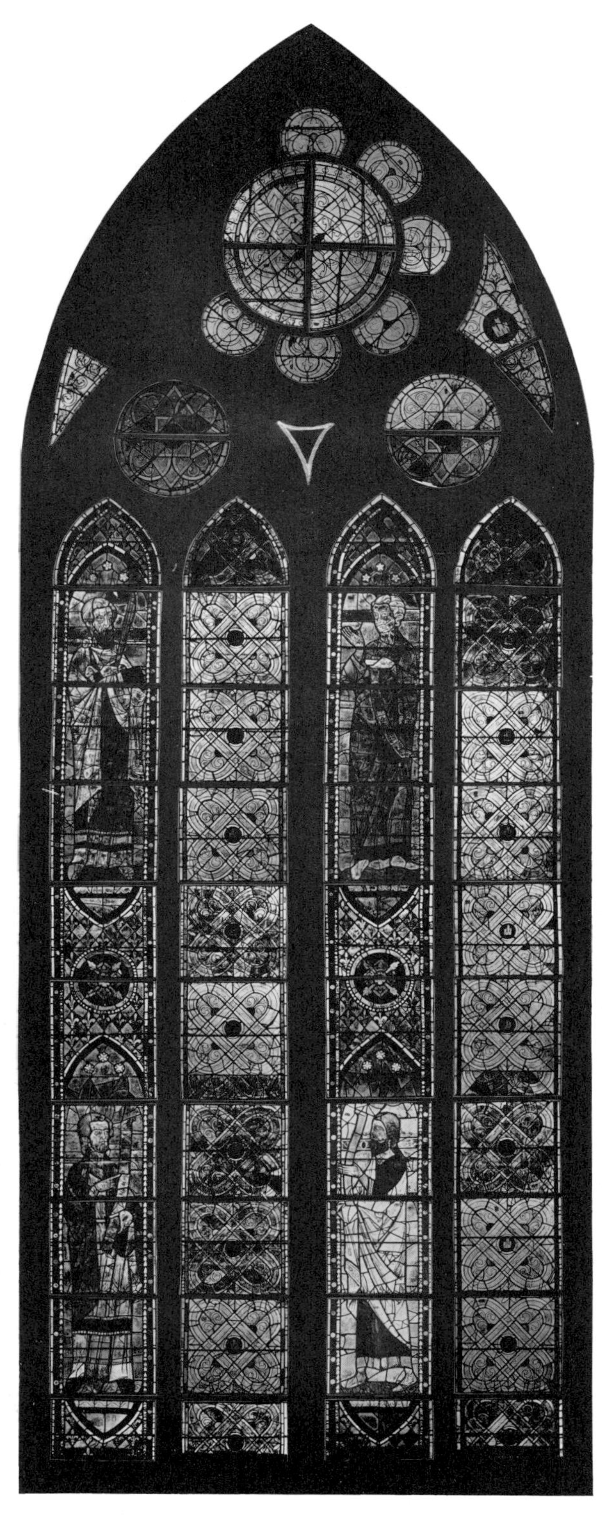

PLATE 25 Choir: Bay 12. *(Paris, Archives photographiques)*

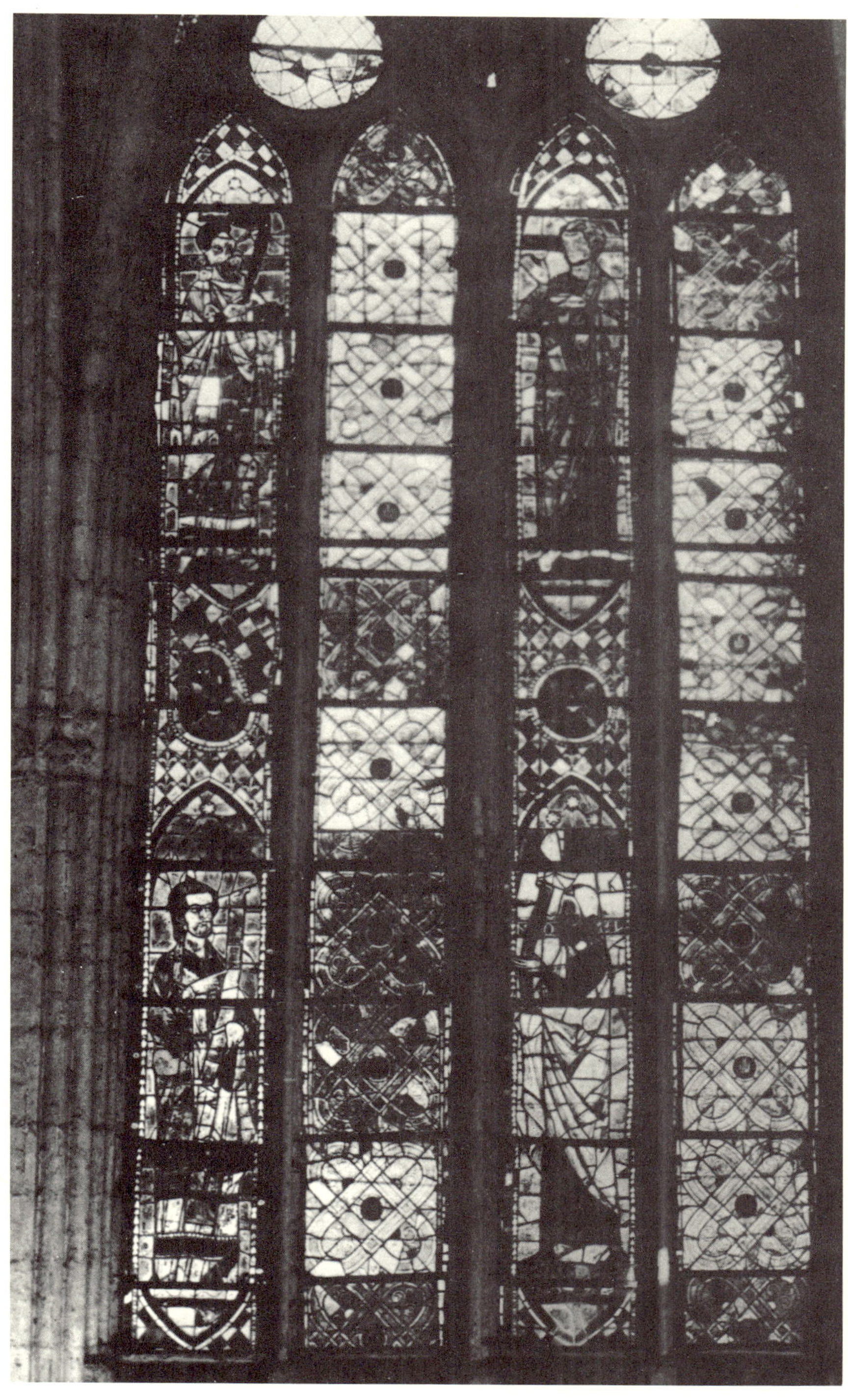

PLATE 26 Choir: Bay 12. Before 1905 restorations. *(Photo from Michon) (Paris, Archives photographiques)*

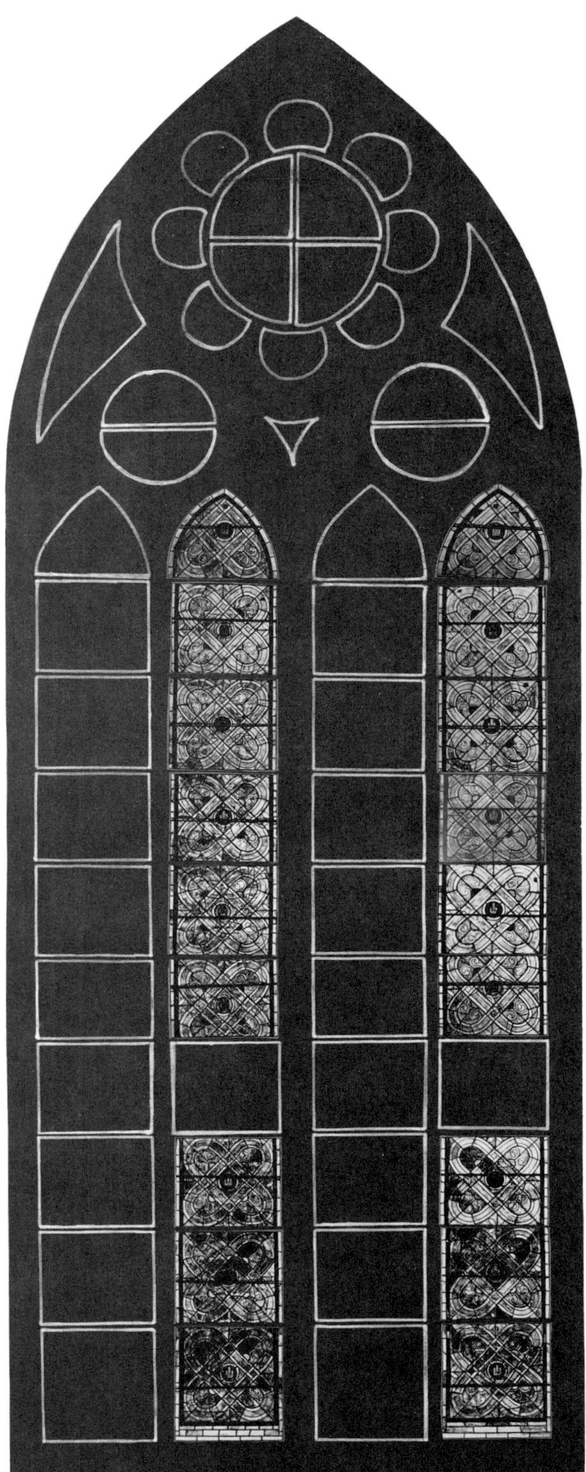

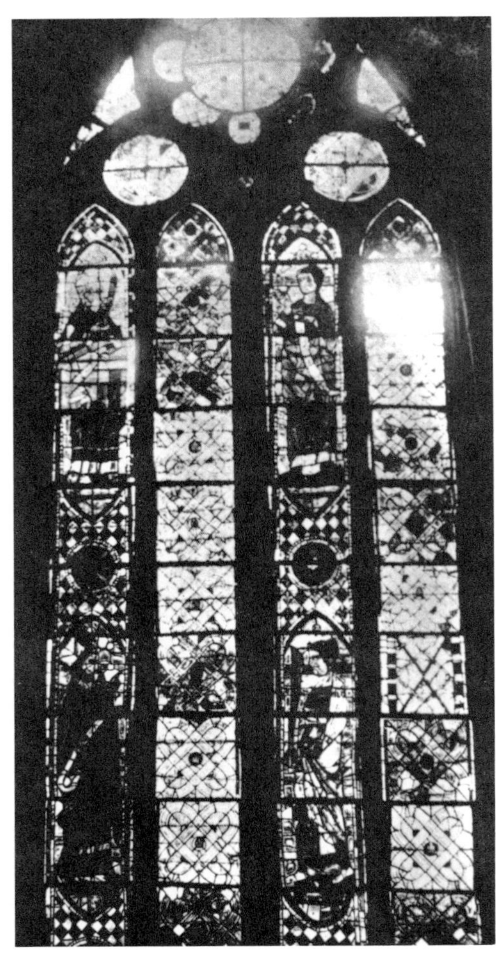

PLATE 27 Choir: Bay 13. Missing glass destroyed in World War II. *(Paris, Archives photographiques)*

PLATE 28 Choir: Bay 13. Before 1905 restorations. *(Photo from François Lorin studio) (Paris, Archives photographiques)*

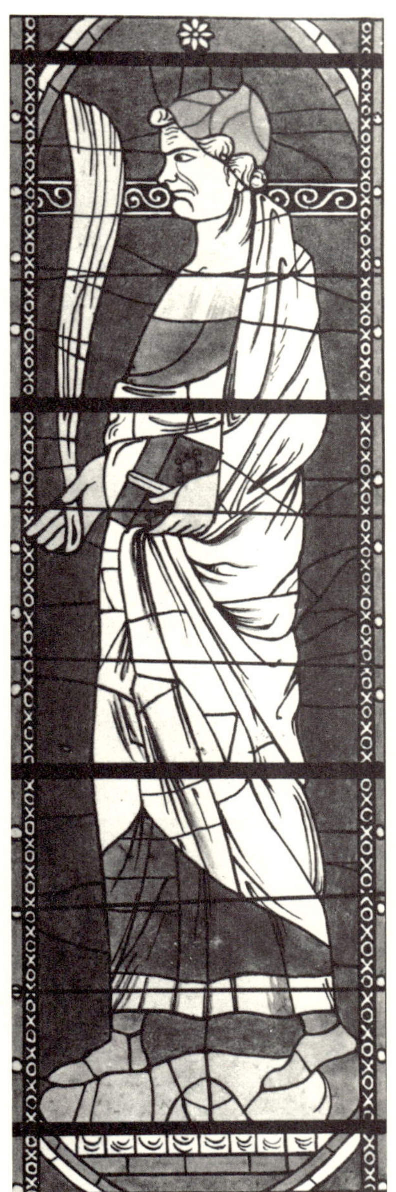

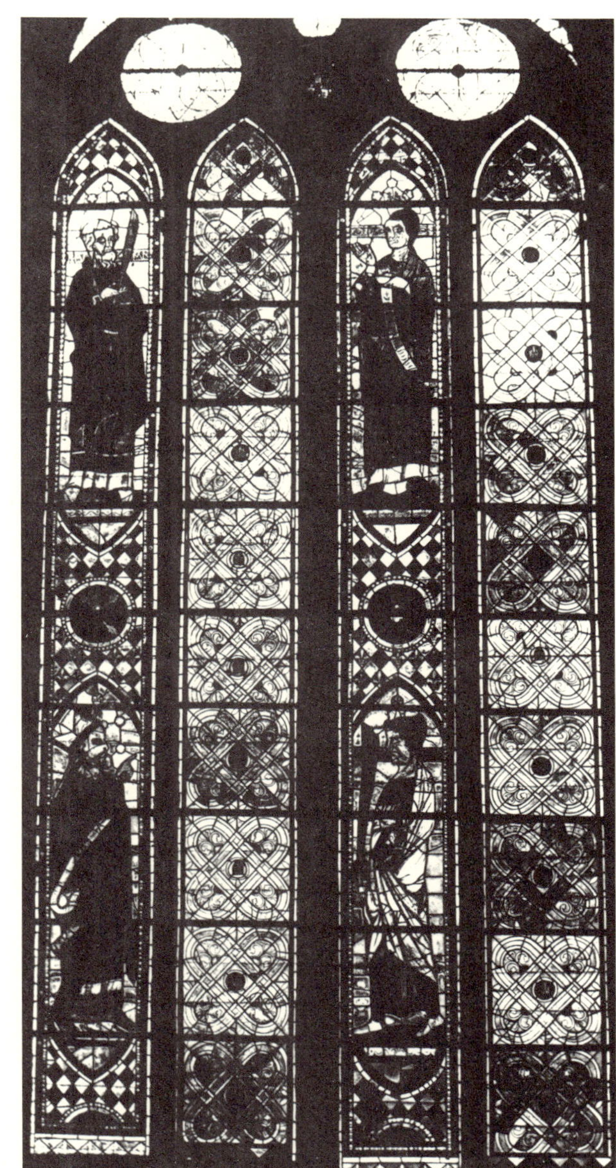

PLATE 29 Choir: Bay 13, detail. *(After F. de Lasteyrie, 1857)*

PLATE 30 Choir: Bay 13. After 1905 restorations (figure lancets now destroyed). *(Photo from Jean Lafond collection) (Paris, Archives photographiques)*

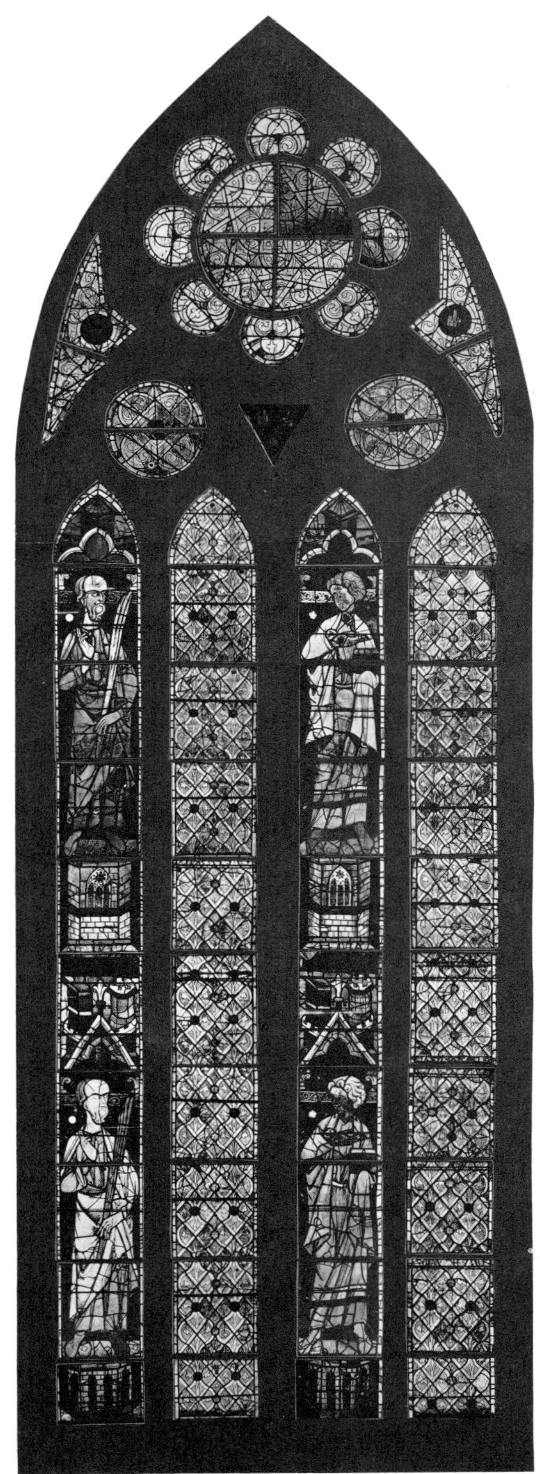

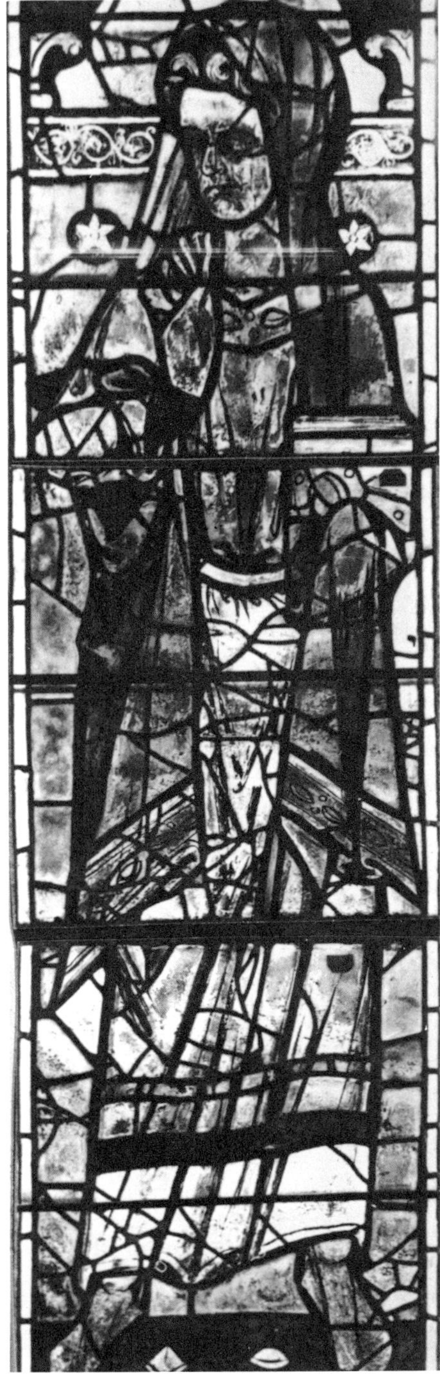

PLATE 31 Choir: Bay 14. *(Paris, Archives photographiques)*

PLATE 32 Choir: Bay 15, figure. *(Paris, Archives photographiques)*

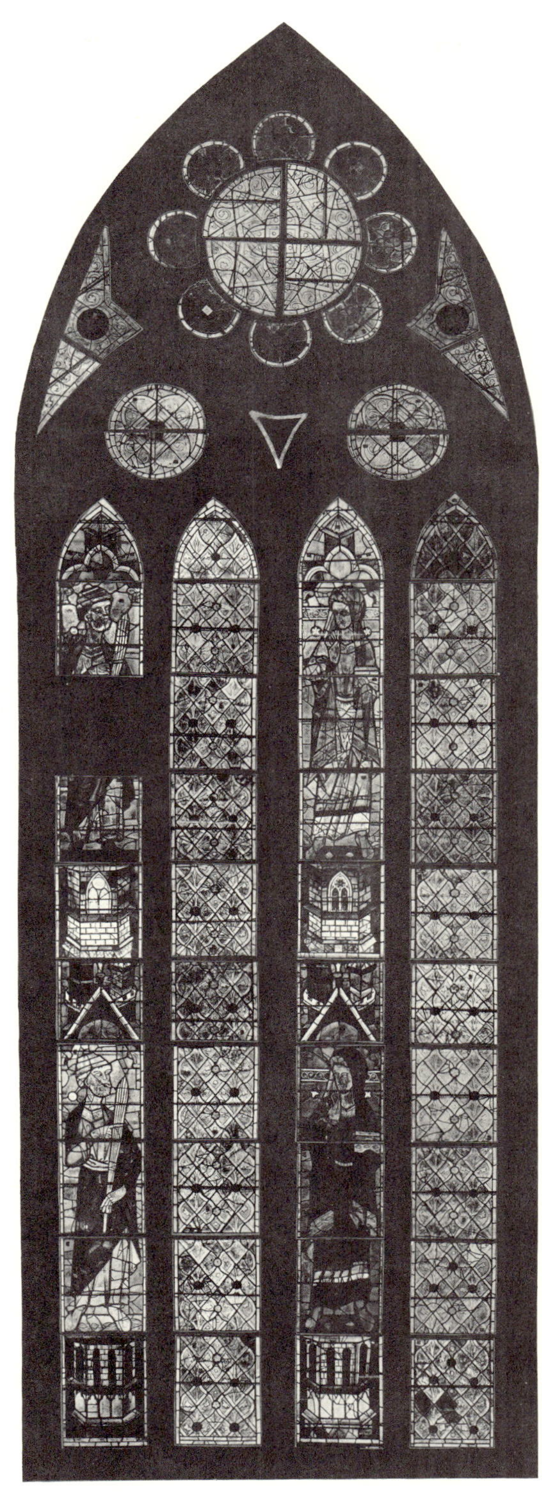

PLATE 33 Choir: Bay 15. *(Paris, Archives photographiques)*

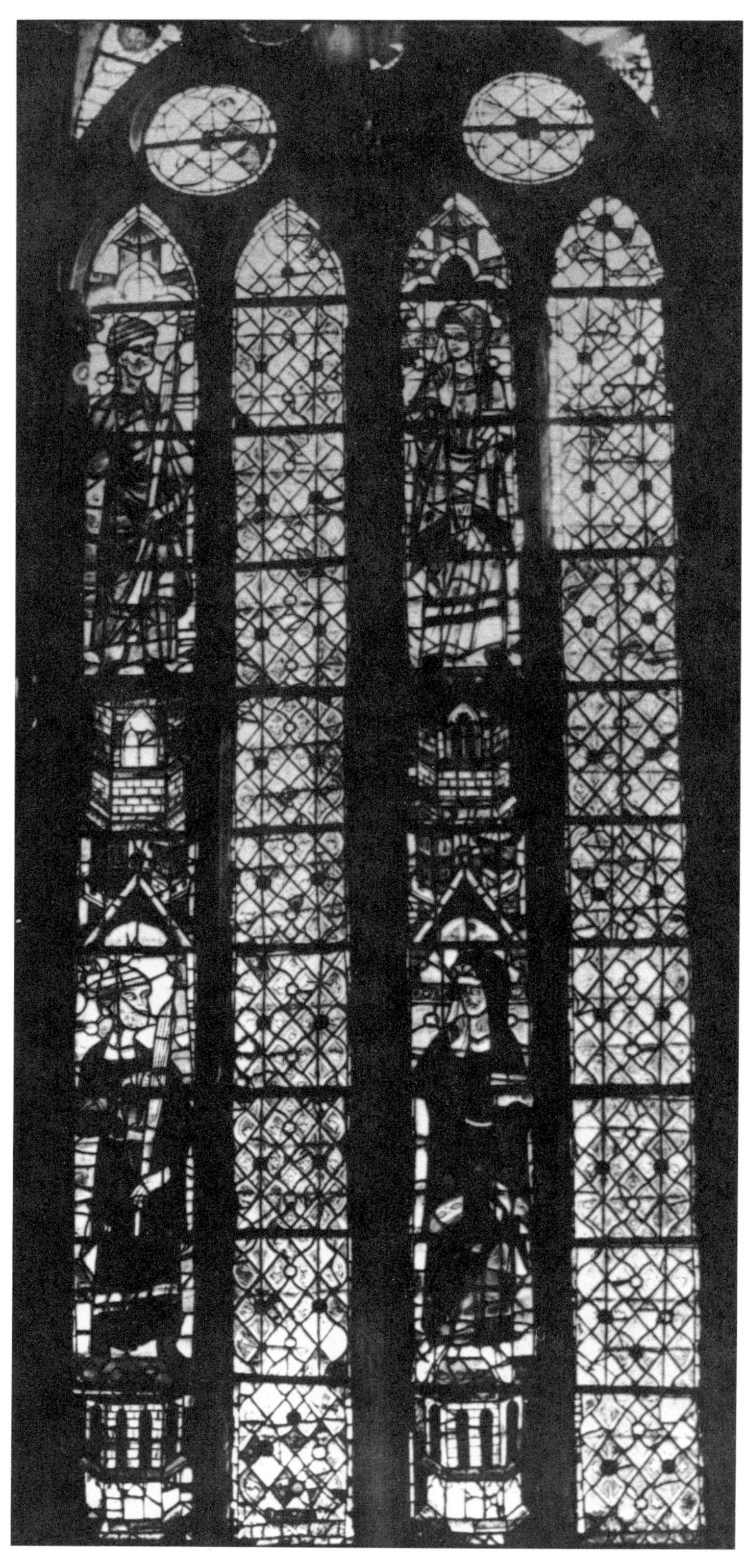

PLATE 34 Choir: Bay 15. Before 1905 restorations. *(Photo from Michon) (Paris, Archives photographiques)*

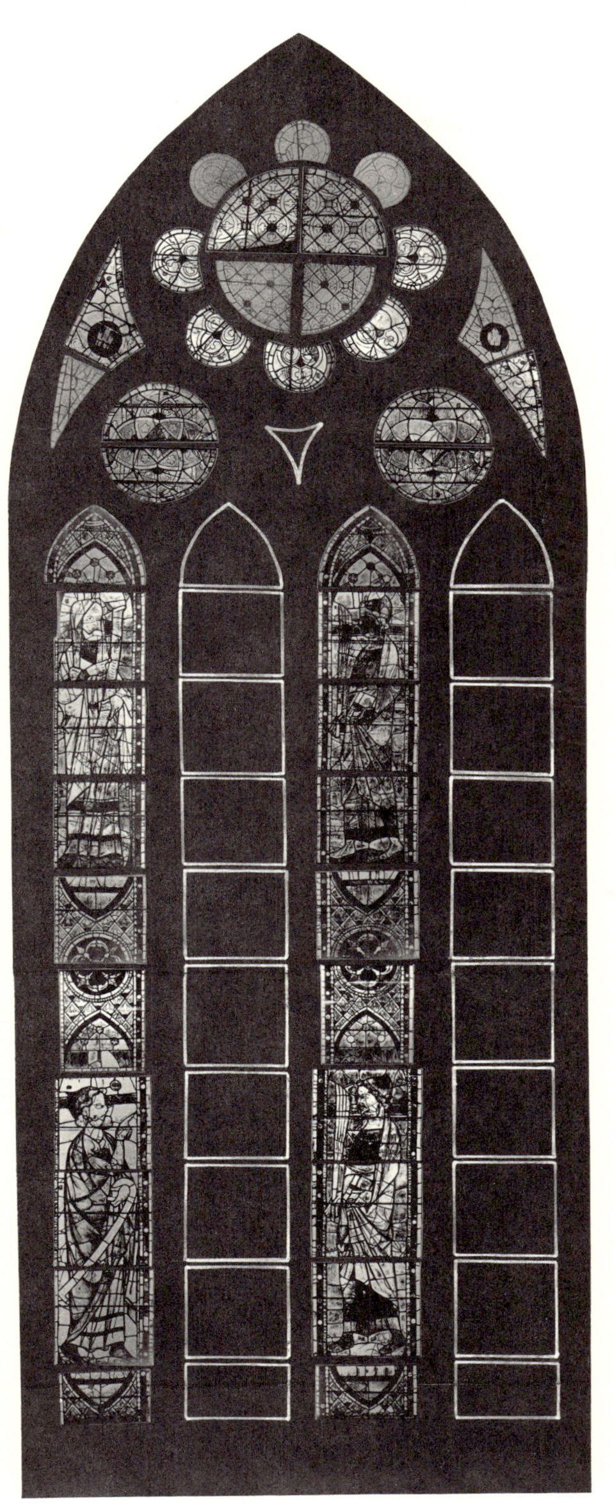

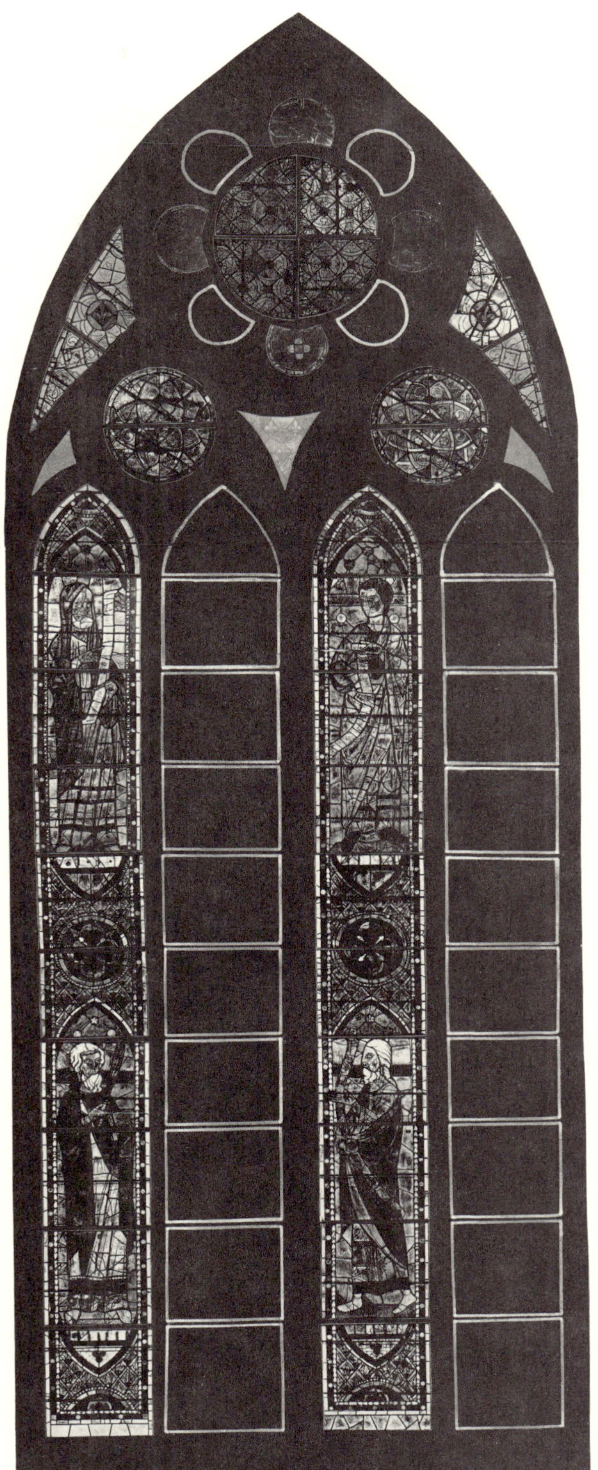

PLATE 35 Choir: Bay 16. *(Paris, Archives photographiques)*

PLATE 36 Choir: Bay 17. *(Paris, Archives photographiques)*

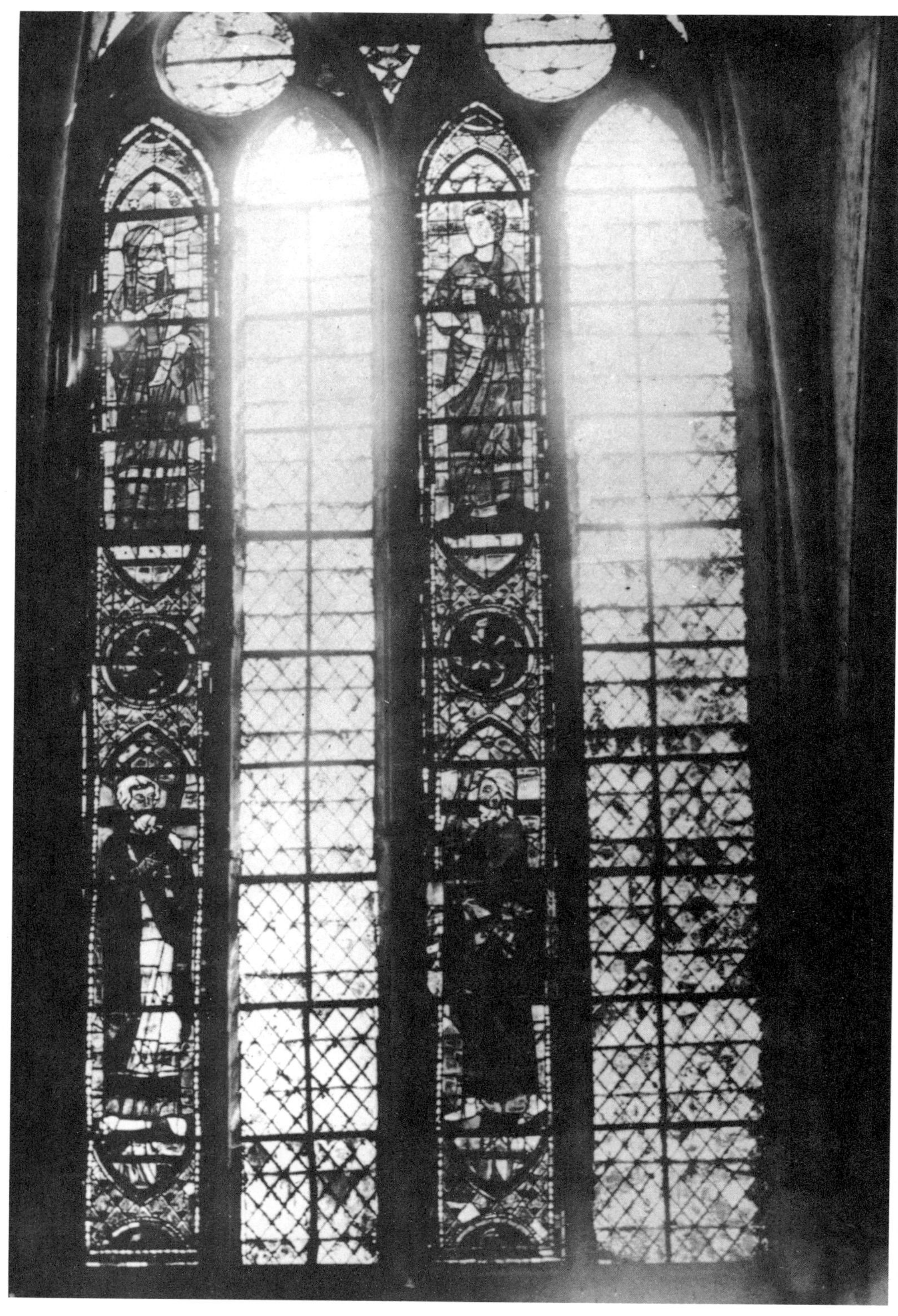

PLATE 37 Choir: Bay 17. Before 1905 restorations. *(Photo from Michon) (Paris, Archives photographiques)*

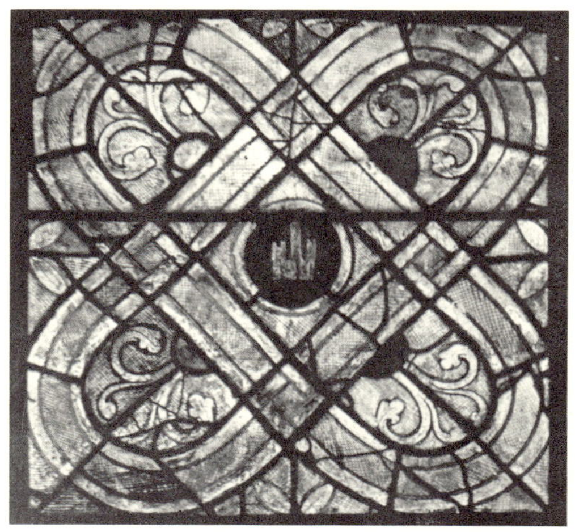

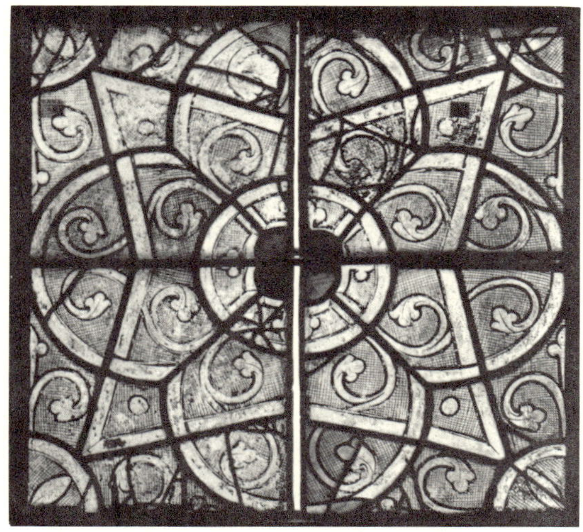

PLATE 38 Choir: Bay 13, grisaille. *(Paris, Archives photographiques)*

PLATE 39 Choir: Bay 11, grisaille. *(Paris, Archives photographiques)*

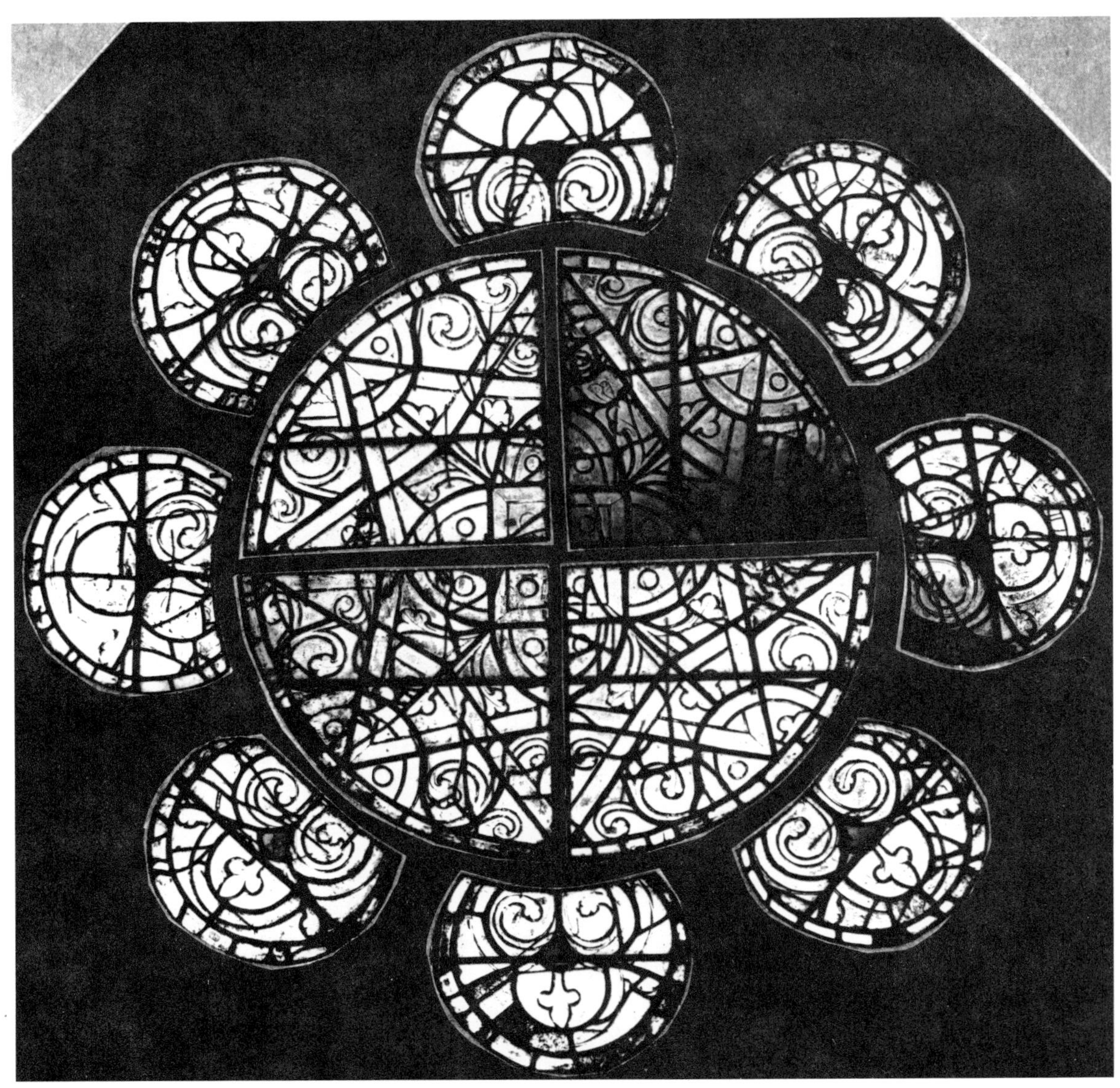

PLATE 40 Choir: Bay 14, tracery grisailles. *(Paris, Archives photographiques)*

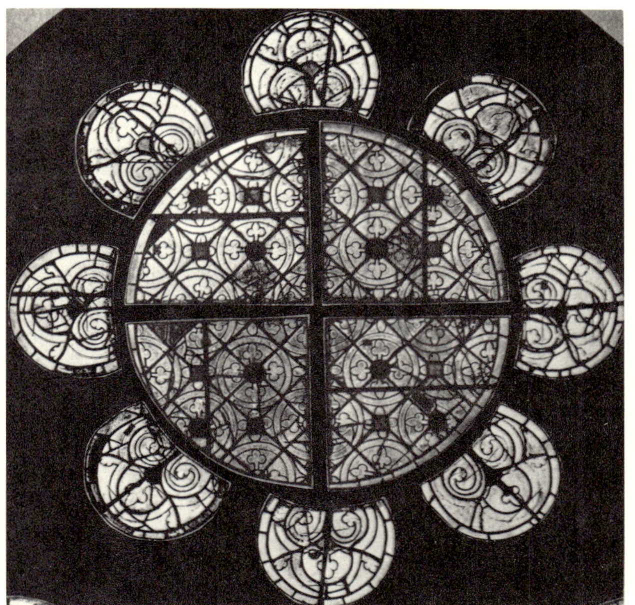

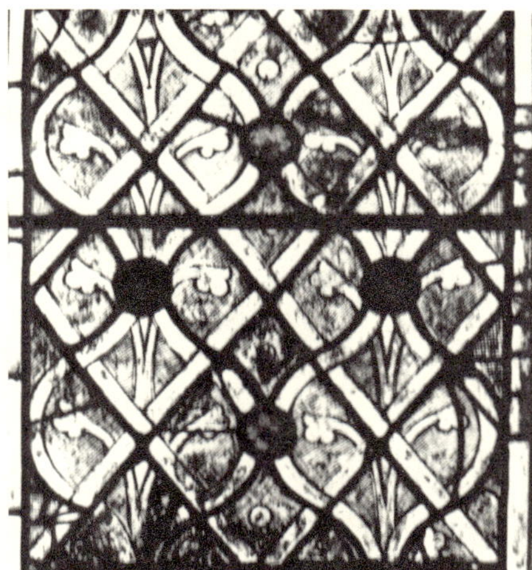

Plate 41 Choir: Bay 10, tracery grisailles. *(Paris, Archives photographiques)*

Plate 42 Choir: Bay 14, grisaille. *(Paris, Archives photographiques)*

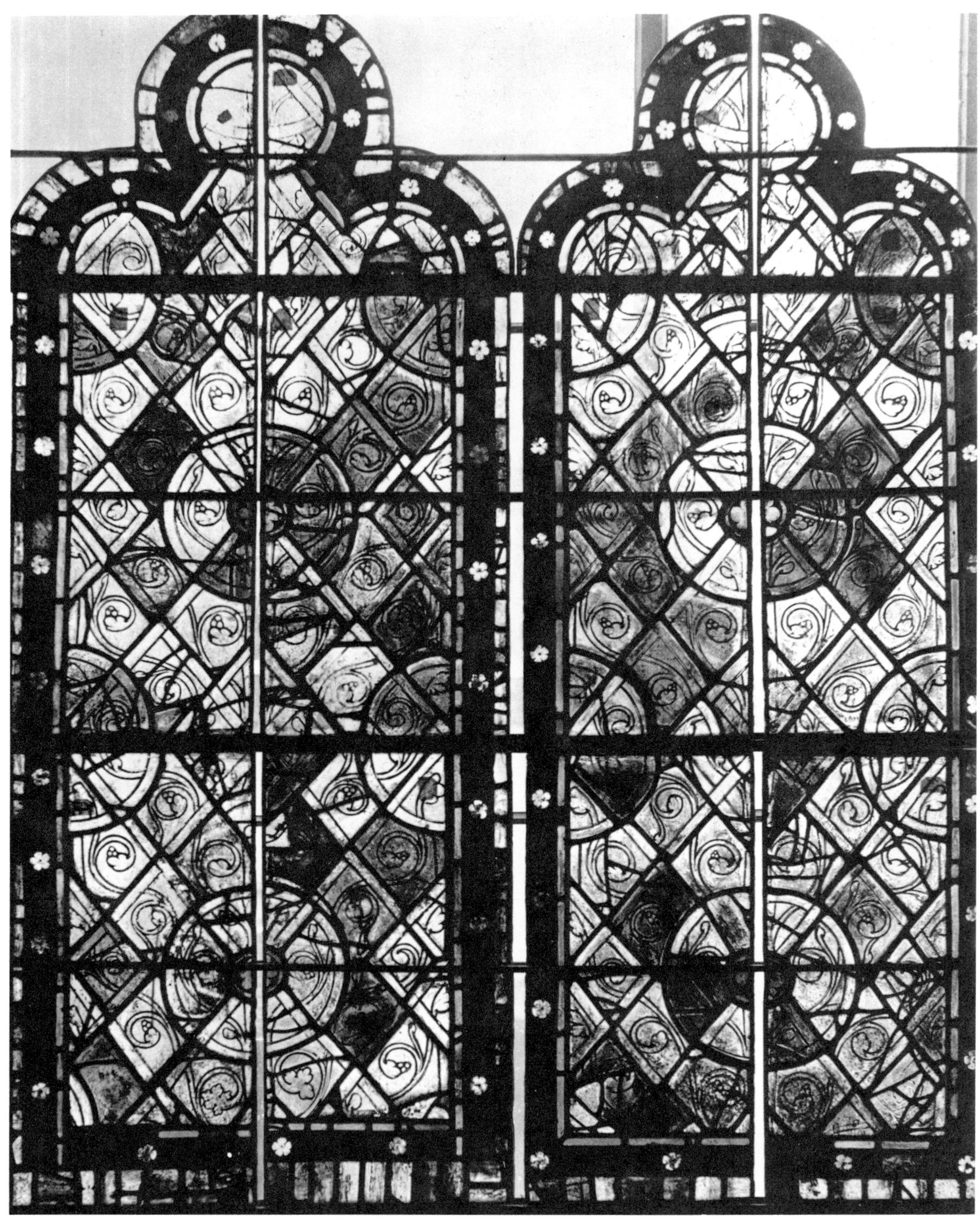

PLATE 43 Choir triforium: Bay 17, grisailles. *(Paris, Archives photographiques)*

Bays 8–13 and 16–17 contain glass which predates the architecture by several decades, while Bays 14–15 were probably designed to harmonize with the older series when the choir was rebuilt. The six names occur in the earlier group, and it is quite possible that in their intended location (the nave clerestory?) all bore names — on bases, above their heads, in the ground? — which have not survived. By the time of their re-use ca. 1270–1275 personalizing attributes were gaining the ascendancy over mere name inscriptions as a device for identification. The four cartoons designed for the eight figures of Bays 14–15 (Pls. IV, 31–33), although each repeated exactly, were slightly more individualized: one figure is bald (Jonah?),[5] one wears a peculiar layered cap, and two seem to be women, possibly the Sybil.[6]

Daniel and Ezekiel, two of the greater prophets, and Habakkuk, a lesser one, were extremely common in thirteenth-century prophet cycles in sculpture and glass. The patriarch Balaam was not at all rare in the early thirteenth century,[7] but his popularity seems to have abated in later art. He is not found in the extensive prophet cycle in the clerestory of Saint-Urbain de Troyes ca. 1275, nor in the north rose of Notre-Dame (1255). Balaam was considered to have prophesied the Nativity. He was mentioned in early sermons on the Virgin[8] and was regularly among the procession of prophets in medieval dramas.[9] His presence at Saint-Père among the few named figures helps confirm a pre-1250 date for the choir glass.

Enoch, the father of Methuselah, is a rare participant in medieval prophet cycles. Thirteenth-century illustrations of his assumption occur occasionally, but as a large single figure in an Old Testament series he appears only in the late-twelfth-century remnants from Canterbury[10] and the early-thirteenth-century medallions of the Virgin chapel at Lyon.[11] No less than Balaam, his presence adds weight to an early dating for the Saint-Père choir glass.

As stated previously, it is impossible to tell with certainty whether the figure called "NOEL" is Noah or Johel. Isolated figures of Noah were rare, but do occur at Canterbury in the late-twelfth century (NOE),[12] on an ivory casket of the first half of the thirteenth century (NOE),[13] and at Saint-Urbain de Troyes (NO . . . E).[14] Johel, one of the minor prophets, is found in glass among the patriarchs in the Bourges clerestory (IOHEL) and at Saint-Urbain de Troyes (IOEL).[15]

Influence of the processions of patriarchal figures in ecclesiastical drama on the Saint-Père group is only slight.[16] None of them carries an attribute as did the processional actors. Whereas the Daniel in the choir window corresponds to the type of clean-shaven youth described in the thirteenth-century Laon mystery play,[17] Habakkuk, described in the playscript as bearded and hunchback, is also young and smooth-faced at Saint-Père.[18] So is Enoch, who lived 365 years, and

Ezekiel, who is customarily presented in art wearing a beard in reference to God's commandment to shave his head and beard.[19] The fact is that the cartoons were copied and the prophets' names inserted indiscriminately. Daniel and Enoch are from the same cartoon; so are Habakkuk and Ezekiel. The cartoons for Noah/Johel and for Balaam also have been used elsewhere but without inscriptions.

There is no clue as to why these six patriarchs were selected. They present an odd conglomerate of major and minor prophets, types of Christ and of the Assumption, patriarchal annunciators of the Nativity. It seems more likely that they were *not* selected, that the six names were retained haphazardly in the process of reworking the older series for its new position in the choir. In its original location, which from circumstantial evidence of size, type, dating, and design seems to have been the nave clerestory, the Saint-Père Old Testament figures probably formed an important series of the stable stylistic type known from such familiar medieval sites as Bourges early in the thirteenth century, Saint-Urbain de Troyes later in the century and another half-century later still, in the second quarter of the fourteenth century, at Saint-Ouen de Rouen.

NOTES

1. See Chapter II for discussion. On the lost glass of Bay 13, see Chapter I, fn. 52.

2. Many but not all of the prophets were sainted by the church. In the thirteenth century, however, prophets were frequently combined, haloed and unhaloed, in an indiscriminate manner. At Saint-Père all of the haloed prophets who are identified by name (Daniel, Habakkuk, Enoch, Ezekiel) were actually saints. The figure in Bay 12 called "NOEL" (Pl. 24), however, has no halo, although both Noah and Johel (both of the possible identifications) were sainted.

3. See fn. 1, this chapter. The six inscriptions were probably renewed during the 1905–1908 restorations, as nineteenth-century authors report them variously. "NOEL," called Johel by Bulteau (pp. 293–299), is probably the figure identified by Clerval as Moses (A. Clerval, *Guide chartrain,* 4th ed. [Chartres, n.d.], p. 234). He is not Moses, who from the twelfth century regularly wore horns; see Arthur Watson, *The Early Iconography of the Tree of Jesse* (Oxford, 1934), pp. 26ff.; Ruth Mellinkoff, *The Horned Moses in Medieval Art and Thought* (Berkeley, 1970), pp. 65–71; stained glass of ca. 1255, Le Mans, upper ambulatory of south hemicycle, Bay j; stained glass of fourteenth century, Saint-Ouen, illustrated in Lafond, CVMA France IV, pl. 54. "EZEKEEL" is called Malaléel (Willemin, see my Pl. 22; Poisson, p. 417) or Malachi (Bulteau). Clerval refers to an Elisha who is apparently the present "EHOH," undoubtedly Enoch (H = N, as in the DAHIEL at Saint-Père; H = CH, as in EZEHIEL of Notre Dame north rose). See: Louis Grodecki and Jean Lafond, *Les vitraux de Notre-Dame et de la Sainte-Chapelle de Paris, Corpus Vitrearum Medii Aevi* France I (Paris, 1959), pp. 47, 51, G–4 and R–1. The only nineteenth-century identification which cannot be accounted for is an Aaron which Bulteau says was on the south side of the choir.

4. See discussion, Chapter II.

5. Elijah and Elisha were occasionally shown bald, but Jonah was by far the most common

smooth-pated patriarch. Jonah's baldness is based ultimately on the Rabbinical *Midrash Jonah,* which says: "The intense heat in the belly of the fish had consumed his garments, and made his hair fall out." (Louis Ginzberg, *The Legends of the Jews,* transl. Henrietta Szold [Philadelphia, 1936], IV, p. 252). Carl-Otto Nordström ("Some Jewish Legends in Byzantine Art," *Byzantion,* XXV–XXVII [1955–1957], pp. 487–508) gives examples in Christian art: (a) Byzantine manuscript, the Theodore Psalter, 1066 A.D., Brit. Mus. Add. 19352, fol. 201r (illustrated pl. IX); and (b) Catalan Bible of first half of the eleventh century, Bible of Sant Pere de Roda, Bibl. Nat. ms. lat. 6, III, fol. 83r (see also Carl-Otto Nordström, "Rabbinic Features in Byzantine and Catalan Art," *Cahiers archéologiques,* XV [1965], pp. 179–205, fig. 11 on p. 196). I am indebted to Professor George Stricevic for the Nordström reference.

6. Erythraea was the only sybil shown in thirteenth- and fourteenth-century French art, according to Emile Mâle, *L'art religieux du XIIIe siècle en France,* edition Livre de poche, v. 2 (Paris, 1958), pp. 352–355. She was occasionally included with the prophets as a herald of the Last Judgment. A sybil was customarily included in prophet dramas. See Watson, pp. 20ff. and Appendix I, p. 148.

7. Balaam is one of the embrasure statues on the north porch, right portal, of Chartres, and is among the patriarchs on an ivory casket from Saint Ived-de-Braine, 1200–1250 (Cluny Museum, illustrated in Adolph Goldschmidt, *Die Elfenbeinskulpturen* [Berlin, 1923], Plates III, pl. XII [62e]).

8. For example, sermons of Honorius d'Autun (*PL* clxxii, see especially col. 846); and Pseudo-Augustine, "Sermo contra Judaeos, Paganos et Arianos" (*PL* xlii, col. 1117). See Watson, p. 23.

9. Watson, pp. 148–149, Appendix I, lists four prophet dramas.

10. Rackham, *Canterbury,* Pl. I.

11. Professor Robert Branner stated that "Enoch" is the one thirteenth-century inscription legible on an archivolt of the Last Judgment portal of Notre-Dame, Paris.

12. Rackham, *Canterbury,* pl. 5c.

13. Ivory casket from Saint Ived-de-Braine, Cluny Museum (see fn. 7, this chapter).

14. Abbé O.-F. Jossier, *Monographie des vitraux de Saint-Urbain de Troyes* (Troyes, 1912).

15. *VF,* fig. 39 (p. 64).

16. Enoch and Noah are not part of the prophet procession in drama usually, in any case. Ezekiel and Joel are not commonly found. See Watson, Appendix I; also pp. 16, 22, 27ff., directed against Mâle.

17. "Daniel: adolescens, ueste splendida indutus," Laon, Bibl. Comm. ms. 263 (Ordo prophetarum), in Karl Young, *The Drama of the Medieval Church,* II (Oxford, 1933), p. 145. Daniel on the north porch of Chartres, left portal, is bearded.

18. "Abacuc: barbatus, curuus, gibosus," Young, II, p. 145. Bibl. Nat., ms. lat. 16746, fol. 7v, Bible of Saint-Bertin de Saint-Omer, twelfth century; the two beardless prophets are Daniel and Habakkuk (Watson, pl. XXIII).

19. Ezekiel is bearded in the Bourges clerestory (Silvain Clement and A. Guitard, *Vitraux de Bourges* [Bourges, 1900], pl. XXXIX) and in two windows in Chartres Cathedral (Delaporte Plates, III, pl. CCXXXII and pl. CCI).

{ CHAPTER VIII }

Hemicycle: Lancets – Iconography

A SPLENDID fanfare of monumental apostles and martyrs in heady color fills the clerestory windows of the Saint-Père hemicycle (Pl. I). Six of the seven bays are still glazed, each presenting four sizeable canopied male saints. The axial bay (Pl. 3) includes a standing Virgin and Child and a Crucifixion with Mary and John in the same canopy format, the focus of this proclamation of the power and vitality of the Church on Earth.

None of the saints bears a name inscription. Although many were designed from the same cartoons,[1] each bears an attribute or detail of costume which serves to individualize him to some extent. In spirit these huge figures have a greater affinity to the monumental sculpture groups of High Gothic cathedral porches than they do to contemporary stained glass, an effect which probably stems from their profusion in such a concentrated space, and from the sense of mass which is a major element of their style. The coloration is brilliant and unrelieved. There is no grisaille in the hemicycle clerestory for the same reason that there are no inscriptions. These saints were meant not to be studied individually, but to overwhelm as a group. They form a glory eminently suitable for the apse.

As noted in Chapter VI, a program of hemicycle glazing in which the Virgin and Child and the Crucifixion are flanked by apostles and prelates of the Church is particularly noteworthy in Saint-Remi and the Reims Cathedral campaigns (dating up to ca. 1240). The idea appears to have come to Saint-Père from there, and is one more indication of a strong Eastern French source for the style of the earliest figures in the choir and for the interest in combining grisaille and color. Whereas the stylistic borrowings were further developed at Saint-Père, the iconographic program of the great Rémois monuments shriveled and weakened. The Virgin and Child and the Crucifixion at Saint-Père are surrounded by a chaos of apostles and prelates, largely unidentifiable and offering none of the rich and precise references to local ecclesiastical life found at Reims. That the Rémois programs influenced Saint-Père seems undeniable, but equally evident is the passage of a generation and more in time, and the more casual view toward iconography which occasionally surfaces in art native to the West of France.

Few of the figures on the hemicycle are easy to identify. Among them are apostles, abbots, bishops, a deacon, and a pope, but except for those in the axial bay they are not arranged in any readily discernible order. Most apostles' attributes appear at least twice (ax, pike, cross, fuller's club). The prelate-saints, except St. Peter as Pope, carry no identifying attributes.

The four figures of each bay are as follows (listed in order, top right, top left, bottom right, bottom left):

Bay 1: Virgin and Child; Crucifixion with Mary and John; St. Gilduin; St. Louis of France (Pl. 3).

Bay 2 (north): St. Peter as Pope; apostle with palm; archbishop saint; apostle with sheathed sword (Pl. 4).

Bay 3 (south): Apostle with cross; St. Paul (with bare sword); apostle with curved stick (fuller's club?); apostle with ax (Pl. 6).

Bay 4 (north): Apostle with ax; apostle holding bare sword by the blade;[2] bishop saint; apostle with fuller's club (Pls. V, 8).

Bay 5 (south): Apostle with pike; apostle with palm; apostle with cross; St. Barnabas with flame? (Pl. 10).

Bay 6 (north): Abbot saint; apostle with pike; abbot saint; St. Bartholomew with knife (Pl. 12).

Bay 7 (south): Now blind.[3]

Aside from the identified figures of Bay 1 there are one archbishop, one bishop, two abbots, Sts. Peter and Paul, Bartholomew, Barnabas and twelve *other* apostles. The figures of the axial bay will be discussed first, and then some attempt will be made at positive identification of the remaining saints of the apse.

The crowned Madonna in Bay 1 (Pl. 3) holds a scepter in one hand and supports the Child with the other. The Christ Child, with a cruciferous halo, holds a small round object (ball? apple?), which, as it is held downward rather than up, is probably not a ritual object. With the other hand He plays with His mother's veil. The Virgin's stance is frontal, only minimally swayed, and she does not incline toward her Son. The Crucifixion in the left lancet shows Christ in a long loincloth on a tau-cross, His head drooped on one arm, His body bent in an exaggerated curve, and His feet nailed with a single nail. Above Him are a small sun and moon and below are dignified standing figures of the grieving Mary and Saint John.

As discussed in Chapter VI, the two lower saints in this bay, Sts. Gilduin and Louis, are of specific significance to the abbey, the former a local patron saint and the latter one of the earliest representations of the holy king after his canonization. St. Gilduin is a little-known Norman saint who died and was buried in the abbey of Saint-Père in the late eleventh century. He is shown dressed as a deacon, but unlike a deacon, holds a crozier.[4]

The erroneous identification of St. Gilduin as the more familiar deacon-martyr Stephen, probably first made by Dom Bernard Aubert (a sub-prior of the abbey in the late seventeenth century), sowed the single seed from which grew a whole forest of false theories concerning the date and provenance of the Saint-Père glass. As St. Stephen never carries a crozier,[5] the monk-historian explained its presence as evidence that the figure was the patronymic saint of an abbot-donor. If the theory were true it would be an example of some precocity, as the practice of honoring name-saints[6] was not popular in France until well into the fourteenth century. In searching for his hypothetical abbot-donor, Dom Aubert, confronted by a choice between Etienne II, abbot 1394–1416, too late for his purposes, and Etienne I, 1172–1193, conferred upon the latter the honor of donating all the stained glass in the church.[7] *Gallia christiana* incorporated his theory as fact, and it has remained viable to the present time.[8]

The saint's true identity was first revealed by the Abbé Poisson in a local mid-nineteenth-century publication of small circulation[9] and has won a limited acceptance.[10] The theory of the mythical twelfth-century abbot-donor has, however, remained alive as the basis for unfounded speculations about the dating of the prophet series in the choir[11] and the existence of a complete set of lost glazing for the twelfth-century chevet.[12] It is time that the house of cards fell in. The statement in *Gallia christiana* upon which all such theories are based was undoubtedly adopted from the manuscript of Dom Aubert, who built his conclusions on an erroneous identification of the deacon-saint in question. There is unfortunately no firm evidence that the twelfth-century chevet was ever entirely glazed by Abbé Etienne, or indeed by anyone else.[13]

St. Gilduin had tremendous importance for the abbey.[14] Returning from Rome, he had sickened and died at Saint-Père in 1077. His mother was the daughter of Hugues du Puiset, Viscount of Chartres, and his father the seigneur of Dol and of Combourg in Brittany. He had been chosen at an extremely young age to be Archbishop of Dol and had undertaken the trip to Rome to persuade Pope Gregory of his unworthiness for such an office. On the return trip he was stricken with fever while visiting relatives of the Chartrain house of Puiset. He was buried beneath the choir of Saint-Père.

Almost a century later the construction of the new choir, undertaken after the fire of 1134, had to be suspended for lack of funds. During the excavations for the foundations of a temporary wall to enclose the part of the structure already erected, so the story goes, Gilduin's body was discovered in a small vaulted chamber.[15] On May 9, 1165, it was reinterred in a chapel and began to attract pilgrims seeking miraculous cures. Among the first cured was Foucher, Abbot of Saint-Père from 1150–May 17, 1171, a sufferer from gout, under whose abbacy the new choir had been begun. Donations made at the tomb enabled the abbey to continue the construction and ultimately to add a new nave to the completed choir. St. Gilduin was therefore, in a sense, the donor of the abbey's new church and eminently worthy to be honored in its axial window.

His neighbor saint in Bay 1 is another figure of particular interest, St. Louis.[16] Crowned and haloed, he carries a book and a scepter and wears a robe decorated with yellow fleurs-de-lys in lozenges under a mantle lined in vair. Although the face and parts of the hair have undergone at least two restorations in modern times, a Montfaucon engraving shows that the saint originally had a small beard.[17] The figures of St. Louis and St. Gilduin, considerably stiffer and more aloof than the gesticulating group about them, were most likely late additions to the hemicycle, inserted after the Capetian's canonization.

King Louis IX died on crusade in 1270 and was canonized in August of 1297. Whether or not he had taken any specific interest in the construction of Saint-Père during his lifetime cannot be affirmed. It seems altogether likely, however, that his immediate descendants maintained a more than casual interest in Saint-Père, and Philippe-le-Bel may have helped in some way to finance the glazing program.[18]

The sainted king's image relates comfortably to both types of existing early replicas of St. Louis, both in narrative cycles (largely bearded) and in devotional statues (mostly not), a group in which one can observe both a crystallizing iconographic form and an occasional attempt, albeit minimal, at personal characterization.[19]

The saints in the remaining windows of the hemicycle are not arranged in any rigid or logical order. On the south are apostles — eight of them — while on the north, along with seven more apostles, are two abbots, a bishop, an archbishop, and a pope. Even this partial separation of sheep and goats has been broken down by the recent discovery of debris of a bishop saint (Pl. 15) probably removed from Bay 7 on the south.[20] The only other discernible pattern to suggest itself would be the placement of all non-apostles in lower positions, as they were before the Bartholomew and an abbot-saint of Bay 6 were interchanged during the ca. 1905 restorations (Pl. 9).

The single pope is Peter with his double key (Bay 2, Pl. 4), and opposite him in Bay 3 (Pl. 6) is an apostle who can only be Paul, with bald head and bare sword. Together they flank the axial bay. They are, of course, the abbey's patron saints, found together on the abbey seal,[21] a pairing which was general throughout the middle ages.

All of the other prelate-saints are presented incognito. The guidebook lists of names are uniformly guesswork,[22] as the figures carry no inscriptions or specific attributes. The nave series includes among its similar pope-, abbot- and bishop-saints a handful who bear names, but no valid reason exists for transferring these identifications to the hemicycle. The stylistic, and apparently the iconographic, development in the church traveled in the other direction.

The barefoot apostle figures of the hemicycle, however, do carry attributes. Not including the Peter and Paul already mentioned, there are fourteen of them, only one of whom can be positively identified: Bartholomew with his knife (Bay 6, Pl. 12), one of the earliest apostles to receive a standardized attribute. Another one, the lower left apostle of Bay 5 (Pl. 10), can be tentatively labeled Barnabas. He carries a large white object, presently unpainted, which may be either a stone, his customary attribute in the fourteenth century, or a flame, an attribute of which the Saint-Père nave series (Bay 28, Pl. 83) includes one of the extremely rare examples.[23] Barnabas with a flame was a rare specialty of the Western school of glass painting, found at Vendôme and Evron (Pl. 90) as well as Saint-Père.[24]

The attributes carried by the remaining twelve apostles are: two palms, two crosses, two fuller's clubs, two axes, two pikes, one bare sword, and one sheathed sword. All of them had been introduced into Gothic art by the late thirteenth century as part of a general movement to attempt differentiation between apostles formerly provided with nothing more specific than a book or martyr's sword. Consensus with regard to identifying attributes, slow to develop, certainly had not been reached by the end of the thirteenth century when the Saint-Père windows were designed. The iconographer introduced into his series of hemicycle figures a variety of attributes but apparently did not conceive of them clearly as identifying labels. The existence of two of many of them, usually from different cartoons, is evidence for this assumption.

The palm, for example, was a rare attribute of St. John[25] during the transitional period, but never served any other apostle.[26] It clearly derives from the apocryphal text of Pseudo-Melito, "De Transitu Beatae Mariae,"[27] in which the palm, given by the angel Gabriel to the Virgin at the annunciation of her death, is carried by John in her funeral cortège. Are both apostles who carry it — in Bay 2 and in Bay 5 (Pls. 4 and 10) — therefore intended to be St. John?

Of the two crosses, one would certainly indicate St. Andrew, one of the earliest apostles to receive a set attribute. He appears with the Latin cross in Bay 24 of the nave (Pls. 72, 74), as he was commonly depicted during the thirteenth century. The other cross could stand for any of several apostles whose attributes were in flux at the time, including Philip, James the Less, Simon, and Peter.[28] The fuller's club, traditional attribute of James the Less,[29] occasionally served Judas Thaddeus as well.[30] The ax was sometimes carried by Matthias[31] and was a somewhat tardy attribute of Matthew, who until the start of the fourteenth century customarily held a sword;[32] both Judas Thaddeus and Simon were occasionally provided with axes as well. The pike or lance was a common attribute of Thomas during the latter part of the thirteenth century, but Judas Thaddeus, Matthew, and Matthias occasionally appeared with one in the fourteenth century.

For swords, the general attribute of the middle ages connoting violent death, identification is even less defined.[33] St. James in the early thirteenth century frequently carried a sheathed sword, such as the one shown in Bay 2 (Pl. 4), but by 1300 it would be odd not to find some detail of pilgrim's garb to individualize him.[34] Bare swords could indicate Thomas, Philip, Matthew, and Matthias in the thirteenth century, the last named more commonly holding his by the point, as he does in nave Bay 28 (Pl. 83) at Saint-Père.

The confusion is such that no solution is likely. The mere fact that sixteen apostles, including Peter and Paul, appear, indicates that the artist had no clear idea of the specific identities of all of his figures. Even discounting Paul and Barnabas, who were not among the original twelve, his group still numbers fourteen. We are a long way from the precise lists dictated in the late fifteenth century.

The windows are more important as an example of the growth of interest by the end of the thirteenth century in attributes themselves. At the beginning of that century, except for Peter, Paul, Andrew and Bartholomew, the apostles held only books, and their number fluctuated easily. Fourteen or fifteen was not an unusual number to find if space permitted. As we can see from examples in which the saints were identified by inscriptions, the group often included evangelists, Paul, Barnabas and other disciples not strictly qualifying as apostles.[35] In general, with rare exceptions, only the inscribed names differentiated them one from the other. Attributes appear intermittently but with no consistent development during the mid-thirteenth century.[36] By the end of the century most apostles carry attributes other than books, but by no means always the same ones. The idea definitely had taken root, however. The refinement and crystallization of the group and of their individual labels was to occupy the whole of the fourteenth century. In the Saint-Père hemicycle, where not a single figure of the amorphous group carries only a book, this transitional moment is epitomized.

Another interesting feature of the Saint-Père group is the juxtaposition of early and late, common and rare attributes. St. James with nothing but a sheathed sword is *retardataire* by 1300. The palm of St. John is a rarity which may have had special currency in the Western glazing school.[37] Barnabas is a saint who certainly did so (see Pl. 90). The axes, pikes and crosses were precocious and perhaps indiscriminate emblems of most saints until many decades of the fourteenth century had passed. On the other hand, attributes were often adopted according to traditions, where they existed, hence, Bartholomew with his knife, Peter with his keys and papal raiment, also Paul with the bald head, and Andrew with a Latin cross. Iconography is in transition in Saint-Père as surely as is the Gothic style.

The original iconographic program for the hemicycle was thus, basically, one of Rémois origin and rather general appeal: the Virgin and Child and the Crucifixion, as emblems of the Infancy and Passion, surrounded by a selection of apostles and prelate-saints. The inclusion in important flanking positions of the abbey's patrons Peter and Paul, one shown as an apostle and the other as a prelate, drew the only topical reference. It is only in the relegation of martyrs to a quite secondary role that one senses the character of Saint-Père — clearly not a monastery strong on evangelical fervor, but rather one with temporal power and the aspirations which accompany it. It was the addition to the axial bay of the equivalent figures of Sts. Louis and Gilduin which was to provide for us the unambiguous statement of the abbey's position, its royal connections, its "personality" as an institution.

NOTES

1. See list of hemicycle cartoons, Chapter III.

2. At Bourges, St. Paul holds a bare sword by the blade. For illustration see Marcel Aubert, *French Cathedral Windows,* pl. XVII (apse, south side). At Saint-Père, however, the bald apostle in Bay 3, who, with Peter opposite, frames the axial bay is undoubtedly Paul.

3. Remnants exist of one of the four lost figures, a bishop-saint. See: Chapter I, fns. 15 and 25.

4. The present crozier head is a restoration made ca. 1905. Photographs taken before the

restorations at that time (see Pl. 5) clearly show the deacon-saint holding a staff with a bulbous top curving toward him. Dom Aubert, whose visual descriptions are reliable, reports a crozier in 1672, although he mistakenly identifies the saint as Stephen: "St. Estienne revetu en diacre une crosse en la main comme patron dudit abbé Estienne . . ." (ch. 90).

5. The nearest approximation among his attributes would be the bannered staff found infrequently in late medieval Italian paintings and manuscripts.

6. The earliest dated example known to me is a lost fresco of 1290 in the Charterhouse of Paris, where Jean the Baptist presented Jeanne de Châtillon to the Virgin; see Lillich, "Vendôme," fig. 6 and fn. 51.

7. "Apres que le corps de l'abbé Foucher (1163–1171) fut inhumé les moines de St. Pere, elurent pour abbé Etienne leur confrère. . . . Cet abbé apres son election fit achever l'eglise, et notamment il fit faire les vitres du choeur et de la nef. . . . L'ouvrage de ces vitres embellit entierrement l'eglise, et quand l'abbé Estienne n'auroit fait faire que cela en l'abbayé de St. Pere, il seroit digne d'une eternelle memoire." (Dom Aubert, ch. 90.) See Chapter I, fn. 4.

8. *Gallia christiana,* VIII, col. 1226: "Stephanus I sedebat anno 1172. Ecclesiam vitreis fenestris ornavit, eique supremam manum imposuit." Guérard reiterates the theory in his famous edition of the Saint-Père cartularies (v. 1, p. cclj), and it can be found in many nineteenth- and twentieth-century guidebooks. The most recent examples are *VF,* p. 165 (Marcel Aubert) and Elizabeth von Witzleben, *Stained Glass in French Cathedrals* (New York, 1968), p. 46.

9. Abbé Jean-Charles-Benjamin Poisson, *Chroniques de l'abbaye royale de Saint-Père-en-Vallée* (Chartres, 1957):

> Il y a donc apparence que le diacre crossé qu'on a pris pour saint Etienne, en faisant honneur des verrières actuelles . . . à l'abbé Etienne, successeur de Fulcher, n'est autre que saint Gilduin, diacre également, et de plus évêque nommé de Dol, dernier titre dont la crosse est le symbole. Qu'on n'objecte pas qu'au lieu d'une crosse à la main (footnote: "Cette crosse dont parle d. Aubert a disparu; ça été, à n'en pas douter, par les réparations qu'on a faites au vitrail") le personnage représenté sous les habits de diacre devrait avoir une croix, marque de l'archiépiscopat dans les sculptures et les peintures du Moyen-Age; il y avait longtemps déjà que Rome avait décidé que le vrai métropolitain de Bretagne était l'archévêque de Tours (footnote: "En 1199, par le pape Innocent III.") et que les évêques de Dol avaient usurpé un titre qui ne leur appartenait pas; on se conformait donc dans la légende à la décision du suprême Pontife. Louis IX, la gloire de la monarchie française, et Gilduin, la gloire de Saint-Père, furent placés au lieu le plus éminent, l'un sous le Christ . . . l'autre sous la Vierge . . . (pp. 389–390).
>
> *Also:* . . . un saint diacre; autrefois il avait une crosse à la main, ce qui indique un évêque: ce symbole montre évidemment qu'on a voulu représenter Saint Gilduin, jeune diacre, archévêque nommé de Dol, qui, à l'époque où furent placés les vitraux, n'était plus qu'un évêché, le Pape ayant terminé la grande question de la primauté entre elle et Tours. Saint Gilduin avait été le bienfaiteur de cette église de Saint-Pierre par les nombreuses offrandes qu'il avait attirées à son tombeau; on lui devait son achèvement, il était juste de lui donner place au milieu des saints patrons (p. 414).
>
> *Also:* Les chroniques de Saint-Père [i.e., Dom Aubert] qui attribuent à l'abbé Etienne Ier l'achèvement du monument à la fin du XIIe siècle et la pose des verrières, donnent le diacre pour Saint Etienne, patron de l'abbé, et le roi de France pour Louis VII, ce brûleur d'église. Elles prenaient la crosse du diacre comme indication que c'était le patron de l'abbé, explication un peu forcée, pour ne pas dire extraordinaire. Mais les verrières sont beaucoup plus récentes; elles sont du XIVe siècle. . . . J'ai cherché un autre abbé du nom d'Etienne; le second du même nom ne se rencontre dans la liste des abbés de Saint-Père qu'au com-

mencement du XVe siècle, Etienne II le Baillif, époque trop rapprochée pour faire à celui-ci l'honneur des verrières (p. 414, fn. 1).

10. See: Abbé Victor Pasquier, *L'Eglise et l'abbaye de Saint-Pierre de Chartres, notice historique et guide* (Chartres, 1921), and a more recent guidebook signed "V.P.," *Eglise Saint-Pierre de Chartres, ancienne abbatiale des moines de Saint-Père-en-Vallée* (Chartres, 1954), p. 41. Louis Réau adopts the identification in *Iconographie de l'art chrétien,* III, pt. 2 (Paris, 1958–1959), pp. 592–593. The Canon Yves Delaporte, in conversation in 1960, also referred to the figure as St. Gilduin. See also Popesco, p. 48 and fn. 16, where he confuses St. Louis with the deacon saint.

11. The earlier writers were more skeptical. Willemin in 1806 stated simply that the whole church clearly does not date ca. 1170, and suggested a fifteenth-century date for the nave windows (pp. 38–39). Mérimée in 1836 simply dismissed *Gallia christiana*'s dates and attribution to Abbot Etienne; he dated the triforium grisailles thirteenth century, the choir windows contemporary with the cathedral (for him ca. 1300), and the nave windows ("fort mutilés, mais d'une belle harmonie de couleur") probably late fifteenth century. (Prosper Mérimée, *Notes de voyages* [Paris, 1971], pp. 264–266.) It was in 1857 that one of the great pioneers in stained glass studies in France, Ferdinand de Lasteyrie, unable to reconcile the "twelfth-century donor" of *Gallia christiana* with the existing windows of the hemicycle, suggested the prophet series in the choir as the abbot's donation (p. 40). He further stated on this evidence that the choir prophets were the largest known figures for their date, which he took to be the 1180's. He was parroted by Olivier Merson in 1894 (p. 75) and by Bushnell in 1914 (p. 116), although Hugh Arnold had punctured his trial balloon in 1913: ". . . The choir had been glazed in 1172." [Arnold's footnote]: "Lasteyrie would have it that the existing windows represent this glazing — an extraordinary mistake for him to make — but it is just possible that they contain figures from the older windows." The upper part of this choir was, however, pulled down in 1270, and rebuilt with large traceried windows . . ." (pp. 185–186 and fn. 1). Arnold has not laid the mythical abbot-donor to rest, only relegated his "donation" to the limbo of lost glazing. With his customary astuteness he sensed that the prophet figures of the choir might have been re-used, as they undoubtedly were, although in attributing them to Abbot Etienne he has made a mistake as extraordinary as de Lasteyrie's.

12. The theory that the Abbé Etienne donated glass which was destroyed "during the Revolution," was first suggested by the Abbé Bulteau in 1850 (p. 293) and has never seriously been challenged. See for example Lorin, "Médaillon du XIIe siècle," p. 509.

13. One twelfth-century panel has been found at Saint-Père, used as a stopgap. It is the subject of a handsome study by Paul Popesco, discussed in Chapter I. Popesco (p. 48) treats Bulteau's hypothesis about losses during the Revolution with a healthy suspicion. He suggests that, if such a twelfth-century glazing had existed, it had disappeared before Dom Aubert's 1672 chronicle, which does not mention any lower windows. Popesco's efforts to reconstruct a window design from the medallion, and to suggest an original location within the chevet, remained tentative (see esp. his fn. 9).

14. It is perhaps only fair to outline the specific importance of St. Stephen (the former identification of the figure) to the abbey as well, for which there are miscellaneous bits of evidence: (a) The head of St. Stephen is listed among the abbey's relics in the inventory of 1399. (See de Mély, V [XXXVII] [Jan. 1887], p. 64, who suggests that the head may have been a gift of the seigneurs de Puiset returning from crusade.) (b) The next surviving inventories, of 1559 and 1665, although they do not list the head, do include an arm-bone of St. Stephen. Dom Aubert is the untrustworthy source for two other items: (1) He identifies the three corner statues of the cloister built by Abbé Etienne II in 1407 (now destroyed) as Peter as Pope, Paul, and 'Stephen as deacon holding an abbatial crozier as patron of Abbé Etienne.' (On the destroyed cloister see

Bienvenüe, pp. 7–27, who states p. 14 that Elie Lambert believed the three lost statues to have been thirteenth-century.) (2) Dom Aubert identifies the remains of an old chapel on the church's exterior, at the easternmost bay of the north nave (in ruins at time of his writing and since destroyed) as the chapel of St. Stephen. He reports that this chapel or a more primitive one occupied that spot from the very beginnings of the abbey in the sixth–seventh centuries. According to tradition, he continues, the chapel originally had been a martyrium situated in a cemetery, dedicated to St. Stephen and containing bones of the first Chartrain martyrs. The abbey church of Saint-Père and the parish church of Saint-Hilaire (built adjacent to the north of Saint-Père and razed in 1801) were constructed to either side of the ancient martyrium (Dom Aubert, ch. 116).

15. See discussion Chapter I.

16. Lillich, "Saint Louis." There can be no doubt that the figure represents the "glory of the Capetians" in spite of a certain skepticism voiced in a review of that article (see "Chroniques," *Bulletin monumental,* CXXV [1970], pp. 156–157). The review appears to be of the abbreviated French synopsis rather than of the article itself, as it contains a succession of misrepresentations of published fact and opinion (e.g., the author is attacked because the photograph in fig. 2 does not show an obvious beard, although fn.2 explains the window's deteriorated condition at that time. It is fig. 3, an eighteenth-century engraving, which shows the beard).

17. Lillich, "Saint Louis" fig. 3. For other contemporary images of St. Louis bearded, see p. 252 and fns. 12–15 of the same article. The heated debate over whether in fact a portrait of St. Louis exists revolves with needless passion about the unfortunate word "portrait"; that early bearded images (and unbearded ones, too) exist is undeniable. For still one more example, see the manuscript of Vincent de Beauvais, Dijon, ms. 568 (329), fol. 9r. See: Jean-Pierre Babelon, "La France de Saint Louis," *Archeologia,* XXXVII (November–December 1970), p. 10.

18. For documentation see Chapter VI; see also Lillich, "Saint Louis," pp. 251–252.

19. The possibility of real portraiture is completely discounted by Alain Erlande-Brandenburg, "Le tombeau de Saint Louis," *Bulletin monumental,* CXXVI (1968), pp. 7–28 (who claims the unbearded Mainneville statue is a portrait statue of Philippe-le-Bel). I am more inclined to regard the depiction of Saint Louis' beard as a timid first step toward realistic portraiture. My assumption, stated in the "Saint Louis" article, that the tomb statue was standing, and is depicted in the Hours of Jeanne d'Evreux in the Cloisters, was attacked by Erlande-Brandenburg, *Société nationale des antiquaires de France, Bulletin* (1970), p. 226 and fn. 5; that assumption has since been superbly buttressed by the solid work of Georgia Sommers Wright, "The Tomb of Saint Louis," *Journal of the Warburg-Courtauld Institutes,* XXXIV (1971), pp. 65–82.

20. Lillich, "Découverte," pp. 28–32.

21. See seal appended to Arch. Nat. J227, no. 37 (1300 A.D.) (Doüet d'Arcq, *Collection de sceaux,* VIII, no. 8186).

22. Bulteau, pp. 297–298, is the source of most of the later guidebooks.

23. Barnabas' flame in Bay 28 is yellow. In the clerestory of Saint-Ouen in Rouen, second quarter of the fourteenth century, he carries a red flame. See Lafond, CVMA France IV, pp. 227–228 and pl. 67. Other examples of Barnabas holding a flame or fire are: (a) psalter from East Anglia, second half of the fourteenth century, in Vienna, Nat.-Bibliothek, Cod. 1826, fol. 154v, illustrated in Montague Rhodes James, *The Bohun Manuscripts* (Oxford, Roxburghe Club, 1936), pl. LVI (c); (b) a figure (Barnabas?) shown in flames on archivolts of central portal, Auxerre, late-thirteenth–fourteenth century; (c) two vaguely identified examples in Maurice and Wilfred Drake, *Saints and Their Emblems* (London, 1916), p. 16, showing the saint burned to death or near a fire. See Chapter X, Bay 28.

24. See Chapters IV and V. Vendôme's Barnabas is illustrated in Lillich, "Vendôme," fig. 3.

25. Bay 24 of the Saint-Père nave (Pl. 72) shows St. John with a palm. Its use at Saint-Père clearly derives from Tours, where an unnamed, unbearded apostle in the triforium carries a

palm. It has been suggested that the stub remaining in St. John's hand on the south porch jambs of Chartres Cathedral was originally a palm (Peter Kidson, *Sculpture at Chartres* [London, 1958], p. 41); this point remains problematical, however. Infrequent in early Gothic art, the palm of St. John is very rarely found as late as the early fourteenth century, the date of its use at Saint-Père. Other late examples: (a) Freiburg Cathedral statues on nave piers, thirteenth–fourteenth century; (b) English embroidered cope, first quarter of the fourteenth century, Butler-Bowden collection, Chesterfield (A. Christie, *English Medieval Embroidery* [Oxford, 1938], pl. CXXXVI and fig. 137); (c) St. Elizabeth shrine, The Cloisters, made in France ca. 1340–1350.

26. The "palm of martyrdom" was given to many saints but never to apostles, who, if undifferentiated, carry books, rolls and/or swords.

27. Translated in M. R. James, trans., *The Apocryphal New Testament* (Oxford, 1953), pp. 209–216. A Latin text probably dating from the fourth century, based on earlier Coptic and Greek versions, it was summarized (and hence disseminated in the West) by Gregory of Tours ca. 590 in "De gloria martyrum" (according to T. S. R. Boase, *The York Psalter* [New York, 1962], p. 8).

28. It is conceivable that the cross of Bay 5, the lower part of which is modern, was originally a carpenter's square, in which case the saint would be Thomas. Cf. Pl. 10 with Pl. 11, which shows debris in the middle panel of the figure.

29. "S. Jacobus" in Bay 24 of the nave (Pl. 72) carries a fuller's club. "S. Jaco_us Mino_" of Bay 28 (Pl. 83), however, carries a staff. There is also a "S. Jacobus" in Bay 20 (Pl. 55) holding an ax.

30. Sculptured retable, Cistercian church of Doberan, fourteenth century, illustrated in Hans Wentzel, *Die Lübecker Plastik bis zur Mitte des 14. Jahrhunderts* (1938), pls. 64–71 (14); statues in right choir, Vienna, Cathedral of St. Stephen, reworked in fifteenth century.

31. An early example is the metal reliquary triptych of the Pfarrkirche at Mettlach, from a Benedictine monastery (ca. 1220) (Hermann Schnitzler, *Rheinische Schatzkammer* [Düsseldorf, 1959], II, pl. 17).

32. He does so in Bay 20 of the nave (Pl. 55) holding it by the point. Matthias also holds a sword by the point in Bay 28 of the nave (Pl. 83).

33. It seems likely that apostles were first given swords (supplementing or replacing the books or phylacteries common in the twelfth century) on the Chartres south jambs, where they stand not only in their usual role as witnesses of the Last Judgment but also as the first martyrs and confessors (central portal: Last Judgment; side portals: Martyrs Portal, left, Confessors Portal, right). The apostles were martyred, and did confess Christ by their lives, and so serve as prototypes for both groups of saints (cf. Matthew 10:28 [martyrdom] and 10:32 ["confession"]). Adolf Katzenellenbogen, *The Sculptural Programs of Chartres Cathedral* (Baltimore, 1959), p. 80.

34. The figures of St. James in the nave are equally *retardataires*.

35. The Bourges series includes Paul, Matthias, Barnabas, Luke and Mark. Either Paul or Matthias was the customary replacement for Judas Iscariot. The series of twelve at Châlons-sur-Marne (ca. 1275) includes Paul *and* Matthias. Nine carry attributes other than books. Saint-Ouen, in the fourteenth century, has sixteen; see discussion by Lafond, CVMA France IV, p. 180.

36. Because of the mutilations and restorations of embrasure statues such as those of Chartres and Amiens, the most reliable evidence must be sought in other media. Several of the very early examples of specific attributes are German. See Rhenish metal reliquary of ca. 1220 (Schnitzler, II, pl. 17).

37. See Tours triforium windows, where the apostles are likewise not named.

{ CHAPTER IX }

Hemicycle: Tracery Medallions—Iconography

THE hemicycle tracery of Saint-Père glorifies Christian martyrdom in a set of medallions as handsome in design as they are unusual in form and program. The tracery of each bay contains three quatrefoils, two of the trio containing scenes of martyrdom while, in the uppermost, an angel flying upside-down holds out two crowns of heavenly reward (see Pl. 13). The tracery lights thus "read horizontally" across the bays as an independent program, rather than, as more commonly found, as themes related directly to the lancets beneath, as isolated subjects, or even unthematic filler. The tracery quatrefoils add a distinctive voice to the chorus in praise of the Church on Earth, as presented by the hemicycle as a whole.

The bays are united by the repetition, in the upper quatrefoil of each, of the *ange porte-couronne.* The cartoon is repeated identically in all bays of the group, even the axial one where it surmounts not two martyrdoms but the Annunciation and Nativity of Christ.[1] In contrast to many of the martyrdoms, the *ange porte-couronne* was a familiar Parisian motif in the thirteenth century,[2] and one particularly adaptable to irregularly formed tracery lights.

The series of tracery medallions directly below the angels contains, except for the Annunciation and Nativity of Bay 1, scenes of martyrdoms of important saints. Six bays of the original seven remain. The iconographic program of martyrdoms, unlike the angels presenting crowns, is unusual for the medium of stained glass. Series of apostles and martyrs were, of course, one of the staples of Gothic church decoration; in the glass medium such series were particularly well suited to fill the regulated patterns of odd shapes provided by rose windows. The south rose of Notre-Dame, ca. 1260, contains rings of angels, apostles, martyrs, confessors, and virgins, encircling Christ and the Evangelist symbols, in a program which parallels that of the cathedral's portal sculpture. In his discussion of the rose, however, Jean Lafond[3] rightly underscores the very important point that the saints appear there as single, standing devotional figures and not in scenes of their martyrdoms.

Isolated martyrdoms occasionally are included in tracery glazing,[4] sometimes illustrating the death-scenes of standing saints below, sometimes with little or no connection either to the subjects of the lancets or of other tracery lights. Tracery glass is usually of secondary importance in an ensemble, often filled with grisaille or diaper and probably the work of assistants. The program at Saint-Père is very unusual on several counts, not only because the tracery medallions are a highly coherent glazing series in their own right, but because the quality of the designs and of their execution is uniformly high. Furthermore, the martyrdoms are presented in tableau-like scenes with sparse detail, as ideograms, rather than in the looser, narrative manner common in stained glass medallions of the period.

The subjects are as follows:

Bay 1: Annunciation and Nativity (Pl. 3).
Bay 2 (north): Crucifixion of Peter; Beheading of Paul (Pl. 4).
Bay 3 (south): Beheading of John the Baptist; Stoning of Stephen (Pl. 6).
Bay 4 (north): St. Lawrence on the grill; St. Vincent thrown into the sea (Pl. 8).
Bay 5 (south): Crucifixion of St. Andrew; the second martyrdom is lost[5] (Pl. 10).
Bay 6 (north): St. Eustace in the burning bull; St. Bartholomew being flayed (Pls. 12, 13).
Bay 7 (south): (now blind).

The series contains several martyrdoms definitely not in the mainstream of French High Gothic iconographic practice. The presence of these, in addition to other factors — choice and conjunction of saints in an unusually structured program for the tracery location, the form of the quatrefoil medallion, and the spareness of the tableaux already noted — lead one to search for a possible model which the artist could have employed. The assumption is, on evidence, that such a model was (at least in its sources) non-French — perhaps English.

While such a hypothetical model could have been a portable object in any number of media, a number of archaisms in the scenes suggest either an object earlier in date or one in a medium such as embroidery, which seems to cling to older formulae longer.

Bay 1

The Annunciation appears in the customary classic simplicity of the thirteenth century (Pl. 3). Mary and the Angel stand facing one another. The messenger gestures and the Virgin, holding a book, inclines her head. A chair fills the right lobe of the quatrefoil. The focus, dignity and lack of apocryphal clutter, are typical of the period.

The Nativity (Pl. 3), on the other hand, exemplifies an earlier iconographic type. The Virgin reclines in the foreground; Joseph sits to the right, gesturing. She is oblivious of the Child, who is swaddled and placed on an altar behind her, framed by the heads of an ox and an ass. The group is strongly reminiscent of the twelfth-century west window of Chartres.[6] While most of these features, singly or in combination, lasted well into the thirteenth century, the presence of them all together in a work dating ca. 1300 is unusual and strongly suggests reliance on an archaizing model or one earlier in date.

Bay 2

Adjacent to the axial bay on the north are martyrdoms of the abbey's name-saint Peter and his companion Paul (Pl. 4). St. Paul is kneeling on one knee in prayer. The executioner behind him places one hand on the saint's shoulder and, with the other, swings high his sword. The scene is iconographically austere for ca. 1300. In France throughout the thirteenth century and even before, Paul was frequently shown blindfolded in reference to the episode of the veil of Plautilla, or with his head already severed, probably in reference to the story of the three miraculous springs.[7] The absence of such apocryphal detail, although not workable evidence for a specific source, certainly is atypical for the window's period.[8] French examples of a similar austerity date from a half-century or more earlier.[9]

The Crucifixion of Peter in the neighboring medallion of Bay 2 (Pl. 4) is a much greater and more engrossing puzzle. St. Peter, in a long robe, hangs upside-down on the cross. Two symmetrically-positioned executioners nail his feet with claw-ended hammers. The left figure stands before the cross with his back to the spectator; the other is shown in profile straddling the crossbar.

Because the question of the Gothic representation of the Crucifixion of

Peter is such a complex one, I will attempt to outline the subject and its development briefly, and some of the issues involved, before placing the medallion of Bay 2 in context. The issue is a particularly pertinent one because at Saint-Père there are two Crucifixions of St. Peter, the one under discussion and another in Bay 22 of the nave (Pl. 59), each of which partakes of a different tradition.

There are at least two variables in any representation of the scene: the method of attachment to the cross, either cords or nails; and the positioning of the executioners, either symmetrically (usually standing and attaching the feet) or asymmetrically (most commonly, one standing working on the feet and another, on the other side of the cross, crouching and affixing a hand). No religious text states whether Peter was tied or nailed to the cross. It is commonly stated by French scholars that in thirteenth-century France Peter was depicted as tied with cords,[10] and in the art forms of manuscript illumination and sculpture this is largely true. In glass, although cords are the more usual form, the statement cannot be applied so absolutely. Still, it is probably correct to say that the nailed crucifixion, by the High Gothic era, ultimately relies on a non-French tradition, wherever it occurs.

Tony Sauvel, in an article in the *Bulletin monumental* in 1938,[11] organized examples into two traditions based on the symmetrical or asymmetrical placement of executioners (regardless of whether they employ cords or nails and hammers). The latter, he believes, derives ultimately from the mosaics of the basilica of St. Peter in Rome (chapel of John VII, 705–707),[12] and appears in early medieval art in such works as the Sacramentary of Drogo.[13] Although Sauvel did not pursue matters so far, it can be said that this asymmetrical type became the basis for German Gothic representations and is found quite as universally there in the thirteenth century as the tied crucifixion is in France.

The symmetrical group — of which the medallion of Bay 2 of Saint-Père (Pl. 4) is a late example — Sauvel considers to be based on English models of the Romanesque period. The Benedictional of St. Aethelwold[14] is such a work, one which had a clear influence on the continental side of the channel, and he suggests that all symmetrical examples in France are ultimately based on such Anglo-Saxon, "barbaric" art (as opposed to Carolingian, "classical" art). He delineates two groups of twelfth-century French sculpture, one in Languedoc[15] and the other in Aquitaine 'under Queen Eleanor,'[16] which adhere to this basic placement.

While his arguments concerning the transmission of the formula from Romanesque England to, say, Languedoc, are not completely persuasive, it suffices for our purposes to understand that in twelfth-century Europe the two "nailed" traditions were centered in Germany (asymmetrical) and the Aquitaine (symmetrical). The French High Gothic formula of a tied crucifixion seems to have almost completely obliterated both types in the major arts in France.

In provincial schools and in less monumental media the nailed traditions seem to have resisted longer. Thus it is that the Burgundian windows in the first half of the thirteenth century reproduce the German type, a situation which will be discussed with Bay 22 of the nave, which also contains an example (Pl. 59). And windows in the Angevin area in the twelfth century, and in the school of the West in the thirteenth, maintain the Aquitaine tradition, culminating in the hemicycle medallion which is the ultimate subject of inquiry here.

The following windows in the West of France show Peter nailed to the cross by symmetrical executioners:

a) Poitiers, Crucifixion window (ca. 1165): four executioners, two crouching, one on each side, nailing the hands; two up on ladders, one on each side, nailing the feet.[17]
b) Angers, north choir, Bay 24 (Peter window), ca. 1225–1235: one executioner stands left (on crossbar) nailing the feet; one stands right (on crossbar) nailing the feet.
c) Tours, choir clerestory (Peter window), 1257–1270's: one executioner stands left, nailing feet; one stands right, nailing feet.[18]
d) Saint-Père, hemicycle, Bay 2, ca. 1290–1300 (Pl. 4): same placement as Tours.

The medallion of Saint-Père seems to be one of the few clear-cut examples in the church of a format passed on by the glazier himself from windows he knew, in his medium. The window he remembered was very likely at Tours. Saint-Père is thus the final highly sophisticated version of a local Western variant of the scene in the glass medium, probably originating at Poitiers.

Bay 3

Flanking the axial bay on the south are medallions of the Beheading of the Baptist and the Stoning of the protomartyr Stephen (Pl. 6). In a representation which remained standard throughout the Gothic era, St. John kneels before his prison while his executioner, sword in hand, grasps him by the hair.[19] In accordance with Mark VI:27 he is always beheaded in or in front of his prison.

Stephen kneels praying while two flanking figures stand and stone him, one holding stones in a bag (or in a fold of his garment?). The saint has a maniple over his arm, and one of the stones is "attached" to his head. All details were current by the thirteenth century, although the simplification of the angry crowd to two men and the inclusion of the maniple[20] became increasingly common in the second half of the century.

The "framing" design, that is, the inclusion of stoners on both sides of the saint, had a long history in all media and was maintained well into the fourteenth century.[21] It was more common to French thirteenth-century sculpture[22] and stained glass[23] than to manuscripts, where the stoning group customarily appears to the left.[24]

Bay 4

Vincent and Lawrence, the two other deacon-martyrs who with Stephen enjoyed universal homage in the middle ages, are honored in the medallions of Bay 4 (Pl. 8). St. Vincent, nude and weighted about the neck with a millstone, is being tossed from a sailboat by one of two figures therein. In the Tours clerestory the scene is shown similarly, but with a sailless boat.[25] A boat with sail of the Saint-Père type does appear at Tours, however, in the St. Eustace window of the same clerestory series.[26]

St. Lawrence lies nude, face up, on his grill, two men holding him and tormenting him with forked poles. The horizontal ladder-type grill[27] seen at Saint-Père was a long-lived and immutable type found from the twelfth through the fourteenth centuries.[28]

Two features of the medallion are unusual: the absence of a man or men working bellows, and the winged helmet of one of the executioners. Concerning the bellowsman, at least one such figure customarily participates in the scene during the thirteenth century, not only in France but throughout northern European art.[29] His omission at Saint-Père probably was not caused by cramped quarters — a tiny bellowsman is included in the equally crowded Eustace martyrdom of Bay 6 — but by imitation of a model without a bellowsman. One possibility in the same medium and same general area of France would be the window in Angers Cathedral (ca. 1230–1235),[30] but it remains only a possibility. English examples in other media should also be mentioned.[31]

The winged helmet seems more clearly to be of ultimately English origin. Two other examples of such an unusual helmet can be cited, both from the early fourteenth century and both of English origin or influence. One is the famous Queen Mary Psalter[32] and the other an embroidered hanging *(opus anglicanum)* from the church at Harlebeke, Belgium.[33] The winged helmet thus could be another clue to an ultimately English source for the martyrdom cycle.

Bay 5

Of the two martyrdoms of Bay 5 only the crucifixion of St. Andrew remains (Pl. 10).[34] The saint, in a long robe, is being tied to a horizontally placed Latin cross

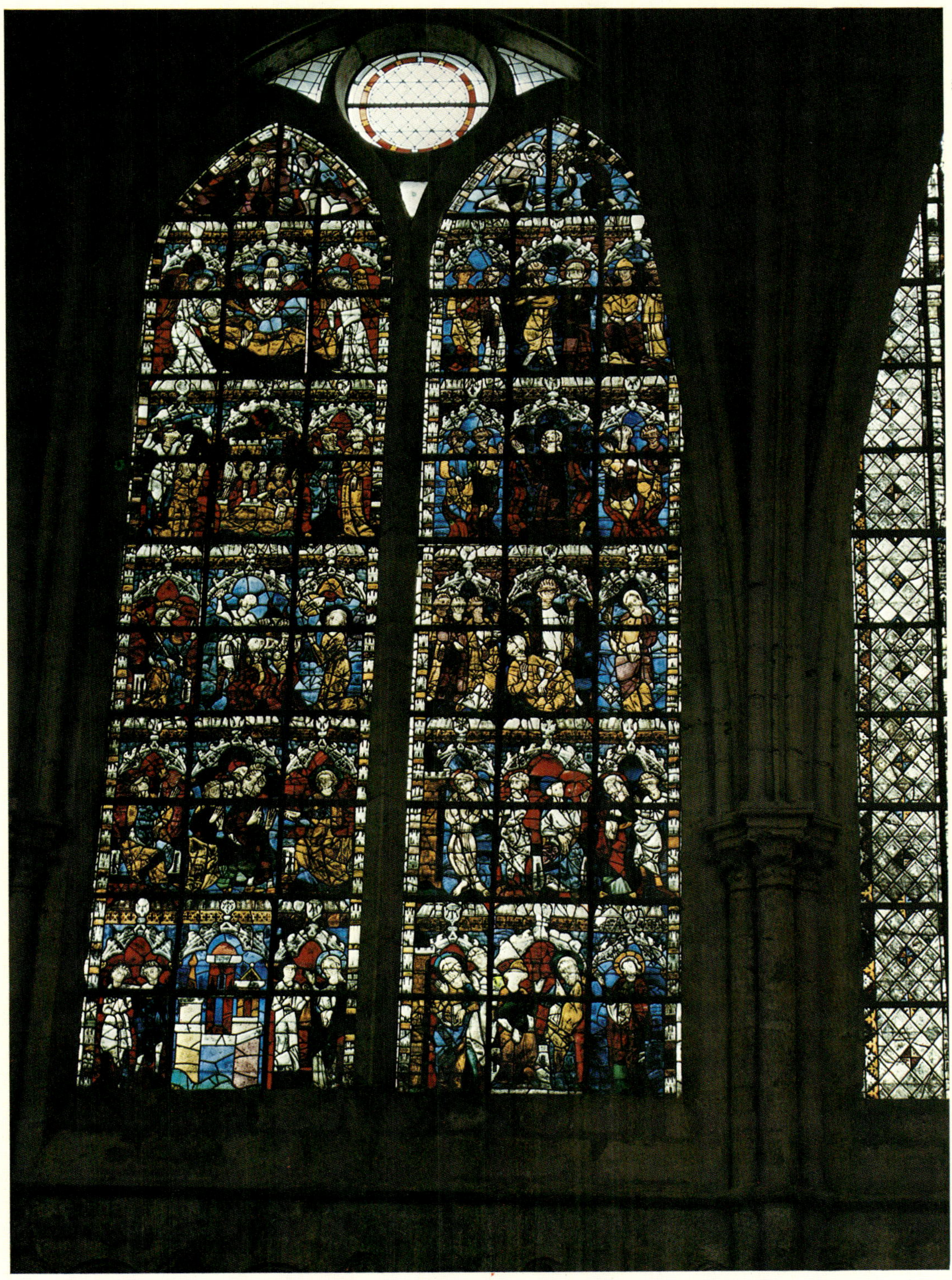

PLATE VIII Nave: Bay 27. St. Catherine and St. Agnes window. *(Edouard Fièvet)*

by two executioners standing behind it.[35] They turn their backs slightly to one another as one ties the saint's feet and the other his upper hand, both employing some sort of tightening tool.

In the thirteenth century little conformity had been reached in representing the details of Andrew's crucifixion; the cross was shown sometimes upright,[36] upside-down,[37] horizontal as at Saint-Père, sloping at an oblique angle,[38] or even occasionally as the saltire-cross which was to assume the saint's name.[39]

In the major High Gothic monuments of France the upright Latin cross was the rule. In media other than sculpture the horizontal cross was only slightly less common in the thirteenth century.[40] The high number of examples of Benedictine origin is an indication that the horizontal cross possibly may have sprung from such a monastic source.[41] By the thirteenth century, however, it had spread beyond the orders and had undergone several variations. A number of set formats can be traced, notably a design with single executioner standing behind the cross,[42] a design with executioners shown rather awkwardly crouching both above and below the saint's body,[43] and the more sophisticated arrangement which appears at Saint-Père and in the Uppsala cope (Pls. 91, 93), in which two standing executioners turn their backs to one another.[44]

Bay 6

Bay 6 honors Sts. Eustace and Bartholomew (Pls. 12, 13). Eustace and his wife and two children are lined up nude in the bronze bull of their martyrdom, below which is a tiny figure working bellows. The cult of Eustace in France was inaugurated in the twelfth century by the translation of his relics to Saint-Denis, and was popularized later by the Golden Legend. His martyrdom is depicted frequently in thirteenth-century windows and sculpture.

The grouping of the scene most probably stems originally from Greek manuscripts of the Menologium of Basil, where the family is clothed and the children stand in front of their parents.[45] The late twelfth-century window at Sens repeats the Greek formula. By the end of the thirteenth century several changes had been standardized: the family was shown nude and was lined up in a row, and executioners working bellows, as well as a tyrant, were often included. The two representations at Chartres Cathedral, which differ in detail, illustrate the fluid state of the iconography in the early thirteenth century. On the south porch (west side of pier I) the family is shown nude and a man works bellows to the right, but the parents still stand behind the children.[46] In window 62 (Chartres north nave) the clothed family is seated side by side, two men are tending bellows, while two others grasp Eustace,[47] like the two men flanking Eustace at Sens.

After 1250 the group usually appears much as it does at Saint-Père. The Tours clerestory contains such an example,[48] and an even closer group is found in a relief of the first half of the fourteenth century from the Abbey of Saint-Denis.[49]

The flaying of Bartholomew, shown in the other quatrefoil of Bay 6 (Pl. 12, 13), achieved no such standardization of format.[50] In the Saint-Père medallion the saint is shown nude, face up, on a table or trestle, two executioners standing behind him and working on his limbs with knives. The scene is misidentified in most current guidebooks and in the *Archives photographiques.*[51] Although the scene is less explicit than was often the case, the presence of a second, darkened left arm below the first identifies it with certainty as the flaying of Bartholomew.

Bartholomew, shown seated or tied to a column in Byzantine and early German art, sometimes standing in Italian examples, was usually depicted reclining in France, Flanders and England. He reclines either on the ground, on a sloping stretcher, or on a table. The most coherent iconographic group[52] shows Bartholomew on the ground, looking very much like an octopus with limbs doubled in number and going in all directions.

The martyr is shown at Saint-Père, however, nude on a trestle. While similar trestles occur in Liégeois psalters[53] (where Bartholomew wears a charming checkered loincloth), the combination of nude saint on trestle can be found only in German and late-English examples.[54] The inconclusive evidence — alas! — proves only that the Saint-Père type is not French *au fond.*

One hesitates to make judgments where many links of evidence are obviously missing. A number of the martyrdoms of Saint-Père take forms similar to those in the Tours glazing or in other High Gothic monuments (Annunciation, John the Baptist, Stephen, Vincent, Eustace). A disturbing handful, on the other hand, do not. The Nativity and the martyrdom of Paul are shown in earlier formats, which had been superseded by ca. 1300 by newer types in French art. The martyrdoms of Lawrence and Andrew contain irregular details not in the mainstream of French iconographic usage. The Bartholomew medallion is the most clearly non-French of the series.

Much more significant, however, is the program itself. The combination of angels with crowns, the Annunciation and Nativity and saints' martyrdoms is strongly suggestive of a medium other than stained glass. Not only the program, however, indicates this, but the economical and concentrated, almost emblematic, form of the scenes. The Tours and Angers medallions which have been referred to in comparison, in all cases include the usual auxiliary figures (such as crowned, enthroned tyrants observing, extra executioners, and witnesses).

The martyrdom series of the Saint-Père hemicycle, it can be said, is atypical for its medium, for its date, and for its location high up in the clerestory. It is atypical precisely because it is a more closely-knit, coherent series in subject matter than is customary in tracery lights of clerestories of *any* date, but particularly of transitional or fourteenth-century glass ensembles. The artist has united, by subject matter, the tracery lights across all the hemicycle. The effect achieved iconographically is therefore, in a general sense, similar to that often achieved in glass of the same period by stylistic means: i.e., a horizontal "banding" which reads across parts of several windows, thereby breaking up the internal unity within the bay which was more typical of the earlier period. Tracery lights (and particularly those under the high vaulting of the church) were not ordinarily considered important enough for such a full treatment; in fact, they are often filled with grisailles or isolated subjects by lesser craftsmen. In sum, Saint-Père is, inexplicably, a carefully organized and precisely, even tightly drawn set of images particularly unsuited for its position in the uppermost lights of a very tall chevet. It is not, in a phrase, a glazier's "solution," as a comparison with the Parisian narrative windows of the Tours clerestory underlines without doubt.

We have evidence, it seems clear, of the use of a model from another medium. What medium, what sort of object? Presumably portable, an ecclesiastical object which depicts a similar conjunction of subjects — the combination of Infancy scenes with saints' martyrdoms and crown-bearing angels — in a similarly abbreviated, emblematic fashion and probably in a medallion format. Psalters, particularly those of the archaizing Liégeois group[55] of the second half of the thirteenth century (see for example Pl. 94), frequently couple scenes of Christ's life with saints' martyrdoms. In addition, the Liège group places the martyrdoms in medallion borders.

Copes of the type produced in Eastern France from the third quarter of the thirteenth century present an alternative hypothesis. These copes, from the Verdun or Lyon region, combine roundels or quatrefoils filled with Infancy (and Passion) scenes with martyrdoms, and include as well many forms of angels, some bearing crowns. The technique and very probably much of the iconographic detail of this group were absorbed from *opus anglicanum,* of which the French copes are early continental imitations. All scenes are depicted in simplified, tableau-like forms which befit the medium. An example would be the Uppsala cope of ca. 1270 (Pls. 91–93), containing thirty medallions of martyrdoms including those of Peter (nailed with symmetrical executioners), Paul, John the Baptist, Stephen (one stoner), Lawrence, Andrew, and Bartholomew (on the ground) as well as the repeated motif of an angel holding two crowns.[56]

Did the acquisition of a luxurious new cope — or perhaps the gift of an impressively decorated manuscript[57] — inspire the programming of the Saint-Père tracery lights? The question finds no sure answer. What remains from iconographic sleuthing is only meager, but undeniable, evidence of a strong guiding spirit, a skillful and adaptable artist, and an atypical model of foreign influence.

NOTES

1. Christ's Incarnation is the core of the lancet program below as well, the axial bay presenting the Virgin and Child, and the Crucifixion with Mary and John.

2 Zone 4 of the south rose, Notre-Dame, has two medallions of angels carrying two crowns (Grodecki and Lafond, CVMA France I, pl. 12 [H19]). Many of the tracery lights of the choir clerestory of Le Mans, a monument combining stained glass of Parisian and Western influences, also contain the angel motif. See also the manuscript of the Vita S. Dionysii, Bibl. Nat. nouv. acq. fr. 1098, fol. 34r (dated 1250, from Abbey of Saint-Denis); and the Sainte-Chapelle dado.

3. See Grodecki and Lafond, CVMA France I, p. 54 and fn. 6.

4. Note especially the martyrdoms included among the amorphous subjects of the clerestory tracery of Saint-Urbain de Troyes. It has, however, been heavily restored.

5. The quatrefoil contains a simple rosette design inserted during the ca. 1905 restorations. Photograph taken before restoration shows confused debris in the light (Pl. 11).

6. Illustrated in Marcel Aubert, *French Cathedral Windows,* pl. V. The window is dated ca. 1145. Note the draped bed, which is retained at Saint-Père.

7. The latter type apparently derives ultimately from the frescoes of the porticus, Basilica of St. Peter (see Cod. Barb. lat. 2733, fol. 138, illustrated in Josef Wilpert, *Die romischen Mosaiken und Malereien der kirchlichen Bauten* . . . [Freiburg, 1917], text vol., fig. 140).

8. French examples of Paul blindfolded: Poitiers Crucifixion window (ca. 1165); Chartres, Bay 32, central apse (Delaporte and Houvet, Plates I, pl. LXXXVIII); Rouen, thirteenth-century sacristy window, in Georges Ritter, *Les Vitraux de la Cathédrale de Rouen* (Cognac, 1926), pl. XXVI. Paul with head already severed: 1317 manuscript of the life of St. Denis, Bibl. Nat. ms. fr. 2090–92, II, fol. 64v (illustrated in H. Martin, *Légende de Saint Denis* [Paris, 1905], pl. XXV). The late thirteenth-century English "Huth" psalter (Brit. Mus. Add. 38116, fol. 12v, illustrated in Burlington Fine Arts Club, *Exhibition of Illuminated Manuscripts* [London, 1908], pl. 42) also shows Paul blindfolded.

9. See: Lyon window (1181–1192) (illustrated in Lucien Bégule, *Les vitraux du moyen âge . . . dans la région lyonnaise* [Paris, 1911], fig. 14); Troyes Cathedral, ambulatory chapels ca. 1240's; early thirteenth-century Latin Moralized Bible (Ile-de-France), Oxford, Bodleian, 270b, fol. 121v.

10. Emile Mâle, *Les saints compagnons du Christ* (Paris, 1958), p. 107, states flatly that this was French practice. Réau (v.3, pt. 3, p. 1097), in surveying international medieval practice, draws the overly hasty conclusion that both nails and cords were used with no special national formulae evolving.

11. Tony Sauvel, "Le crucifiement de Saint Pierre," *Bulletin monumental,* XC (1938), pp. 337–352.

12. The saint was shown already having been nailed to the cross by one executioner (Cod. Barb. lat. 2732, fol. 75v, in Wilpert, p. 399, fig. 136). Cf. frescoes of porticus, Old St. Peter's (Cod. Barb. lat. 2733, fol. 137, in Wilpert, fig. 139), where Peter is shown, having been nailed to the cross, but no executioners are included. Italian art continued to omit the executioners.

13. Bibl. Nat. ms. lat. 9428, fol. 86r (illustrated in Sauvel, p. 341). It should also be mentioned that the "asymmetrical" type seems to be described in the Byzantine Guide to Painting published by A. N. Didron, *Christian Iconography* (New York, 1968, reprinting 1st ed.), II, p. 367: "some nail his hands, others his feet."

14. Brit. Mus. Add. 49598.

15. This group differs from the Benedictional of St. Aethelwold in that it depicts executioners nailing, while the manuscript shows executioners tying an already nailed Peter. Examples: (a) capital, cloister of Moissac, ca. 1100; (b) capital from Saint-Pierre-des-Cuisines; (c) capital, church of Duravel (Lot). Sauvel, pp. 345ff.

16. The Aquitaine group depicts executioners in the same placement (symmetrically), but in a less realistic, more symbolic manner. Examples: (a) tympanum reliefs, Aulnay-de-Saintonge; (b) relief, Pont-l'Abbé-d'Arnoult (Charente-Inf.). Both examples date second half of the twelfth century. In addition, one should mention fragments of the Crucifixion of St. Peter in frescoes at Tavant (one executioner visible, nailing) and at Nohant-Vicq (the hands have nail wounds; two standing executioners attach the feet with a rope). There is also an example in Norman Sicily, in the mosaics of Monreale (symmetrical executioners nailing). This mosaic is one of the subjects found at Monreale but not in the more Byzantine series of the Palatinate Chapel. See Otto Demus, *The Mosaics of Norman Sicily* (London, 1949), pl. 81A, p. 299.

17. Sauvel (pp. 350–351) includes the Poitiers window with examples from Aquitaine, but remarks that it is very original.

18. Illustrated in: Bourassé and Manceau, pl. X; Boissonnot, pl. VI (colored drawing).

19. In a few French thirteenth-century examples the executioner merely touches the saint's head. See: (a) Clermont-Ferrand window, illustrated in Henri du Ranquet, *Les vitraux de la cathédrale de Clermont-Ferrand* (Clermont-Ferrand, 1932), color drawing opp. p. 132); (b) Rouen Cathedral, St. John chapel (Ritter, pl. II).

20. A maniple is found (for the first time?) in the Huntingfield Psalter, Pierpont Morgan 43, fol. 28r (English, late twelfth century or ca. 1200). By the second half of the thirteenth century, it is a standard feature of French art.

21. It remained viable even after the vogue of Pucelle's sophisticated variation.

22. See Chartres, south porch, martyrs' portal; tympana at Bourges, Notre-Dame de Paris, Mantes, and Reims.

23. See Chartres, Bay 41 (north apse) Delaporte and Houvet, II, pl. CXX) and Bay 170 (north nave) (III, pl. CCLXXI).

24. Flemish and German manuscripts occasionally maintain the "framing" stoners in the late thirteenth century. See, for example, antiphonary executed in 1290 for Cistercian convent in Beaupré (near Grammont, Belgium), Walters Art Gallery, ms. 757–760, III, fol. 125v (Eric George Millar, *The Library of A. Chester Beatty: A Descriptive Catalogue of the Western Manuscripts* [Oxford, 1927–1930], text vol. II, esp. p. 101).

25. Bourassé and Manceau, pl. XIV. One of the figures carries a pole. See also a window from Saint-Germain-des-Prés: Philippe Verdier, *Walters Art Gallery Bulletin,* XIII (1961), no. 5, fig. 23 (p. 61). The saint is regularly shrouded in earlier examples; see Bourges, window in St. Philomena Chapel, illustrated in Martin and Cahier, pl. XIV, and Clement and Guitard, pl. XIX. The earliest example known to me of a shroudless Vincent is the late-twelfth-century bas-relief at Basle, illustrated in Joseph Gantner, *Kunstgeschichte der Schweiz von den anfängen bis zum beginn des 20 jahrhunderts* (Frauenfeld and Leipzig, 1936), I, fig. 184.

26. Bourassé and Manceau, pl. I. For another example see Chartres, Bay 112, south choir clerestory (Delaporte and Houvet, III, pl. XXCC), in which the saint is shown already in the water.

27. Chartres, Bay 121 (north nave clerestory) Delaporte and Houvet, III, pl. CCLXXI); the saint is tied to the grill. See also the Troyes cope, discussed in this chapter, fns. 52 and 56.

28. Chartres Cathedral also contains two examples of the more unusual triangular grill, on pier I of the south porch and in Bay 47, north choir (Delaporte and Houvet, II, pl. CXLI). A variant of the triangular type at Bourges (St. Philomena Chapel) supports the saint tied face

downward (Clement and Guitard, pl. XVII). Could this medallion be misplaced from the Vincent window in the same chapel? Vincent is the saint usually grilled on his stomach. Cf. martyrdom of St. Vincent panel from Saint-Denis (illustrated in *VF,* p. 94).

29. The motif appears as early as Moissac in France: cloister, Gall. D, capital 6, illustrated in Meyer Schapiro, "The Romanesque Sculpture of Moissac," *Art Bulletin,* XIII (1931), fig. 51, p. 306.

30. Hayward and Grodecki, fig. on p. 40.

31. An early English example is the twelfth-century font at Cottam (Yorkshire); see also the Halberstadt cope-fragment, third quarter of the thirteenth century, possibly an Eastern French copy of *opus anglicanum,* Christie, pl. XXXVI and p. 81. The Troyes cope example also has no bellowsman, although it is damaged and therefore inconclusive evidence. See fns. 52 and 56, this chapter.

32. Brit. Mus., Roy 2B VII, fols. 240r, 253r, 261, and others.

33. Brussels, Musée des arts décoratifs (illustrated in Louis de Farcy, *La Broderie du XIe siècle jusqu'à nos jours* [Paris and Angers, 1890–1900], II, pl. 39 [top right]). See also M. Crick-Kantziger, "Nouvelles installations . . .," *Bulletin des Musées Royaux d'art et d'histoire de Belgique,* XVII (1945), pp. 92–93.

34. Speculation on the identity of the lost saint of Bay 5 and the two lost from Bay 7 is pointless. See Chapter VI, fn. 3. Popular martyrs of the medieval church not found now at Saint-Père include Sebastian, George, Christopher, and Blaise.

35. The medallion is mounted incorrectly in the photomontage of Bay 5 in the *Archives photographiques* with Andrew upside-down and the executioners sideways. It is correctly placed in the church itself.

36. Italian art maintains the upright cross throughout the medieval period. See also Königsfelden.

37. The upside-down cross, found rarely in French thirteenth- and fourteenth-century manuscripts, occurs previously in the Menologium manuscript in Jerusalem, Lib. Greek Patriarchs, Saba 208, fol. 91r (eleventh–twelfth century).

38. The "oblique" cross seems to have been a short-lived variant introduced in the fourteenth century at the time when the search for distinctive attributes also began to popularize the saltire cross. The "oblique" cross occurs in an early fourteenth-century breviary executed for the monastery of S. Vaast of Arras (Arras, Bibl. mun., ms. 729, I, fol. 12r) (illustrated in: Georg Vitzthum von Eckstädt, *Die Pariser miniaturmalerei* [Leipzig, 1907], pl. XXIX); and in the fourteenth-century nave windows of the Florentius Church in Niederhaslach (Bas-Rhin).

39. Iconographers formerly dated the introduction of the saltire (i.e., transverse or "St. Andrew") cross in the fourteenth century. It is much more ancient. Fourteenth-century examples outside France are numerous. With rare exceptions, however, the saltire cross does appear to have been unknown in the Ile-de-France until quite late. Exceptions: (a) 1300–1320 manuscript of *Légende dorée,* Bibl. Nat. ms. fr. 183, fol. 106; (b) missal from the Sainte-Chapelle, end of thirteenth century (Lyon, Bibl. mun., ms. 5122, fol. 208r). Not so in Eastern France, where examples from the second half of the thirteenth century occur at Lyon (apse clerestory window, illustrated in Bégule, fig. 58); at Saint-Urbain de Troyes (Bay I, clerestory, tracery rondel); and in the archivolts of Auxerre, central portal. Evidence indicates an origin in Scotland and probable dissemination via pilgrimage badges. In the Edinburgh National Museum is the stone mold for a pilgrim's badge of very primitive design (from cemetery of St. Andrew's Church, North Berwick, East Lothian). The saltire cross appears next in the twelfth century in Yorkshire (font of Cottam Church, East Riding, illustrated — and incorrectly identified — in John Piper, "England's Early Sculptors," *Architectural Review* [England], LXXX [1936], pl. II opp. p. 160). It appears ca. 1250 in a fresco in Winchester (pl. 55 of E. W. Tristram, *English Medieval Wall*

Painting, the Thirteenth Century [London, 1950]); and ca. 1270 in the Oscott Psalter, Brit. Mus. Add. 5000, fol. 8v (Florens Deuchler, *Gothic Art* [New York, 1973], pl. 151). An example in Oxford (Merton College Chapel, window) dates in the second half of the thirteenth century. The motif apparently crossed the channel on threads of *opus anglicanum,* although only later, circumstantial proof for this theory exists: (a) cope fragment, Steeple Aston Church, 1310–1340 (Christie, pls. CXIV, CXVI–CXVIII, fig. 134); (b) Syon cope, first quarter fourteenth century; (c) *opus anglicanum* orphrey vestments from Harlebeke, Belgium, now in Brussels Musée des arts décoratifs (illus. in Christie, pl. CXLV). See also antiphonary from Beaupré (Schoonwert, near Grammont, Belgium) dated 1290 (Baltimore, Walters Art Gallery, mss. 757–760, II, fol. 185r). The extremely early manuscript example mentioned by Réau and identified by Lafond (CVMA France IV, p. 79, fn. 3), the Autun troper, Bibl. Arsenal, ms. 1169, dated 996–1024, remains to be investigated. The subject does not appear, however, among the miniatures of this manuscript listed by Henry Martin, *Catalogue des manuscrits de la Bibliothèque de l'Arsenal,* II (Paris, 1886), p. 321.

40. See, for example, Troyes window, ca. 1225–1235 (ambulatory chapel). On the topic of Andrew's horizontal cross, see Lafond, "Normandie," p. 345 (note carried from preceding page); and Emile Mâle, "Histoire et légende de l'apôtre saint André dans l'art," *Revue des deux-mondes* (October, 1951), pp. 412–420, esp. p. 415.

41. Réau (III, pt. 1, p. 79) also mentions a psalter from Cîteaux, eleventh-century (sic), which is undoubtedly the psalter in Besançon, ms. 54, fol. 22 (illustrated in Mâle, *Saints compagnons,* p. 129).

42. For example: Liège psalter, Pierpont Morgan 183, fol. 12v (see Pl. 94); breviary of second half of the thirteenth century, probably given to the Abbey of Tennenbach (Lucerne, Kantonsbibl., PMsc.4, fol 228v).

43. Examples in stained glass: Chartres, Bay 33, central apse (Delaporte and Houvet, I, pl. XCI); Tours, ca. 1245 (illustrated in *VF,* p. 157); Angers, Bay 9, debris (one figure crouches below head, one below feet, three others standing?); Evreux, late thirteenth century (illustrated in Lafond, "Normandie," fig. opp. p. 344).

44. The Uppsala cope, dated before 1274, is an eastern French imitation of *opus anglicanum.* See: Agnes Geijer, *Textile Treasures of Uppsala Cathedral* (Stockholm, 1964), pp. 23–25; Geijer, "Broderies françaises datées, conservées en Suède," *Les monuments historiques de la France,* XII (1966), pp. 55ff.; Geijer, "Broderies françaises du haut gothique conservées en Suède," in *Festschrift Ulrich Middleldorf* (Berlin, 1968), pp. 32–38; Christie, no. 45, pp. 79–81 and pls. XXXII–XXXV. It is now generally recognized that the Uppsala cope was made in France, perhaps in Lyon. The same iconographic formula occurs in stained glass of Lyon Cathedral. See also: (a) Cluniac breviary, ca. 1300, in Andrew Lang collection, London, illustrated in Burlington Fine Arts Club, 1908 catalog, pl. 84 [#127] and p. 58; and (b) Benedictine breviary from Cambrai, Abbey of Saint-Sépulchre (Cambrai, ms. 102–103, fol. 354r, dated 1295–1296, discussed by Lilian Randall, "The Fieschi Psalter," *Walters Art Gallery Journal,* XXIII [1960], p. 34).

45. See Bibl. Vaticana, ms. gr. 1613, p. 53 (dated 976–1025) and Brit. Mus. Add. 11870, fol. 151r (eleventh–twelfth centuries).

46. Etienne Houvet, *La cathédrale de Chartres* (Chelles, 1919), IV (Portail sud), pt. 2, pl. 67.

47. Delaporte and Houvet, II, pl. CLXXIV.

48. Bourassé and Manceau, pl. I. The nude family is shown in a bunch. A tyrant and executioners appear in the adjacent medallion.

49. Cluny Museum (illustrated in *Le Musée de Cluny,* photocollographie de Chène et Longuet [Paris, 1895–1897], I, pl. 39 [top]). A standing tyrant and a bellowsman are included.

50. This is strange considering that Bartholomew's knife was one of the most stable of apostles' attributes and one of the earliest to emerge.

51. The photomontage of Bay 6 is labeled "St. Apollinaire sur le chevalet." Most guidebooks rely on Bulteau, p. 297.

52. The group has two distinct branches, the earlier being a group of Moralized Bibles of French origin, and the other a number of English works of art in various media. Moralized Bibles: (a) example from Saint-Germain-des-Prés library, first half of the thirteenth century, Bibl. Nat. ms. lat. 11560, fol. 95v; (b) example in French dialect of eastern Champagne, thirteenth–fourteenth centuries, Vienna, Nat.-Bibl. 2554, fol. 27r; (c) example of early fourteenth century, Bibl. Nat. ms. fr. 9561, fol. 78v. English objects or objects of English influence: (a) late thirteenth-century psalter, Brit. Mus. Add. 21926, fol. 11v (Exeter?); (b) English alabaster relief, ca. 1400, Ashmolean Museum; (c and d) Uppsala and Troyes copes, ca. 1275, probably Eastern French copies of *opus anglicanum.* For the Uppsala cope, see fn. 44 supra and Pl. 91, where the scene of St. Bartholomew's flaying is on the right directly below the crucifixion of St. Andrew (horizontal type). For the Troyes cope, see fn. 56 infra; also Jean Taralon, *Les trésors des églises de France,* Musée des arts décoratifs (Paris, 1965), p. 92 and pl. 157; Philippe Verdier, *Art and the Courts, France and England from 1259 to 1328,* National Gallery of Canada (Ottawa, 1972), no. 87 and pp. 165–166. Other examples of *opus anglicanum* could also be cited, and it is reasonable to assume that the two copes of French manufacture reproduced English models.

53. For example, (a) Pierpont Morgan 183, fol. 12v (see Pl. 94); (b) Liège, Bibl. de l'Université 431, fol. 10v, dated 1255–1260 (illustrated in Joseph Brassinne, *Psautier liégeois du XIIIe siècle* [Brussels, 1923], pl. 16).

54. The earliest German example is the "Psalter of S. Elizabeth," dated 1200–1217 and probably executed in the monastery of Reinharsbrun, Mainz (Cividale, Mus. Archeologico CXXXVII, fol. 5r; discussed in Italia, Ministero della pubblica istruzione, *Mostra storica nazionale della miniatura* [Palazzo di Venezia, Rome, catalogue], 2nd ed. [1954], pp. 109–110, #152). English examples include (a) Oxford, Bodleian, Auct. D.4.2, fol. 72v [thirteenth–fourteenth centuries]; and (b) Luttrell Psalter, Brit. Mus. Add. 42130, fol. 107r (ca. 1340) (illustrated in Eric George Millar, *The Luttrell Psalter* [London, 1932], pl. 40c).

55. On Liégeois psalters, see Brassinne, as well as Burlington Fine Arts Club, pp. 57, 68–69. On fol. 8v of one of the earliest (Liège, Bibl. de l'Univ. 431), the Annunciation and Nativity and two other Infancy scenes are surrounded by martyrdom medallions including those of Peter (tied), Paul and John the Baptist. Fol. 10v shows four scenes, including a Crucifixion with Mary and John, encircled by medallions including the martyrdoms of Bartholomew (trestle and checkered loincloth) and Lawrence (bellowsman). Similar notable examples can be found in another psalter of the group, Pierpont Morgan 183 (cf. fols. 9v, 11v, 12v). The group is presumed to have been copied from a mid-twelfth-century psalter of Lambert le Bègue, for use by the Béguines, a circumstance which would explain the retention of earlier iconographic forms in many cases. See the Columbia dissertation (1976) by Judith Oliver, "The 'Lambert-le-Bègue' Psalters: A Study in Thirteenth Century Mosan Illumination."

56. The Halberstadt cope-fragment includes angels and medallions of martyrdoms and scenes of the life of Christ (Christie pl. XXXVI). The Troyes cope is formed of forty-nine quatrefoils of angels, Infancy scenes, and martyrdoms. Although Taralon (*Trésors,* p. 92) seems to indicate that the Troyes cope could be English work, the saints included are clearly French: Denis, Eustace, Blaise, Léger. It is probably a case, like that of the Uppsala cope, of French imitation of English workmanship (even the faces have an English cast to the features). (See Charles Ledit, "Le samit de Troyes," *Zodiaque,* LXVII [1966], p. 1 — the only illustration of the front of the cope, which is damaged.)

57. Liégeois psalters were made in most cases for lay-women, often wealthy. If Saint-Père had such a book, a patronness is indicated.

{ CHAPTER X }

Nave: Standing Figures—Iconography

HALF of the twelve great bays of the nave are fitted out with large, standing saints, arranged four to a window. The six bays which comprise this aggregation alternate strictly with the six color-saturated narratives, giving a slower and more ponderous rhythm to the nave. The iconographic organization of the standing saints, moreover, is fairly rigid, apostles taking their places in the three northern bays (Bays 20, 24 and 28), abbots (Bay 29), bishops (Bay 25), and popes (Bay 21) in the windows on the south. The whole repeats the energetic message of the hemicycle, in a more structured polyphony and a more ceremonial tempo.

Many of the saints retain inscriptions, and the apostles among them bear attributes as well. Precisely the same transitional uncertainty that was evidenced in the identifications in the hemicycle is found among the nave apostles. The artist's (or iconographer's) intentions, however, are clearer in the nave, where both attributes and beautiful Lombardic name-inscriptions are lavished on the apostle group. The confusions are therefore the more evident. Whereas one can only guess about the artist's plan in the hemicycle, inscriptions in the nave make the program clearly evident, and the success or failure of its execution easily gauged.

THE APOSTLES IN THE NORTH NAVE

The twelve apostle-figures are as follows (top to bottom, left lancet first).

Bay 20: PHELIPPE, THOMAS, JACOBVS, MACIEV (Pl .55)

They carry, at present, a pike, bare sword,[1] ax and sheathed sword. It seems highly probable that the upper two figures (Philip and James) have been interchanged with the lower two (Thomas and Matthew).[2] If so, the attributes originally would have been: Philip with a bare sword, Thomas with a lance or pike, James with a sheathed sword, and Matthew with an ax — all quite standard for the thirteenth century, except that Matthew's ax would be slightly precocious. The most likely period of an accidental interchange of panels was the late seventeenth century at the time when, in the course of restoration, this bay and Bay 21 opposite (Pl. 57) were "improved" by having their colored diaper framing panels (still visible at the tops of the lancets) replaced with clear glass.[3]

Bay 24: IOHANNES EVANGELISTE, ANDREAS, JACOBVS, BARTHOLEMEVS (Pls. 72, 74)

John with a palm,[4] Andrew with a Latin cross, James with a club, Bartholomew with a knife. Andrew's cross and Bartholomew's knife were among the earliest attributes to be defined. The Latin form of the cross follows customary thirteenth-century French practice. The palm of paradise was a short-lived attribute of John, uncommon by the turn of the fourteenth century. The source is clearly Pseudo-Melito, "De Transitu Beatae Mariae," an apocryphal legend of the Virgin's Assumption, in which John carries the palm given to her at the annunciation of her death.[5]

The club was common to James the Less and to Judas Thaddeus, but on rare occasions given to James the Greater, probably in confusion with his more usual (for ca. 1300) pilgrim's staff. Which saint is here intended? Clearly the latter; the window has a border of his shells in both lancets.[6]

Bay 28: MATHIAS, JACO_VS MINO_,[7] IVDAS, BARNABAS (Pls. X, 83)

Matthias holds a bare sword by the point, James the Less holds a staff, Judas holds a rope, and Barnabas has a yellow flame. This window is by far the most interesting of the series for the study of attributes "in the making," as it contains apostles who were less well known and not so frequently represented. Matthias, the apostle called to replace the Lord's betrayer in the original twelve, customarily relinquishes his place in medieval series to Paul. His attribute never really crystallized, and he can be found holding an ax, halberd, lance, or sword. James the Less is holding the staff, which, by the late thirteenth century, was becoming one of the common, pilgrim attributes of James the Greater.[8] Undoubtedly confused by the shifting iconography of his time, the Saint-Père artist has provided in the nave a full complement of Jameses: a James with sheathed sword in Bay 20 (Pl. 55) (an early-thirteenth-century attribute); a James with club, in a border of shells, in Bay 24 (Pl. 72) (the club being the developing attribute throughout the thirteenth century for James the Less); and a James the Less in Bay 28 (Pl. 83) holding the staff, which was coming into vogue as part of the pilgrim's garb adopted for James the Greater by the final decades of the thirteenth century.

Barnabas was, like Matthias, a rarity in apostle circles. Not a member of the original twelve but attached to them as a kind of deputy, he suffered martyrdom by stoning and being burned. His attribute in the Bourges and Chartres[9] clerestories is merely a book; in the fourteenth century he occasionally carried stones.[10] Reference to fire or flames is more unusual.[11] A specialty of the later Western school of glass-painting, Barnabas with a flame is found at Vendôme and Evron (Pl. 90) as well as twice in Saint-Père (Pls. 10, 83).[12] It occurs later in Normandy, at Saint-Ouen de Rouen (ca. 1325ff.).[13] The local popularity of Barnabas is difficult to account for, and his flame may have been a happy invention of a Western artist or iconographer, based on a text such as Voragine.

The Judas with a rope (Pl. X) is perhaps another invention, and a more startling one. The attribute is very unusual, one can even say unique. The clerestories of Saint-Ouen de Rouen include a St. Mark holding a rope, the only other known example of this attribute.[14] There is textual basis for the latter, as, before his martyrdom, the evangelist was dragged through the streets of Alexandria by a rope around his neck.[15] Judas Thaddeus, on the other hand, had no connection with a rope and is never shown with one. Who is it, then?

Astonishing as it may seem, the "IVDAS" in the Saint-Père nave is probably Judas Iscariot. Judas Iscariot was hanged by a rope, and the depiction of his hanging (Matthew, XXVII:5, Acts I:18) was enormously popular in medieval art.[16] The insignia later became crystallized in at least two Italian manuscripts of the fourteenth century in which Judas, at the knees of the personification Hope (Spes), appears with a piece of rope around his neck.[17]

The confusion of Judas Iscariot with Judas Thaddeus was probably not unknown in early Gothic art, nor was the confusion concerning the identity, as a single individual, of the duo-named Judas Thaddeus. The simplest proof of the latter issue is the occasional practice of including both a "Judas" figure and a "Thaddeus" figure in apostle groups, the former often being the one accompanying Simon.[18] Choosing only from apostle groups in media where inscriptions were used at an early date (i.e., ivories, reliquaries, embroideries), it is possible to cite the following list where the two names (usually rendered as Ivdas and Thadevs) are borne by two separate figures:

(a) Chasuble of St. Etienne and of Queen Gisela, Budapest National Museum (eleventh century): IVDAS, SIMON, TADEVS, etc.[19]

(b) Ivory casket, Turin, Sabauda Gallery (twelfth–thirteenth century): SIVDAS (next to Simon), STADEVS (between Philip and Barnabas).[20]

(c) Metal reliquary casket of St. Honoratus, treasury of Servatius church, Siegburg, Cologne, ca. 1200:[21] IVDAS (next to Simon), IUDEUS(?) (between James and Matthew).

(d) Ivory casket from Cologne, Louvre, 1200–1250:[22] IVdAS (next to Simon), THAdEVS (between James and Barnabas).

(e) Ivory casket, Leningrad, Hermitage Museum, 1200–1250:[23] IVdAS (next to Simon), TAdEVS (between Matthew and Barnabas).

(f) Portable walrus-ivory altar, Rhenish (Cologne), Cleveland Museum of Art (ca. 1200 or before):[24] S̃CSIVDAS and SC̃ƌV̲DAS.

(g) Portable enamel altar ("altar of Gregory"), from the Abbey of Siegburg (twelfth century):[25] IVDAS (between Matthias and Matthew); THADEV' (next to Simon).

(h) Embroidered cope-fragment, Steeple Aston church, 1310–1340:[26] THADE (next to John, on section 2), IVDA (on section 3).

In relating the above confusions to Saint-Père, it should be remembered that the apostle group of the nave is quite amorphous and, in this way, typical for its date. It comprises twelve saints, but among them are a Barnabas and a Matthias, and three Jameses. There is no Simon, no Peter (no Paul either).

I would like to suggest sources for the iconographer's choice of apostles, both literary and visual. That the confusion of the "two Judases" lasted through the thirteenth century is witnessed not only by the *opus anglicanum* cope listed above (h) but from the litany in a Liégeois psalter (Bibl. Nat. ms. lat. 1077, fol. 142v) listing "Sce Thadee" (after Simon) and "Sce Juda" (between Luke and Barnabas). I have suggested at the end of Chapter IX that such a cope or a psalter provided ideas for the hemicycle windows. Also possible is the influence of some Byzantine art work in the Saint-Père treasury, containing the so-called "historical series" of apostles. This group includes Matthias and also, with a halo, Judas Iscariot.[27] The halo of Judas finds no more reasonable explanation.

In choosing attributes for the apostles thus chosen, the artist was a man of his time, straining for precision and individualization at a period when there was as yet no rubric to consult. He adopted the few which had already become traditional: Bartholomew's knife, Andrew's cross. He followed current trends, some of which were to enjoy only a brief vogue: John's palm, Thomas's lance, Matthew's ax (assuming as suggested earlier that the apostles of Bay 20 were originally interchanged, the attributes being completely chaotic otherwise). He embalms at least one attribute which was *retardataire* by ca. 1300: James's sheathed sword (Philip with a sword could also be placed in this category). Matthew's ax, on the other hand, is precocious for the date. The confusion of Jameses is total: two of them carry a sword and a club, while the one specifically labeled James the Less has a staff (a minimal nod given to the crystallized James-Pilgrim iconography, and here bestowed upon the wrong James).

The Saint-Père glaziers demonstrably worked from manuscript sources in other windows, and it seems likely that the rope attribute created for Saint Judas was suggested by a miniature of Judas Hanged, perhaps one in a Liège psalter (see fn. 16).

THE SAINTS IN THE SOUTH NAVE

The ecclesiastical saints in the three southern bays of the nave carry no attributes and often have no inscriptions.

Bay 21: Two pope-saints (S GREGORI, S SILVESTER), Virgin and Child, donor Laurent Voisin (Pls. VII, 57)

Bay 21 is the only window on the south where all of the figures are still identifiable, as well as being the only one to include divergent subject matter. The saints are Popes Gregory and Silvester; the other figures are the Virgin and Child, and a kneeling donor, the Canon Laurent Voisin.

The papal saint S GREGORI (Pl. VII) may be Gregory VII (1073–1085) rather than the Church Father, who is more frequently identified by a dove on his shoulder. Gregory VII was the pope to whom St. Gilduin, the abbey's patron, journeyed to decline his bishopric. Gregory VII's inclusion here would therefore imply a connection similar to that between Sts. Clement and Denis in Bay 23. It is also conceivable that a political theme was invoked. A Cluniac, Gregory VII was the pope who humbled Henry IV at Canossa in 1077,[28] the lesson of which the Capetians never forgot. It is impossible to say at what precise moment in the decade of Philippe-le-Bel's bullying of Clement V this kind of political flattery would have been appropriate, however.

Although proof is lacking, the otherwise surprising choice of S SILVESTER as the other pope-saint could possibly be another such political maneuver. Silvester's general medieval following, not inconsiderable, is usually assumed to be based upon the accidental fact of his feast falling upon New Year's Eve. He had a particular importance at Chartres, however, where he has been identified among the jambs of the cathedral's Confessors' portal, south transept.[29] He is also depicted in a bas-relief on the Cathedral (south porch, right pier) in the act of baptizing Constantine, the first Christian emperor. The Capetian political mystique had long involved references to Charlemagne,[30] the "New Constantine." Although the hypothesis cannot be refined or substantiated, the odd pairing of Popes Gregory and Silvester could be a subtle reference to the complicated relations between pope, abbey and crown under Philippe-le-Bel: Gregory, who had wished to empower Gilduin; and Silvester, who had empowered the antecedent of the king.

Bay 21 is the only window in the series of nave saints where a donor is shown, and it has been done without breaking the visual pattern. The Canon and the Virgin to whom he prays take their places democratically among the standing saints of the nave. The Canon in fact kneels, although his figure is quite as large and conspicuous as the others.

The inscription behind his head reads: MAGISTER LAVRENCIVS CAPITERIVS CARNOTENSI_.[31] Laurent Voisin was capiterius (chefcier or dean) of the cathedral of Chartres by 1293[32] and died in the winter of 1314–1315.[33] Beneath his feet are depicted two windows of the doublet-and-rose design, a style which was out-of-date long before ca. 1300. They may be taken to be illustrations of the nave windows in which the canon's image is found, possibly an indication that his gift included two windows. If this theory is valid, the second window would unquestionably be Bay 20 across the nave (Pl. 55). Bays 20 and 21 are the only windows of the series of standing saints to be filled originally with colored diaper instead of grisaille framing panels.[34]

Bay 25: Four bishop-saints (S MARTINVS, SEnT LVBIN[35] and two without inscriptions). (Pl. 75)

The two missing names may have been removed when the four late coats of arms now visible in the grisailles were installed. Two of them are the arms of Hélie de Bourdeilles (1423–1484) and the other two those of either François (34th abbot of Saint-Père from 1522–1540) or Christophe de Brilhac (32nd abbot, 1491–1514), all of whom were, at one time in their careers, bishops.[36]

St. Martin of Tours was one of the most popular saints in thirteenth-century France and in medieval art was always shown with a crozier. In Bay 25 he holds a cross-staff rather than the usual crozier, probably a substitution when the heads of the four bishops were replaced during an old restoration. (The cross touches Martin's head.)[37]

St. Lubin was a bishop of Chartres in the sixth century. He is included twice in the cathedral: Bay 63 in the north aisle, given by the tavern-keepers;[38] and a bas-relief on the Confessors' portal, south porch. He was also included in the missal of the usage of Saint-Père discussed in Chapter VI.

The two bishops now incognito might have included St. Nicholas, a bishop-saint beloved in the thirteenth century, who is not otherwise represented in Saint-Père, or any number of local saints such as Piat, Hilaire, Germain[39] or more probably Fulbert,[40] who was buried at Saint-Père near the high altar.

Bay 29: Four abbots, (only one, SEnT MOR, now named). (Pl. 84)

Large standing figures of Maurus are not common even in Benedictine establishments. The extraordinary clarity and legibility of the inscription, considering the heavy damage and restoration throughout the window, makes his identification suspect. It is possible that the inscription was repainted after the abbey joined the Congregation of Saint-Maur in 1650, probably during the restorations to the church fabric and windows undertaken shortly thereafter in 1654–1659.[41] On the other hand, Maurus was included in the missal referred to above (Chartres, Bibl. mun., ms. 519), and in the clerestory windows of Saint-Ouen de Rouen (ca. 1325ff.).

Any conjecture about the identity of the other three abbot-saints would be pure guesswork. One can only presume with some certainty, on the basis of the present confused leading patterns above their heads, that originally they were all named.

The beatified churchmen of the south side of the nave show the same reasoned organization which was evidenced in the apostles group on the north. They were grouped according to their status, and without much doubt they were named. Unfortunately, largely as a result of historical accidents, so few names are left or are reliable that they offer us little insight into the life of the monastery at the time when the windows were designed. The circumstance is to be regretted. A knowledge of which bishop- and abbot-saints rated special veneration by the abbey at the beginning of the fourteenth century might have illuminated a relationship which seems to have emerged between the abbey community and the cathedral at the beginning of the fourteenth century, after a period of strife lasting more than a century.[42] Two canons of the cathedral — Laurent Voisin and Nicolas de Maison-Maugis[43] — contributed heavily toward the glazing of the nave of the abbey-church. The abbot of Saint-Père was one of the executors of Laurent Voisin's will. Lubin, beatified bishop of Chartres Cathedral, is among the nave saints. Evidence of a new and closer relationship between the Abbey of Saint-Père and Chartres Cathedral is tantalizing but also meager.

CONCLUSION

The iconography of the standing figures of the nave is clearly an ordering and patterning of the apsidal chorus. An improvement was probably intended. In the nave the sainted ecclesiastics are arrayed on one side, neatly subdivided into abbots (Bay 29), bishops (Bay 25) and popes (Bay 21), while the apostles are grouped on the other side, facing them. Many of the latter carry not only attributes similar to those shown in the hemicycle, but name-inscriptions as well. In the case of the prelates, who carry no personal attributes, these nave inscriptions, in a handsome "Lombardic," have little relevance to the comparable figures of the hemicycle. One may assume, if one likes, that the anonymous abbot-saints of Bay 6 of the hemicycle include St. Maur, as does nave Bay 29; or that the undefined apsidal bishop and archbishop are Martin and Lubin, as in Bay 25 of the nave. But wishful thinking is the only basis for such assumptions.

In dealing with the two groups of apostles there is a little more evidence to go on: the attributes held in common in both ensembles. It is tempting and probably correct, for example, to assume that St. Barnabas with flame and inscription (Bay 28) copies a St. Barnabas with flame but no inscription in Bay 5 of the hemicycle. A further extension of this sort of analogy is dangerous, however. The iconographic relationship was more probably the following: the nave artists (and patrons) wished to copy and also to clarify the identities of the figures of the hemicycle. They did copy the attributes shown there, some of which had become standard and some of which were becoming archaic in the fast-moving iconography of the time. Then names were bestowed, and it is these names which reveal the same state of iconographic flux and confusion perceptible in the hemicycle. It is disappointing — but realistic — to accept the nave not as the long-lost "key" to the hemicycle (and other ensembles)[44] but as a near-contemporary derivation.

NOTES

1. The bare sword is difficult to see, and is often described in guidebooks as a T-square. See, for example: Jean Villette, *Chartres* (Chartres, 1948), p. 38; Bulteau, p. 294; Clerval (5th ed.), p. 198; Mâle, *XIIIe siècle* 1958 ed., II, p. 303 (chart).

2. The figure panels would be interchangeable but not the inscription panels, the designs of

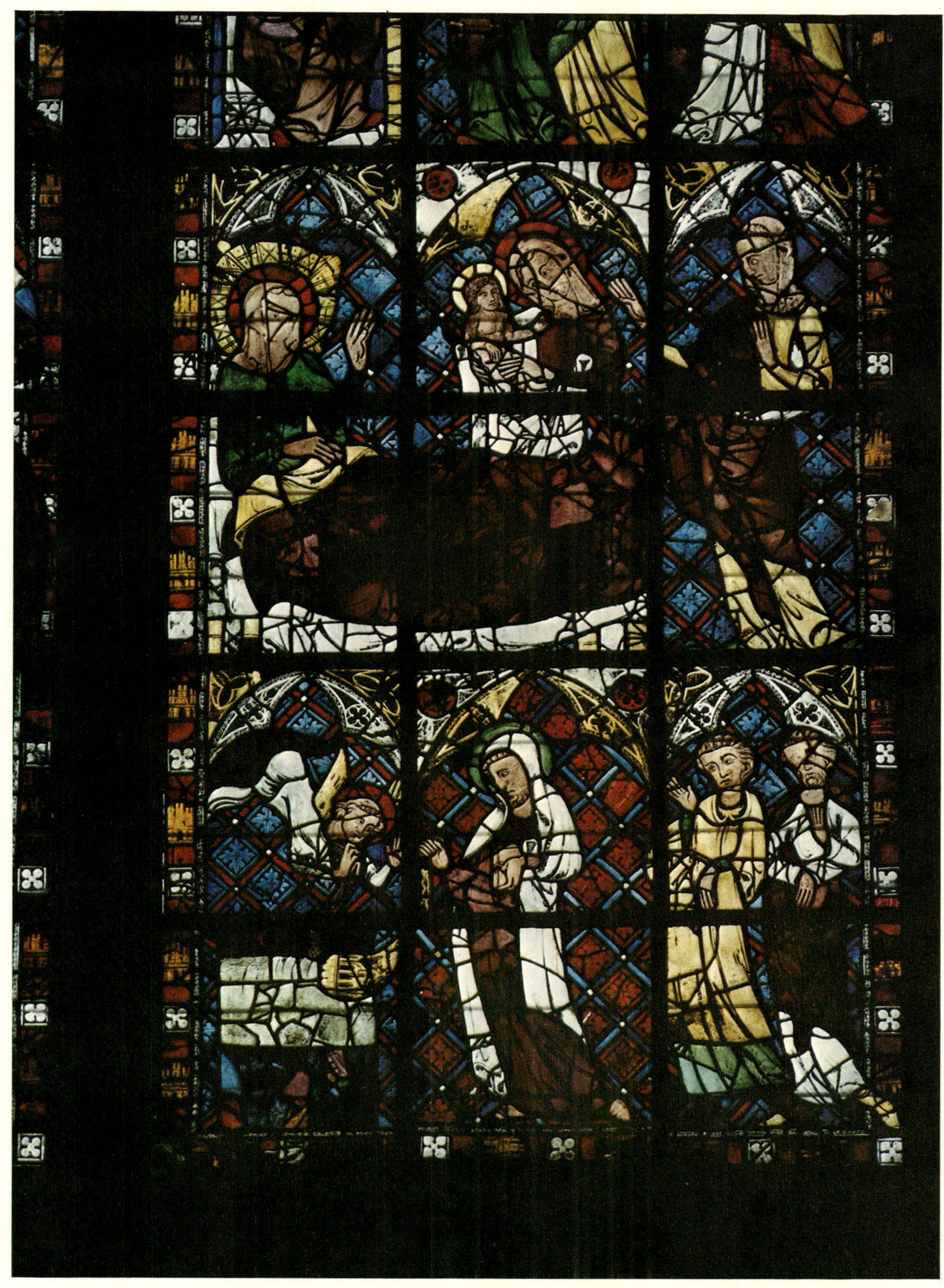

PLATE IX Nave: Bay 26. Baptist window, Annunciation to Zacharias; Nativity of Baptist *(Edouard Fièvet)*

which vary between the upper and lower rows.

3. The diaper was there untouched in 1672, when it was described by Dom Aubert (ch. 90). It was undoubtedly gone by the nineteenth century, notwithstanding Guérard (I, p. cclij), who probably drew his information from the Dom Aubert manuscript rather than from observations *in situ*. Bulteau (1850, p. 293) and Poisson (1857, p. 423) both describe Bays 20 and 21 without diaper. See Chapter I at fn. 29.

4. It has been described erroneously in guidebooks as a pen because of its small size (see Bulteau, p. 294; Clerval [5th ed.], p. 198).

5. The palm is also found in the hemicycle of Saint-Père, Bays 2 and 5 (Pls. 4 and 10). See Chapter VIII, fn. 27.

6. See *VF*, color pl. XVII.

7. This inscription was almost illegible to the spectator in the nineteenth century. Poisson (p. 419) omitted it; he describes Matthias and Barnabas in place, lists the figure in James the Less's place as 'probably S. Jude' and refers to the figure in Judas' position simply as 'another apostle.' Were Judas and James the Less interchanged? The inscriptions must have been mutilated in any case. Note that in this bay the inscriptions occur near the saint's head, not above it as in Bay 20 and elsewhere. Thus, even if the figures were out-of-place, their names would not have been shuffled.

8. See Bourges apostles series; panels possibly from the chapel of Château de Rouen (ca. 1260–1270), in Cluny Museum. St. James has a pilgrim's hat and staff, and shells are set into the ground.

9. For illustration of Chartres see Delaporte and Houvet, III, pl. CCLII.

10. Barnabas with a stone: brass of Albrecht Hövener, 1357, Nikolaus church in Stralsund; brass of Burkhard von Serken in Lübeck Cathedral, ca. 1350; trecento panel (Florentine school?), Vatican Pinacoteca storeroom (see P. d'Achiardi, *I quadri primitivi della Pinacoteca Vaticana* . . . [Rome, 1929], pl. CXXVII).

11. See discussion in Chapter VIII, at fn. 23.

12. See Chapter V.

13. Lafond, CVMA France IV, pl. 66 and p. 227 listing examples. See fn. 14, this chapter.

14. See Lafond, CVMA France IV, p. 227, fn. 6. Saint-Ouen and Saint-Père, both influential Benedictine abbeys in the middle ages, maintained a relationship of fraternity and association in prayer during the thirteenth century. See Brossier-Géray, "Le rouleau mortuaire de Guy Ier, Abbé de Saint-Père de Chartres, 1231," *Bulletin de la Société dunoise,* III (1875–1880), pp. 236–237, which states that Saint-Ouen was among the abbeys entered in the mortuary roll of Guy I (Abbot of Saint-Père 1200–1231). Saint-Ouen also includes another rare attribute found otherwise only in glass of the school of the West, the Barnabas holding a flame (see discussion supra).

15. Drake, p. 83, lists several examples of St. Mark dragged by the neck and strangled. See discussion in Lafond, CVMA France IV, p. 227.

16. Thirteenth-century examples of Judas Hanged: a) Moralized Bible, Bibl. Nat. ms. lat. 11560, fols. 4r, 51v, 221v (first half of the thirteenth century); b) Bible of Bredelar (1238–1241), Darmstadt Landesbibliothek Ms. 824, 825 (Hanns Swarzenski, *Die lateinischen illuminierten handschriften des XIII. Jahrhunderts in den ländern an Rhein, Main und Donau* (Berlin, 1936), pl. 30 [#177]); c) psalter, Liège, Bibl. de l'Univ. 431, fol. 167r (1255–1260); d) psalter (ca. 1295–1304), Cambrai, ms. 102–103; e) Fieschi psalter, Walters Art Gallery, Baltimore, ms. 45, illustration for Psalm 51 (see illustration in Randall, "Fieschi," p. 36 and fig. 5). See Judas Hanged also on the facade of Reims (archivolts of left portal) and at Rouen (tympanum of south portal). Fourteenth-century examples are numerous in almost all media.

17. Judas with a rope around his neck, at the feet of Hope: a) Milan, Bibl. Ambrosiana, B. 42 inf., Giovanni d'Andrea, Novella in libros Decretalium, fol. 1r (dated 1354, miniatures

painted by Niccolò da Bologna) (illustrated in: Paris, Bibl. Nat., *Trésors des bibliothèques d'Italie IVe-XVIe siècles* [Paris, 1950], pl. 10 [no. 108]); b) Vienna, Nat.-Bibl., Ser. Nov. 2639, Convenevoli de Pratis?, Poemata, fol. 2r (fourteenth century).

18. Simon and Judas Thaddeus shared martyrdom and the same feast, October 28. The order of the Canon of the Mass is Matthew, Simon, Judas Thaddeus, Matthias.

19. de Farcy, II, pl. I.

20. Paris, Petit Palais, *Trésors d'Italie* (Paris, 1952), #129. The museum describes it as Rhenish, thirteenth century (Acc. n IN 183).

21. Names inscribed but figures now lost. Otto von Falke and Heinrich Frauberger, *Deutsche Schmelzarbeit des Mittelalters und andere Kunstwerke der Kunsthistorischen Ausstellung zu Düsseldorf,* 1902 (Frankfurt am Main, 1904), pl. 59.

22. Adolph Goldschmidt, *Die elfenbeinskulpturen* (Berlin, 1923), III, pl. XXI (61c); ex coll. Revoil, acq. 1828.

23. Goldschmidt, III, pl. XXIII (64b).

24. Goldschmidt, IV, pl. LXXVI (302d); also William Milliken, "Two Medieval Objects from the Rhineland. . . ," *Cleveland Museum Bulletin,* XIV (1927), pp. 56–63 and figs. 60, 61. The letters are sometimes jumbled or reversed, i.e.,

HEVSTAM (Matthew!)
SAƆV⅃ (Luke)

25. Hermann Schnitzler, *Rheinische Schatzkammer die Romanik* (Düsseldorf, 1959), II, pl. 154; the object is now in the treasury of St. Servatius. Note that, in the case of the other object from Siegburg, (c) supra, it is Ivdas who is next to Simon.

26. Christie, pl. CXV; Donald King, *Opus Anglicanum, English Medieval Embroidery,* Victoria and Albert Museum (London, 1963), p. 36.

27. On the two series of apostles in mature Byzantine art, see Demus, p. 318. To the core group of eight (Peter, James, John, Bartholomew, Philip, Andrew, Thomas, Simon), the "liturgical series" adds Paul, Matthew, Mark, and Luke, while the "historical series" adds James the Less, Matthias, Judas Iscariot, and Thaddeus. On Judas Iscariot shown with a halo in Byzantine art, see Didron, I, p. 156f. For an interesting discussion see Guillaume de Jerphanion, "Quels sont les douze Apôtres dans l'iconographie chrétienne?", *La voix des monuments* (Paris-Brussels, 1930), I, pp. 189ff. In the west Judas Iscariot is haloed (in black) only in Italian painting; see Réau, II, pt. 2, p. 413, as well as Gertrud Schiller, *Iconography of Christian Art* (New York, 1972), II, fig. 105 and p. 38.

28. Philippe le Bel had even been excommunicated in 1303 by Pope Boniface, who died the same year, but by 1311 Clement V's bull *Rex gloriae* wiped that slate clean. On Clement and Philippe see, among many works, the standard by Georges Lizerand, *Clément V et Philippe le Bel* (Paris, 1910). Pope Gregory VII was canonized only in 1606. It was not unknown for a medieval church to represent as haloed, however, religious figures of particular importance to the locale.

29. Yves Delaporte, "Une statue de Saint Sylvestre à la cathédrale de Chartres," *Mémoires de la Societé archéologique d'Eure-et-Loir,* XVIII (1947–1951), esp. p. 63. The Silvester window in Chartres Cathedral was donated by the masons' guild. In Italy, Silvester is often paired with Constantine, as in the Quattro Coronati, Rome, ca. 1246, where the Donation of Constantine is depicted. See also Florence, Santa Croce, the frescoes of Maso di Banco (ca. 1340f.), and his stained glass (G. Marchini, *Italian Stained Glass Windows* [New York, 1956], p. 39, p. 245 fn. 45). The identifications of the jambs of the Notre-Dame Coronation portal as Constantine and St. Silvester have been challenged by William Hinkle, "The King and the Pope on the Virgin Portal of Notre-Dame," *Art Bulletin* XLVIII (1966), pp. 1–13.

30. References to Charlemagne in medieval art have been demonstrated by Rita Lejeune and Jacques Stiennon, *The Legend of Roland in the Middle Ages* (New York, 1970).

31. Ferdinand de Lasteyrie, p. 40, read it as: MAG.ST . . . AVRENTIVS CA. . . . . BITER

. . . CARNOTANSI. (See his drawing, reproduced as my Pl. 58.) Bulteau (1850), p. 296, read "Magister Laurentius capicerius Carnotensis."

32. He had this title in a bill of sale of real estate, Arch. d'Eure-et-Loir, H267, p. 40: "home honorable et sage mestre Lorenz Voisin, chanoine et chevecier en l'église Nostre-Dame de Chartres." He is also mentioned as dean in a document of March 27, 1294 (o.s.), Arch. d'Eure-et-Loir, G 1438 (#8 Cotte A. II — 1294, a sale of houses to Nicolas de Maison-Maugis, himself a donor of stained glass to Saint-Père, by executors of the will of Robert de Troville). See Maurice Jusselin, "Une Maison du XIIIe siècle récemment découverte au cloître Notre-Dame, à Chartres," *Bulletin monumental,* LXXV (1911), pp. 350–395 (for this document pp. 363–364).

33. His will is dated Sept. 1314 (Arch. d'Eure-et-Loir, G 134, Inv. du chap. Caisse LXVII, C, 7 [p. 18]). (The contents of this will are described in E. de Lépinois and Lucien Merlet, *Cartulaire de Notre-Dame de Chartres* [Chartres, 1863], II, p. 233, fn. 2.) He was still alive December 6 (Friday, Feast of "Saint Nicolas d'iver") (Arch. Nat. AB XIX 94, copy of J171 no. 43 bis). A bill of sale by his executors is dated July 31, 1315 (Arch. d'Eure-et-Loir, H1 [I, p. 405]). His anniversary was celebrated March 18 (XV Kalendas Aprilis) by the cathedral (source is a late seventeenth-century compiled necrology, Bibl. Nat. suppl. lat. 31, cited in Lépinois and Merlet, III, p. 65 and p. 9 no. 1; the marginal note that the canon died in 1313 is incorrect). His anniversary was celebrated April 7 by the Abbey of Saint-Père (Lucien and René Merlet, "Dignitaires de l'église Notre-Dame de Chartres," *Archives du diocèse de Chartres,* V [1900], p. 286). The Saint-Père necrologies which these authors made use of (Bibl. Chartres ms. 1031, $1037\frac{7}{D}$, $1038\frac{7}{D}$, and old no. 26–30) were almost all totally destroyed by fire in World War II.

34. See fn. 3, this chapter.

35. Not Urbain, as the photomontage of the *Archives photographiques* states.

36. Hélie de Bourdeilles, b. 1423, was Bishop of Périgueux in 1447, Archbishop of Tours in 1467, Cardinal in 1483, d. 1484. Until the 1953 restoration one of his two escutcheons was surmounted by a red hat with six tassels (1, 2 and 3) (a photograph taken while the panels were being restored in the 1950's exists in the *Archives photographiques* but was not used for the photomontage). François de Brilhac was Archbishop of Aix. His tomb was in the south aisle of Saint-Père, where he had been abbot (1522–1540), and according to Dom Aubert (ch. 121) he 'put colored glass into two nave windows.' His uncle Christophe de Brilhac, 32nd abbot of Saint-Père (from 1491–1514), was Bishop of Orléans from 1504. One of the two de Brilhac escutcheons is surmounted by a bishop's mitre and crozier. See Chapter I at fn. 33 and following.

37. As far as it is possible to tell he was never shown in France with anything but a crozier.

38. Delaporte and Houvet II, pl. CLXXV.

39. These saints have been mentioned because they occur in the missal previously referred to (Chartres, Bibl. mun. ms. 519). St. Germain l'Auxerrois also appears in a cathedral window, Bay 54 (Delaporte and Houvet, II, pl. CXLVI). See Chapter VI, fn. 7.

40. Born ca. 960, Bishop of Chartres from 1006, died April 10, 1028. See Chapter I, fn. 11.

41. Dom Aubert, p. 462.

42. *Gallia christiana,* VIII, p. 353-c, reports an *accord* between the canons and monks in 1225. A document of 1233, reported by Dom Aubert, relates a dispute between them. The canons came in procession to the abbey for the Vigil of Sts. Peter and Paul and found the church not prepared for their arrival. Offended by this negligence, they seized and/or did violence to a reliquary of the arm of St. Ignace (later returned, and in the possession of the monastery in the seventeenth century), two altars, and two manuscripts. See: de Mély, "Les inventaires," IV (XXXVI) (July 1886), pp. 316–317.

43. See the discussion in Chapter I of Nicolas de Maison-Maugis, canon of the cathedral and benefactor of Saint-Père.

44. See Lafond, CVMA France IV, p. 227, fn. 6.

{ CHAPTER XI }

Nave: Narrative Windows – Iconography

ALTERNATING with the six nave windows of standing saints are six equally vast bays spelling out, in abundant color, the legends of Christ and His saints in row upon row of small canopied scenes. The subjects illustrated:

South side: Bay 19 — the Virgin
Bay 23 — Saints Clement and Denis
Bay 27 — Saints Agnes and Catherine
North side: Bay 18 — the Passion
Bay 22 — Saints Peter and Paul
Bay 26 — Saint John the Baptist

The storied windows form the richest group in the church for historical as well as iconographic study. Undoubtedly they were part of a unified campaign dating early in the fourteenth century (ca. 1305–1315), and their variations in quality, style, and approach probably reflect exigencies of haste in a *chantier* modest by cathedral standards. The arrangement, while not rigid, is clearly governed by an overall pattern. The Virgin and Infancy scenes face the Passion across the nave; the saints of particular veneration or meaning for the abbey, Denis (and with him Clement, the pope who authorized his mission) and Peter and Paul, also confront one another. The two female saints occupy the Virgin's side of the nave; the Lord's precursor is placed on the Passion side. In individual windows the stories progress from bottom to top and within the row generally from left to right, in the customary Gothic manner; they vary in which lancet is to be read first.

Many of the lancets contain unusual iconographic detail which indicates a model, sometimes a definite manuscript (as do the Denis window, the Church and Synagogue of the Passion window). At other times there is only a hint of some archaic model as in the Nativity, and many scenes from the Passion window. The Saint-Père narrative windows form an important group of work in a little-understood transitional period, between the High Gothic and the Italianate influences, new techniques, and the tendency to intimacy and sentiment of the fourteenth century. This transitional stance is just as true for the iconography of the windows as for their technique and style. As was the case with both standing figure series in the church, the narrative windows exhibit the beginning of a rejection of standard thirteenth-century forms and a search for fresher ones. The field is ripe for Pucelle and the Pseudo-Bonaventura — but they have not yet come.

A. Bay 19: Virgin

Although the two lancets of Bay 19 (Pl. 51) do not match in format, style, or color harmony, the fact that the Virgin's story unfolds with a smooth transition between the lancets indicates that they were intended, at least ultimately, to form a unity. As the Joachim and Anna lancet precedes the Virgin lancet in style, this intention can be presumed to have been manifest from the beginning of the program.

The two escutcheons (see Fig. 12) in the surmounting rosace are those of Robert IV de Dreux and his wife (or conceivably of their daughter Béatrix).[1] As Robert died November 14, 1282, too early to have been the benefactor in question, the donor commemorated was probably his wife, Béatrix de Montfort-l'Amaury, who outlived him by thirty years, dying March 9, 1312 (n.s.).[2] Although the arms, by their position in the tracery rose, surmount both lancets, the presence of an anonymous abbot-donor in the Virgin lancet (Pl. 53) suggests that the Dreux gift was of the Joachim-Anna lancet only. The house of Dreux-Montfort included no abbot during the early fourteenth century, nor would a male have employed both parents' arms.

Béatrix probably donated the Joachim-Anna lancet before her death, most likely during the first decade of the fourteenth century.[3] The earlier lancet stylistically, it is probably the work of the artist who compiled and completed Bay 22 of the nave[4] (Pl. 59) (a window dated by its donor-portrait 1305–1310), and

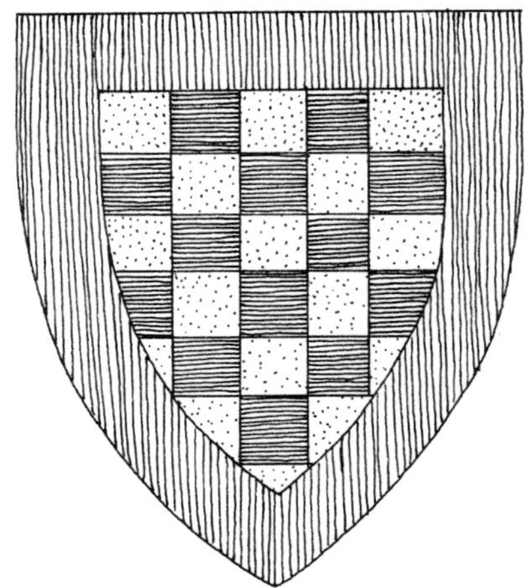

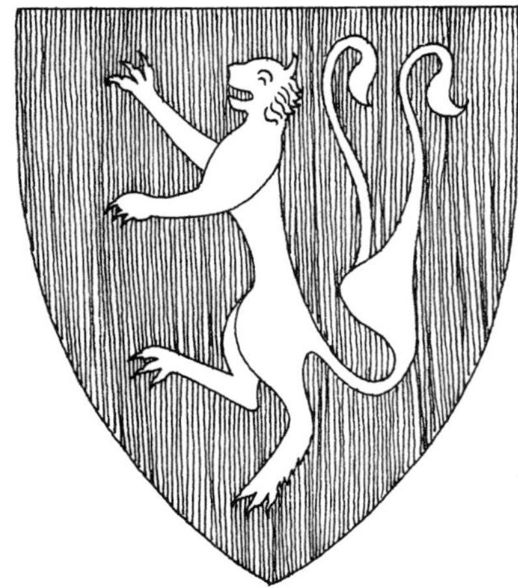

Figure 12 Bay 19: Arms of Dreux and Montfort. (Drawing by Kevin McIntyre)

therefore places early in the nave campaign. The Virgin lancet is undoubtedly a separate gift, possibly by the abbot of Saint-Pére, Jehan de Mantes (donor of Bay 22) or of his successor in office.

The scenes of Bay 19 are arranged from bottom to top, right lancet first. Insofar as there is any movement of the story within the three canopies of each row it is from left to right (i.e., Birth of Mary and her Presentation at the Temple; Annunciation and Visitation).

Joachim-Anna lancet

The story of Mary commences with an elaborate presentation of the apocryphal scenes of her parents. While fairly common in art from the mid-twelfth century on, these scenes never crystallized to anything like the degree that the canonical scenes did. Thirteenth-century works include occasional apocryphal scenes, sometimes one, sometimes another, in no set selection.

The Saint-Père window is extraordinarily complete. In addition to all the established scenes of the Gothic period, it offers some considerably more obscure, comprising a series of notable elaboration for the medium and date. It opens with the prefatory incident, Joachim's offering rejected by the High Priest (Protevangelium I:2).[5] The second row includes two scenes, Joachim retiring to the Wilderness and Anna reproved by Judith (Protevangelium I:4 and II:2–3). Both are uncommon, the latter being one of the rare examples which can be identified in French medieval art. Not even in the apocryphal cycle of Bay 16 of the cathedral, where the special veneration of St. Anne after 1204 is well known, does this scene appear.[6] The text[7] runs:

> And Judith said: How shall I curse thee, seeing the Lord hath shut up thy womb, to give thee no fruit in Israel?

Anna is seated left; Judith stands to the right, sharing the central canopy with the Joachim of the "Retiring to the Wilderness" scene.[8]

The entire row is devoted to the Annunciation to Joachim (Protev. IV:2), an important episode which frequently forms the introduction to a medieval life of Mary. The lesser-known scene of the Annunciation to Anna (Protev. IV:1) is squeezed into a single panel of the following row. The central panel of this row shows that most famous moment of the Joachim-Anna story, the Meeting at the Golden Gate (Protev. IV:4), with Mary's parents embracing one another with dignity before a symmetrically designed medieval "city." Anna has a halo, to indicate an Immaculate Conception. Saint-Père is the earliest of known examples of this detail.[9]

The two female figures under the right canopy, one of them haloed, are very curious. Who is the woman with the halo? The panel is probably out of place. As the scene at the Golden Gate never includes witnesses in northern medieval art, it seems likely that the panel was intended to be part of the Calling of the Suitors scene two rows above.[10]

The fifth row is evenly divided between the Birth (Protev. V:2) and Mary's Presentation in the Temple, the two scenes merging in the extremely cramped quarters of the central panel. The figures belonging to the Nativity of Mary are St. Anne reclining in bed (left panel) and the midwife holding the baby (central panel). The bath of the baby, not mentioned in the texts but frequent in art, is probably omitted for lack of space.

Sharing the central panel with the midwife are Joachim and Anna presenting their daughter at the temple. The Virgin stands on the fifth and sixth steps of a short stairway (central panel) leading up to the draped altar and High Priest (right panel). The only text which mentions steps is Pseudo-Matthew IV, a late (eighth–ninth century) and very popular elaboration of the Protevangelium.[11] Although the priest's hand has been mangled, there is no doubt that the panel was originally designed in the rather awkward form in which it now appears. The artist has tried to show in the same panel the priest standing outside the temple and the draped altar on a high elevation (equal to the top of the stairway) inside. The gesture of Anna embracing her little daughter on the steps, on the other hand, is quite fine.

The sixth row shows the Calling of the Suitors (Protev. VIII–IX).[12] The High Priest, issuing from the temple doors, stands to the left of the draped altar, while Joseph with the flowering rod and another suitor with rod occupy the central panel. The right panel is missing; perhaps it is the panel with two female figures now located two rows below, in which case the haloed female would be Mary. If this hypothesis be true, then the Saint-Père scene follows the format in Chartres Cathedral, Bay 16, one of the few clear examples where the Virgin is present.[13]

The final scene of the lancet is the Marriage of the Virgin, spread across all three panels of the top row. In a scene similar to Chartres Cathedral, Bay 16, the priest, flanked by the wedding couple and four witnesses, grasps a hand of Mary and of Joseph in his own. At the cathedral, the personae are the same (but three of the witnesses are haloed) and there is likewise no altar.

The apocryphal stories of Mary's birth, which had been occasional subjects for art in France since thê mid-twelfth century, were refined and clarified in focus throughout the thirteenth and fourteenth centuries. The completeness and narrative detail of Saint-Père is rarely found in monumental art into the fourteenth century, by which time artists began to lose interest in many of the scenes which had fascinated their predecessors.[14] In stained glass the scenes customarily become abbreviated to the Annunciation to Joachim and the Nativity of Mary.[15] The scene of Judith reproving St. Anne is especially unusual and could indicate that the artist worked directly from a text.

It is not only the all-inclusiveness which makes the Saint-Père window unusual. The scenes run on, the narrative rambles in an unclassified and casual manner which is quite atypical of the fourteenth-century spirit. Did the artist work from a much earlier and similarly uncrystallized visual source, or from an apocryphal text? The detail of Anna's halo at the Golden Gate might indicate the latter.

It is clear that the artist was wrestling with the stylistic problem of how to present stories in the clerestory. Primitive canopies have been employed instead of medallion frames, but the lancet is crowded with rows — there are seven, as in Bay 22, instead of the five used elsewhere in the nave. In his attempt at stylistic organization the artist of the Joachim-Anna lancet was considerably disadvantaged by the amorphous nature of his subject.

Virgin lancet

The extent of his handicap is shown by the juxtaposition of the neighboring lancet (Pls. 51, 53, 54) devoted to the canonical stories of the Virgin, a work by a different artist. The canopies are larger and more elaborate. There are only five rows, each tall enough to be divided vertically into two panels. The included scenes are trimmed in number, increased in size, and presented as tableaux with fewer and more readily distinguished personae. In all fairness it must be pointed out, however, that the iconographic sorting and sifting of Infancy scenes had been accomplished in art by the late thirteenth century. Mary's apocryphal legends never achieved such crystallization.

The scenes selected for the left lancet of Bay 19 comprise:

Row 1 — Annunciation (with donor) and Visitation
Row 2 — Nativity
Row 3 — Adoration of the Magi
Row 4 — Presentation in the Temple
Row 5 — Death of Mary

The Annunciation (Luke I:26–38) occupies the left and central panels of the bottom row, the Visitation taking the right panel (Pl. 53). This somewhat crowded arrangement has the virtue of placing the Annunciate Mary and the kneeling abbot donor together in the central panel. The donor-figure, in fact, takes the place of the chair occasionally found behind Mary, and he is so insignificant that his presence has passed utterly unnoticed in the literature on Saint-Père. Who is he? If, as is most probable, he is an abbot of Saint-Père, then he is most likely Jehan de Mantes, abbot 1305–1310, donor of Bay 22 and probable instigator of the narrative window series of the nave. But the identification must remain circumstantial.

The episodes of the Infancy lancet are, with the exception of one surprising detail, very much works of their times, much more in the mainstream of French Gothic art than the rambling narrative of the Joachim-Anna lancet. Their choice is also typical, with a notable exception: the Dormition (Pl. 54)[16] replaces the standard terminal scene of the Gothic era, the Coronation of the Virgin. It would be audacious to read too much significance into this detail were it not for a much more striking anomaly in Row 2.

Row 2 presents the Nativity, the Virgin lying abed to the left, turning her head away (Pl. 53). The swaddled child lies in the center on a raised crib, a box-like manger rather than an "altar" of the twelfth-century form. Behind Him are the ox and ass. To the right is Joseph, either seated or kneeling (the lower panel, lost, is now replaced by a modern design). A midwife crouches at the foot of the bed, and a lamp is suspended incongruously from her extended arms.

The latter two details (lamp and midwife), like the terminal Dormition, provide clues to an early model, and to the artist's working methods in adapting such models. Although a lamp was more commonly hung above the Child, a lamp suspended below an "altar" type crib occasionally appears in thirteenth-century art. French examples include, in addition to a few manuscripts, stained glass windows from Troyes Cathedral (Virgin chapel, Infancy window, ca.

1210–1215) and Le Mans (Virgin chapel, before 1254). The Saint-Père artist, who evidently had such a scene, or the memory of it, before him, was forced by the proportions of his panel and the presence of the midwife to place the lamp below her arms. It is, actually, correctly placed below the Child on axis with the crib, but appears to be hung inexplicably from the midwife's upper sleeves.

The midwife is the anachronism. Discounting the scene of the Christ Child's bath, which maintained a tenuous popularity through the thirteenth century,[17] the apocryphal midwives who figured so prominently at the Nativity for centuries became increasingly rare as the Gothic era progressed.[18] In Early Christian art the iconography of the midwives, or more particularly of the doubting Salome (Zelomi), had been a firmly established part of the Nativity. The texts from Pseudo-Matthew XIII and Protevangelium XIX:2, 3 and XX:1–4[19] relate the episode, culminating in Salome's cry, "Woe unto mine iniquity and mine unbelief."

The episode easily crystallized into the figure of Salome kneeling or crouching at the foot of the bed, extending her withered arms toward the Virgin. She is usually in front of the crib and supports her arm with the other hand. Ivory objects regularly include the motif from the sixth century on;[20] it was adopted by Roman fresco and mosaic artists in the eighth century;[21] and is found in such well-known early medieval sites as Castelseprio,[22] the Hildesheim doors (ca. 1008–1015), and the bronze doors of Benevento Cathedral (twelfth–thirteenth century). In France it occurs in the Sacramentary of Drogo (Bibl. Nat. ms. lat. 9428, fol. 24v, initial letter), a Metz manuscript of ca. 830 or ca. 850.[23] Strangely enough it was dropped in Byzantium and never became an influence in German Romanesque manuscripts.[24]

By the thirteenth century the figure and gesture, in the few cases where they appear in western art, were universally misunderstood. Some interesting misinterpretations of the motivation of the gesture are to be found, as where Salome, posed correctly, offers the Virgin a bowl, carries the Child, or reaches toward the crib.[25] The Salome figure at Saint-Père is much closer to the Early Christian prototype in placement and posture than anything to be found in France for probably two hundred years.[26] The artist comprehended his model no more clearly than other Gothic near-contemporaries. His Salome no longer supports one arm with the other, but presents them both in a gesture which seems to be one of supplication. It is nevertheless highly likely that he was working from a model of the eleventh century or before.[27]

The crouching midwife of the Saint-Père Nativity (Pl. 53) is an anachronism, as is, to a lesser extent, the terminal Dormition (Pl. 54). To what ancient treasure in the abbey's possession could the artist have referred? The abbey's period of aggrandizement in the tenth century[28] and its close connections with Rome during the twelfth–thirteenth centuries[29] make its ownership of such a hypothetical object quite likely; and there is evidence as well that the local nobility presented relics and treasures on their return from crusade.[30] It is fairly safe to say, at least, that the mystery object was not a product of Gothic France.

B. Bay 23: Sts. Clement and Denis

The two lancets of Bay 23 (Pl. 69)[31] are the work of one artist and have similar formats (five rows of scenes under canopies, each row formed of two layers of panels). The window and its opposite on the north, Bay 22, suffered a dismantling and exodus of panels in the eighteenth century — after 1672 — which was only corrected with the restorations of ca. 1905. To provide more light, the Age of Enlightenment removed the panels bordering the stonework and replaced them with clear glass. Some were placed in unorganized confusion in windows of the ambulatory (Pl. 71) and apsidal chapels.[32] Eleven of them and the lights of the right ogive have been totally lost.[33] The task of replacing the existing removed panels in 1905 was facilitated, happily, by the artist's practice of extending forms across conjunctive panels. It can thus be assumed that most are now in their original relationships, although it is possible that whole rows may be out of order.

The choice of saints is significant. The inclusion of St. Denis, like the St. Louis in the apse and the arms of the house of Dreux in Bay 19, underlines the abbey's close connections with the royal family. Clement, pope and martyr, illustrates another, spiritual connection. The abbey is dedicated to Sts. Peter and Paul,[34] whose story is illustrated in Bay 22, the nave clerestory bay directly opposite the Clement/Denis window. According to medieval belief, St. Denis was converted by St. Paul, and was sent to Gaul by Pope Clement. Clement himself had been converted to Christianity and consecrated by St. Peter. Thus Clement forms the logical link between St. Peter, the abbey's patron and name-saint, and St. Denis, first bishop of Paris and patron of the royal house of France.[35]

St. Clement lancet

The aforementioned theory provides the identification of the first scene of the Clement lancet (Pl. 69), which has been a puzzle to authors. A seated pope with cross-staff and tiara[36] addresses three standing figures, i.e., a standing bishop with crozier and two tonsured monks.[37] All four figures are haloed. The scene, an extremely rare episode in monumental art, is of St. Clement as pope sending Denis and his companions, the deacons Eleutherius and Rusticus, to

Gaul. The presence of haloes on the two attending monks eliminates all possibility that Clement's consecration by St. Peter is intended.[38] The scene of Clement sending Denis to Gaul can be found, exactly reversed, as fol. 34r of the Life of St. Denis executed at the Abbey of Saint-Denis in 1250 (Bibl. Nat. nouv. acq. fr. 1098) (Pl. 97).[39]

The scene is handled quite differently in a later product of the Saint-Denis scriptorium, the Vita S. Dionysii written by the monk Yves and offered by his abbot, Giles of Pontoise, to Philippe-le-Long in 1317 (Bibl. Nat. ms. fr. 2090–92, II, fols. 70v and 80v).[40] The iconographic formulae of the St. Denis legend changed radically between the early thirteenth and the early fourteenth centuries, probably under the impact of the Saint-Denis manuscripts. The Saint-Père window occupies a pivotal position in this change, sometimes adopting the traditional design and sometimes the new solution. This idea and its ramifications will be pursued in the coming discussion of the St. Denis lancet. For the time being it will be enough to note that the scene of the consecration of the saint by Clement clearly follows the 1250 model.

The glazier has simply added clarifying "attributes" — the pope's cross-staff and the bishop's crozier, the chalice in the hands of the priest on the right. It is probable that the crozier crossed in front of the saint is drawn, moreover, from a similar design in fr. 2091, fol. 125r. The glazier has followed the earlier manuscript in extending the papal throne across the division of the framing arcades. Also significant to the window's program is the inclusion, in this particular folio of the 1250 manuscript, of Sts. Peter and Paul in the uppermost corners (Pl. 97); the main scenes of the sending of Denis to Gaul, like the Damnation of Nero above it, are presented by the illuminator as results of the martyrdoms of Peter and Paul, shown receiving martyrs' crowns in heaven. A similar cause-and-effect relationship has been observed at Saint-Père between the facing bays of Peter/Paul and Clement/Denis.

The second row of the Clement lancet shows another uncommon scene, that of the saint's exile to the Crimea. Clement, standing in his boat, preaches to a group of men. The subject is almost unknown in French art.[41]

The following scene is a more common one in Clement cycles, that of the Miracle of the Spring. According to legend, Clement was condemned to break stones in a quarry. His companions were dying of thirst. Clement invoked the Lamb of God, who scratched the ground until a spring burst from the rock. The Saint-Père window, of which the left panel is missing, shows Clement (now largely lost) striking the rock with his pick at the spot indicated by the Lamb (adorned with cruciferous halo). Four companions watch in amazement as the spring gushes forth. The quarry pick is an unusual detail, but otherwise the Saint-Père panels follow the customary arrangement of the popular scene.

The two panels remaining of the fourth row are more puzzling. They are out of place in any case, and the left panel of the row is lost. The most supportable assumption would be that the scene represented is a rare episode in the Clement legend which occurred before his exile. He had converted a woman named Theodora, whose husband Sisinius was furious and tried to prevent their entering the church. Sisinius was thereupon struck blind and had to be led away by a servant. The episode ended as Sisinius ordered his servants to bind Clement, and they, having also been blinded, bound up a column by mistake. Much as the story resembles such popular thirteenth-century fictions as the defeat of Simon Magus by Peter, it was almost unknown in French art.[42] It is found in fragments of a Roman fresco dating ca. 1100, in the nave of the lower church of San Clemente,[43] as follows: Zone 2 shows Clement near an altar, donors and clergy and Theodora at mass. Next to her a servant leads away the blind Sisinius. Zone 3 shows the epilogue, omitted at Saint-Père, in which the blind servants bind up a column in place of the saint.

Is the inclusion of this story, like the midwife of the Nativity of Bay 19, evidence of Roman early medieval iconography somehow reaching Saint-Père? Probably not. The midwife was a pictorial detail borrowed without understanding; the Clement scene was comprehended and translated into contemporary dress. Theodora kneels praying in the central panel, while behind her two servants support her blind husband. In the right panel a servant leads Sisinius away. The lost left panel probably showed Clement at the altar. The artist has given the husband and wife French caps which tie under the chin, of types common in Parisian thirteenth-century manuscripts. Sisinius, moreover, carries a glove, customary Gothic mark of a figure of noble status.[44] The most likely assumption is that the Saint-Père artist constructed the scene from a textual account.[45]

Although the final row has lost two of its three panels, the central remaining panel clearly formed part of the familiar martyrdom scene of Clement, in which the saint is thrown overboard with an anchor about his neck. The customary formula shows a boat in the water, from which two men throw the saint head first, a millstone or anchor tied to his neck.[46] In the remaining Saint-Père panel can be seen the head of Clement attached to the anchor. Issuing from the clouds above is the blessing hand of God in a cruciferous halo. Behind the saint's head is the prow of a boat and below him the waves of the sea.

To the lower left are the legs and feet of a figure crouched on one knee. This figure is in an impossible sideways position. Even allowing for the extreme posture distortions of which the artist of Bay 23 was capable — note, for example, the incredible position of the executioner in the Denis lancet, fourth row from bottom — the crouching figure seems to be turned at a forty-five to sixty-five-degree angle. As the panel was not among those removed and then returned to the window,[47] and is not heavily restored,[48] it must be allowed that the figure has not been rotated.

It therefore seems likely that the crouching figure does not represent one of the men who heave Clement from the boat, but is a reference to another story. One of the most prominent episodes from the Clement legend concerns a submarine chapel built for the saint's body by angels.[49] Annually, on the anniversary of his martyrdom, the sea receded to allow the faithful to visit the chapel. One year a woman who had made the pilgrimage with her son left him sleeping there by mistake. The boy was found safely sleeping in the chapel the following year. Could the questionable figure be the boy lying on his back with one knee bent? If so, the submarine chapel would have appeared, most probably, in the left hand panel of the row.

Generally speaking, in the narrative windows of Saint-Père posthumous miracles, no matter how important a place they customarily occupy in a saint's legend, are omitted or minimized. The submarine chapel of St. Clement provides a case in point. Although one of the major episodes of the legend, it was either omitted altogether or, at best, telescoped into a single (now lost) panel.

The two triangular panels of the tympanum (Pl. 70) contain two angels holding the martyr's beatified soul in a cloth. The format and angels are original; the soul was redesigned in the 1950's by François Lorin to replace a previous restoration in a different style.[50]

St. Denis lancet

The chronicle of the patron of France, introduced in the bottom row of the Clement lancet, continues in the lowermost register of the Denis lancet filling the right side of the bay (Pl. 69). The life of St. Denis is much more familiar matter for French art than the Clement legend. The choice of scenes and their manner of representation altered radically during the thirteenth century, as a comparison of an early cycle such as the Bourges window[51] with some of the fourteenth-century ivories[52] will reveal. It seems likely that the manuscripts produced at the Abbey of Saint-Denis during the period were largely responsible for the changes. The Saint-Père window, now looking forward and now back, is an important monument in the study of the iconography of St. Denis.

Whereas the Clement lancet presents scenes mainly invented from a written account, it is demonstrable that the artist based the Denis lancet on visual models, two Parisian manuscripts produced at Saint-Denis about 1250 (Bibl. Nat. nouv. acq. fr. 1098) and about 1315 (Bibl. Nat. ms. fr. 2090–2092). The former is a "picture-book" life of the saint, written presumably as a "tourist guide" for the abbey's constant stream of noble visitors; the prose text is in the vernacular, while the pictures are accompanied by doggerel Latin titles. The latter manuscript is the lavish Vita S. Dionysii probably produced to the order of the king himself, the final volume being a chronicle of the kings of France. It has been suggested that it was commissioned by Philippe-le-Bel at a difficult moment in his career, at the time of the general uprisings against the taxation of 1314.[53]

Philippe-le-Bel died, however, in 1314, before the commission was finished. His son Louis died in 1316, and it was his second son, Philippe-le-Long, to whom the abbey finally turned over the manuscript in 1317. It had remained in the workshop for such a length of time for a very good reason — so that an interleaved French translation of the Latin text could be prepared and inserted for the benefit of the sons, less well-lettered than their father who had commissioned it. The miniatures would therefore have been available for viewing in the abbey scriptorium for a considerable period of months before the final luxury product entered the king's library in 1317. It is not unreasonable to presume that the two Benedictine abbeys cooperated, and that the Saint-Père glazier was allowed access to the manuscripts at Saint-Denis,[54] possibly with the approval of the king.

The story, begun in the lower row of the Clement lancet, is picked up at the bottom of the Denis lancet. This row contains major restorations including the bishop's face[55] and the whole lower right panel;[56] its identification is therefore more problematical than the rest. Five standing haloed figures line up, the central one a bishop making the gesture of benediction, the left one crossing his arms on his breast in a posture of humility seen elsewhere in the window. The curious fragment still visible at the neck of the figure second from the right probably holds the key to identification.[57] A basket? Pieces of rope or chain?

In the second row of the Denis lancet we are on much firmer ground. Two episodes are juxtaposed — one might almost say "telescoped" — the familiar scene of St. Denis preaching in Paris (left),[58] and, to the right, Denis being attacked by the angry mob. In the preaching scene the glazier has combined details of both manuscripts, adopting the format of the 1250 manuscript (fol. 37v, top):[59] draped altar, listeners seated on low rocks, including one inclining his head on one hand. The placement and gestures of the preaching saint and his companions, however, are much closer to the 1317 manuscript (ms. fr. 2090, fol. 85v),[60] which also includes the head-on-hand figure, but in reverse. See also another preaching scene in the 1317 manuscript (Pl. 99).[61]

The glazier took advantage of the empty space above the seated congregation to squeeze in part of another connected but less common episode, that of St. Denis and his companions being attacked by the mob (or by soldiers). The scene is not included in the 1250 manuscript.[62] The source would appear to be the 1317 version (ms. fr. 2091, fol. 130v), in which a group of figures sits on the ground to the left while Denis and his disciples, behind a draped altar to the right, are being seized by armed soldiers. This folio follows one of the preaching scenes in the manuscript (fol. 111r) (Pl. 99). The glazier chose not to uniform his attackers as soldiers but to conform them to the prefect's henchmen whom he represents in the following row of his lancet.

Row 3 presents the flagellation of Denis and his companions by these henchmen (Pl. 69). The saint, in loincloth and miter, lies stomach-down on a sloping plank, while Eleutherius and Rusticus, also nude to the waist, stand to the right, arms bound. Three men scourge them with knobby rods. The episode of the sloping plank, absent from thirteenth-century window cycles, was familiar to the fourteenth century.[63] It appears, perhaps for the first time, in the 1250 manuscript (fol. 40r, top), where the saint likewise retains his miter (Pl. 98). The inclusion of the disciples at Saint-Père, on the other hand, finds its source in the 1317 manuscript. In ms. fr. 2092, fol. 16v, all three saints are scourged on sloping planks and Denis has lost his miter; on fol. 10v and on fol. 42r, all three are scourged standing nude, arms bound. The glazier has combined the two types and reduced the redundancy to a simple declarative sentence.

Two more episodes are similarly telescoped in Row 4. To the left an executioner shoves the saint head-first into a fiery furnace. In the right panel two mad dogs rush into a crenellated building (doubtless the prison) from outside. In the saint's legend the "test of the wild beasts" occurs first; after the saint has driven them off with the sign of the cross, he is thrown into the oven. Both episodes maintained a continuous popularity in art while changing format radically between the early thirteenth and early fourteenth centuries.

The early type takes place inside the prison,[64] while the later version (possibly introduced in the 1250 manuscript, fol. 41v, top, and very popular in Parisian ivories) is moved to the great outdoors, with a new figure arrangement.[65] The Saint-Père panel is a compromise, undoubtedly dictated by the extreme shortage of space: the animals rush into the prison interior from a verdant landscape barely visible through the door. The glazier has used mad dogs like those of the 1250 manuscript[66] rather than the hairy leonine beasts popular later;[67] he has combined both interior and exterior, connected by a door of the type found in ms. fr. 2092, fol. 24v; and he has omitted the saint altogether!

It is the second scene of the row, the episode of the fiery furnace, which is highlighted. The glazier, clearly an artist who prefers the active to the passive voice, has in this case rejected the format found in both manuscripts (in which the saint sits quietly meditating in the nude inside his furnace).[68] For once he returns to an older glazing tradition traceable in all of the extant earlier windows showing this legend — Bourges, Saint-Denis-de-Jouhet,[69] and Tours. The fur-

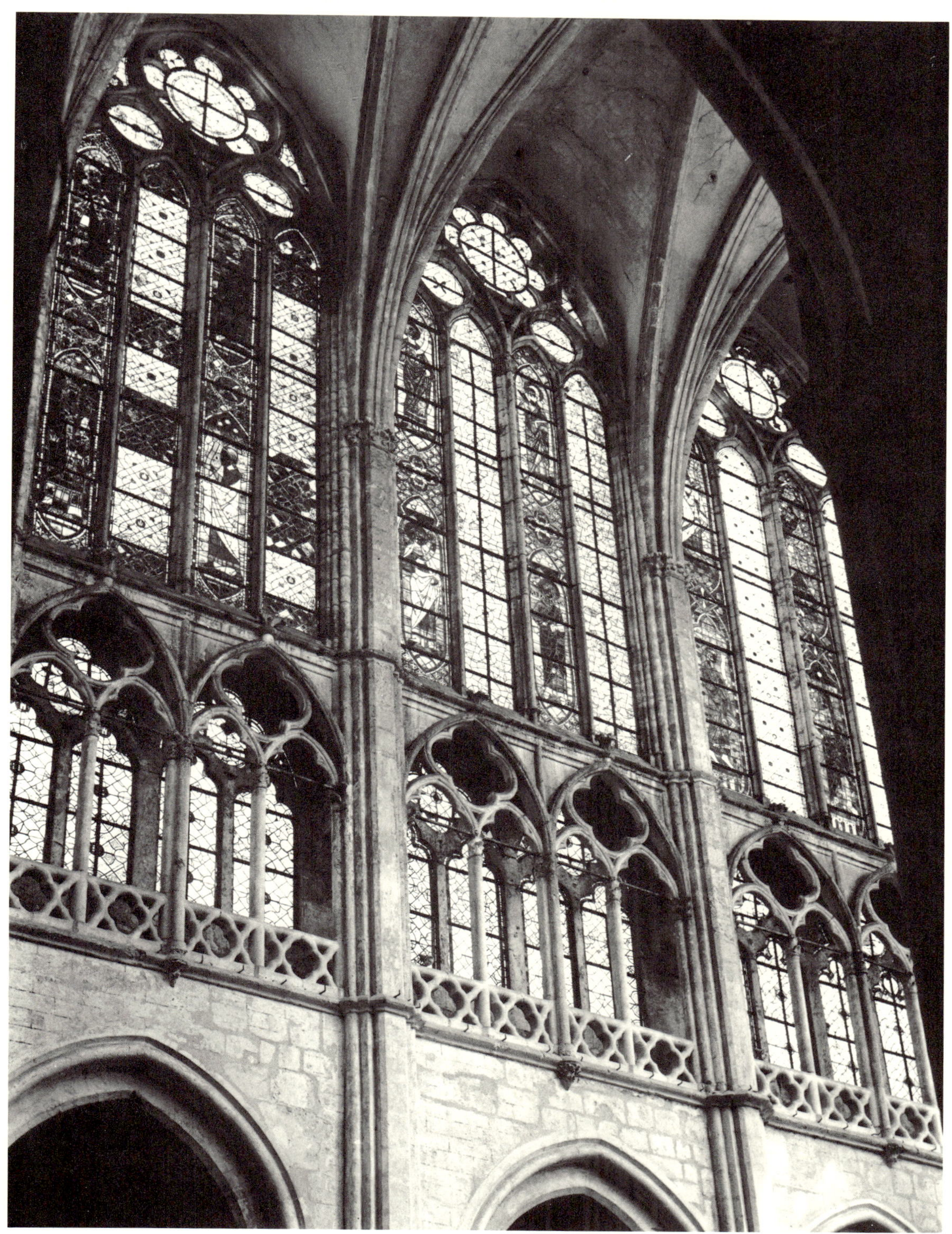

Saint-Père: hemicycle clerestory *(Loïc Martine)*

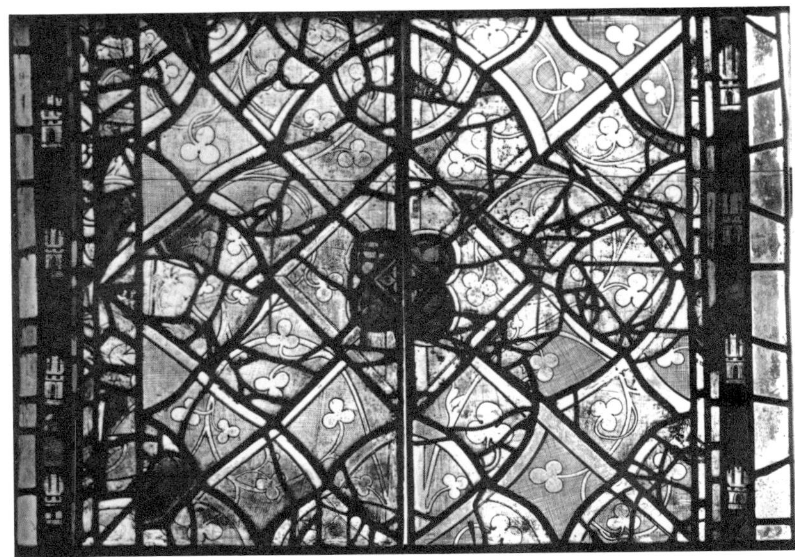

PLATE 44 Hemicycle triforium: Bay 6, grisailles. *(Paris, Archives photographiques)*

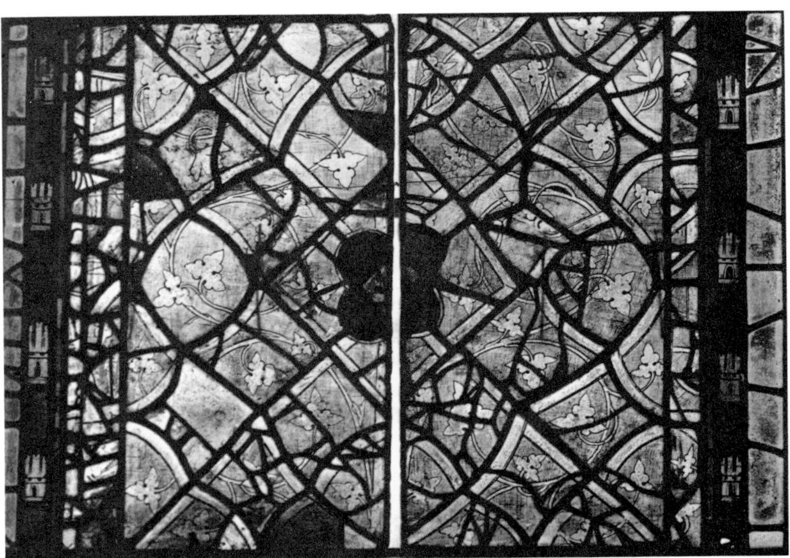

PLATE 45 Hemicycle triforium: Bay 6, grisaille, detail. *(Paris, Archives photographiques)*

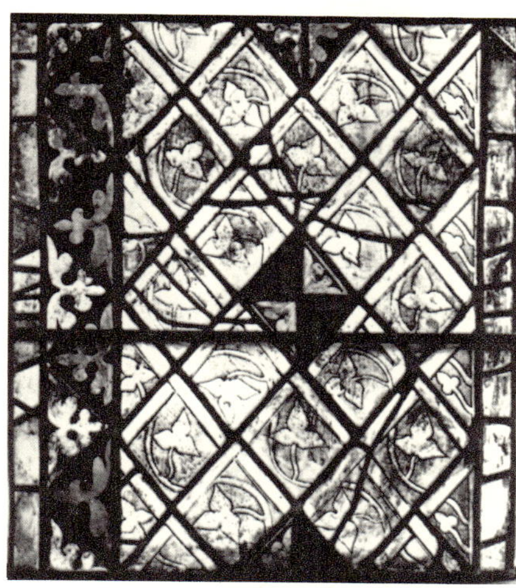

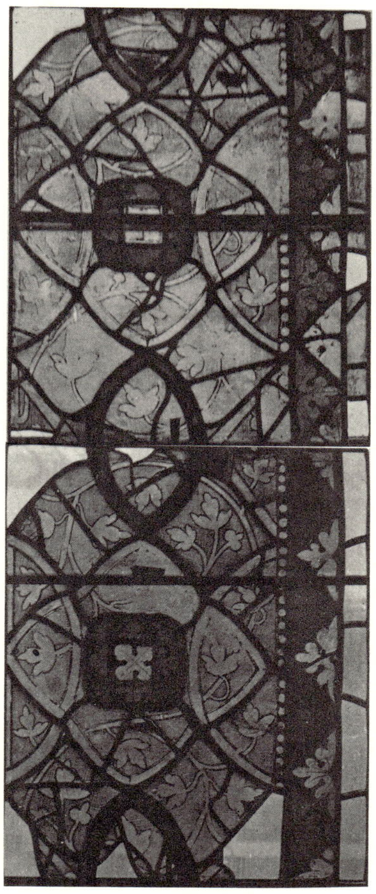

PLATE 46 Nave: Bay 29, grisaille. *(Paris, Archives photographiques)*

PLATE 47 Nave: Bay 28, grisaille. *(Paris, Archives photographiques)*

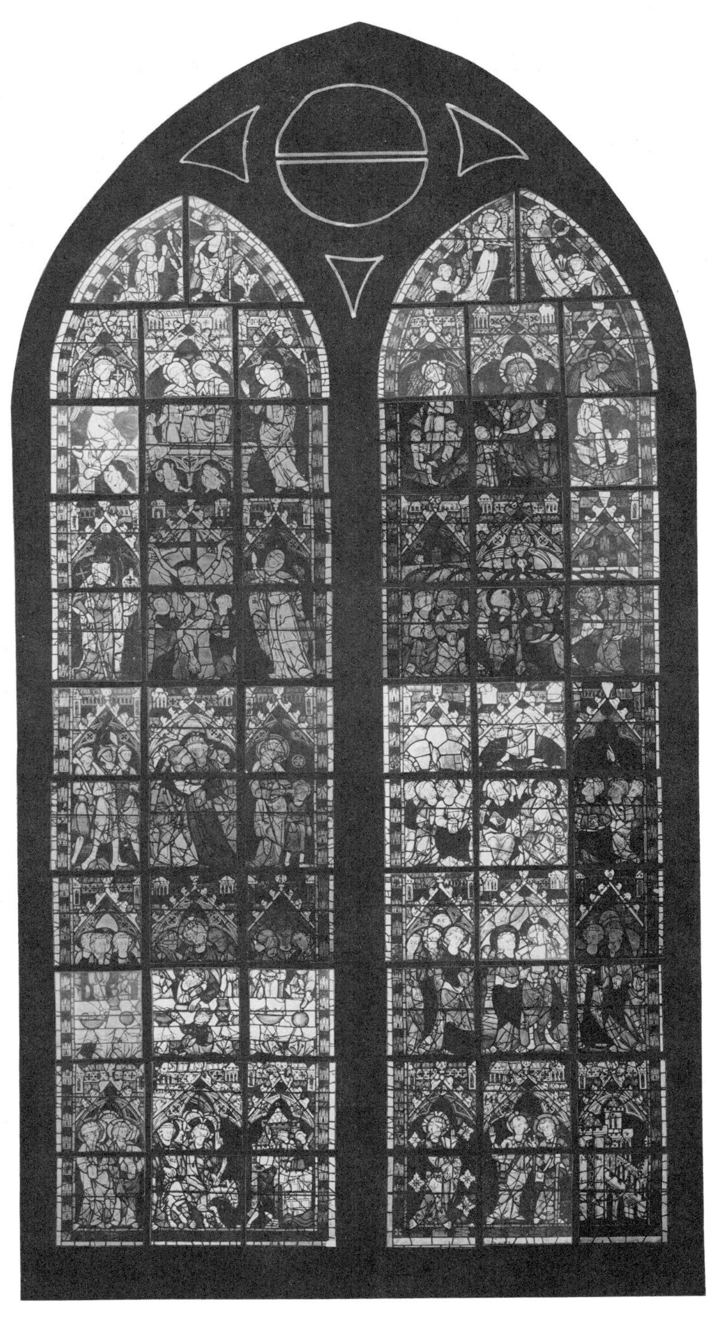

PLATE 48 Nave: Bay 18. *(Paris, Archives photographiques)*

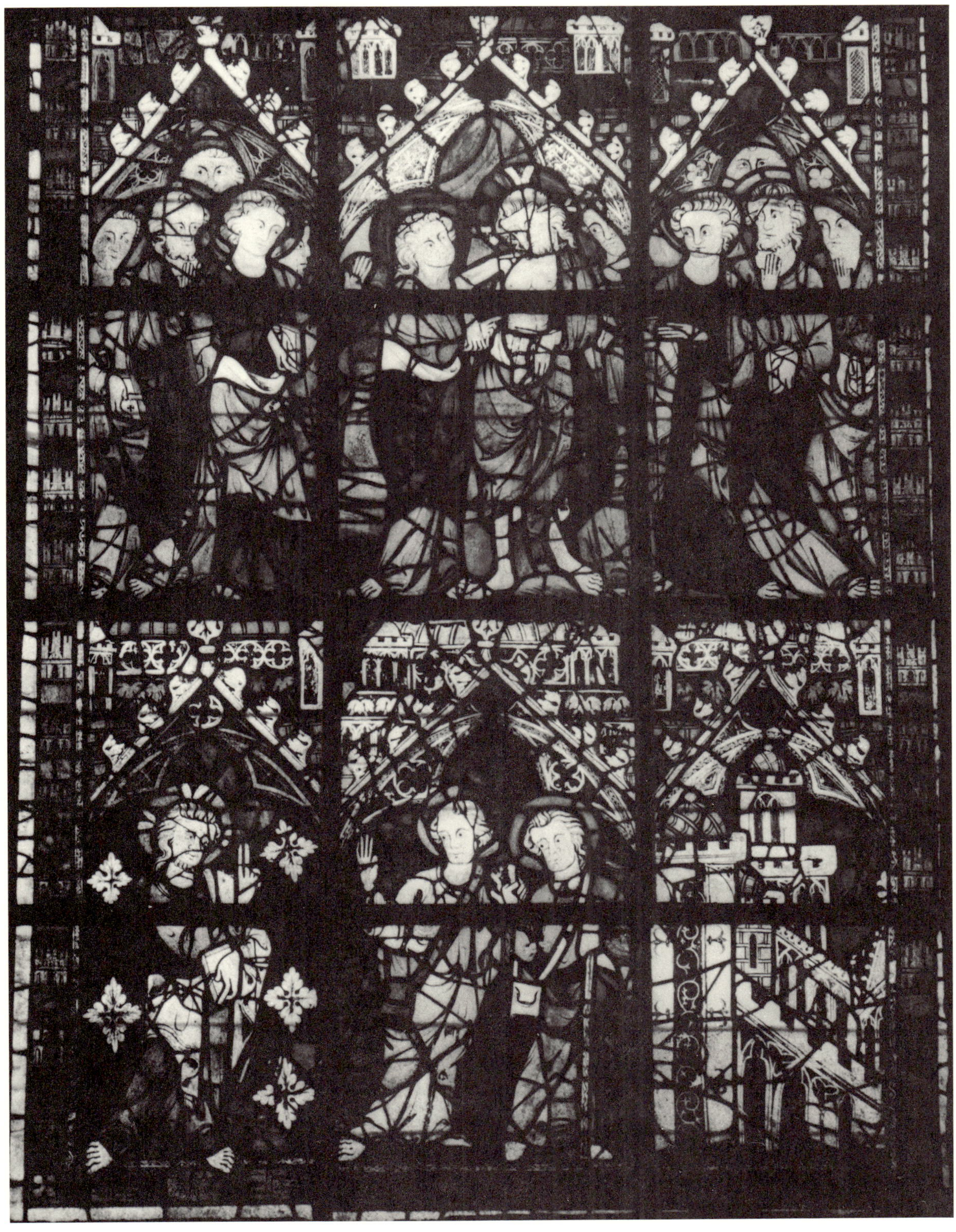

PLATE 49 Nave: Bay 18, right lancet. Passion window: Road to Emmaus, Doubting of Thomas.
(Photo: Edouard Fièvet)

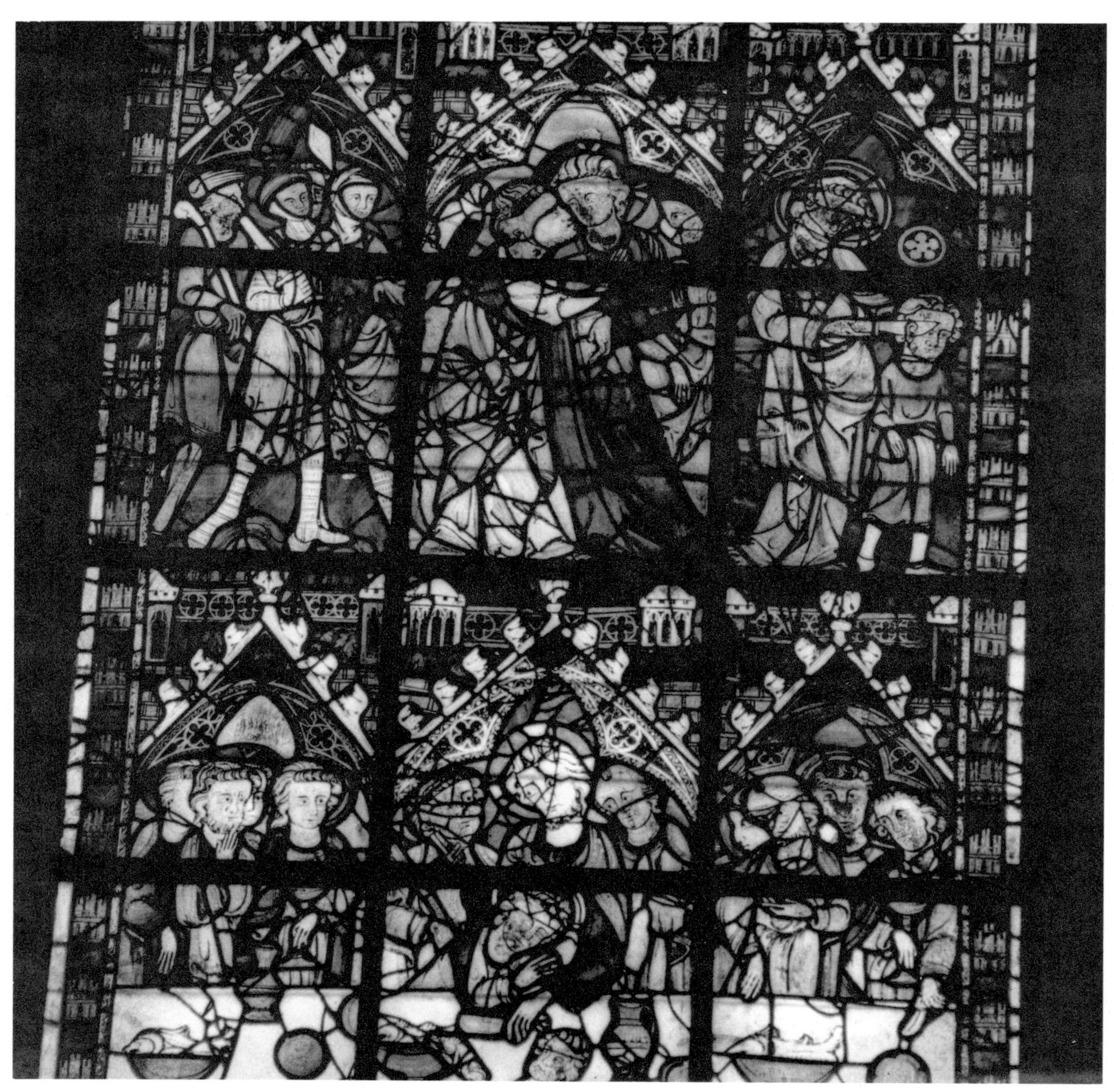

PLATE 50 Nave: Bay 18, left lancet. Passion window: Kiss of Judas and Peter cutting Malchus's ear; Crucifixion. *(Photo: Edouard Fièvet)*

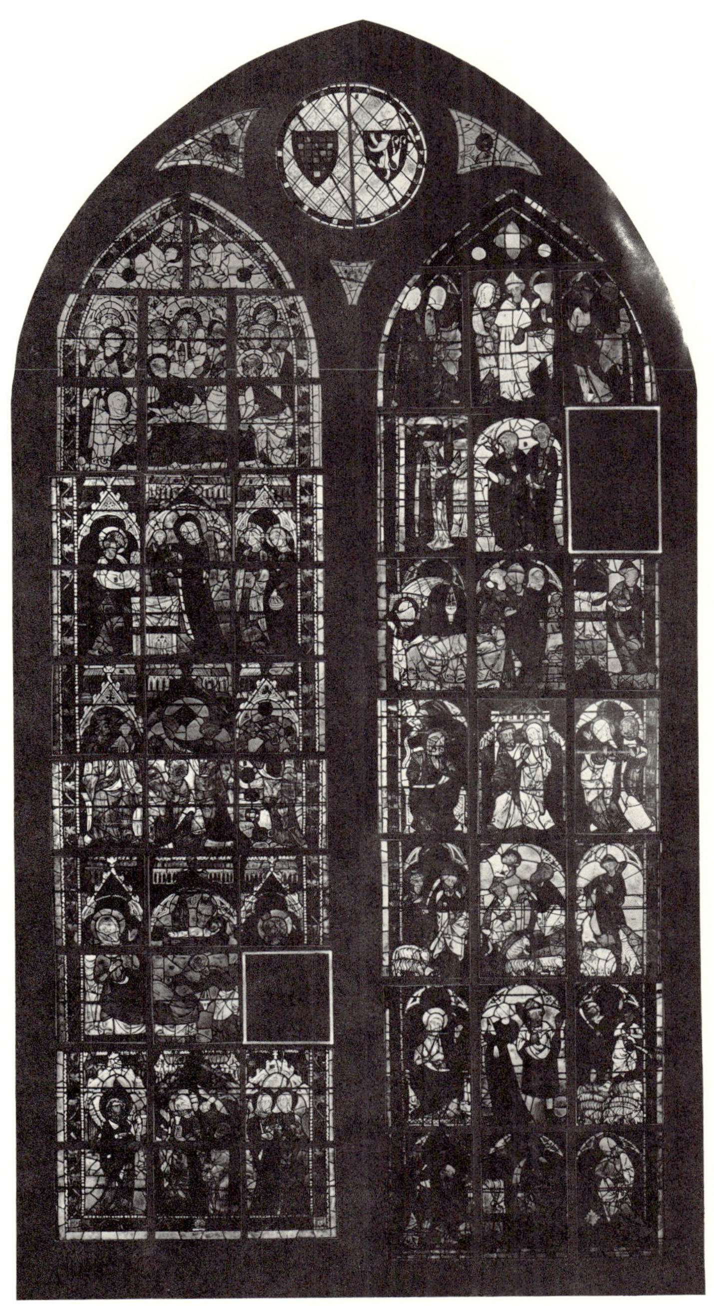

PLATE 51 Nave: Bay 19. *(Paris, Archives photographiques)*

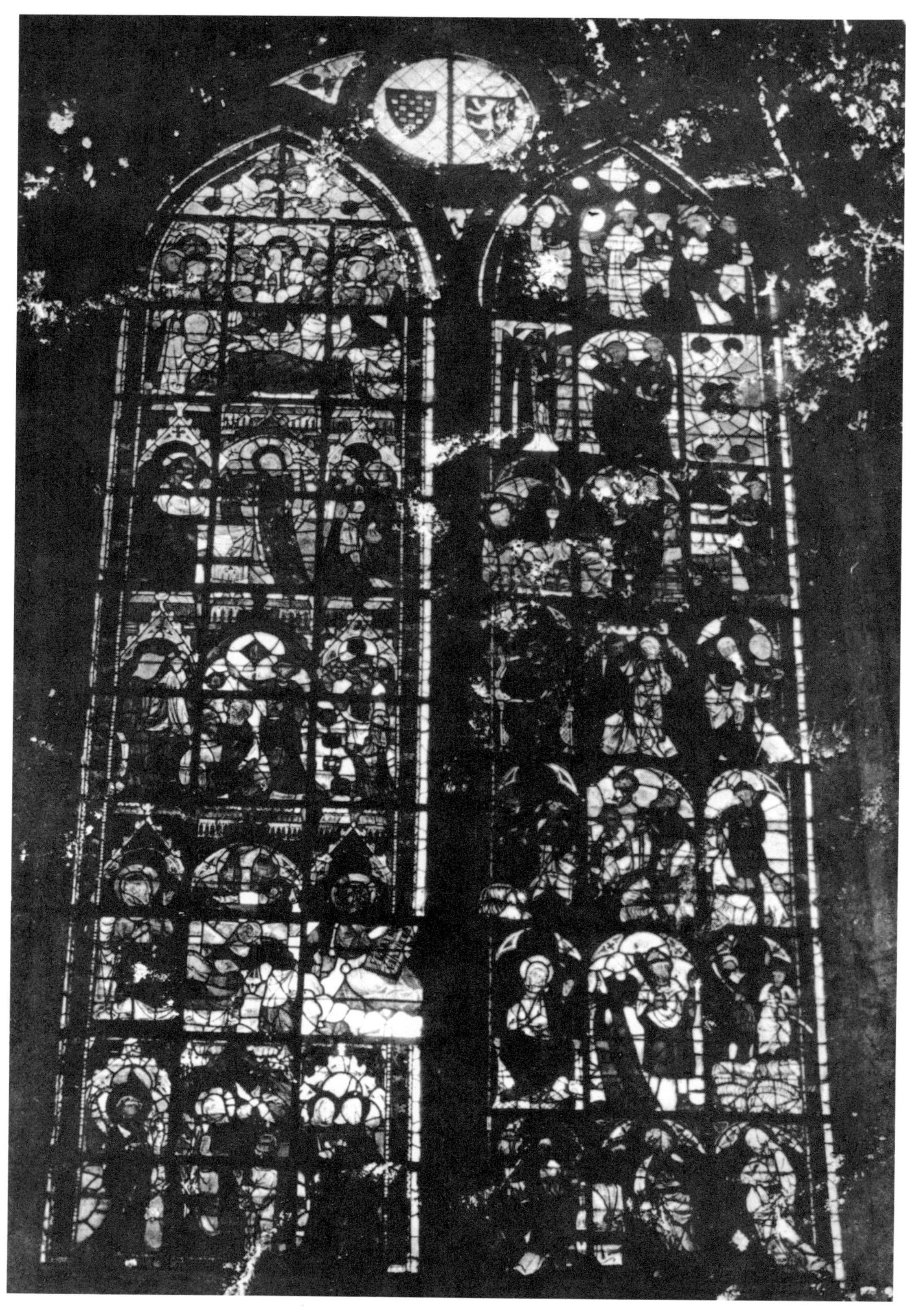

PLATE 52 Nave: Bay 19. Between the restorations of ca. 1905 and the 1950's. *(Photo from Michon) (Paris, Archives photographiques)*

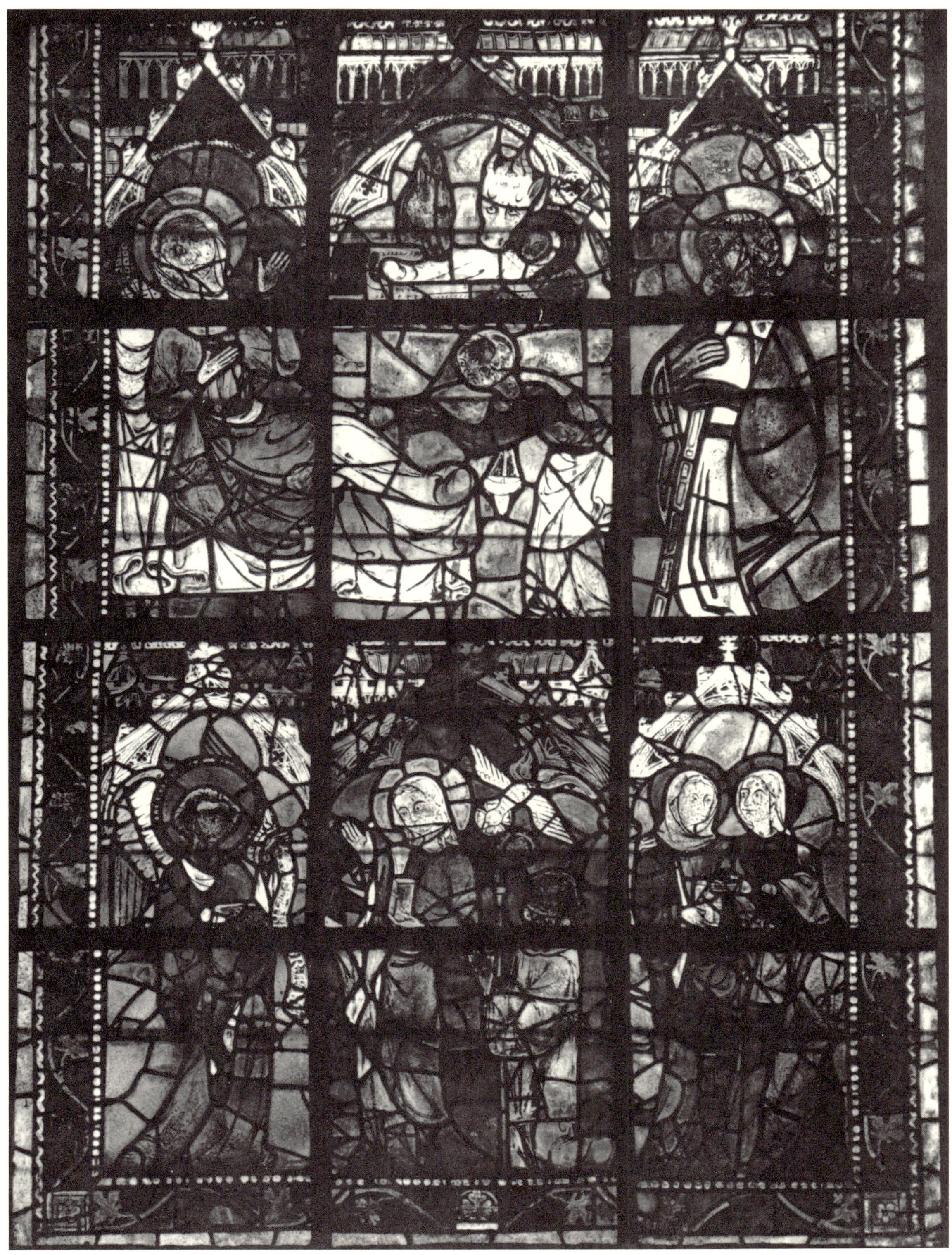

PLATE 53 Nave: Bay 19, left lancet. Virgin window: Annunciation with donor, Visitation; Nativity. *(Photo: Edouard Fièvet)*

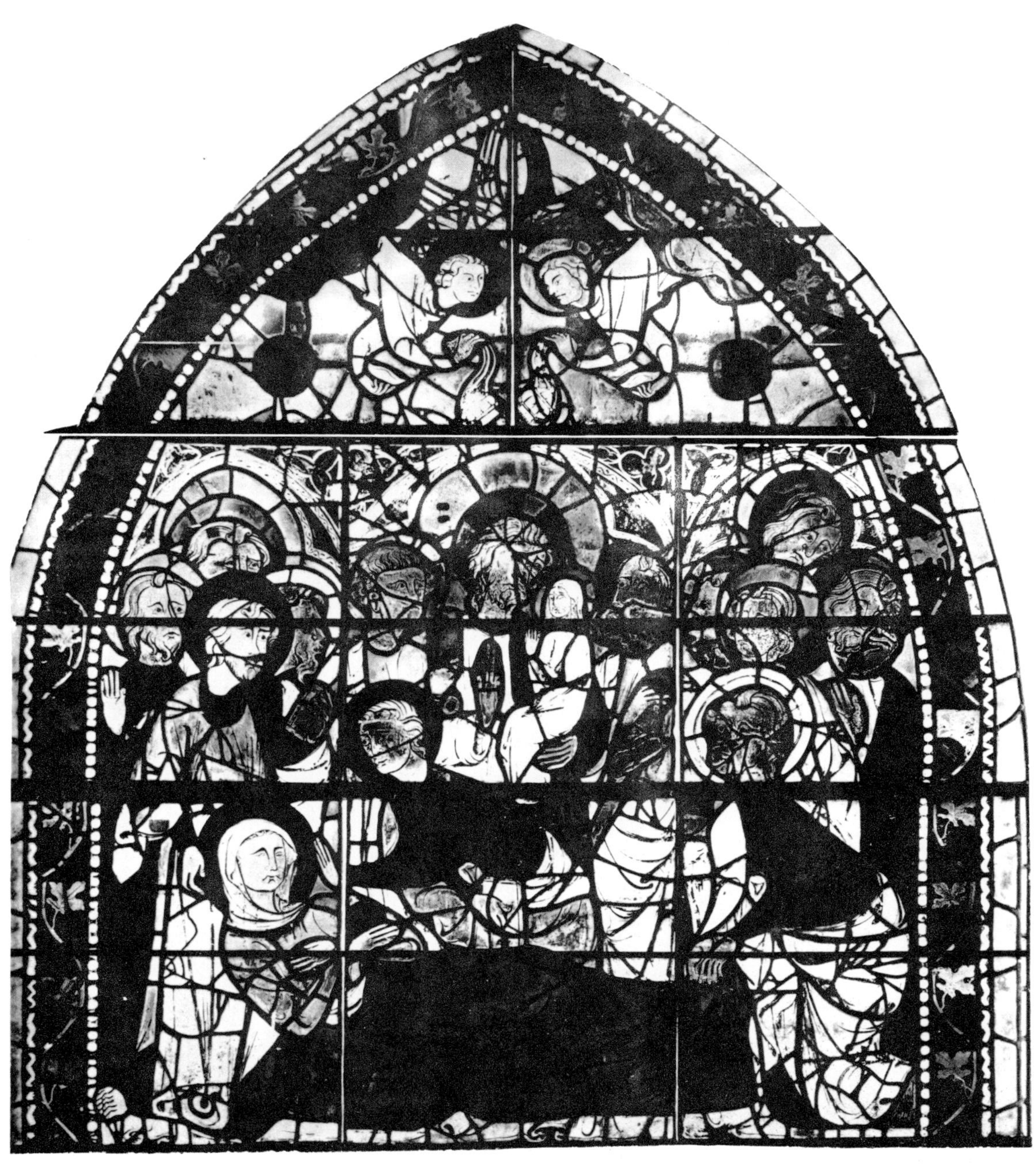

PLATE 54 Nave: Bay 19, left lancet. Virgin window: Dormition. *(Paris, Archives photographiques)*

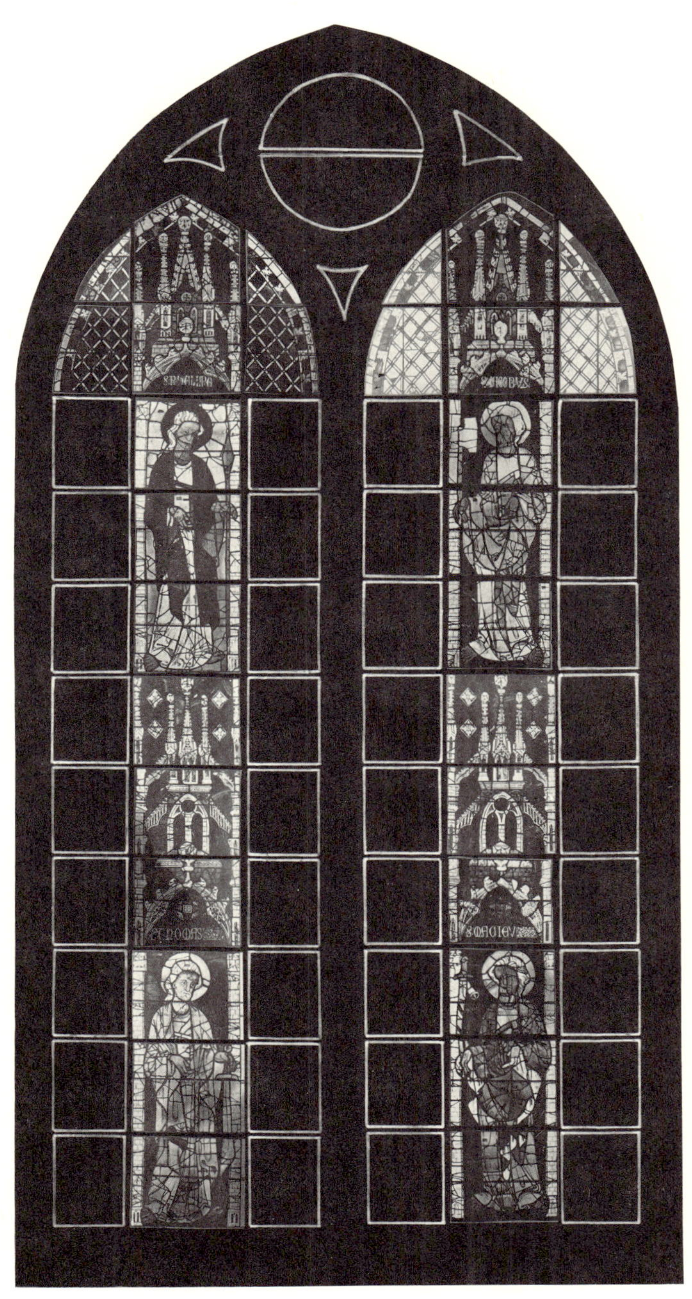

PLATE 55 Nave: Bay 20. *(Paris, Archives photographiques)*

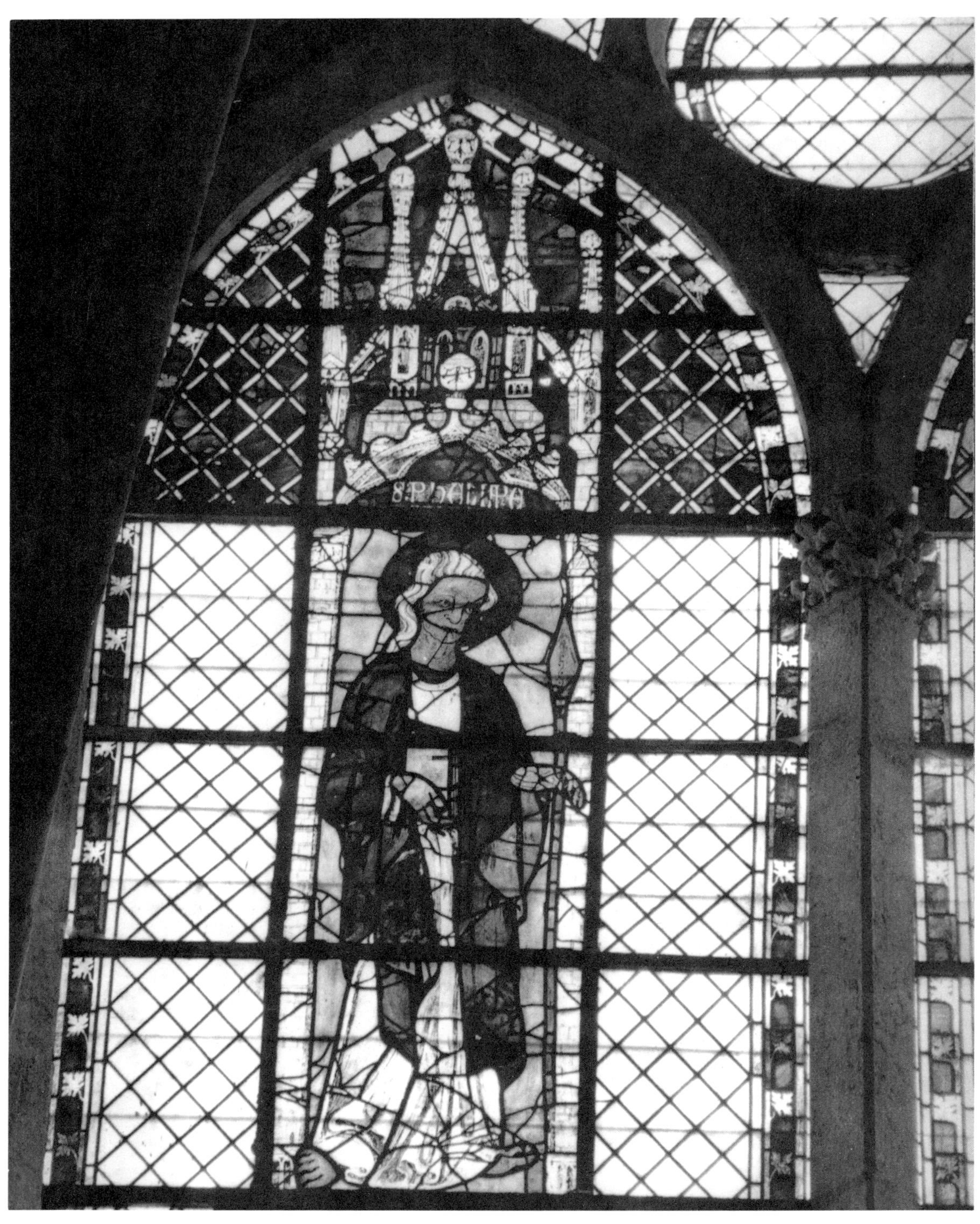

PLATE 56 Nave: Bay 20, left lancet. Remnants of original diaper ground. *(Photo: Edouard Fièvet)*

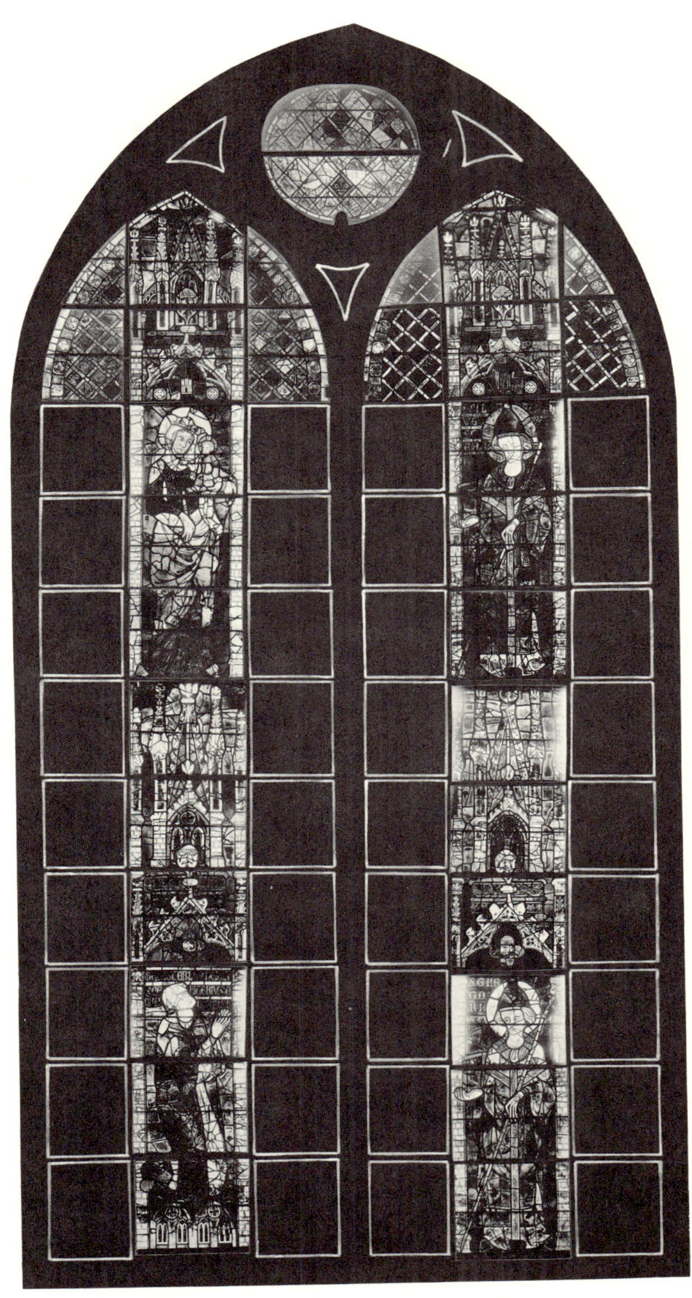

PLATE 57 Nave: Bay 21. *(Paris, Archives photographiques)*

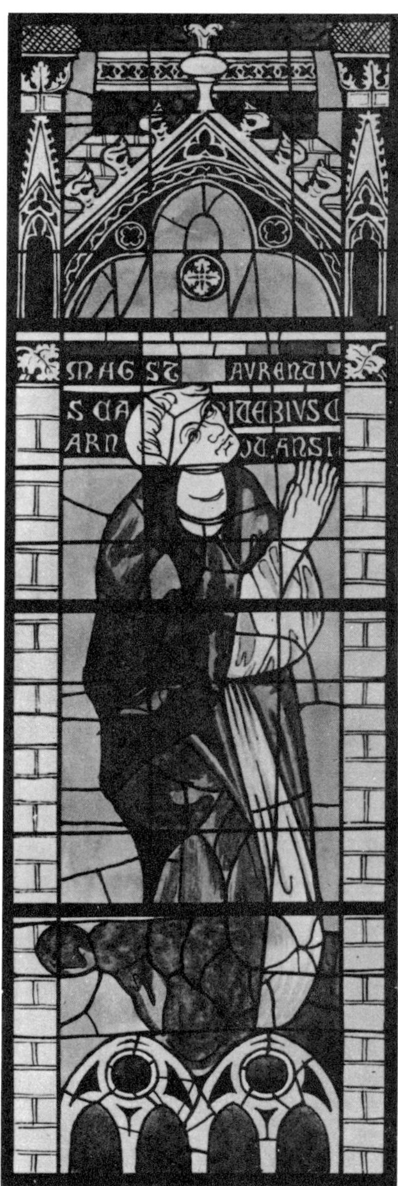

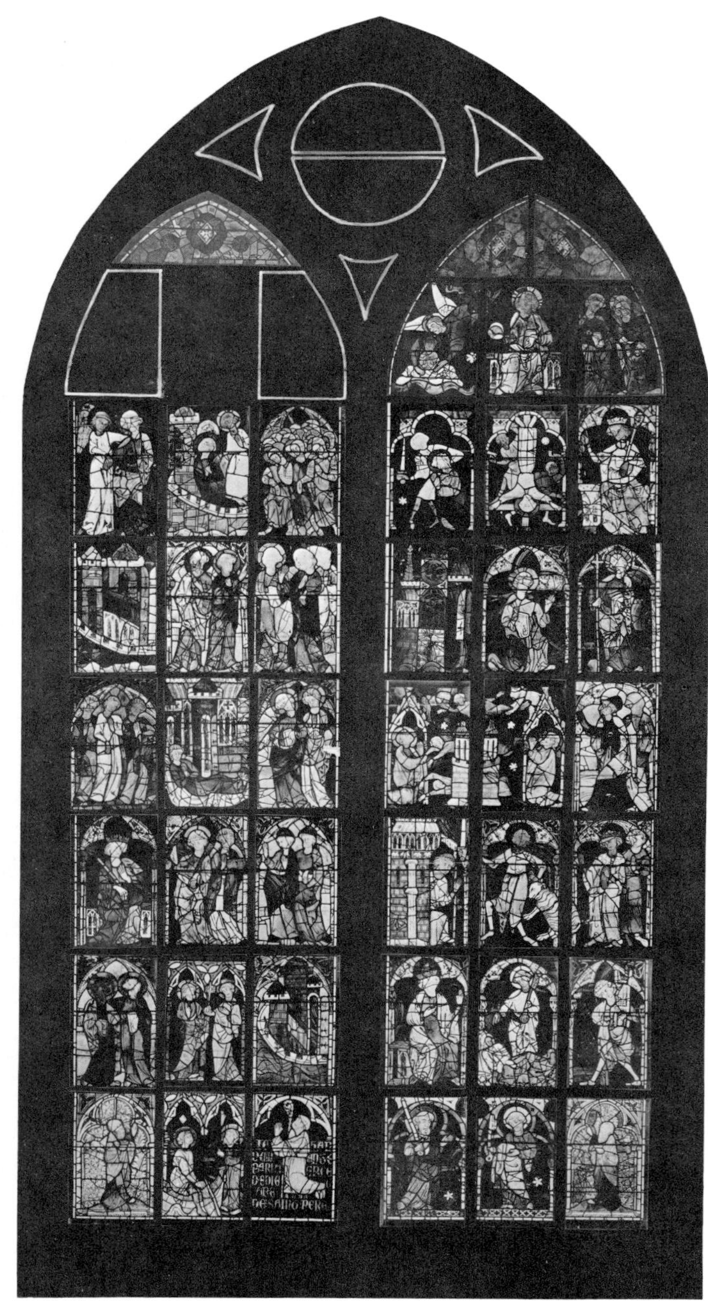

PLATE 58 Nave: Bay 21, left lancet. Donor Laurent Voisin. *(After F. de Lasteyrie, 1857)*

PLATE 59 Nave: Bay 22. *(Paris, Archives photographiques)*

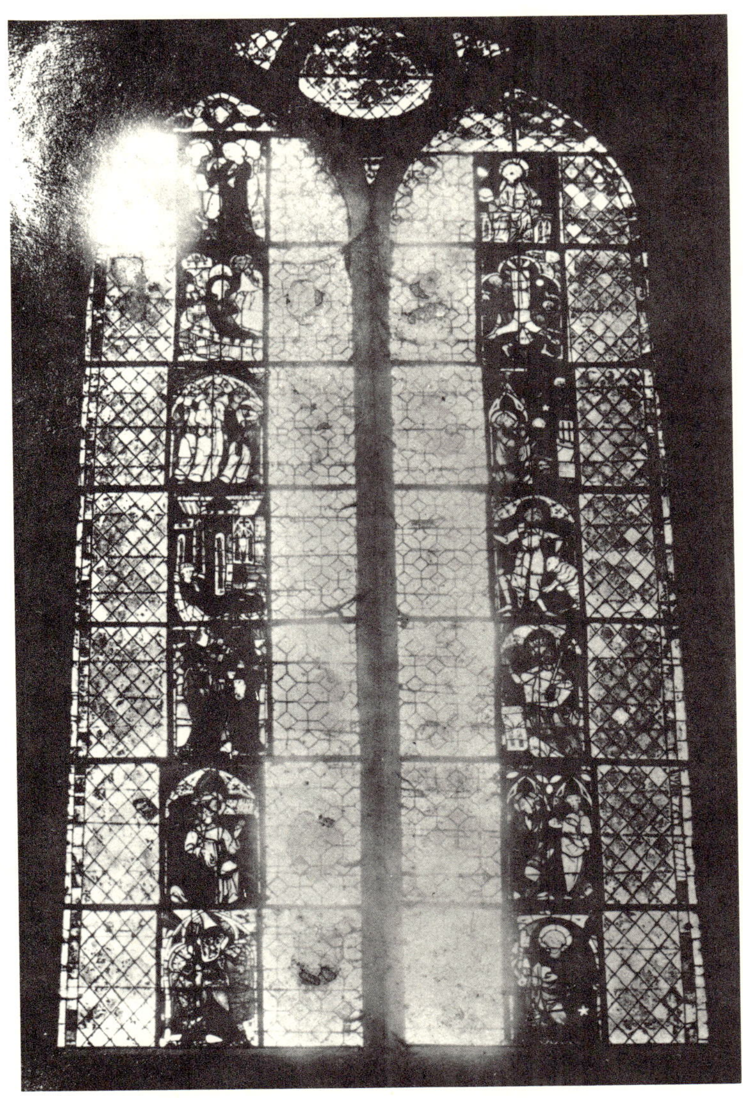

PLATE 60 Nave: Bay 22. Before 1905 restorations. *(Photo from François Lorin studio) (Paris, Archives photographiques)*

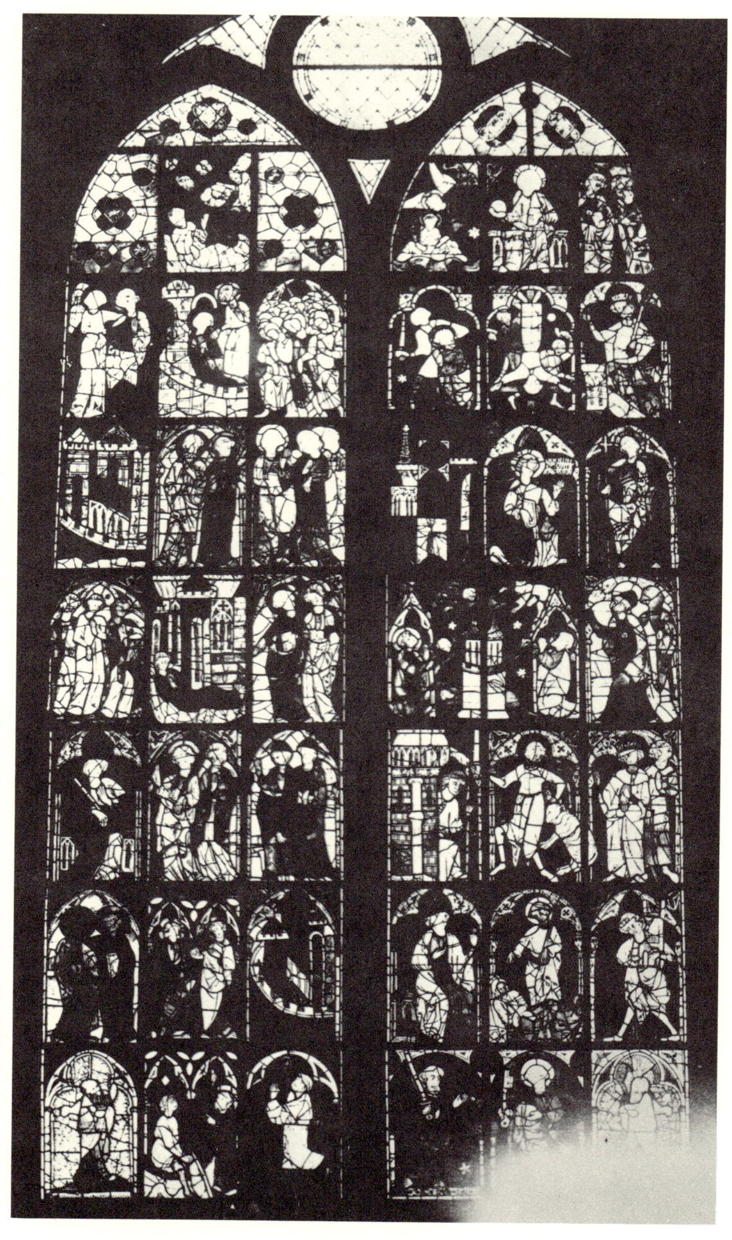

PLATE 61 Nave: Bay 22. Between the restorations of ca. 1905 and the 1950's. *(Photo from Jean Lafond collection) (Paris, Archives photographiques)*

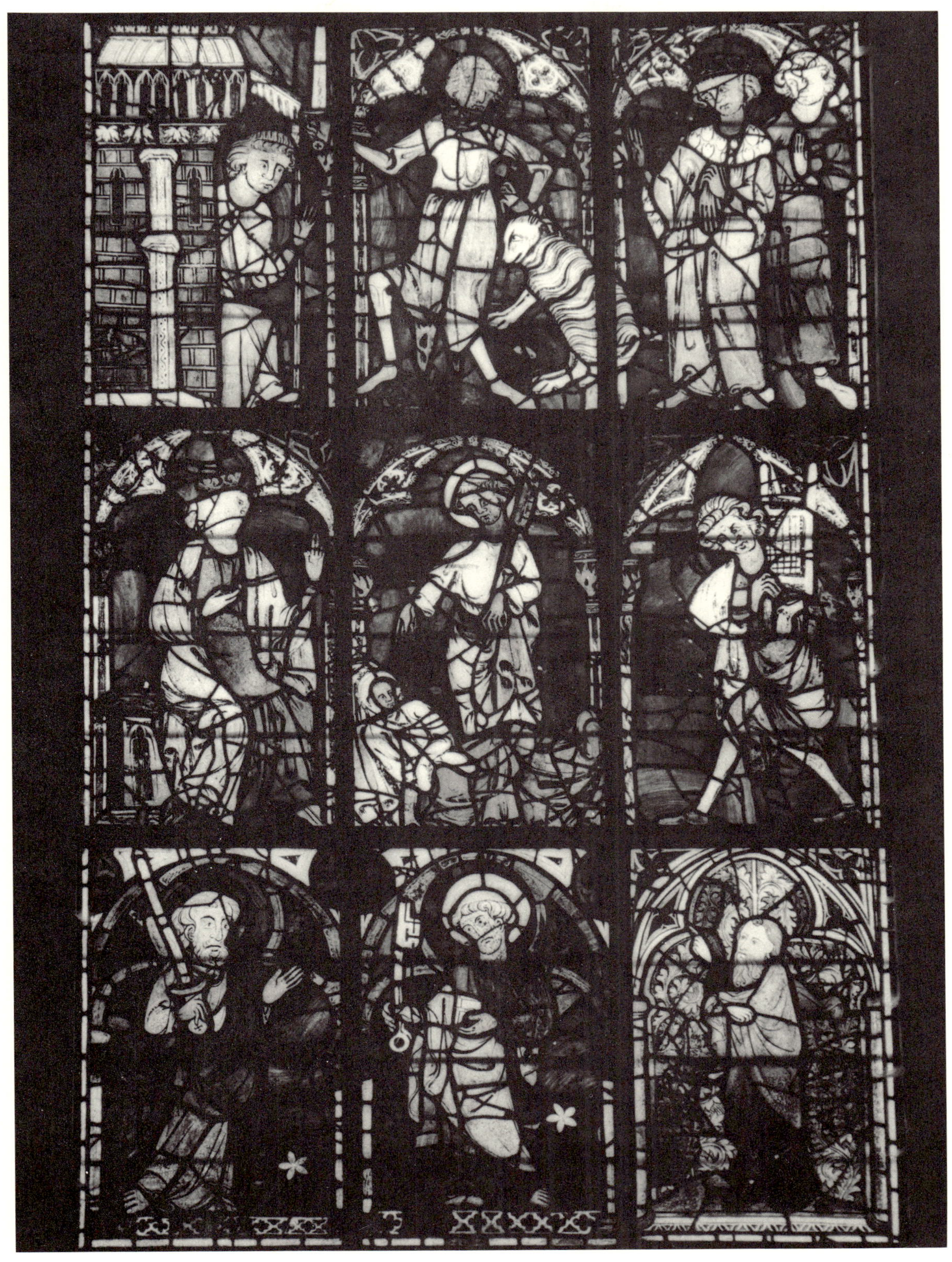

PLATE 62 Nave: Bay 22, right lancet. Peter window: Sts. Peter and Paul; contest with Simon Magus to revive dead youth, Simon's false execution. *(Photo: Edouard Fièvet)*

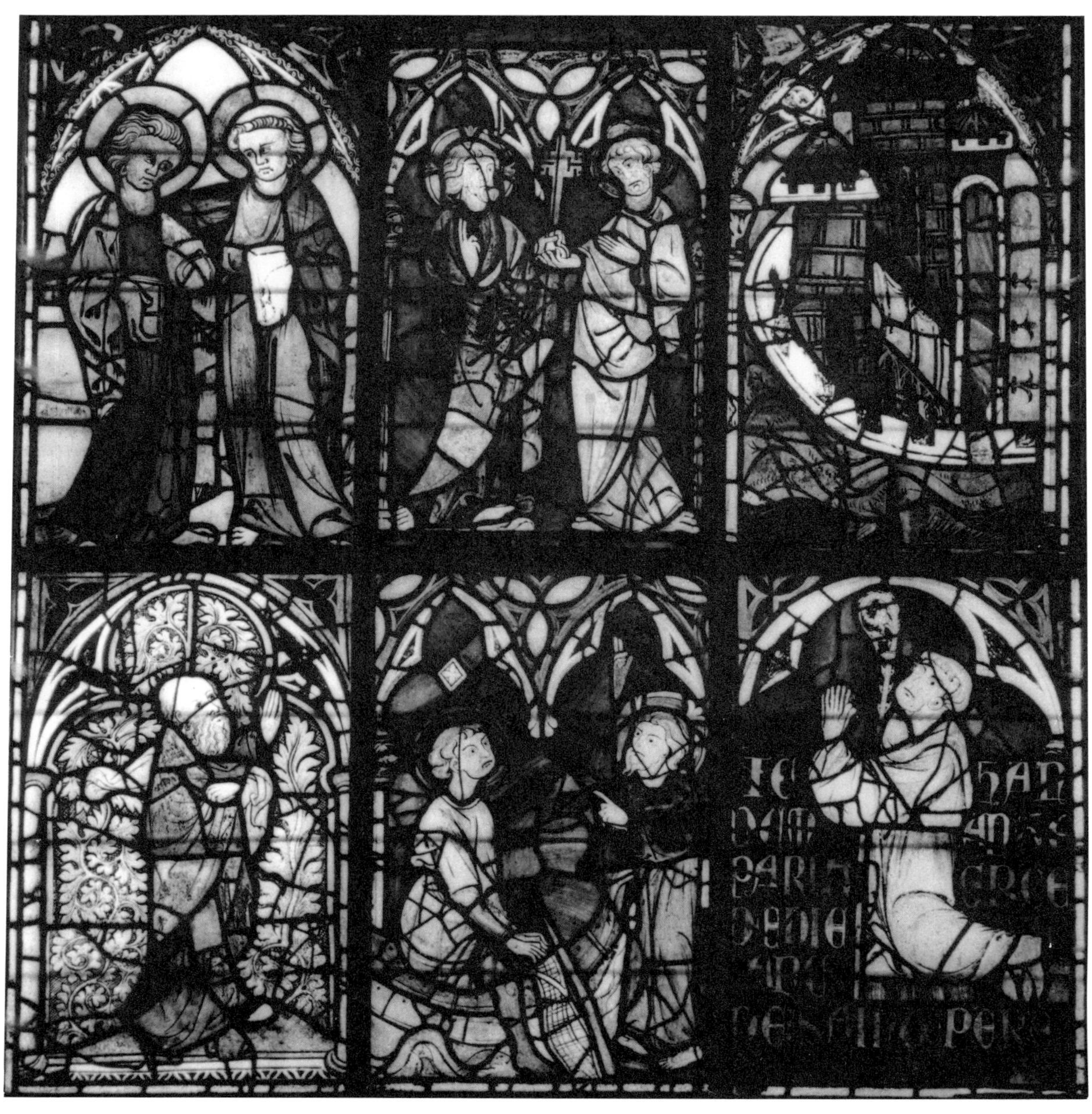

PLATE 63 Nave: Bay 22, left lancet. Peter window: Donor Jehan de Mantes, Calling of Peter; Giving of the keys, etc. *(Photo: Edouard Fièvet)*

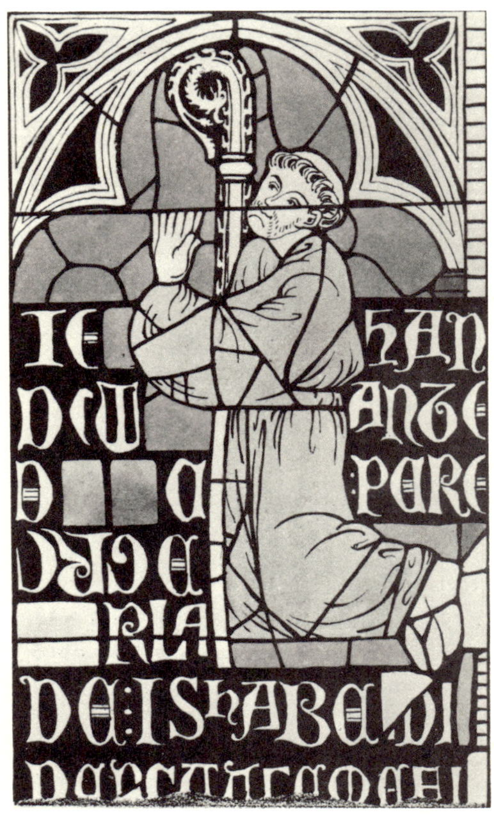

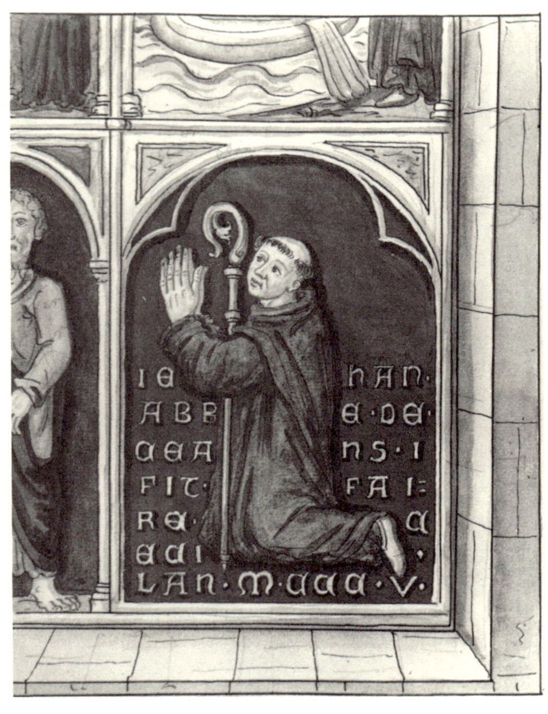

PLATE 64 Nave: Bay 22, left lancet. Donor Jehan de Mantes. *(After F. de Lasteyrie, 1857)*

PLATE 65 Nave: Bay 22, left lancet. Donor Jehan de Mantes. Gaignières drawing. *(Oxford, Bodleian Ms. Gough Drawings-Gaignières 9, fol. 56).*

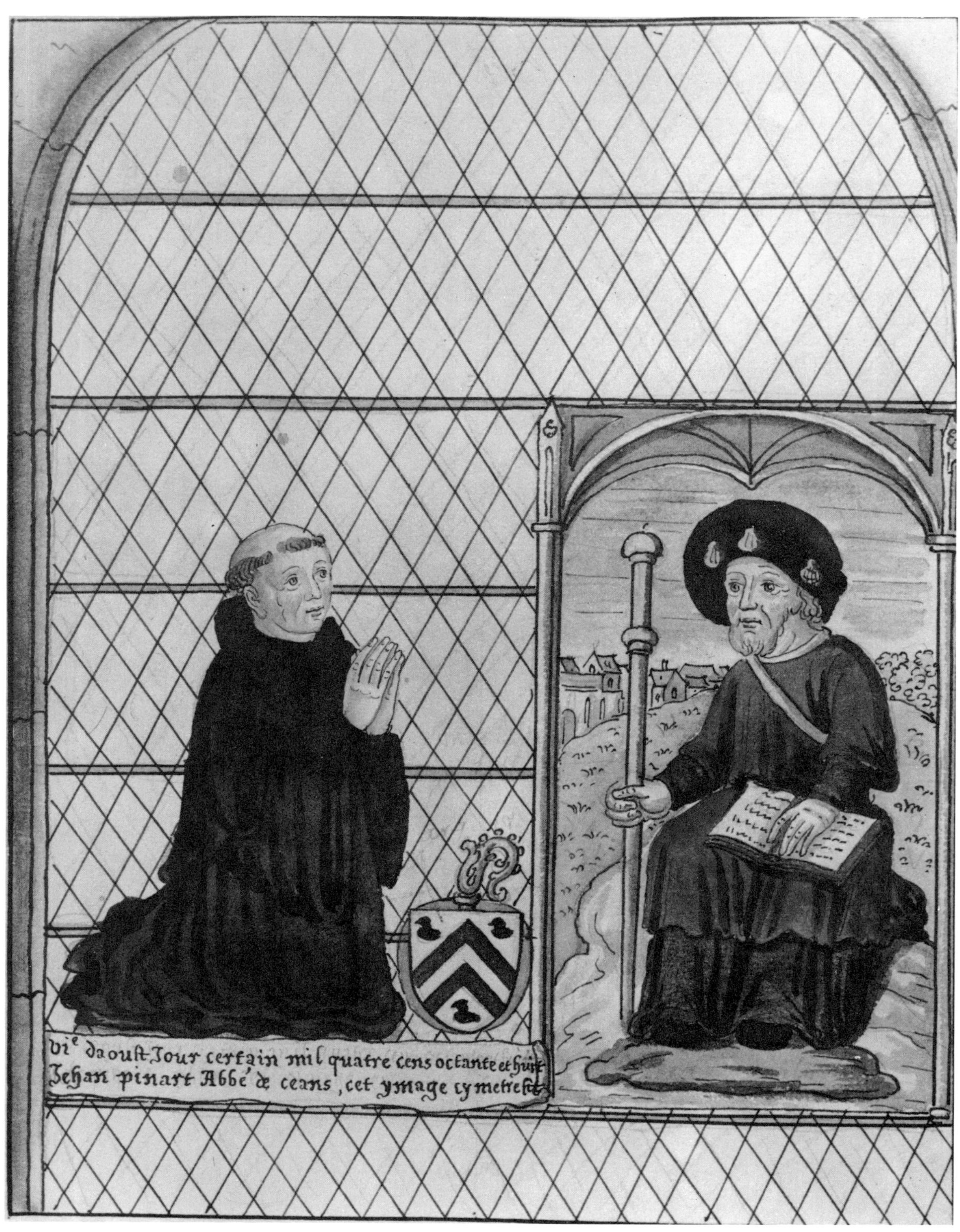

PLATE 66 Saint-Père: lost window of Abbot Jehan Pinart, late 15th century, from aisle (?). Gaignières drawing. *(Oxford, Bodleian Ms. Gough Drawings-Gaignières 9, fol. 57)*

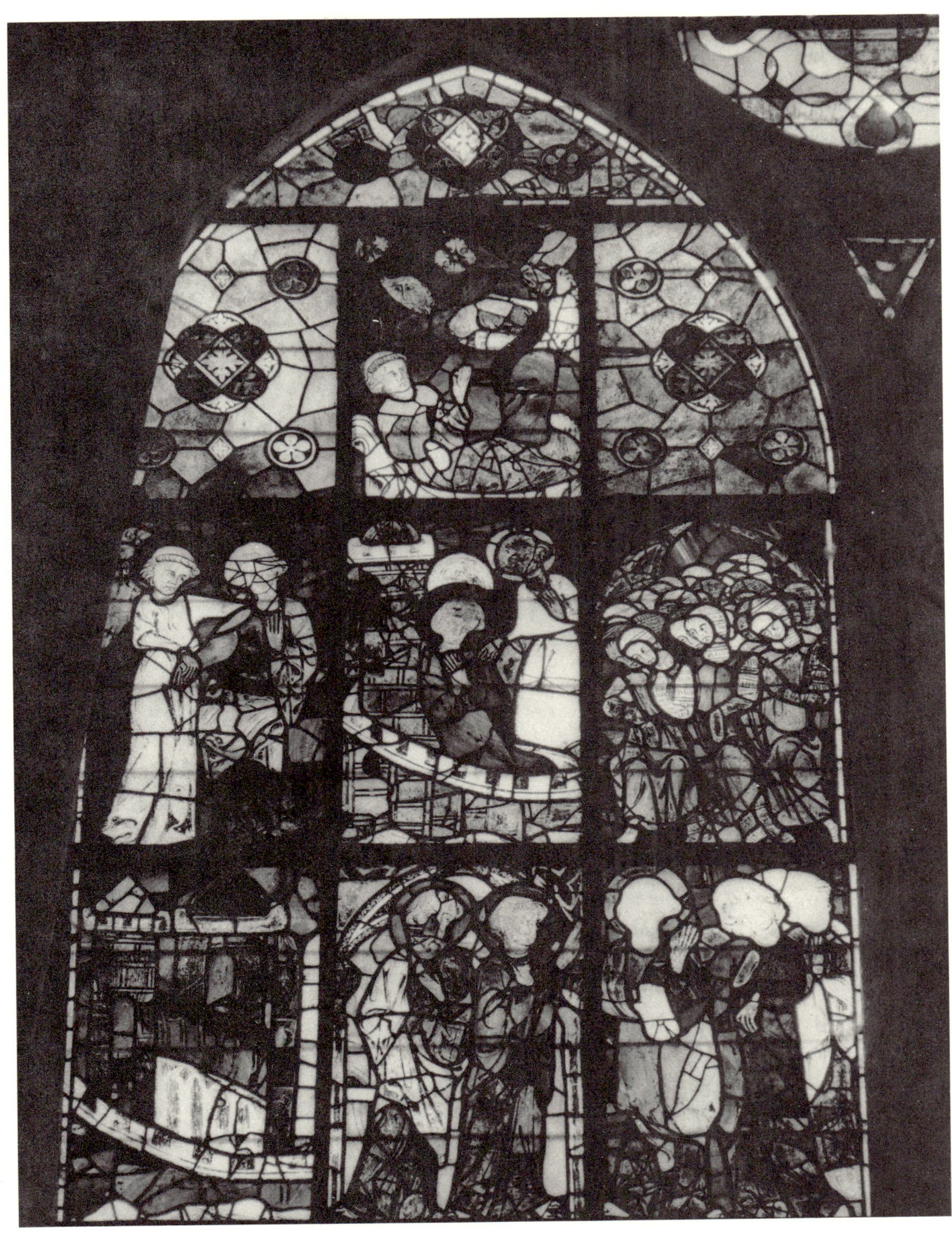

PLATE 67 Nave: Bay 22, left lancet. Peter window: St. Peter in prison. *(Photo: Edouard Fièvet)*

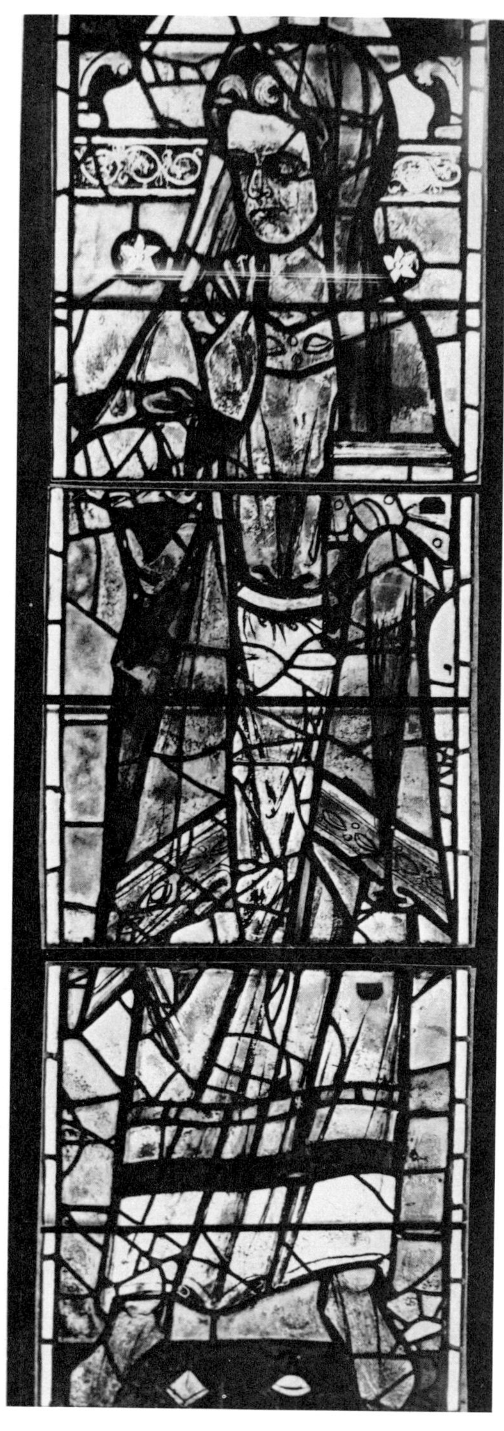

PLATE 68 Nave: Bay 22, right lancet. Peter window: Christ in Majesty receiving Peter's soul; Peter healing with his shadow (?). *(Paris, Archives photographiques)*

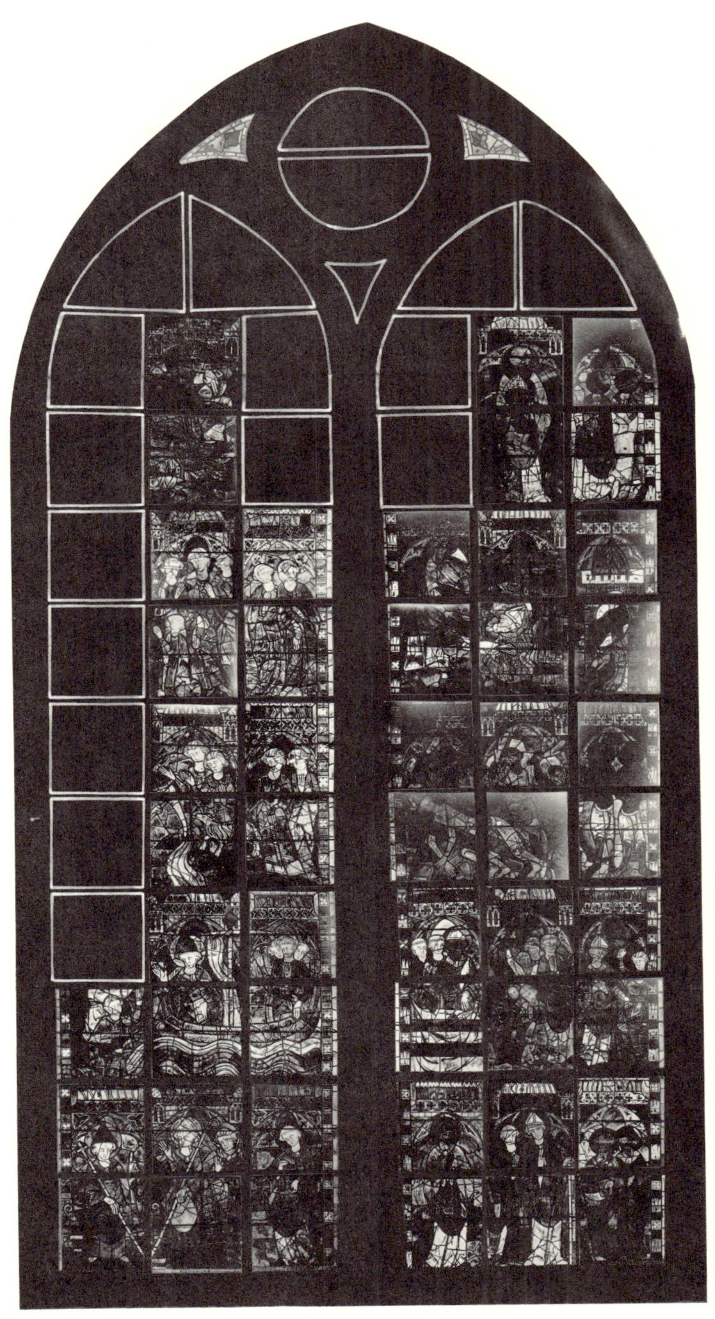

PLATE 69 Nave: Bay 23. *(Paris, Archives photographiques)*

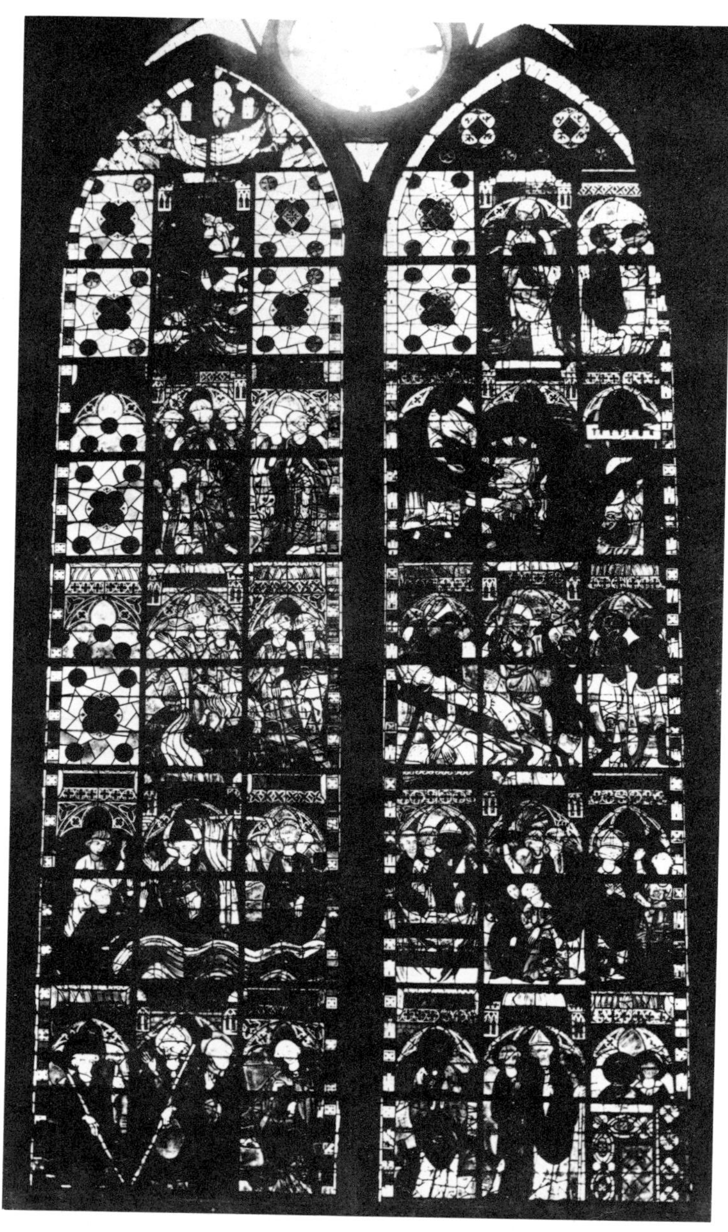

PLATE 70 Nave: Bay 23. Between the restorations of ca. 1905 and the 1950's. *(Photo from Jean Lafond collection) (Paris, Archives photographiques)*

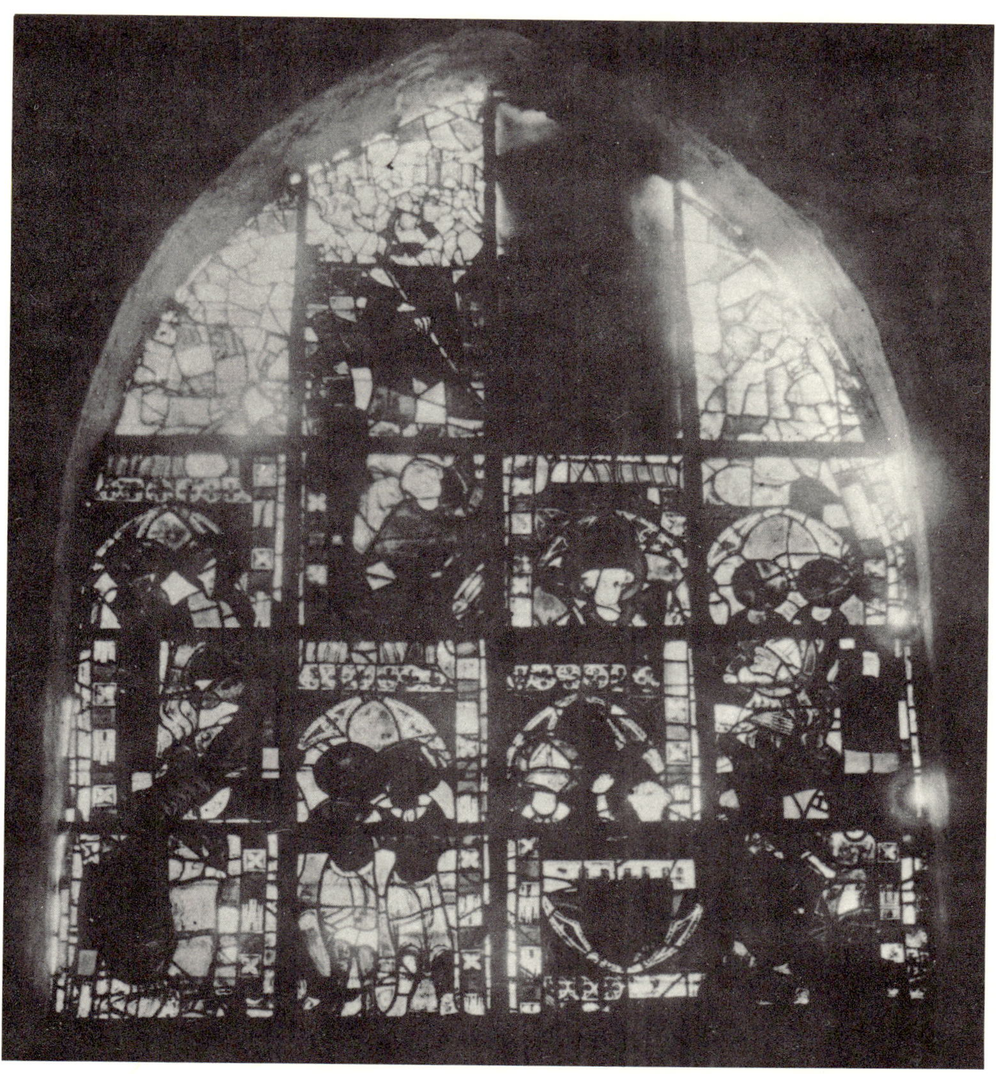

PLATE 71 Ambulatory window. Before the 1905 restorations, showing panels removed from Bay 23. *(Photo from Michon) (Paris, Archives photographiques)*

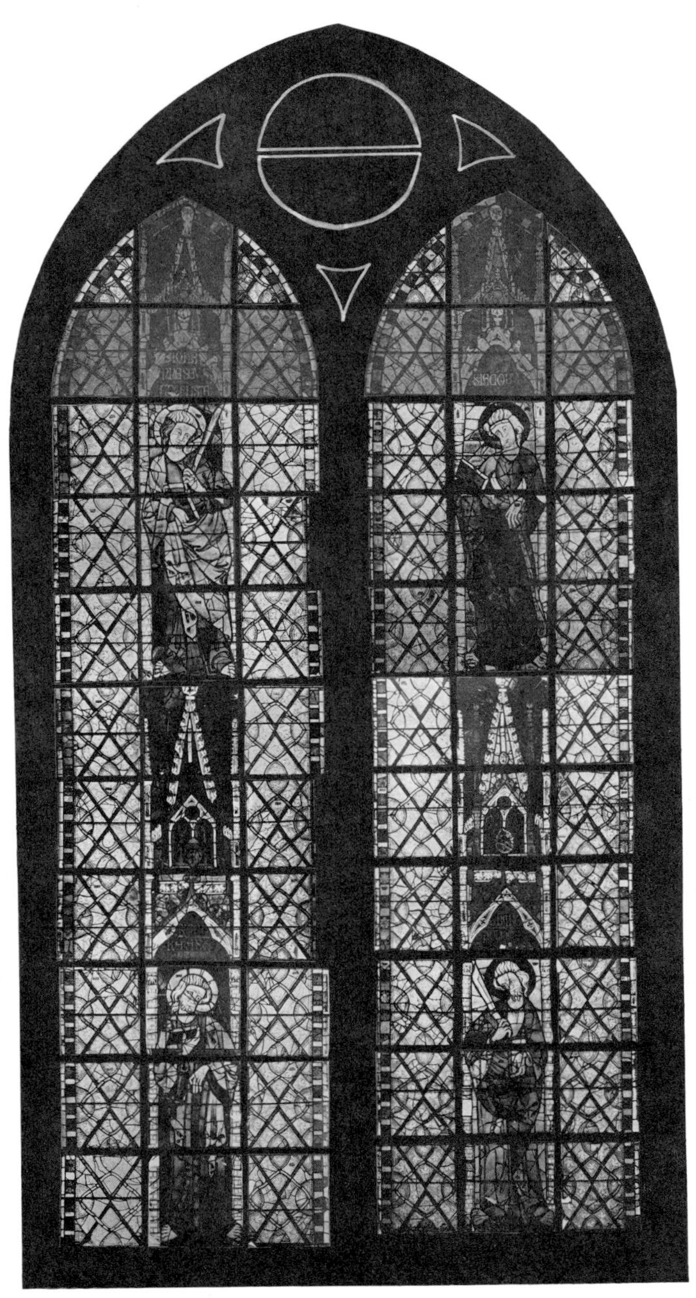

PLATE 72 Nave: Bay 24. *(Paris, Archives photographiques)*

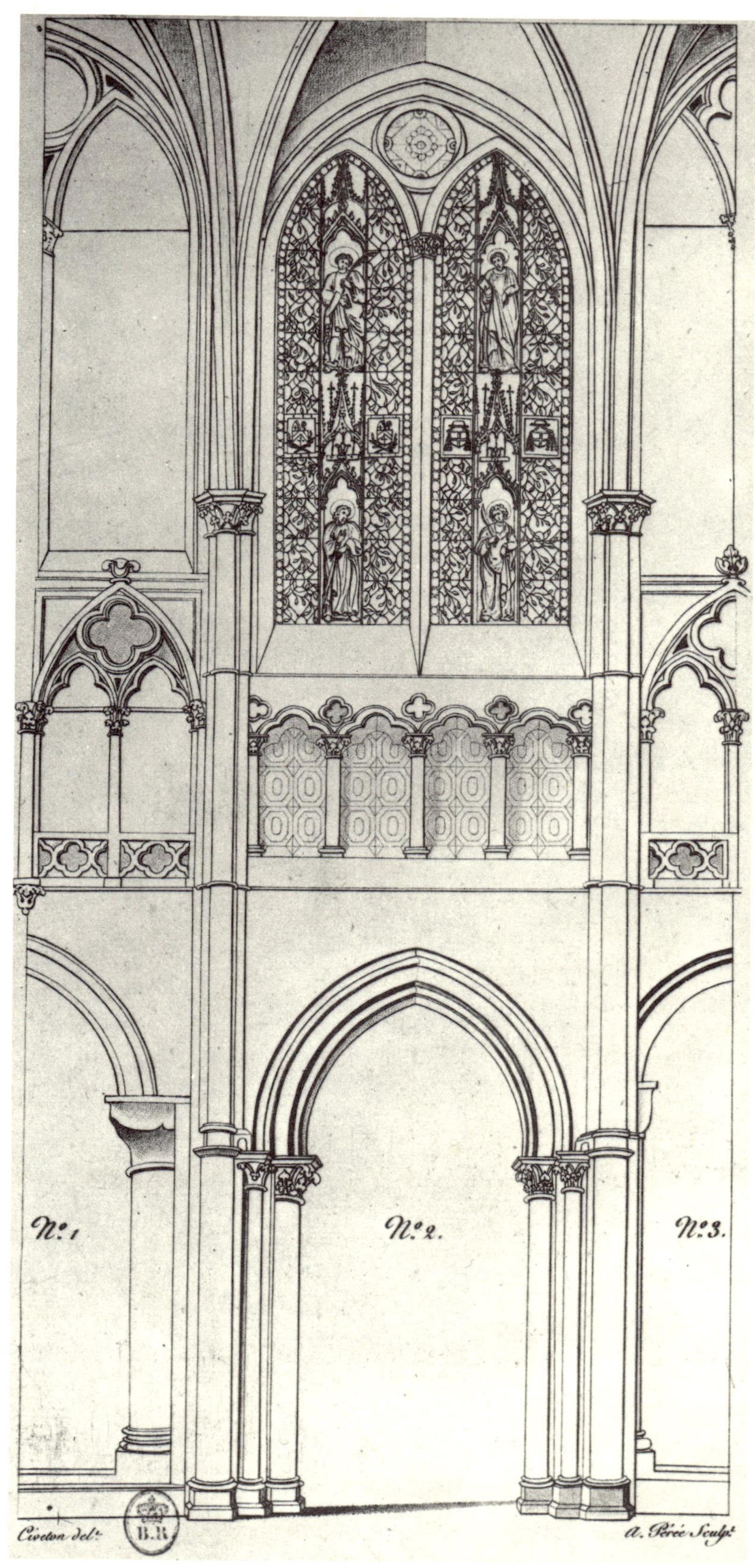

Plate 73 Nave: Bay 24. *(After Willemin, 1806)*

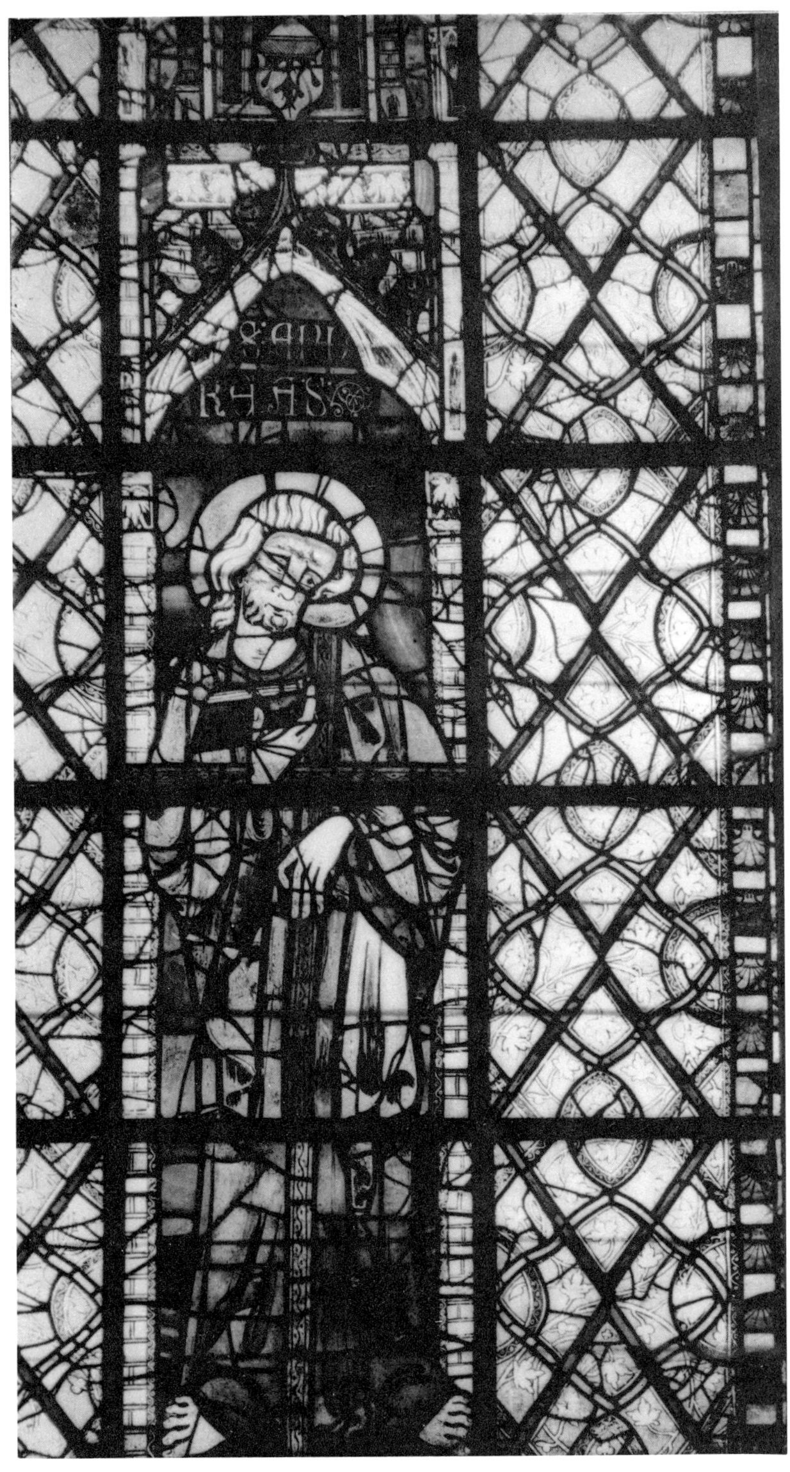

PLATE 74 Nave: Bay 24, left lancet. St. Andrew. *(Photo: Edouard Fièvet)*

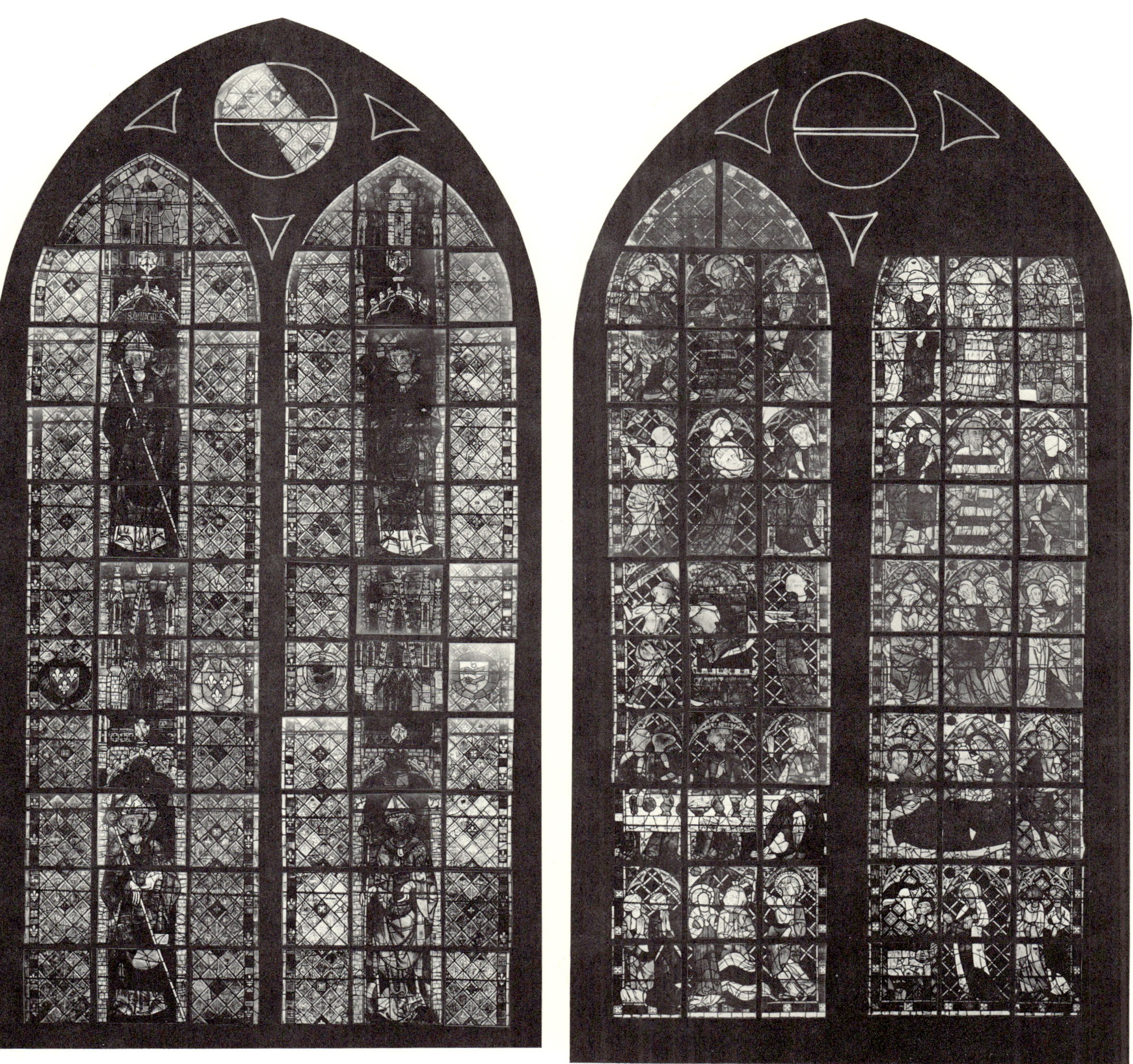

PLATE 75 Nave: Bay 25. *(Paris, Archives photographiques)*

PLATE 76 Nave: Bay 26. *(Paris, Archives photographiques)*

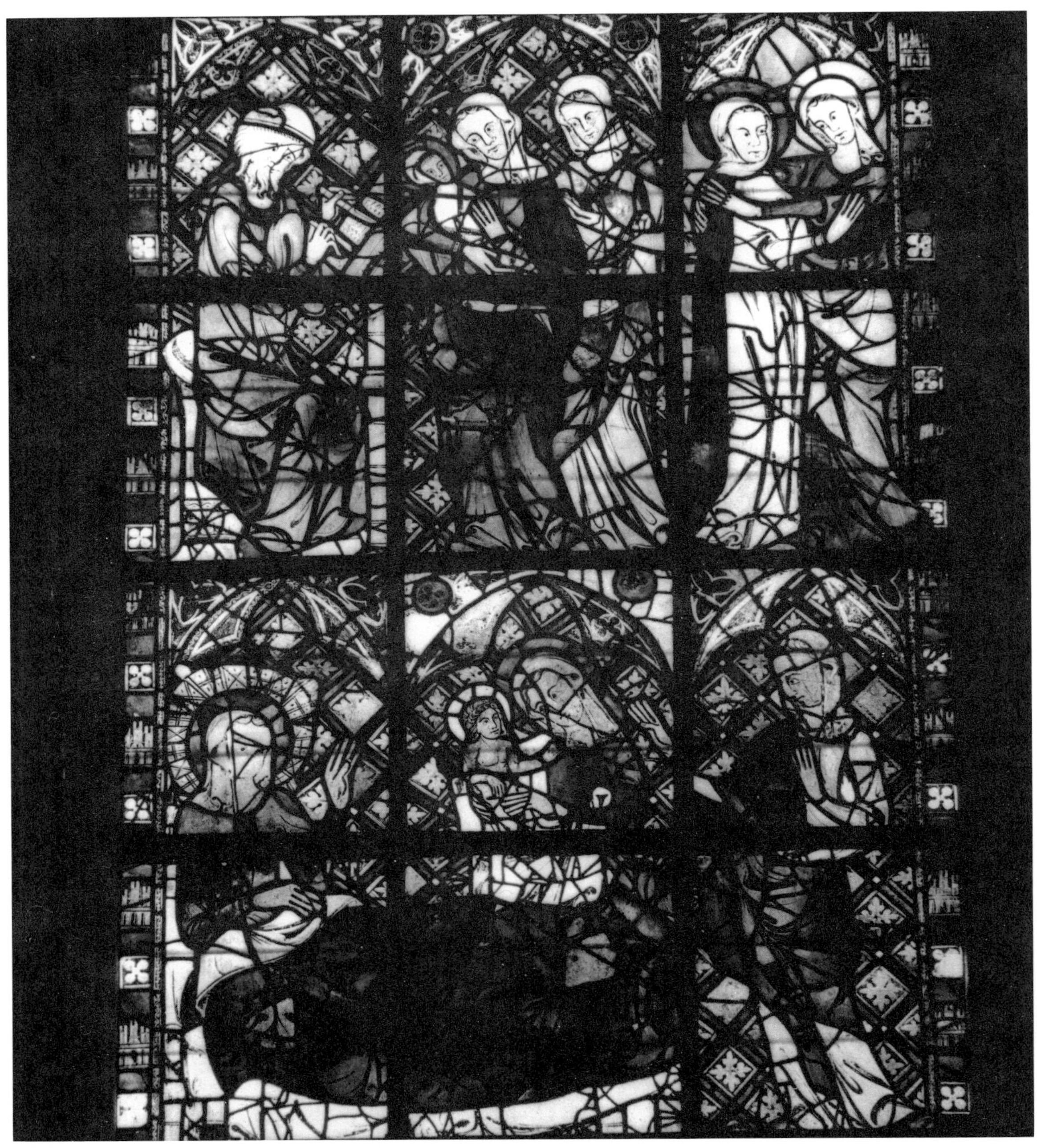

PLATE 77 Nave: Bay 26, right lancet. Baptist window: Birth of Baptist; Visitation, Naming by Zacharias. *(Photo: Edouard Fièvet)*

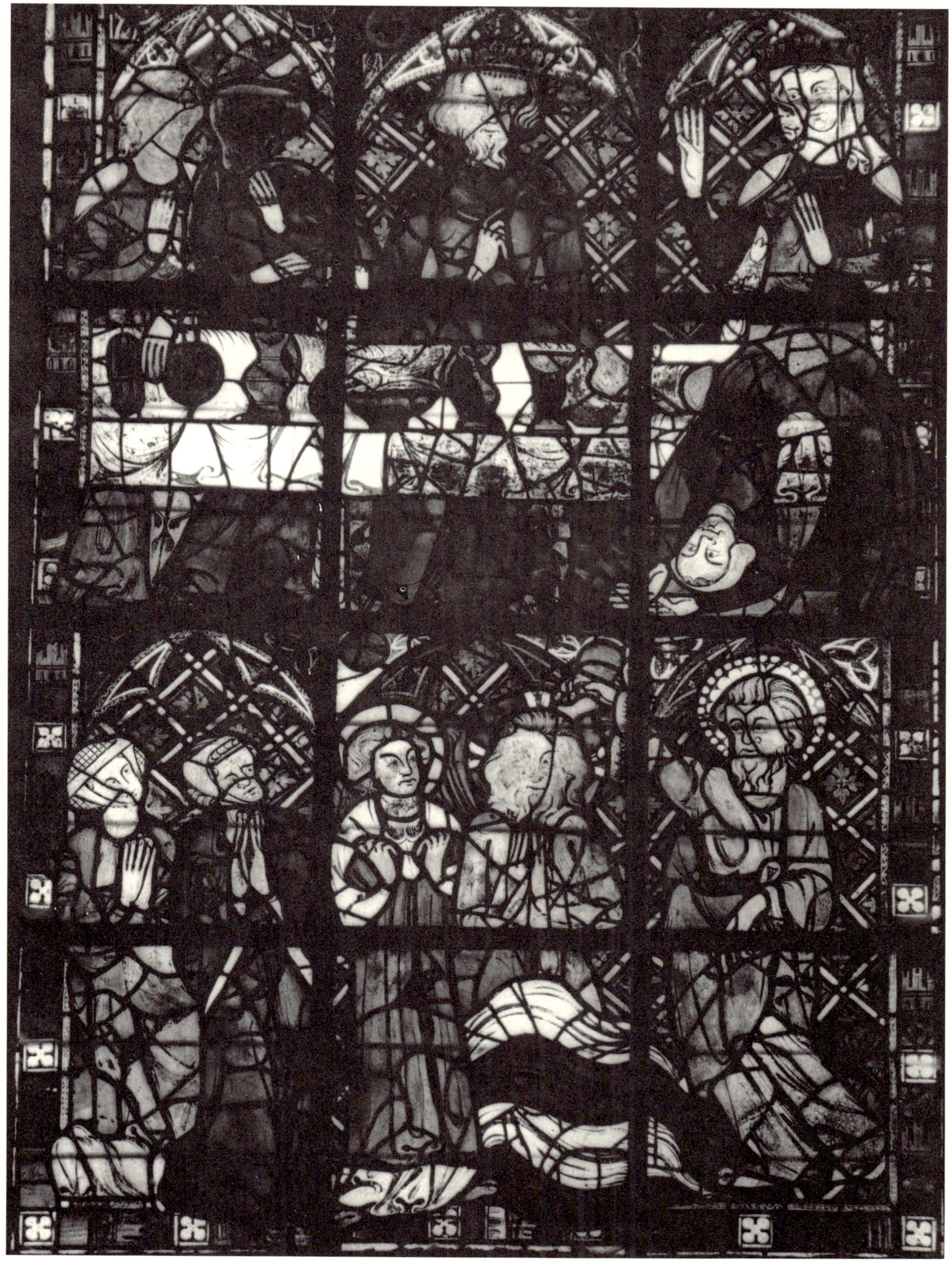

PLATE 78 Nave: Bay 26, left lancet. Baptist window: Baptism of Christ with donors. *(Photo: Edouard Fièvet)*

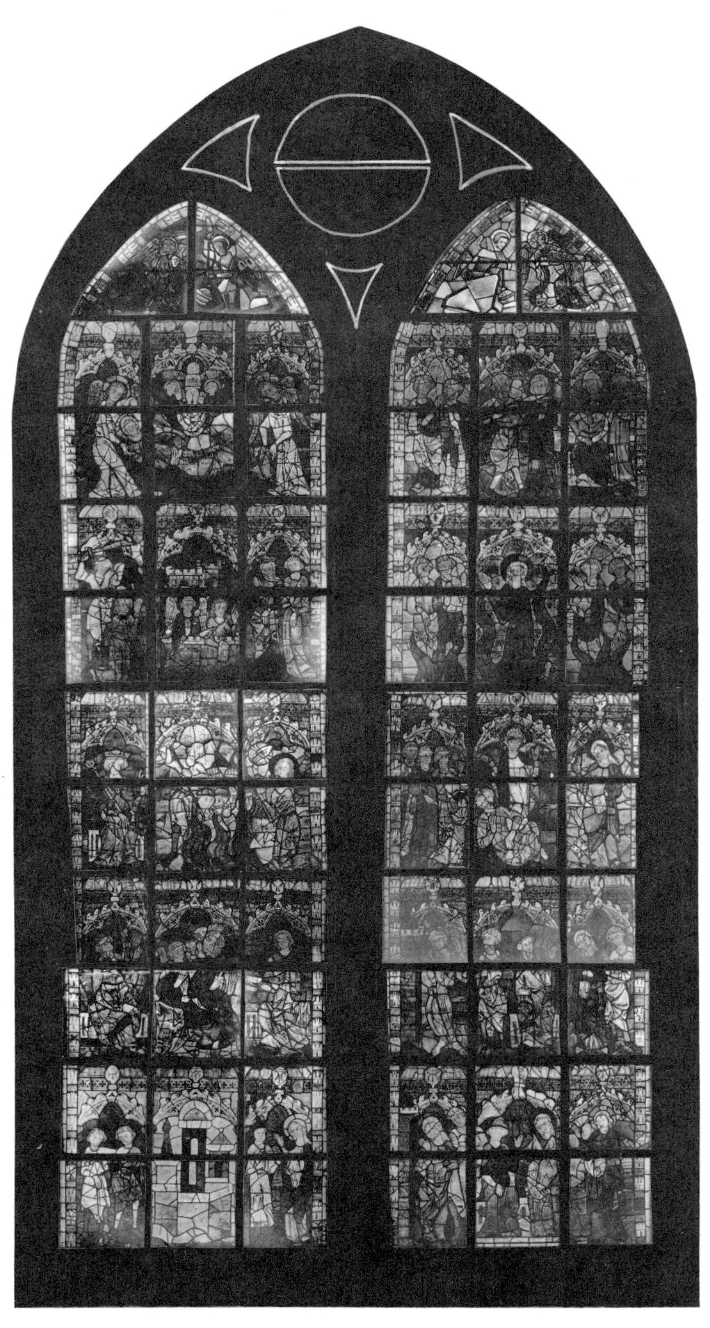

PLATE 79 Nave: Bay 27. *(Paris, Archives photographiques)*

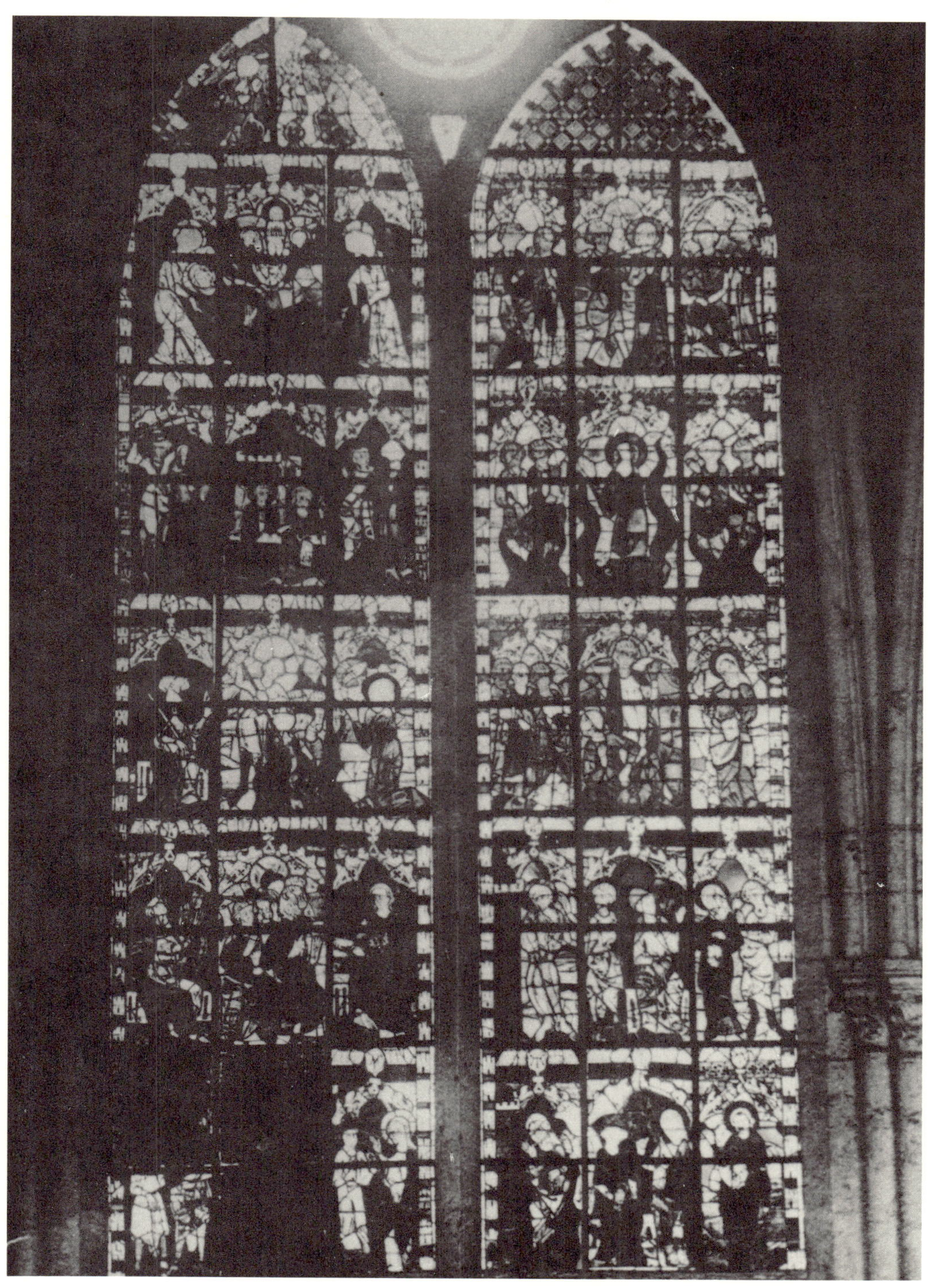

PLATE 80 Nave: Bay 27. Before 1922 (after ca. 1905?). *(Photo from Michon) (Paris, Archives photographiques)*

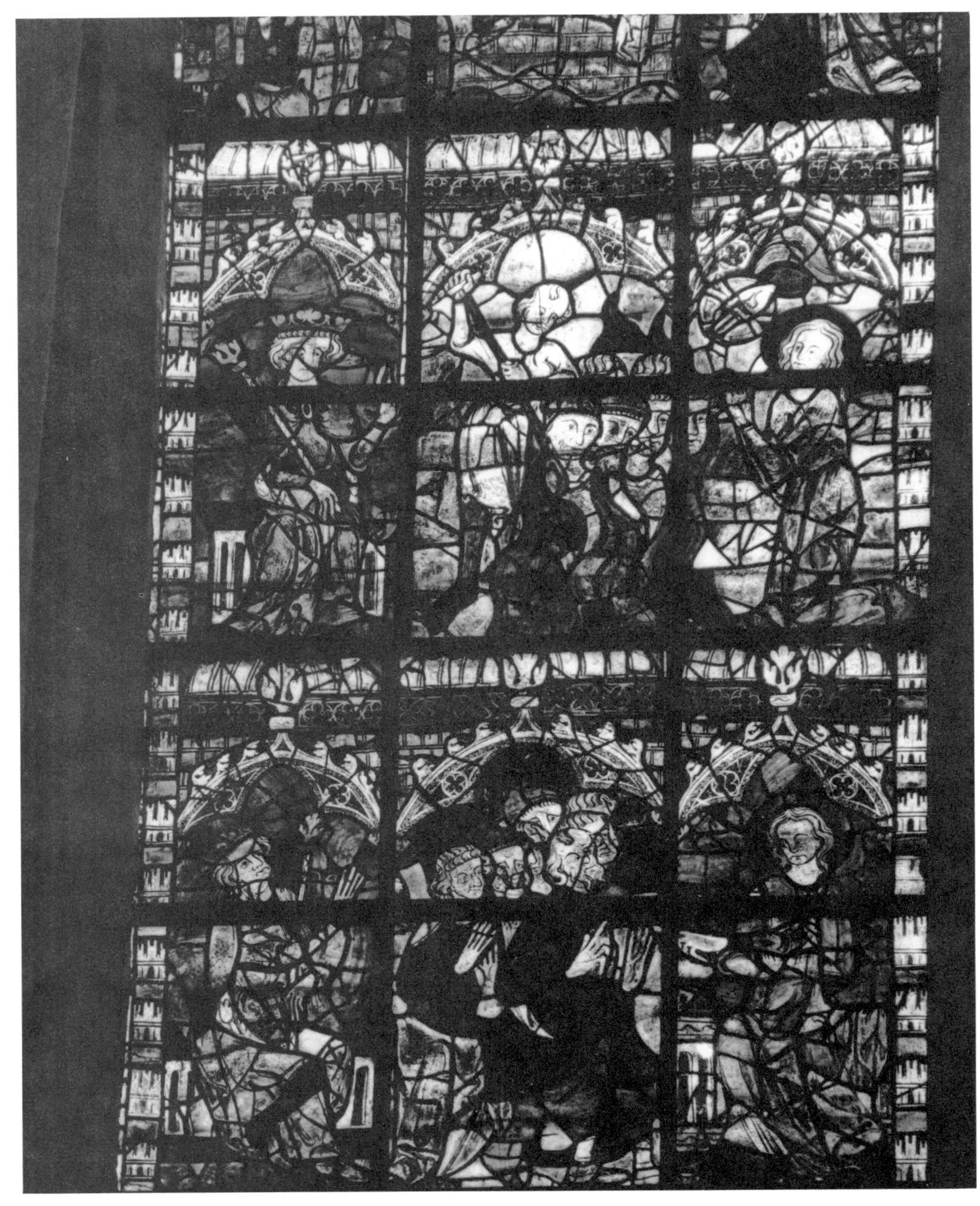

PLATE 81 Nave: Bay 27, left lancet. Catherine window: Dispute with philosophers, their execution. *(Photo: Edouard Fièvet)*

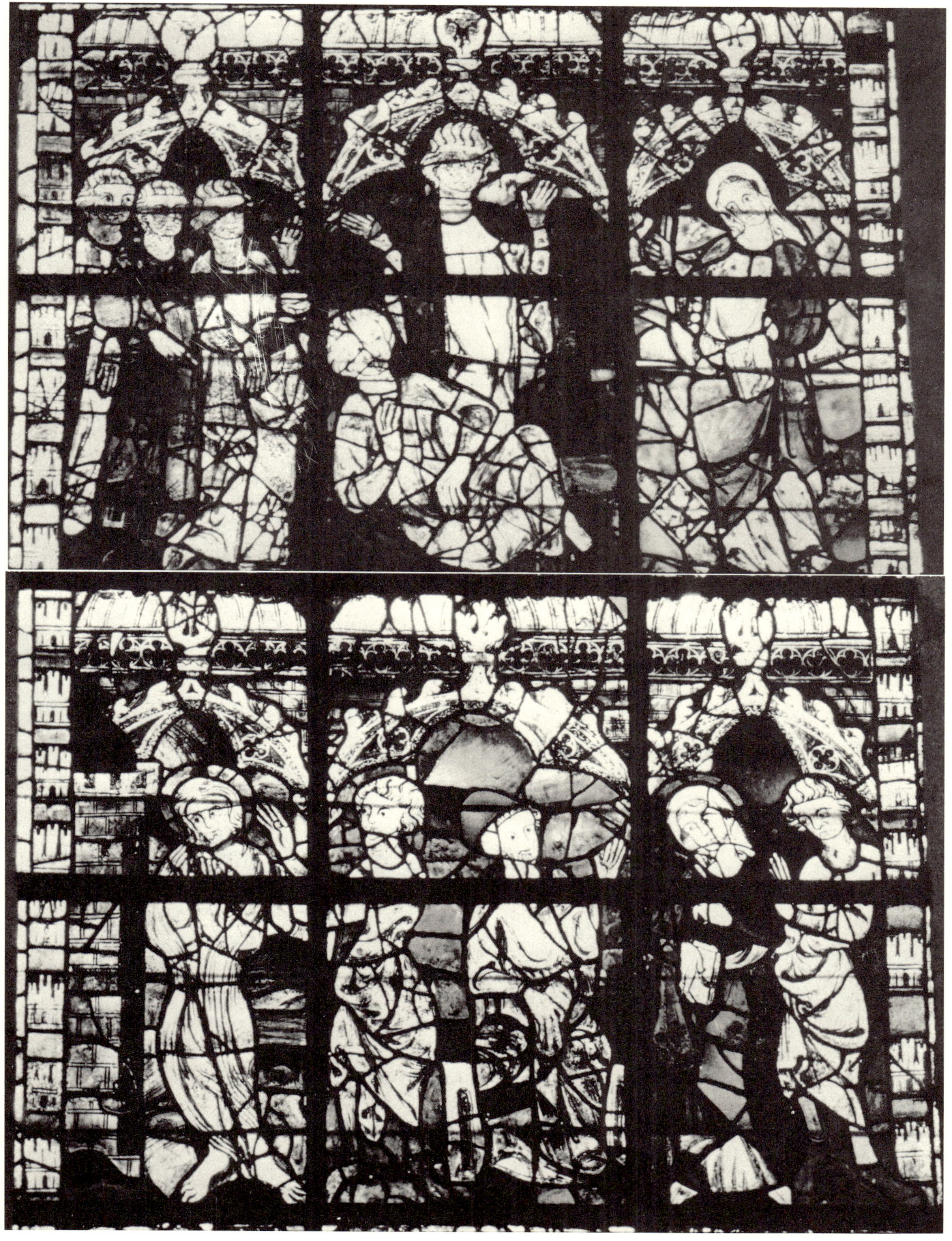

PLATE 82 Nave: Bay 27, right lancet. Agnes window: Agnes clothed in her hair, suitor struck down in brothel. *(Photo: Loïe Martine)*

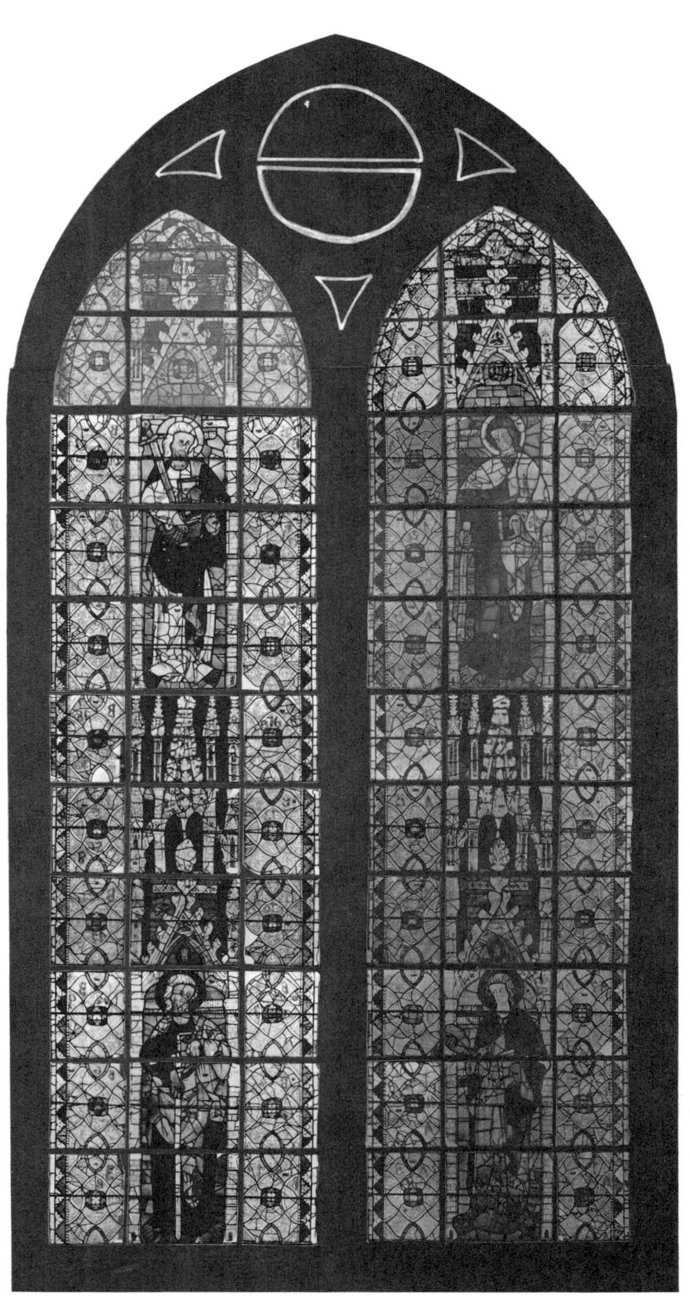

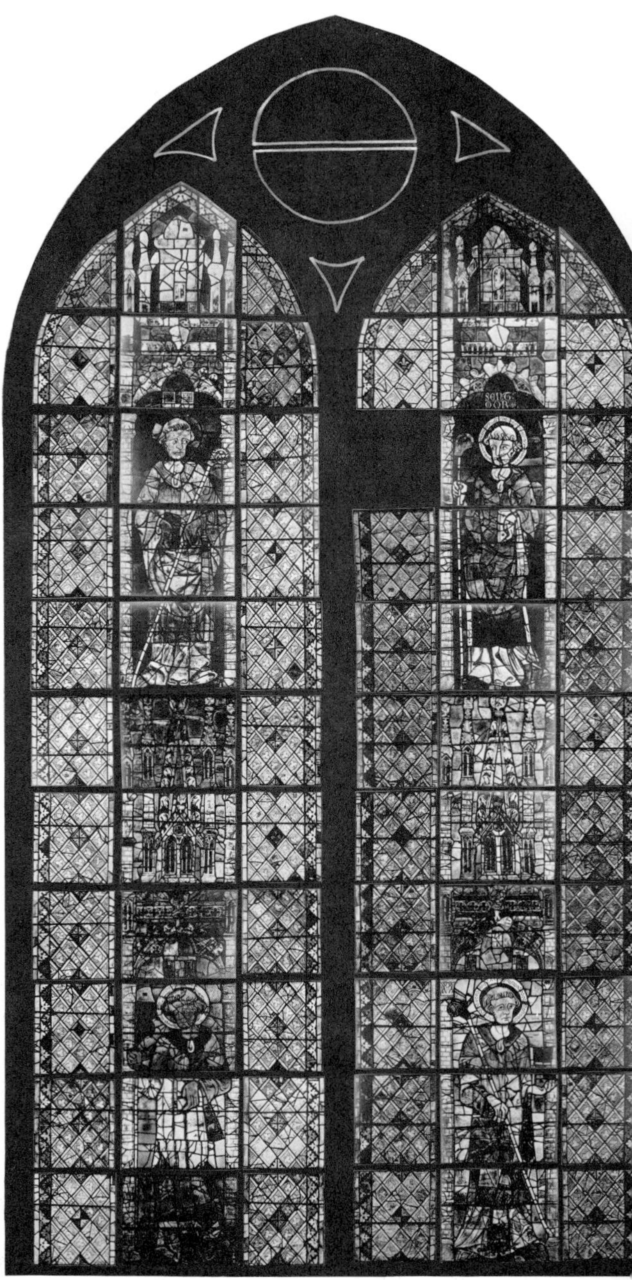

PLATE 83 Nave: Bay 28. *(Paris, Archives photographiques)*

PLATE 84 Nave: Bay 29. *(Paris, Archives photographiques)*

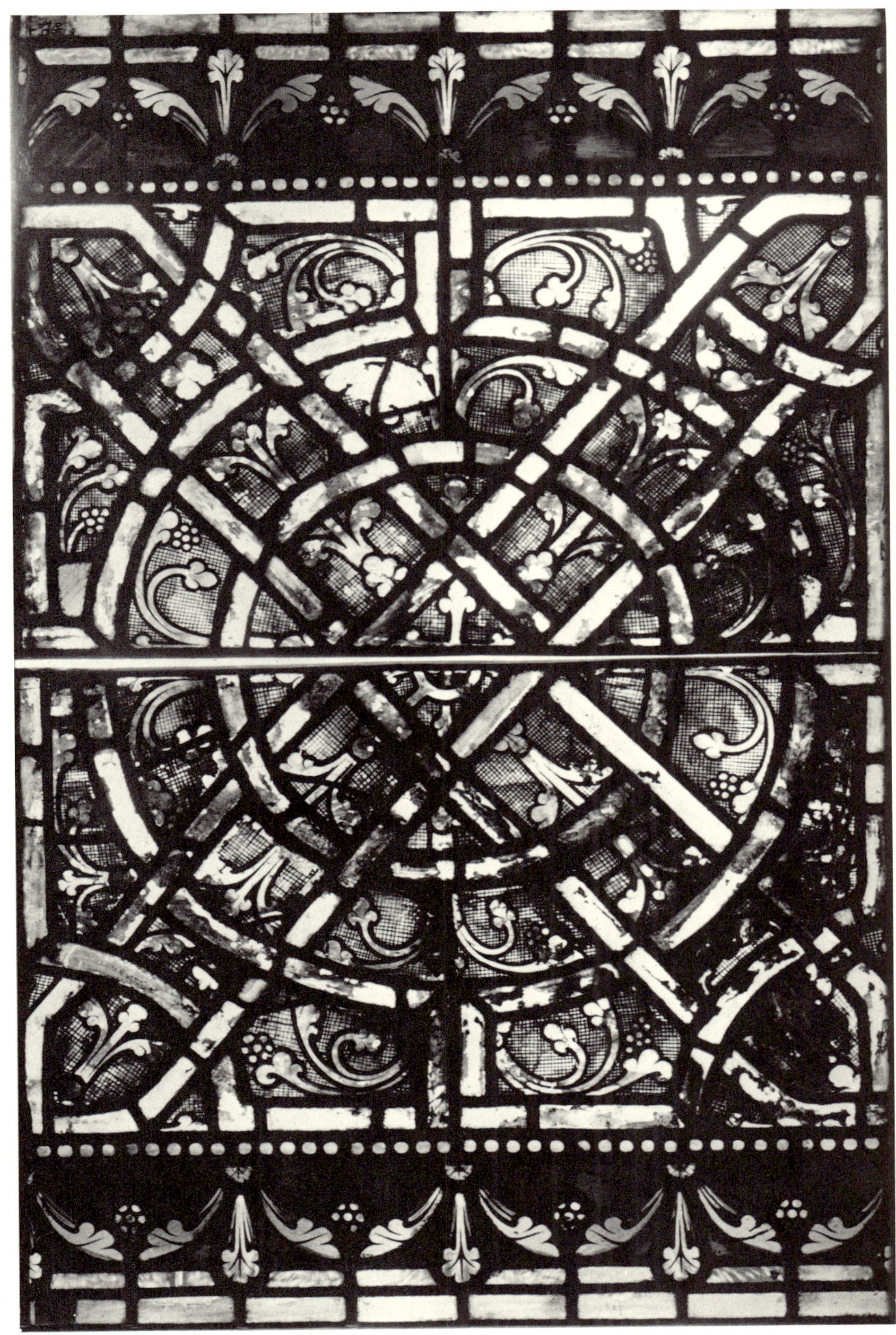

PLATE 85 Troyes Cathedral: grisaille. *(Paris, Archives photographiques)*

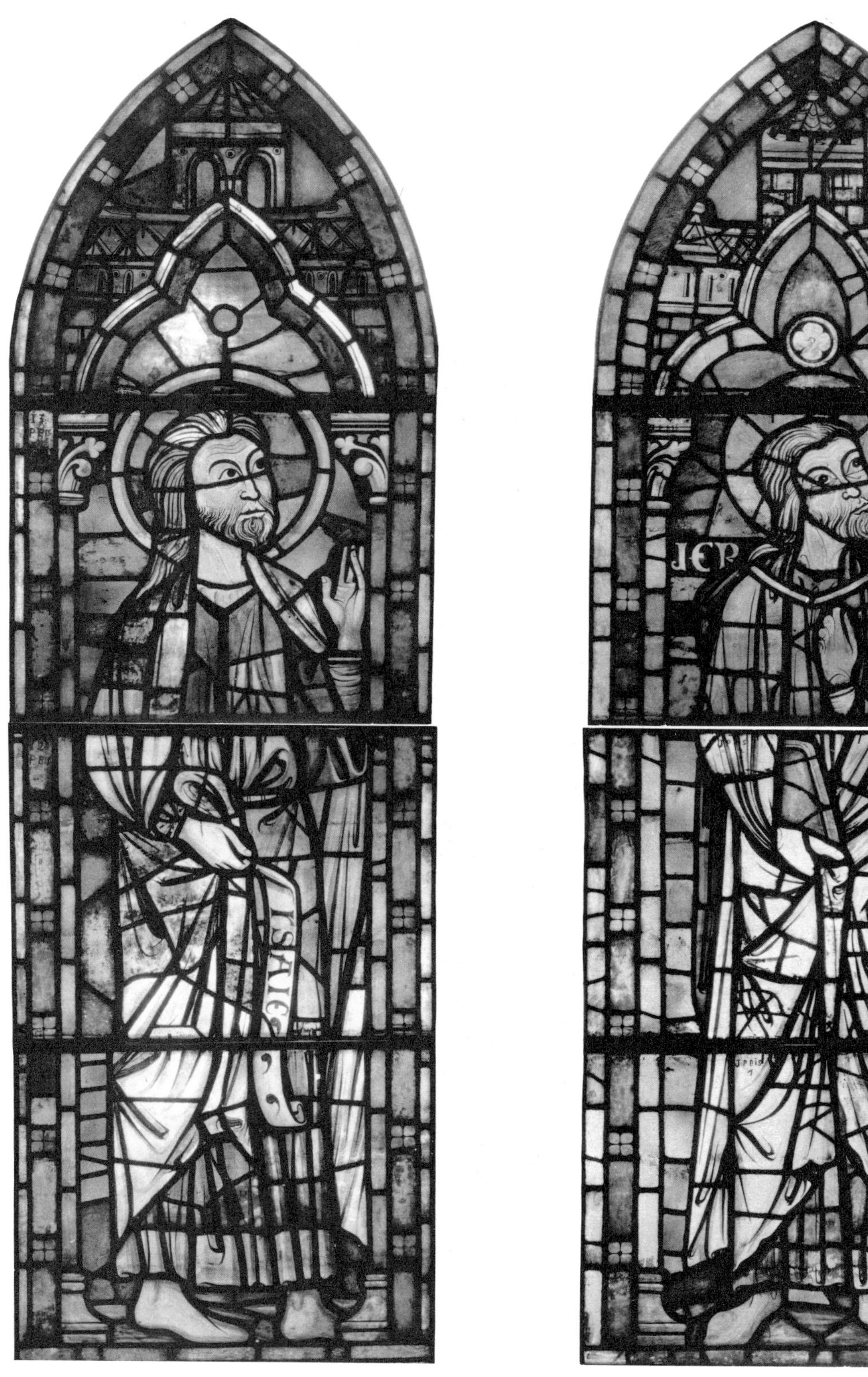

PLATE 86 Troyes Cathedral: triforium of axial bay. *(Paris, Archives photographiques)*

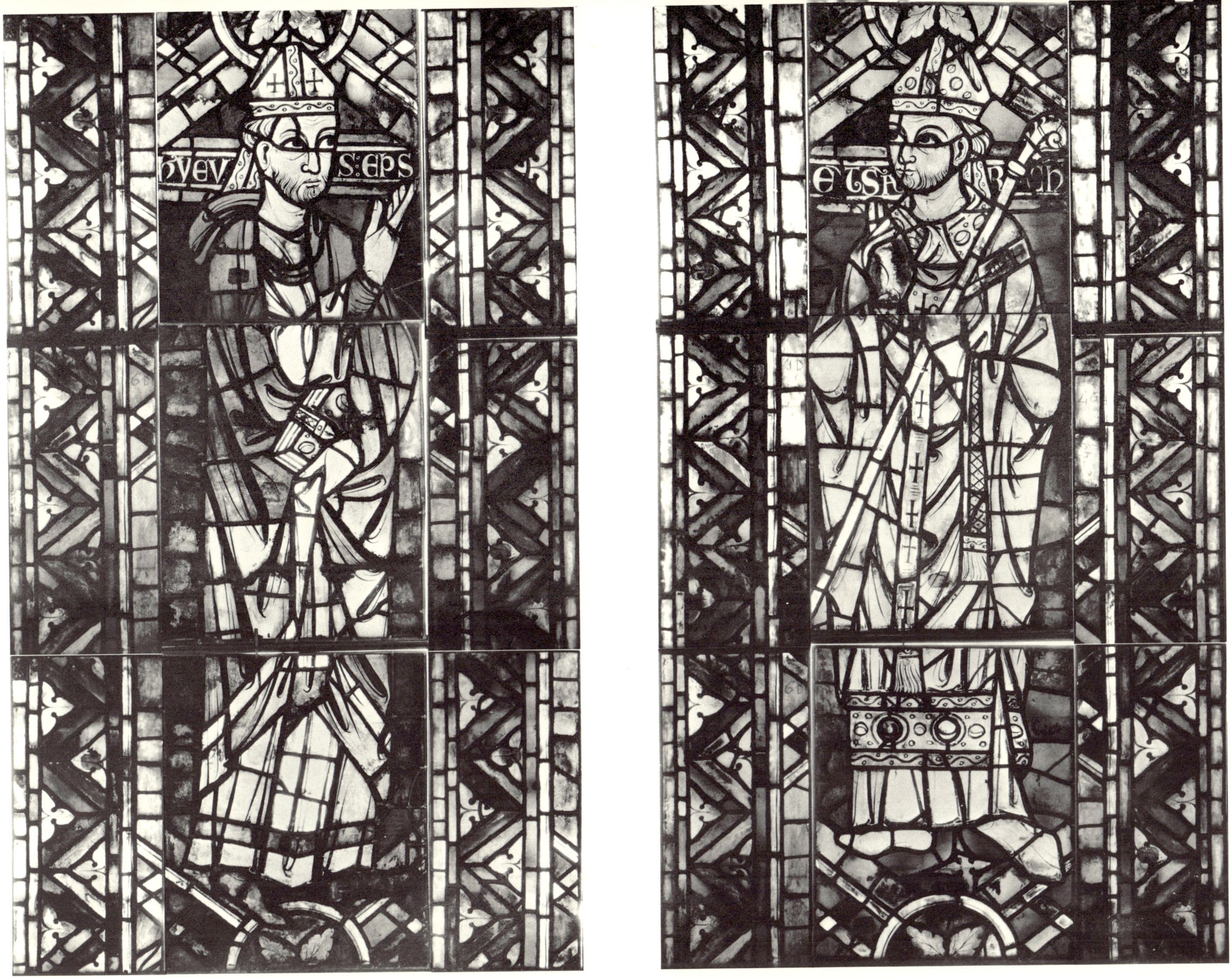

PLATE 87 Troyes Cathedral: north choir clerestory. Bishops and Kings window. *(Paris, Archives photographiques)*

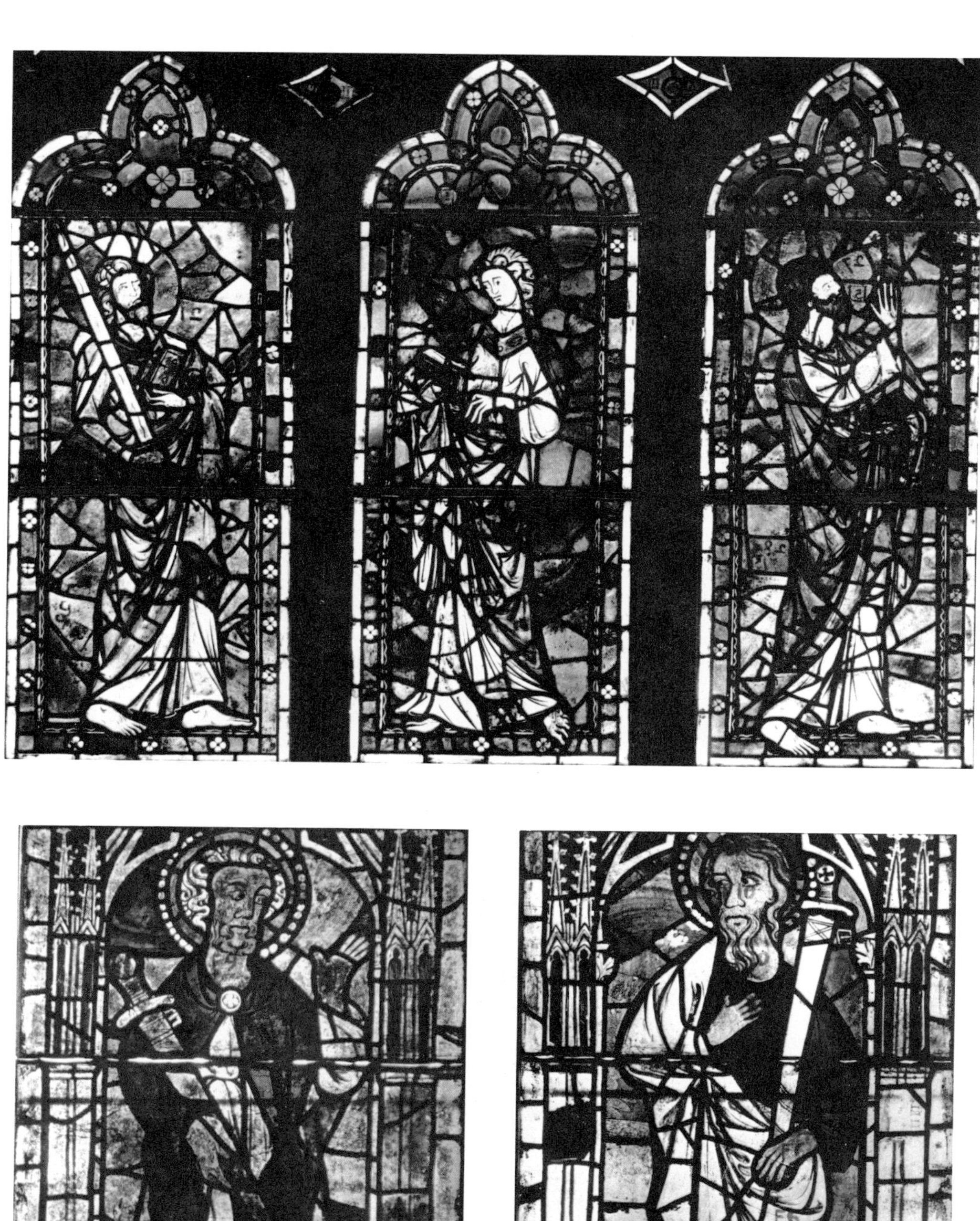

PLATE 88 Tours Cathedral: north hemicycle triforium. *(Paris, Archives photographiques)*

PLATE 89 La Trinité, Vendôme: north choir clerestory. Two apostles. *(Paris, Archives photographiques)*

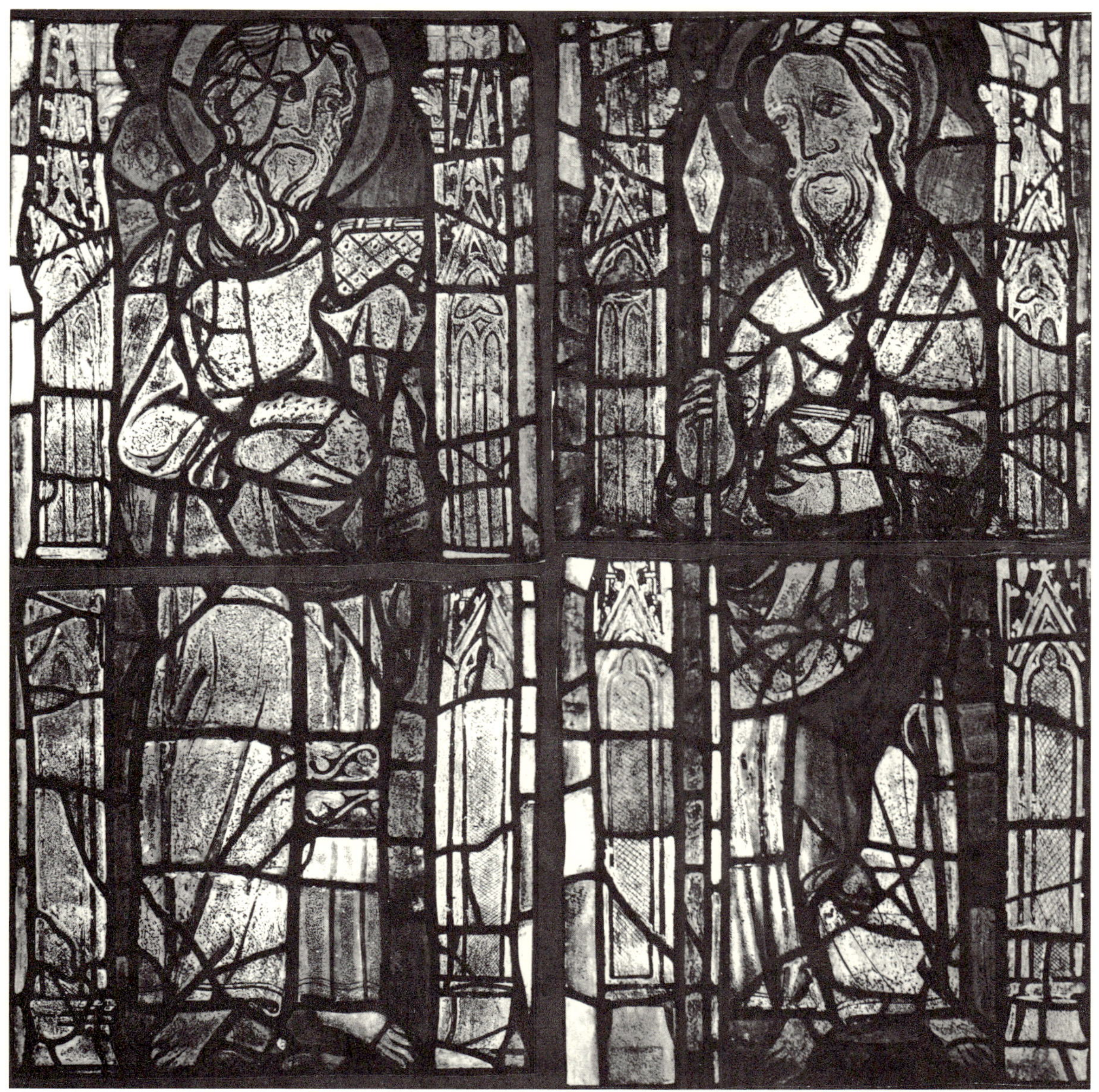

PLATE 90 Evron: north choir clerestory. Two apostles. *(Paris, Archives photographiques)*

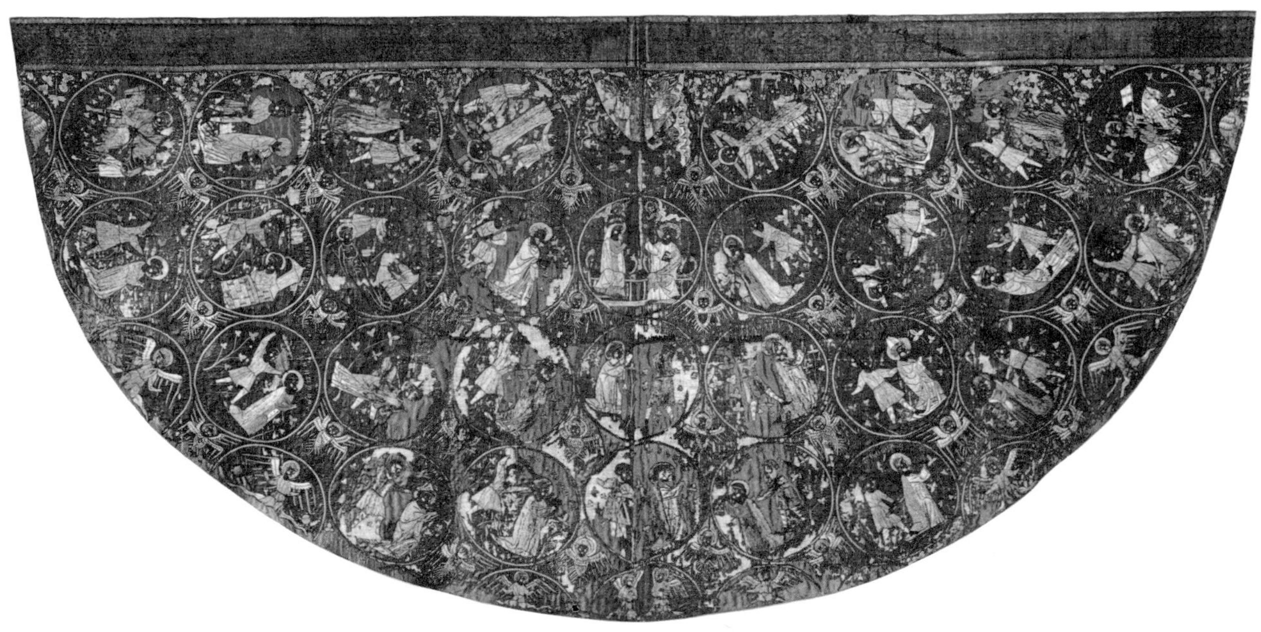

PLATE 91 Uppsala cope. (Uppsala Cathedral) *(Photo: Antikvarisk-Topografiska-Arkivet)*

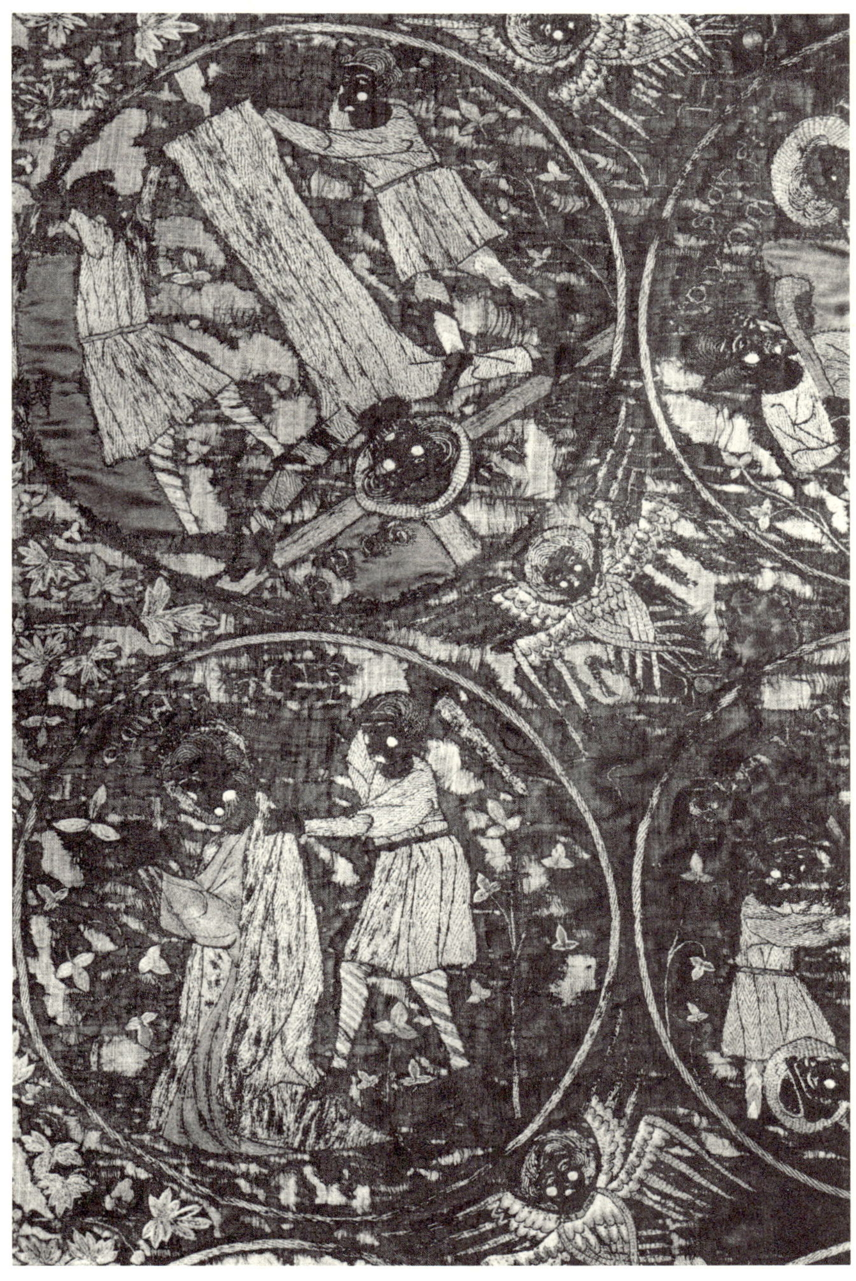

PLATE 92 Uppsala cope: martyrdom of St. Peter. (Uppsala Cathedral) *(Photo: Antikvarisk-Topografiska-Arkivet)*

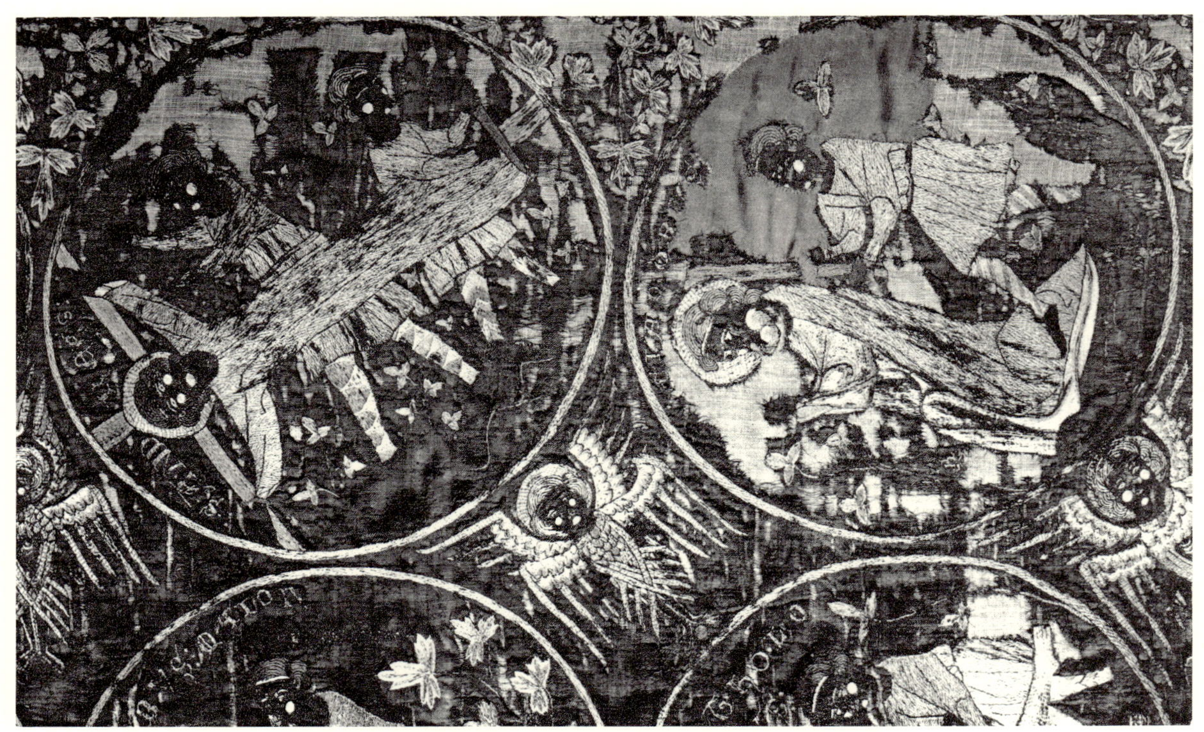

PLATE 93 Uppsala cope: martyrdom of St. Andrew. (Uppsala Cathedral) *(Photo: Antikvarisk-Topografiska-Arkivet)*

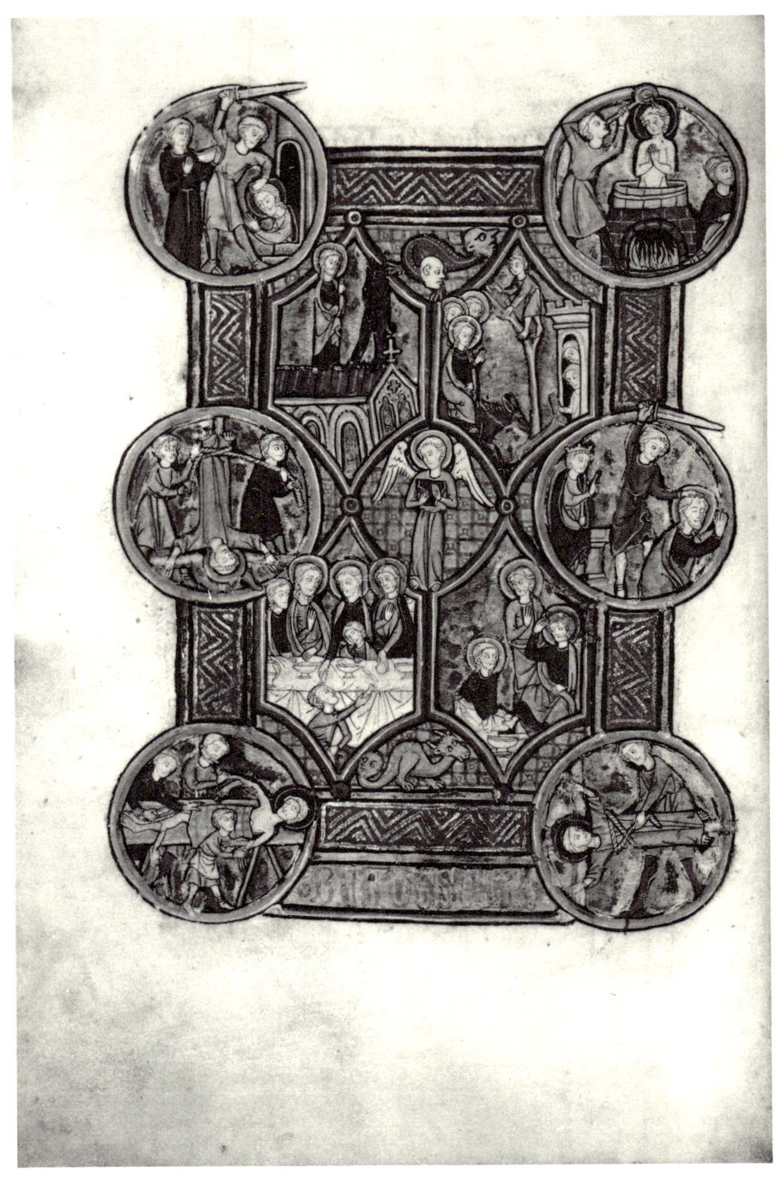

PLATE 94 Psalter. Pierpont Morgan Ms. 183, fol. 12v. *(Pierpont Morgan Library)*

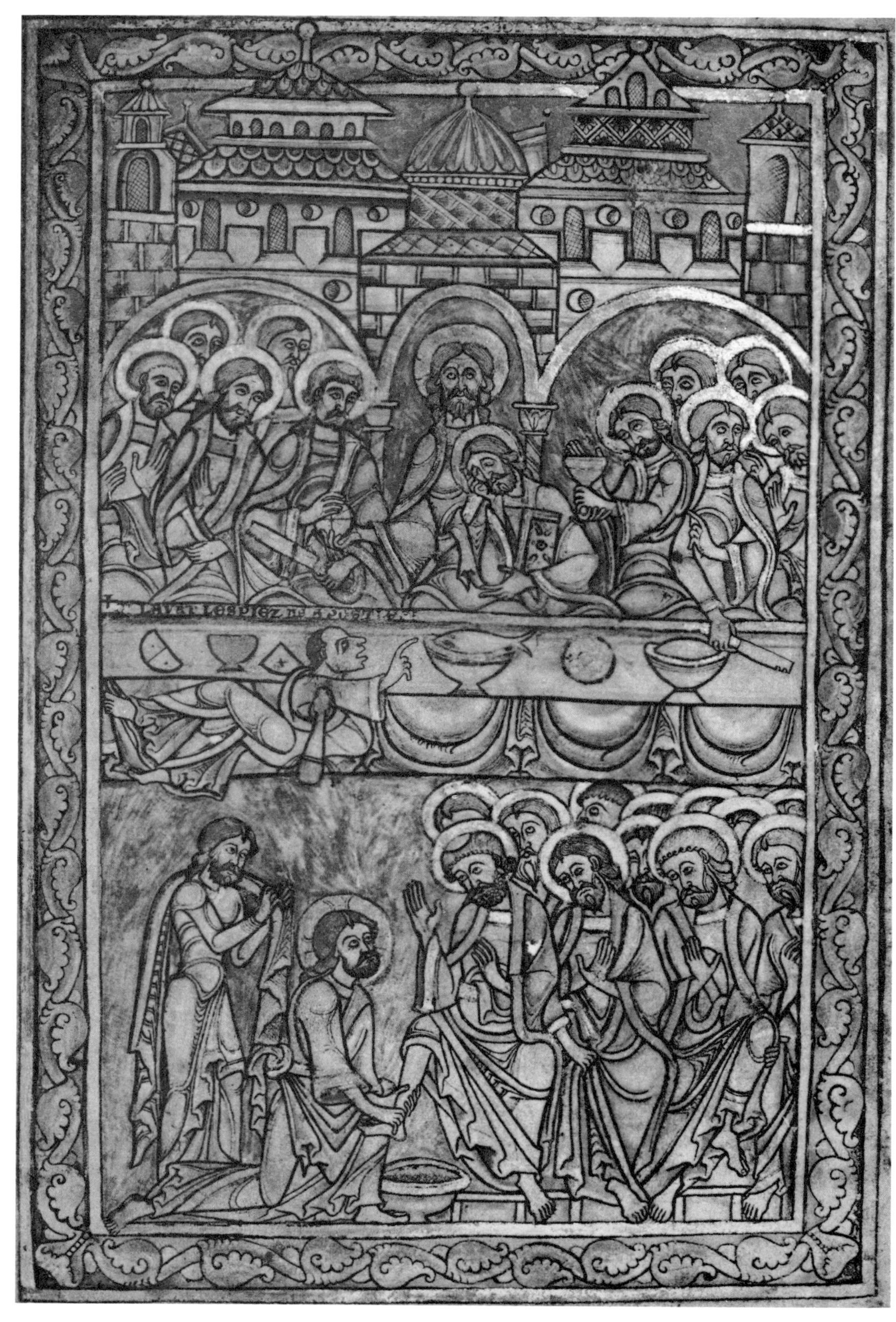

PLATE 95 Psalter of St. Swithin's Priory. British Museum, Cott. Nero C.IV, fol. 20r. *(British Museum)*

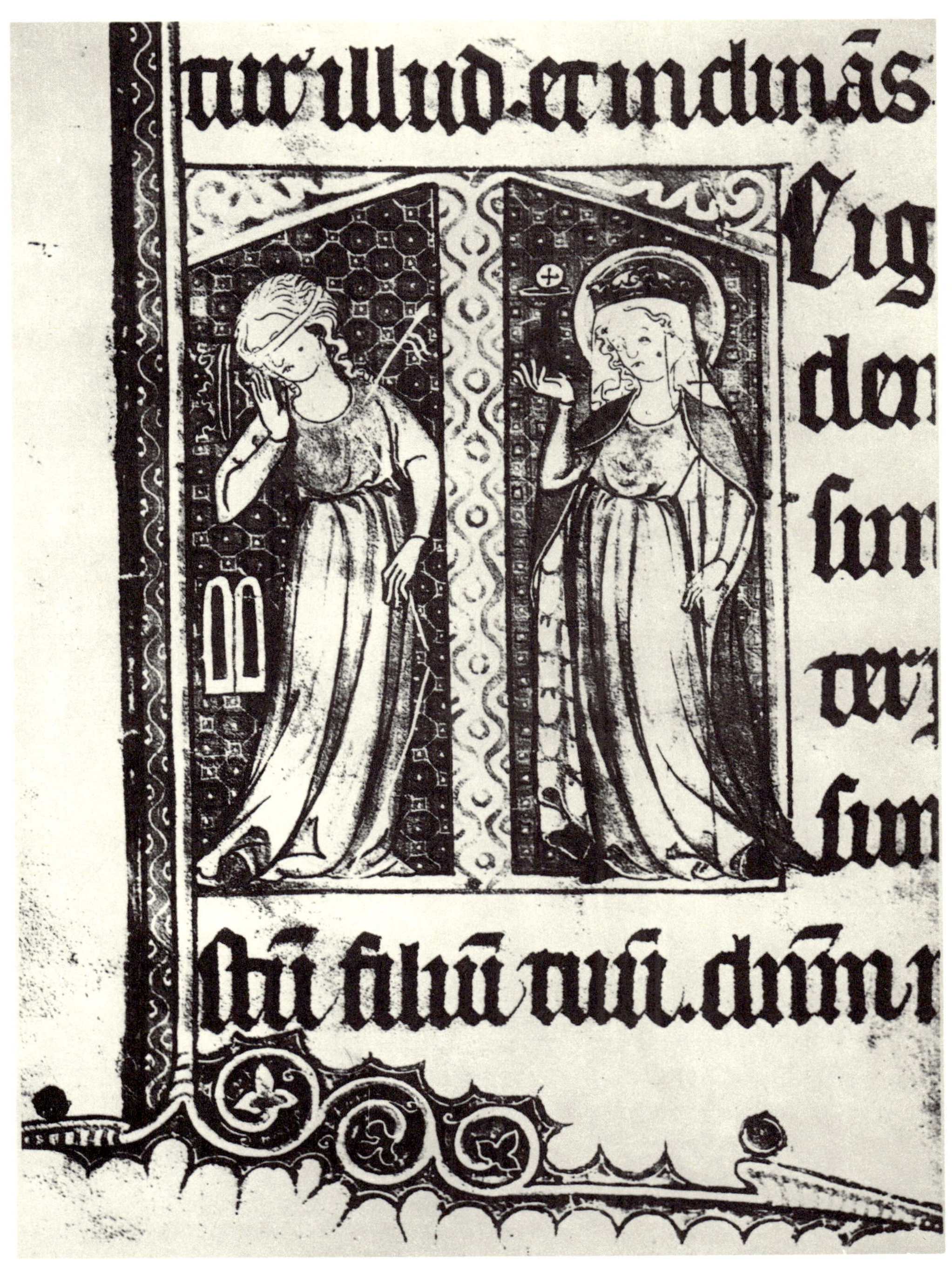

PLATE 96 Missal of Chartres Cathedral, early 14th century. Destroyed in World War II. Chartres, Bibl. Mun. Ms. 502, fol. 189v.

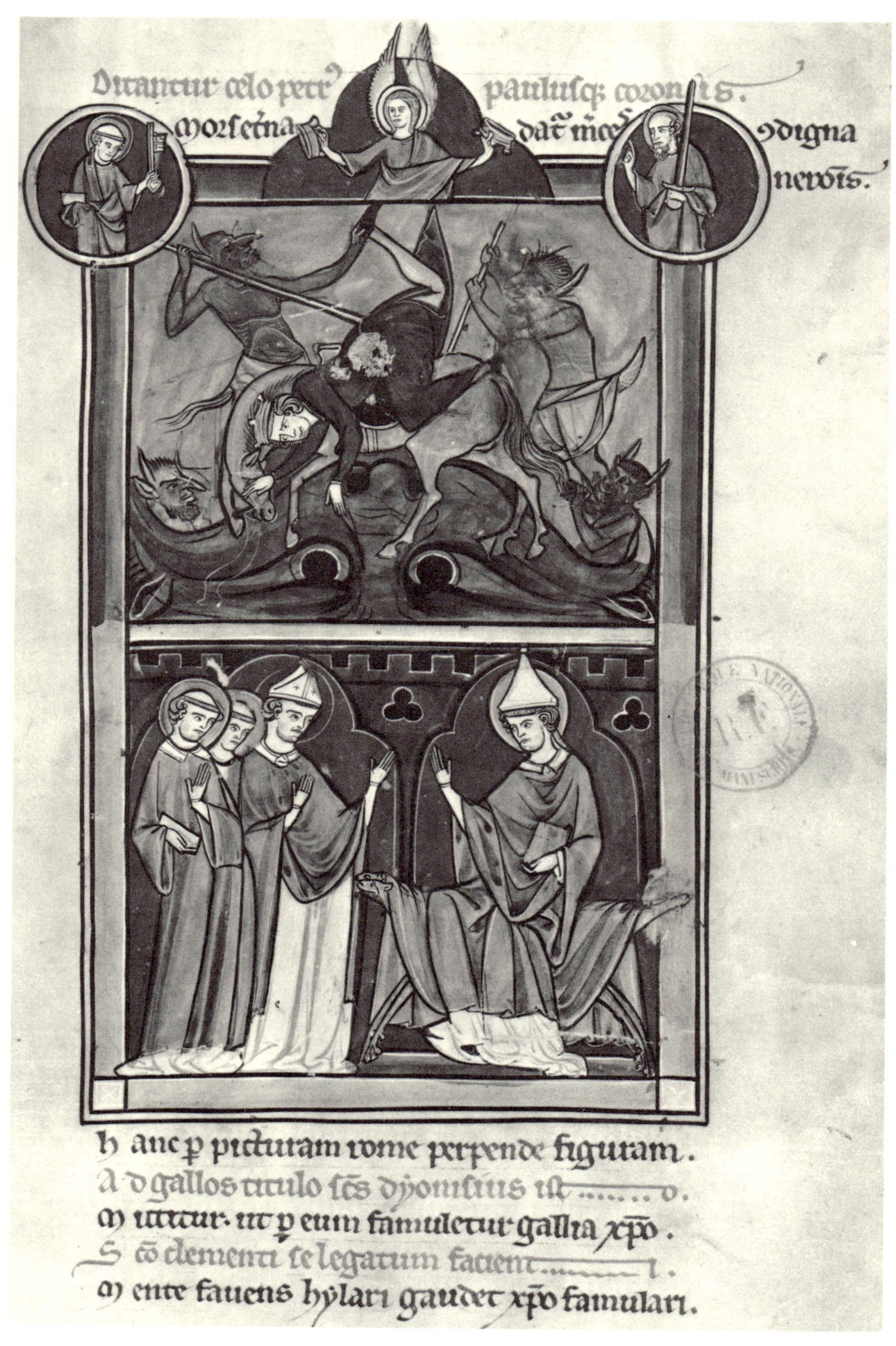

PLATE 97 Life of St. Denis: Denis sent to Gaul by Pope Clement. Paris, Bibl. Nat. n.a.fr. 1098, fol. 34r. *(Paris, Bibliothèque nationale)*

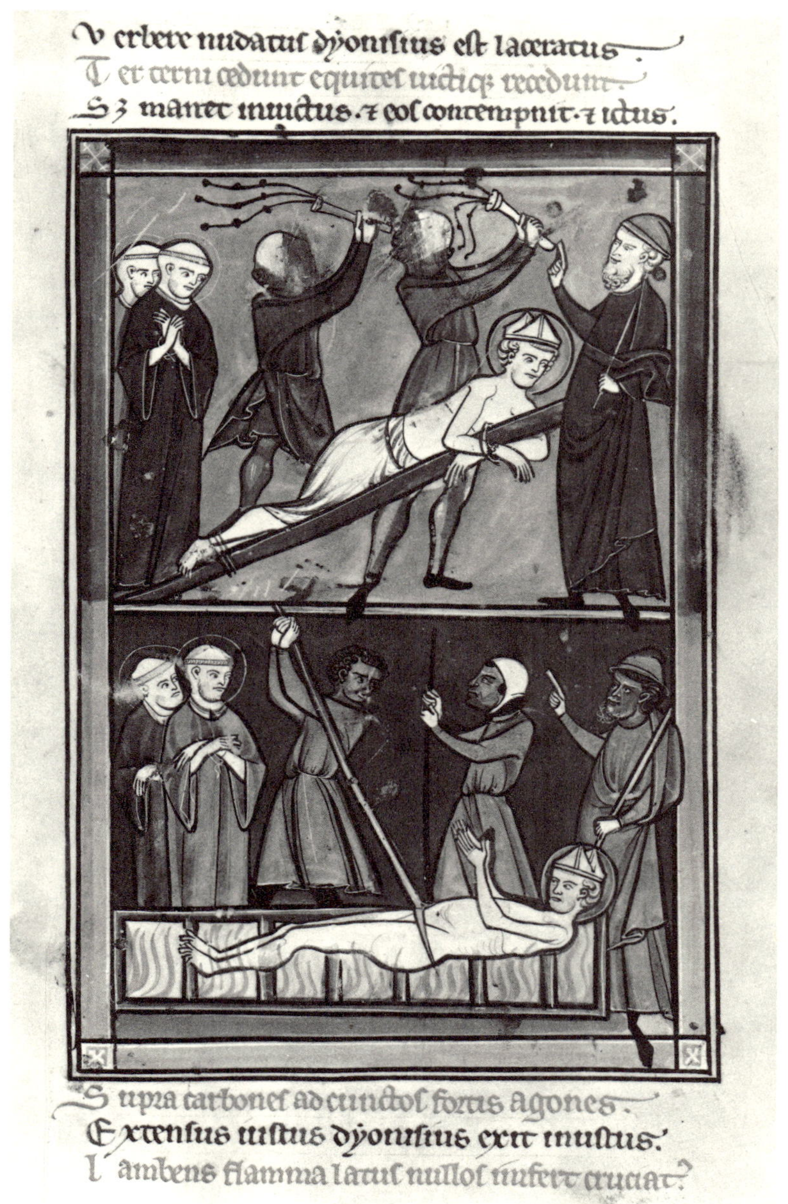

PLATE 98 Life of St. Denis: martyrdom of the saint. Paris, Bibl. Nat. n.a.fr. 1098, fol. 40r. *(Paris, Bibliothèque nationale)*

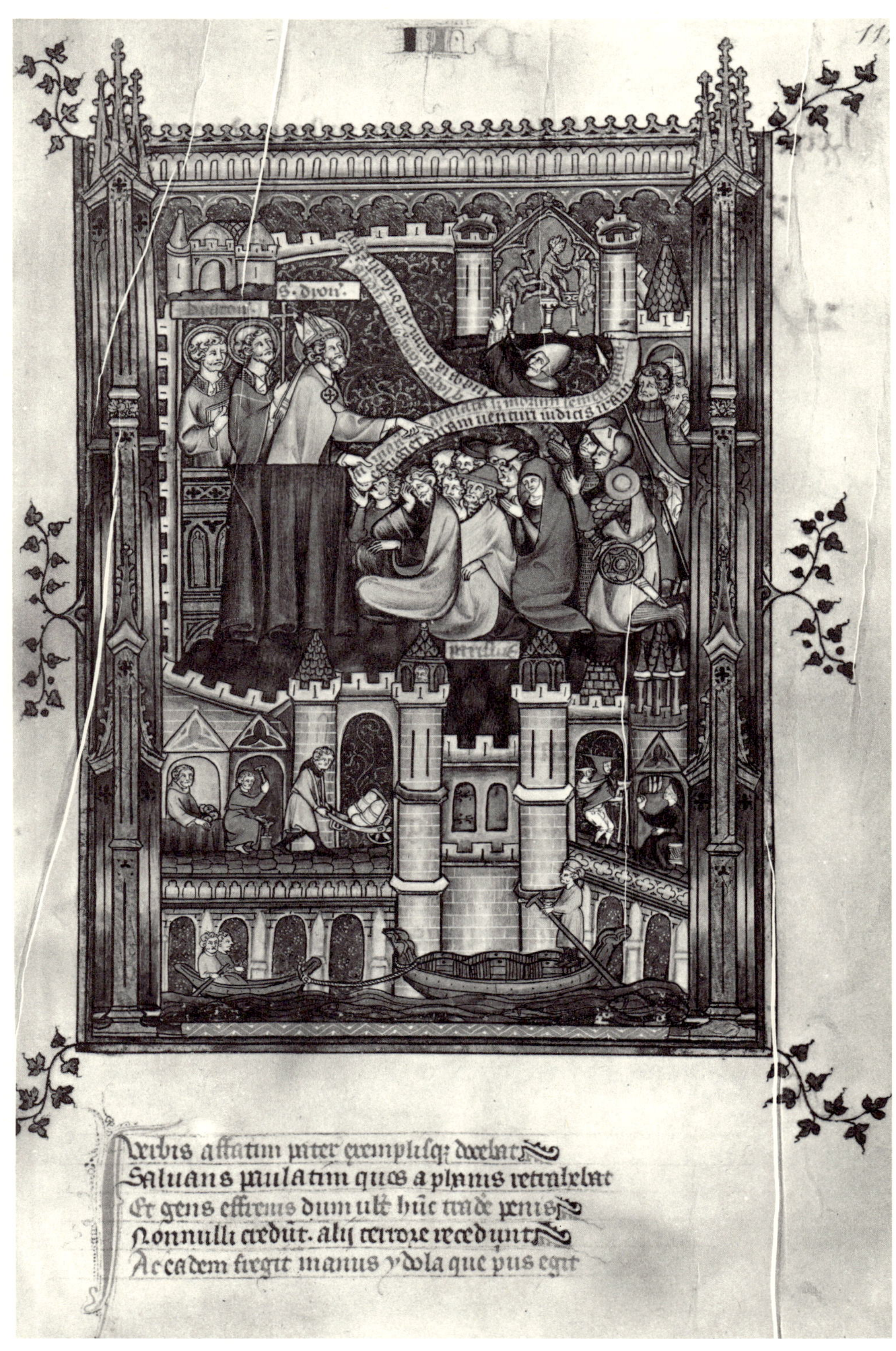

PLATE 99 Life of St. Denis: the saint preaching in Paris. Paris, Bibl. Nat. fr. 2091, fol. 111r. *(Paris, Bibliothèque nationale)*

nace is to the right; St. Denis in bishop's vestments is being pushed miter-first into its mouth by an executioner.

The final row, which has lost the left-hand panels, presents Eleutherius and Rusticus kneeling in prayer, haloed but headless (right panels); and Denis standing in formal frontal pose, also haloed but headless, holding before him his fully mitered head. The kneeling disciples resemble those found in the 1317 manuscript (ms. fr. 2092, fol. 48v), where they flank the kneeling saint. The central panel of St. Denis "head in hands" has little narrative character about it; the saint presents his head as an attribute, very much in the manner of a monumental jamb or devotional statuette. He is nevertheless probably derived from the 1317 manuscript (ms. fr. 2092, fol. 53v, bottom), where he similarly has a halo but no head.[70] One can deduce from both manuscripts that the lost left panels of the row contained an angel or angels.

The saint presents his entire head and not just the cranium. The reference is to the famous debate over relics between the Abbey of Saint-Denis and the Cathedral of Paris, a controversy waged with increasing venom during the Gothic era until its culmination in 1410 in the presentation of the dispute before the Parlement of Paris. At issue was the authenticity of the relic held by the cathedral, namely the cranium of the saint, the abbey claiming to possess — in two separated parts, of course — his entire remains. The saint holds his cranium, for example, in the early stained glass of Saint-Denis-de-Jouhet,[71] also at Tours;[72] it is noteworthy that he does so, in fact, in a missal of the usage of Saint-Père, of the first half of the fourteenth century.[73] The glazier has chosen to throw in his lot with the Saint-Denis manuscripts[74] both of which, not surprisingly, consistently depict the whole head and not just a slice from the sinuses up.

Although the glass of the ogive of the Denis lancet has been lost, it can be assumed, as a dénouement to the story, that it showed a composition like that of the adjoining Clement lancet — namely, angels bearing a soul (or souls) to heaven in a cloth. The souls of Sts. Denis, Eleutherius, and Rusticus are thus carried in the 1317 manuscript (ms. fr. 2092, fol. 48v).

In choosing episodes of the saint's legend for illustration the Saint-Père artist completely omitted several major incidents. The most significant of these are the martyrdom on the grill, the miraculous Last Communion in prison, and the saint's headless march up the hill of Montmartre guided by angels. The first of these scenes, although included in the elaborate 1317 manuscript (ms. fr. 2092, fol. 22v), was losing popularity by the fourteenth century, being easily confused with the grilling of other saints. The last, the headless march, was possibly deleted in accordance with a general prejudice which can be noted at Saint-Père against posthumous miracles. The glazier probably decided against the miraculous communion because it lacked drama. The study of his work makes clear what selective use he made of his materials; space was at a premium in his lancet, and it was to stand over fifty feet from the ground. Hence he was required to choose from among the abundant episodes and illustrations only those which reduced readily to dramatic symbols.

The connection between the window and the 1317 manuscript in particular, raises many interesting questions about the manner in which the influence of such an important manuscript was disseminated throughout the contemporary artistic world. It provides an example, in a period in which the role of individual creation (as against the maintenance of traditional patterns) is but poorly understood, of the imaginative use by a skilled artist in one medium of important works produced in another. In each row of the window the artist has telescoped details from several manuscript folios. His compositions, as a result, are often difficult to sort out iconographically although usually quite successful as visual arrangements. In the second row, however, the combination of scenes produced an unfortunate muddle, particularly in the central panel where details of two episodes overlap. The fourth row and remaining panels of the fifth, on the other hand, are clear, balanced compositions which suit their exalted position in the clerestory. To achieve dramatic simplicity, narrative details had to be eliminated to such an extent that the episodes have been reduced almost to symbols. Two savage beasts rush through a door; the saint's headless companions kneel in prayer.

It is interesting to note how the dramatic and symbolic qualities of the scenes increase as the legend moves ahead. The artist apparently designed the episodes in sequence and learned much about clerestory window design in the process. There is nothing dramatic about the first row; nor is there much economy about the more dramatic scenes of Row 2. By the third row the glass designer had hit his stride. The top three rows of the Denis lancet are among the finest achievements of the church. Bay 23, of an intense coloration and expressionistic draughtsmanship and presenting a complicated series of stories in dramatic and economical shorthand, is a stunning example of clerestory glazing. Not only do its drama and sweep suit their high placement, but the borrowed compositions are not merely successfully transplanted but invested with new life.

C. Bay 27: Saints Agnes and Catherine

The final narrative bay on the south side of the nave is devoted to the two virgin saints Agnes and Catherine (Pls. VIII, 79). With the exceptions of the Virgin and St. Anne they are the only female saints represented in the church.[75] There is nothing unusual about their selection; Agnes and Catherine and a third virgin Cecilia were the most universally popular female saints in medieval art. They clearly personify virginity at Saint-Père, Agnes the simple innocent and Catherine the wise intellectual.

Bay 27 suffered relatively little from the displacements and rearrangements visited upon much of the nave glass. Except for minor restorations, such as heads, throughout the window, only the lower row of the Catherine lancet seems to have suffered a notable loss. Its central panel and the upper light of the left panel are missing.[76] Moreover, it seems likely that the lower right panels of the two lancets have been interchanged. They would be more logical iconographically if exchanged, and the hairstyles of the saints would conform within the lancet. The head (original) in the panel presently in the Agnes lancet resembles the head (original) in the Catherine lancet, Row 2, right (Pl. 81). Note the flowing uncovered hair and downturned mouth.[77] The head of the panel presently in the Catherine lancet, unfortunately, is new, but is draped with the same white mantle found in all the original Agnes heads: Agnes lancet, Row 1, left; Row 2, right, only part of head original; Row 3 (old glass but features probably repainted); Row 4 (part of face and neck new but mantle original). Pl. 82 illustrates Rows 2 and 3.

St. Agnes lancet

Although St. Agnes enjoyed a universal popularity in medieval times, the standing figure of the saint was much more common than her legend in art. It is therefore the Golden Legend, rather than thirteenth-century monuments, which offers the most complete contemporary version of the legend for comparison with Saint-Père. The Greek and Latin traditions of the Agnes legend differed significantly in such details as the saint's age and the method of her martyrdom. Parts of each were adopted by Voragine, and the Saint-Père window follows him rather closely. To press the point further, the very selection of Agnes for the window facing the Baptist (Bay 26) reflects a familiarity with Voragine, who opens his account by stressing the play on words of Agnes and *agna*.[78]

Jacopus da Voragine was born in Genoa about 1228–1230 and spent his life in religious orders in northern Italy, dying in 1298. A French translation of his "Legenda sanctorum" (for example Bibl. Nat. ms. fr. 183, dated 1300–1320) existed by the early fourteenth century. The Agnes lancet of Saint-Père appears to be an early example of its direct influence.

If the panels in the lower rows were interchanged in the manner suggested earlier, the lower row of the Agnes lancet would illustrate the episode of Agnes refusing the offer of jewels by the prefect's son Procopius (right — now in Catherine lancet), his father Symphronius calling on her in his son's behalf (center), and Agnes thereafter being seized by his guard (left). The latter figure, whose head is a restoration, wears a knee-length robe of the type seen on servants and executioners (cf. longer robes of prefect's son and his companions, Row 3). The brick building shown at the border of the left panel is probably the proconsul's tribunal to which Agnes is taken.

Row 2 (Pl. 82) illustrates two episodes. To the right Agnes and the guard appear before the prefect, who offers her the choice of sacrificing to Vesta or being locked in a brothel. To the left is the Miracle of the Hair. Agnes stands clothed only in ankle-length blonde hair, between an astonished guard and a crenellated brick building representing the brothel (or the tribunal?). Both episodes are drawn from the Golden Legend. Although in art Agnes and the prefect are not customarily shown in confrontation twice, Voragine clearly states that the prefect called on the maiden in his son's behalf.[79] Unable to convince her to marry his son he then employed a more official manner of coercion. It would appear that the Saint-Père artist has interpreted the text in showing the prefect's actions as a father (first row, center) and as a governmental authority (second row, right) separately. The Golden Legend also popularized the Miracle of the Hair, which is not mentioned in the Greek version of Agnes's life and did not become common in art until later.[80] A comparison of the Saint-Père lancet with other rare Gothic examples of the Agnes legend[81] shows how much more closely it follows the Voragine text.

The following three rows illustrate three more episodes related in the Golden Legend. Row 3 takes place in the bordello where the prefect's son and his friends have followed Agnes. The saint stands, miraculously clothed by angels, to the right. The young man, attended by his friends, lies prostrate in the central panel, having been throttled by the devil the instant he entered the room. The precise moment depicted is that of his resuscitation. Agnes raises her hand in benediction and the youth's eyes are open. The Saint-Père artist has followed Voragine except in the detail of Agnes's robe, the dazzling white of Voragine not being an easy effect to manage in stained glass. This Agnes wears gold.[82]

In Row 4, Agnes has been thrown into the fire, flames of which are dividing and burning the pagans instead. She kneels in prayer in the central panel between flames which are quite literally divided, while fire consumes two standing youths on either side. In the final row an executioner thrusts a dagger into her throat (central panel) while the seated prefect and an attendant (his son?) observe on the right and two youthful witnesses stand to the left.

In the lancet's tympanum are two censing angels matching a similar pair in the Catherine lancet. In both pairs the outer angels are original, the inner ones handsome modern designs by François Lorin (see Pls. VIII, 79). Previously (see Pl. 80), the two medieval angels had been combined in the lights of the Catherine ogive, and the Agnes ogive filled with a simple diaper not of medieval origin.[83]

St. Catherine lancet

Complete cycles of the legend of St. Catherine are less rare in French Gothic art than those of Agnes. Catherine's story was occasionally represented in conjunction with that of St. Margaret, as at Chartres[84] and later in the century in medallions at Fécamp[85] and in the east window of Dol (Ille-et-Vilaine). Other cycles in glass are found at Angers[86] and at Rouen.[87] The Saint-Père lancet (Pls. VIII, 79), which is complete except for portions of the first row, presents the story in its regular thirteenth-century form. The most unusual feature of the iconography is the absence of any reference to the wheel torture, the well-known episode of the legend which produced the attribute usually carried by St. Catherine.

The bottom row of the lancet has lost its central panel and the upper light of the left panel. The right panel should probably be interchanged with the panel in the same position in the Agnes lancet, which shows a standing haloed female figure with uncovered hair. The subject of the row may have been Catherine disputing with the Emperor Maxentius,[88] a frequent introductory scene (see Chartres Cathedral Bay 26, Fécamp, Dol).

A suggested reconstruction of the original layout of the row would be:

a) right panel: Catherine disputing (the standing saint now in the Agnes lancet).[89]
b) central panel (lost): Emperor Maxentius enthroned?
c) left panel: two witnesses or guards (upper light modern).

Row 3 (Pl. 81) illustrates the scene following the confrontation with Maxentius, i.e., Catherine's dispute with, and conversion of, the fifty philosophers. She sits to the right, the emperor left, and the group of philosophers between them. All three panels are in excellent condition.[90]

The episode is concluded in Row 3 where, in the presence of the emperor (left) and the praying Catherine (right), an executioner thrusts the converted philosophers into the fire (Pl. 81). The scene of the burning of the defeated philosophers enjoyed a constant popularity in Gothic art, no less in the fourteenth century than earlier.

The fourth row presents Catherine in prison accompanied by an angel (center), converting her two visitors, the Empress Faustina and Porphyrius, captain of the guard (right). The space is shared by another scene, that of

Catherine's beheading (left). Both episodes were standard in Catherine cycles. That of the prison visit varies in detail, but the gesture of the executioner grasping Catherine's hair appears in such disparate examples as Chartres Cathedral (Bay 26) and the Queen Mary Psalter about a century later (Brit. Mus., Roy. 2B, VII, fol. 283v).

The final episode of the lancet is that of angels carrying Catherine's body and soul to Mount Sinai. Although the tradition that the head and body were carried separately sometimes appears in art,[91] the unsevered body, as at Saint-Père, is found occasionally.[92] In later art the scene was often reduced to the two angels bearing the soul.

The two unusual features about the Catherine lancet are: a) the total absence of reference to the wheel torture and b) the importance accorded the episode of the philosophers (two complete rows out of five). The former seems especially surprising when one considers that the wheel torture had, by the end of the thirteenth century, provided the saint with an easily recognizable attribute which was to remain constant for centuries to come. The wheel torture is found in cycles as early as the Angers window (ca. 1190),[93] and by the date of the Saint-Père clerestory, examples of the wheel as attribute are current.[94] A Gothic cycle omitting the wheel episode is rare indeed.[95]

The Saint-Père artist not only deleted the wheel torture but the torture by beating as well. The space he gained thereby was allotted to the debate between the virgin saint and the fifty philosophers. Catherine was esteemed as a dialectician in Gothic France, even appearing on the seal of the Sorbonne. Although the lancet contains no hint of a donor, the stress given to this side of her character seems to reflect the wishes of a theologian-donor connected with the cathedral school in Chartres. Such a benefactor was the Canon Nicolas de Maison-Maugis, known by documents to have given the sizeable sum of 300 Chartrain livres during the first decade of the fourteenth century to provide windows for the nave of Saint-Père.[96] There is, unfortunately, nothing but iconographic evidence to support a specific connection of the Catherine-Agnes window with the canon's benefaction.

D. Bay 18: Passion of Christ

The story of the sacrifice of Christ occupies both lancets of Bay 18 (Pl. 48), commencing in the lower row of the left lancet and running bottom to top through five rows and the tympanum of both lancets. The window is beautifully preserved and its coloring and architectural decoration mark it as the most advanced work, stylistically, in the church. All the more striking on that account is the iconography, in most cases traditional or even *retardataire* for its date. The artist seems to have followed closely a model which, on the evidence of several details, may have been a pen-illuminated manuscript of the late twelfth century.

The scenes of Bay 18 run as follows:

Left lancet:	Row 1	— Entry to Jerusalem
	Row 2	— Last Supper
	Row 3	— Betrayal and cutting of Malchus' ear
	Row 4	— Crucifixion with Church and Synagogue
	Row 5	— Holy women at the tomb
	Tympanum	— *Noli me tangere*
Right lancet:	Row 1	— Appearance on the road to Emmaüs
	Row 2	— Doubting Thomas
	Row 3	— Ascension
	Row 4	— Pentecost
	Row 5 and tympanum	— Last Judgment

Aside from certain iconographic relics here embalmed, such as the Three Marys at the tomb in place of the Resurrection, and the Road to Emmaüs without (and in place of) the Supper, the series is most notable in its lack of scenes dealing directly with the "Passion" of Christ in its narrower sense. In the eleventh century such episodes as the Flagellation, Bearing of the Cross or Crown of Thorns were unknown in French art; in the twelfth century they were rare. The taboo occasionally applied even to the Crucifixion itself, when in the context of the narrative life of Christ; the subjects, in such cases, skipped from the Kiss of Judas directly to scenes concerning the Resurrection and Appearance at Emmaüs.[97] By the thirteenth century, however, the Passion scenes had gained a secure place in the iconography of Christ's life. It is very unusual by the fourteenth century not to find at least the Flagellation. The completeness of the Saint-Père cycle makes the total omission of references to Christ's suffering the more noteworthy. It provides the first bit of evidence in building a case for the use of a considerably older model.

The entry to Jerusalem (Matthew XXI:7–9, Mark XI:7–10; Luke XIX:35–38; John XII:12–16) is the customary introduction to the Passion. Christ sits astride the ass, holding a palm branch in His left hand and blessing the crowd with His right. Behind Him is Peter, with the key, and other disciples. Before Him in the right panel is the city gate, with two figures on the ramparts holding palms and the feet of a third[98] who originally, most likely, laid a cloak beneath the ass's feet.

The interesting feature in this otherwise quite traditional scene is the palm carried in Christ's hand. Although an infrequent detail in Gothic art, it occurs often enough in the twelfth through the fourteenth centuries to be considered a standard variation. In most examples where Christ carries a palm, the disciples do so as well. This is not the case at Saint-Père, where the only palms other than Christ's are those held by the two welcoming figures atop the city gates.

Since Mâle's iconographic study of French thirteenth-century art it has been accepted generally that these palms, not mentioned in the Gospels, derive from the Palm Sunday processions of the medieval church:

> Ce qui prouve clairement que la représentation de l'Entrée à Jérusalem a été déterminée par la Liturgie, c'est qu'au XIIe et au XIIIe siècles les apôtres qui suivent Jésus sont représentés avec des palmes à la main. Or si l'Evangile dit que les Juifs accueillirent Jésus-Christ avec des branches d'arbre, il ne dit pas que les apôtres en portaient. La palme aux mains des apôtres était destinée à rappeler la procession du dimanche des Rameaux. Ex.: chapiteau de Chartres, vitrail de Bourges.[99]

I believe that there is another source — more specifically a source for the palm carried by Christ Himself — which made a contribution to the scene's representation.

In the Entry to Jerusalem in Greek and Syrian gospel books, Christ often carries a roll in His left hand. While it is usually tucked in His lap, occasionally He holds it up.[100] Rare examples of such a roll occur in Western art from an early date.[101] Meyer Schapiro[102] has remarked in a more general context that people in the middle ages were still aware that the roll had preceded the book, and perhaps for this reason the roll (as opposed to the book) symbolized the Old Testament — apostles carry books, for example, while prophets have rolls.

Whatever its origin, very early in its development the roll in Christ's hand began to be depicted with a thong or palm leaf[103] emerging from the top, as in the precocious example in the "Cambridge Gospels" (sixth–seventh century).[104] More commonly by the Gothic period, in the infrequent examples where Christ and/or the apostles carry objects, the objects have evolved into whips, sticks or long leaves, not always readily identifiable. The important point to note (see Fig. 13) is that in each case they are undeniably distinct from the palms carried in the same scene by the onlookers.[105] In a late example (Luttrell Psalter, Brit. Mus. Add. 42130, fol. 90r, ca. 1340), Christ and the disciples hold flowering branches while the observers carry nosegays.

Generally speaking, however, the Gothic age abandoned such fine distinctions. Christ's palm, at Saint-Père, is only slightly rounder and more tubular at the stem than those of the welcoming bystanders. The metamorphosis of the Eastern roll into the familiar palm of the Palm Sunday procession was complete.

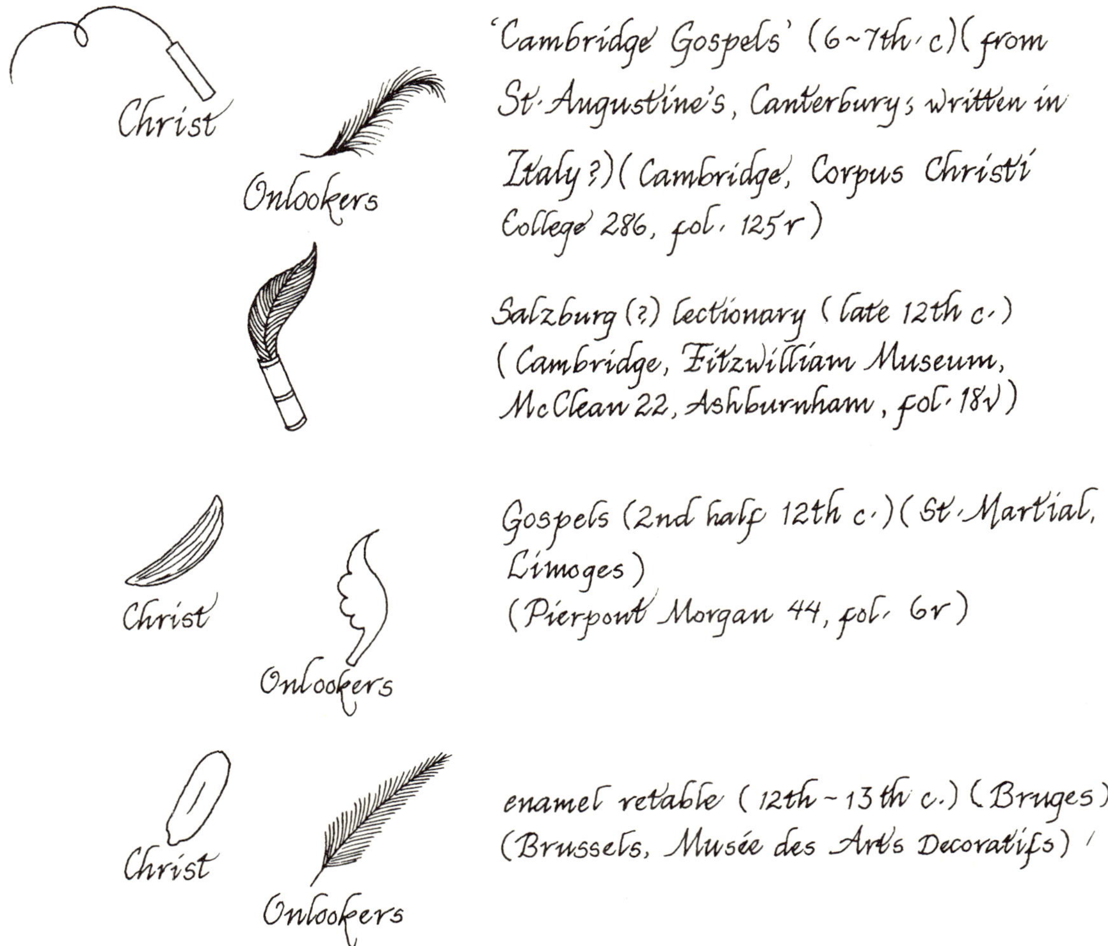

Figure 13 Entry to Jerusalem: palms held by Christ (and/or apostles) and by onlookers. (Drawing by Kevin McIntyre)

The source of the motif at Saint-Père is, however, problematical. It will have been noticed that all of the footnoted examples in the preceding paragraphs are either foreign or, if French, no later than the twelfth century. At Chartres itself there are two mid-twelfth-century examples, in the cathedral's west window and west sculptural frieze.

The scene is not represented at all in the cathedral's thirteenth-century windows or sculpture, on the other hand. One is left with the supposition that the model used at Saint-Père was either foreign or no later than twelfth-century (or possibly both), but there the question must rest for the moment.

Row 2 (Pl. XI) illustrates the Last Supper (Matthew XXVI:20–29; Mark XIV:17–25; Luke XXII:14–38; John XIII:12–27; I Corinthians XI:23–25). Christ, flanked by the apostles, dines at a long narrow table, upon which are seen jugs, loaves of bread and plates of fish. John leans upon the Lord's breast while Judas sits isolated before the table, helping himself to a fish from a nearby bowl.[106] Christ, gesturing to Peter at His side, offers something across the table to Judas with His other hand. It is neither the plate mentioned in Matthew (XXVI:23) or Mark (XIV:20) nor the sop of the Gospel of John (XIII:26).[107] Nor is it a fish, such as the one depicted at Bourges.[108]

Could it be Judas' moneybag? It is necessary to consider such a startling identification after a comparison of the object with examples of the Last Supper where Judas carries a moneybag, as at Laon[109] or at Chartres.[110] Judas's moneybag usually has the appearance of a club or ten-pin decorated with two horizontal lines. What is being represented in linear art is actually a bag with ties, the horizontal lines indicating the top of the bag where the drawstrings are.[111]

The Saint-Père artist seems to have represented such a bag without knowing it, i.e., turned anti-gravitationally sideways and entirely colored gold (not only the bag but the "ground" space between the bag's drawstrings), indicating that his model would necessarily have been an uncolored drawing. An example of such a drawing may be found in the Psalter of St. Swithin's Priory, Winchester (Pl. 95), dated 1150–1160.[112] Judas points to a fish in a bowl with one hand, holds the moneybag with the other. The moneybag resembles a fringed ten-pin. Christ ignores him, instead offering a loaf to the disciple on his dexter side. It is possible that the Saint-Père artist found both such elements in his source — that is to say, both a Christ offering an object and a "ten-pin"-like moneybag. He combined them without comprehending their identities, a confusion likely only if the bag and the space between its drawstrings were indistinguishable by color. The occurrence of such a drawing in the St. Swithin's Psalter is notable, since there is evidence in the apse medallions of Saint-Père of the use of a model, perhaps a psalter, of northern and possibly English origin.

Row 3 (Pl. 50) of the left lancet shows the Betrayal, including Peter cutting off Malchus's ear (Matthew XXVI:47–52; Mark XIV:43–47; Luke XXII:47–54; John XVIII:2–12). Peter is the only apostle represented. To the left are four soldiers with weapons, several of them in chain mail. Christ occupies the central panel, the betraying Judas on one side and a soldier on the other. To the right are Peter and Malchus. The story is told in tableaux rather than dramatic narrative. The object behind Judas's head is probably the lantern often found in that position in Gothic art.

By far the most interesting feature of the row is the figure of Malchus, who is depicted child-sized, legs short and unbent. The customary Gothic arrangement of Peter and Malchus shows Malchus smaller because he is kneeling or crouching.[113] Although the body is often unanatomical, with legs too short for the torso, the knees are always bent to some degree. In the fourteenth century, in order to preserve this ancient grouping and still have room for his feet, Malchus often lies down.[114]

At Saint-Père, on the other hand, the little Malchus stands absolutely erect. Indeed he has the aspect of a circus dwarf, with large head and torso and truncated legs. It is necessary to seek in the twelfth century or earlier to find comparable depictions of Malchus. Romanesque sculpture provides a few examples,[115] as does an occasional Romanesque manuscript.[116] The figure survives in one work almost contemporary with Saint-Père (ca. 1315–1335), an *opus anglicanum* embroidery[117] in which a dwarf-like Malchus stands almost upright while Peter actually slices his ear, as in the window. Whether the source for the window was such a work of English embroidery or a portable art object from an earlier period is impossible to say. The preponderance of archaisms in the iconographic detail of Bay 18 would lend weight to the latter hypothesis.

The Crucifixion with Church and Synagogue occupies Row 4 (Pl. 50). The central panel shows Christ on the cross, His head inclined and His body, draped in a long loincloth and nailed by three nails, forming an S-curve. The scene is stripped of narrative or symbolic detail; only dignified figures of the Virgin and St. John are included.

The figures of Church and Synagogue which flank the central panel are of great interest. Each completely fills its panel, looming larger than the Crucifixion itself; one presumes that they were drawn from a different source. They are represented in the standard manner, the Church crowned and holding a cross-staff, Synagogue blindfolded with the broken lance, her crown toppling from her head and the tablets of the Law dropping from her hand. One detail which is not at all standard is the object carried by the Church. In place of the customary chalice[118] she presents an elaborately traceried doublet-and-rose window! There was local precedent for such a glazier's fancy. In Chartres Cathedral Bay 59 (north nave)[119] Ecclesia carries the model of a church.

While Church and Synagogue were commonly included in Crucifixions throughout the thirteenth century, the precise source for the Saint-Père figures seems to have been a manuscript. The figures are strikingly close to those adorning the "Te igitur" initial of the Missal of Compiègne, ca. 1250 (Bibl. Nat. ms. lat. 17318, fol. 173v),[120] and of an early fourteenth-century missal from Chartres Cathedral (Chartres, Bibl. mun., ms. 502, fol. 189v; see Pl. 96).[121] In these initials the Crucified Christ is not depicted, which would account for the difference of scale at Saint-Père, the artist employing different sources for his Crucifixion group and for its flanking symbols. While the earlier Compiègne initial would seem to represent the ultimate source of the symbols, it is more likely that the Chartres missal, contemporary with the window, was the direct model. Note especially Ecclesia's vair-lined cloak and the tablets of the Law.

The top row of the left lancet (Pl. XII) shows the Three Marys at the Tomb (Mark XVI:1–7), a common scene in the early Gothic period.[122] By the mid-thirteenth century[123] it had largely been replaced by the moment of Resurrection itself, when Christ stepped from the Tomb,[124] or more rarely both were shown in conjunction.[125] By the early fourteenth century, date of the Saint-Père windows, the Holy Women at the Tomb had almost totally disappeared from French art.[126]

The Saint-Père artist has represented his archaizing subject in full traditional detail. The angel, holding a short cross-staff, sits on the Tomb to the left. Behind it are two haloed women and to the right is a third, all carrying ointment jars. Although the jars have been copied by rote — they appear quite flat and angular — the type is clear. The first holy woman touches the shroud resting on top of the Tomb. Below the Tomb, or more accurately framed within the three trefoiled arches of the tomb facade, are three tiny figures of sleeping guards. Only the infrequently found hanging lamps have been eliminated from the standard Romanesque formula.

The Tomb itself and the sleeping soldiers have been modernized to conform to the early fourteenth-century taste. The customary three cavities of the Tomb,[127] which had their origin in the medieval appearance of the Holy Sepulcher itself,[128] and by the Gothic period were occasionally rendered as decorative niches,[129] have been transformed into elaborate High Gothic trefoiled arches with traceried spandrels.[130] The sleeping soldiers are contemporary warriors in chain mail armed with lances, shields, and swords. While it was common practice by the thirteenth century to represent the sleeping guards in medieval battledress, their shields customarily bore an idealized rosette pattern. At Saint-Père the escutcheons are patterned after contemporary coats of arms. That of the central soldier appears to be the rampant lion of Béatrix de Montfort-l'Amaury, donor of Bay 19 (see Fig. 12). The right shield is bendy in a border and the left one is charged with a cinquefoil, in a border SA. bezanty. The rendering of the shields in grisaille without tinctures makes any positive identification impossible, as all three were standard heraldic patterns[131] by ca. 1300.

The tympanum of the left lancet contains the *Noli me tangere* (Mark XVI:9–11; John XX:14–18). The Magdalene kneels in prayer. Christ, chest bared, holds a cross-staff. The episode of Christ appearing to Mary Magdalene enjoyed a long and fairly stable iconographic history and was shown in this manner well into the fourteenth century.[132]

The cycle continues in the bottom row of the right lancet (Pl. 49) with Christ's appearance on the Road to Emmaüs (Mark XVI:12–13; Luke XXIV:13–27). In the left panel is Christ, His hand raised in blessing. The two disciples, carrying pilgrims' staves and pouches, occupy the central panel. City architecture behind a gate appears to the right. Rare as it is to find Christ without a pilgrim's staff or hat, it is rarer still to find the scene at all by the beginning of the fourteenth century, when it had all but disappeared. The popularity of the Emmaüs episode reached a peak in the narrative accounts of the twelfth century and began to wane during the thirteenth. By ca. 1250 the introductory scene of the Road to Emmaüs, shown at Saint-Père, had largely been dropped, its infrequent occurrences almost always in conjunction with the Supper scene which followed it.[133]

There is no Supper at Saint-Père. The artist either omitted it intentionally or followed a model which included only the scene of the Road to Emmaüs. Such works, although rare, include two with demonstrable affinities to the Saint-Père glass. The first, a psalter of ca. 1250 (Liège, Bibl. de l'Univ., ms. 431, fol. 11v), is one of the Liégeois manuscripts which have been discussed in Chapter IX in connection with the tracery medallions of the Saint-Père apse. The other is a fourteenth-century Italian manuscript of the Pseudo-Bonaventura Meditations (Oxford, Corpus Christi ms. 410, fol. 159r). Pseudo-Bonaventura reached France by the first decade of the fourteenth century, and while it made little impact at Saint-Père, it does appear to have been known there.[134] The hypothesized source for the Emmaüs panels cannot be pinned down further.

The Incredulity of Thomas follows in the second row (John XX:25–29) (Pl. 49). St. Thomas and Christ occupy the central panel flanked by two groups of apostles. Both stand, and Christ, grasping the disciple's hand in His own, thrusts it into the wound. This ancient and dramatic gesture,[135] which appears infrequently throughout the long course of Gothic art, was by no means in the mainstream of French thirteenth-century iconography. Christ more passively bares His wound in the Chartres and Tours Cathedrals windows, and on the Notre-Dame choir screen.

Although the coercive gesture of Christ thrusting Thomas's hand into the wound was common in English art from the late thirteenth century on, this late English group[136] may be easily distinguished from Saint-Père: the Thomas kneels, Christ holds a cross-staff, and there are no witnesses, the scene thus resembling a *Noli me tangere*. Saint-Père follows a different form, the sources of which are obscure, in which there are witnesses but no cross-staff, and both participants are more or less standing.[137] Two vastly different early thirteenth-century manuscripts exhibit this type: (a) the ca. 1230 psalter "of Blanche of

Castille," Arsenal fr. 1186, fol. 26r, of possible English or Picard origin;[138] and (b) a Jacobite lectionary from the Syrian rock-cut monastery of Mar Mattaï, finished 1220.[139] Since neither of these manuscripts conforms to the Saint-Père window in other details of the Passion cycle, they would appear to be clues only to the early date and non-French provenance of the model which the glazier employed.

The iconographic detail of greatest interest in the next two scenes (Ascension and Pentecost) is the same — namely, the absence of the Virgin Mary. In both rows the apostles appear seated, holding books. Above them in the Ascension (Luke XXIV:50–51; Acts I:6–11) are Christ's feet, a graphic and theologically rather primitive symbol which retained its popularity throughout the Gothic era.[140] Above the apostles of the Pentecost (Acts II:1–4) hovers a bug-eyed dove from which emanate rays much like maypole streamers. Neither scene is among the inspired creations of the artists of Saint-Père, and certainly the horizontal row format is uncongenial to the "verticality" of the two stories.

It was presumably for this reason that the apostles of the Ascension, who customarily stand, were seated like their counterparts in the Pentecost. The absence of the Virgin is more difficult to explain. Although not always included in the Ascension in early medieval art, the Virgin from the twelfth century customarily took part.[141] Similarly, although not always included in the Pentecost in the Romanesque period,[142] by the mid-thirteenth century in France the Virgin was a regular participant in that scene as well. The streamer-like rays typical of twelfth-century works[143] had likewise given way by the mid-thirteenth century to "tongues of fire" of the sort found in the Sainte-Chapelle (Bay H6).[144] The ribbon-type rays and the absence of the Virgin in both rows mark Saint-Père as an archaizing work for its date in the early fourteenth century.

A unique example of the two scenes without the Virgin can be found in the Apostles window of Chartres Cathedral (hemicycle, Bay 34).[145] The iconographic focus of the cathedral window, however, is sharply trained on the apostles themselves. Many distracting story-lines, such as Peter-Malchus and even to some degree Judas,[146] are eliminated. The latent and pervasive Mariology already present in other early thirteenth-century works has been sacrificed in the Chartres Apostles window for the same reason. But the Saint-Père lancet concerns itself with the Passion of Christ, not specifically with the apostles. As the remainder of the scenes in the two windows are totally disparate, it must be concluded that the source of the Saint-Père window was some other more traditional twelfth- or early thirteenth-century object.

The series of Appearances of Christ in the right lancet is capped in the top row and tympanum by the Last Judgment. In the central panel the seated Christ bares His wounds, flanked by small praying figures of the Virgin and St. John.

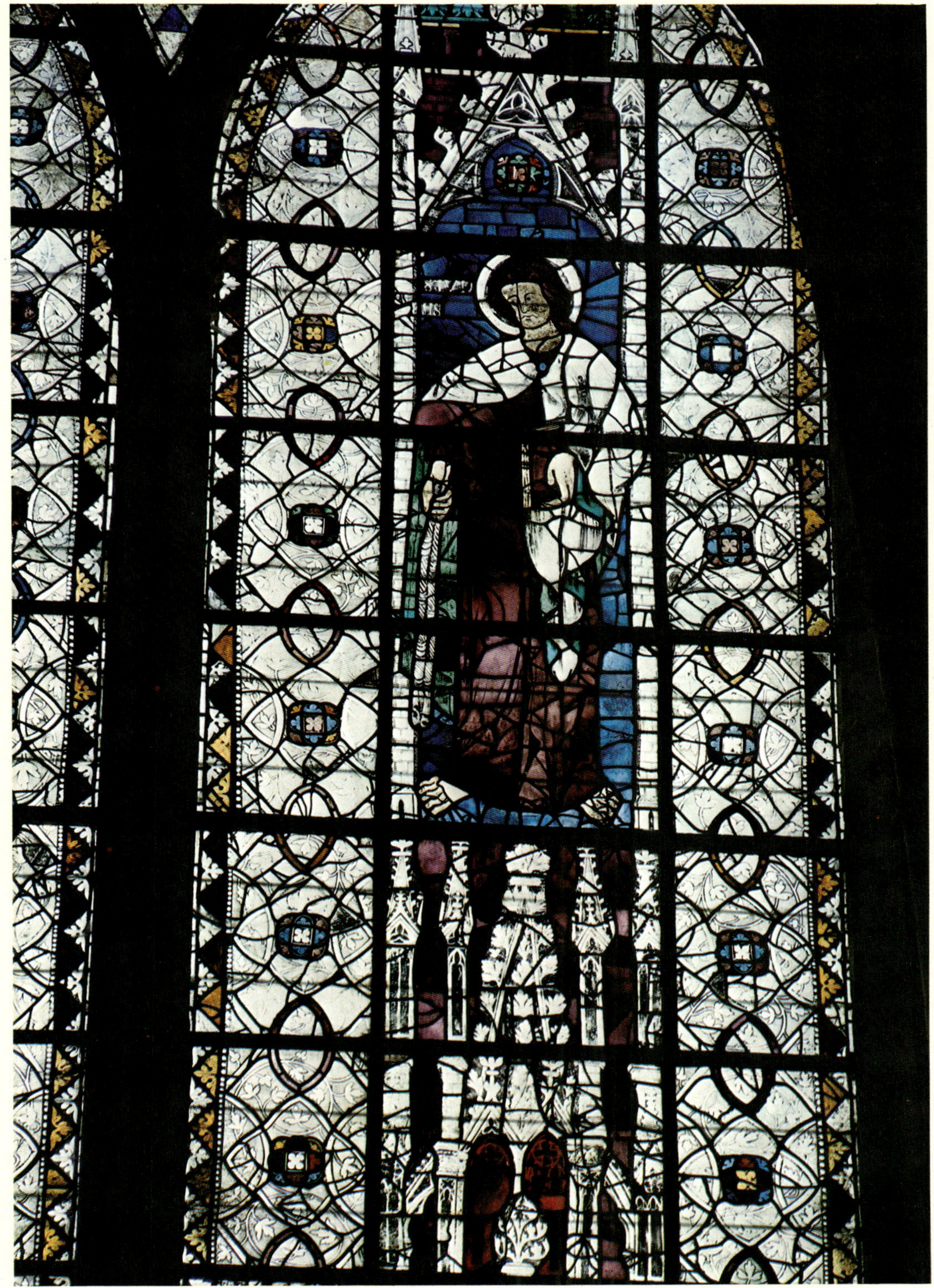

PLATE X Nave: Bay 28. St. Judas (right lancet, top). *(Edouard Fièvet)*

To the sides, two angels with oliphants call the dead from their tombs. Four nude souls arise in attitudes of prayer. Above, in the tympanum, four angels bear the cross, lance, scourges, Crown of Thorns and three nails.

Although the scene expands into the tympanum panels, it is accorded scarcely more importance than any of the window's other episodes. That the Last Judgment was occasionally included in series in such a democratic manner can be seen from a few thirteenth-century works where it is no more focal or grandiose than its neighboring scenes.[147] The iconographic form is the one current in France from the last years of the twelfth century through the fourteenth. Only the small size of the Virgin and John gives the slightest hint of an early model.[148]

The conclusions to be drawn from an iconographic study of Bay 18 are elusive. Almost every scene in some way is peculiar for its date. Even the choice of scenes is unusual for the early fourteenth century, by which time the Scourging of Christ, Bearing of the Cross, Crown of Thorns and other scenes of Christ's suffering had become common in such a series.[149] The relegation of the Virgin to a distinctly minor role is also noteworthy for a period when the cult of Mary was riding the crest. The Holy Women at the Tomb and the Road to Emmaüs scenes, as well as the dwarf Malchus, were definite archaisms by ca. 1310. Strong circumstantial evidence suggests that the window was modeled closely on a work of perhaps a century earlier.

The frequency of specific and minute details, such as the palm carried by Christ in the Entry to Jerusalem, Judas' moneybag in the Last Supper, the ointment jars of the Holy Women, the lantern in the Betrayal, leads to the further assumption that the source was probably a small, carefully rendered object such as a manuscript. It is even possible to suggest, on the evidence of the mistaken coloring of Judas's moneybag, that the model was in black and white. Details such as the "coercion" of the Doubting Thomas indicate that the model was not French. Only the out-of-scale Church and Synagogue, probably drawn from the "Te igitur" initial of a contemporary Chartrain missal, break with the pattern of uniform archaism in the Saint-Père window.[150]

Although the choice of scenes and the manner of their representation was largely borrowed, the artist was not blind to contemporary developments, nor did he fail to embellish his material occasionally. The little traceried stained-glass window held by Ecclesia is a charming innovation; and a moneybag held by Christ in the Last Supper is, at the least, inventive. The Crucified Christ, hanging heavily in an S-curve, is a contemporary form.[151] By limiting the material to a single episode per row, the artist presented the Passion cycle much more clearly and dramatically than, for example, the Joachim-Anne lancet of Bay 19 opposite. The window's iconographic relics, indeed, wear quite well.

E. Bay 22: Sts. Peter and Paul

The window of St. Peter (Pl. 59, Figs. 14, 15) consists of two lancets of seven rows each, each row formed of three lights across. The format, stylistically more primitive than the panel design of five double rows found in most of the nave's narrative bays, allows very little space for canopy development above the scenes and encourages small-scale narrative at the expense of clarity and dramatic effect. The only other use of the seven-row format in the church occurs in the right lancet of Bay 19 (Joachim-Anne lancet) (Pl. 51). Both Bay 19 and Bay 22 can be dated by donors to the first decade of the fourteenth century; and as hesitant and only partially successful designs they fall at the commencement of the campaign of nave glazing.

The bay of the abbey's name-saint, like Bay 23 directly across the nave (Pl. 69), suffered dismemberment ca. 1700 and remained in mutilated form until the restorations of 1906–1908. Two vertical strips of panels, probably the outer light of each lancet, were replaced by clear glass and removed to locations in the apse of the church. There they were leaded into the broad windows in a patchwork in no special order, often sideways or upside-down.[152] Luckily, only a few panels were lost in the exodus.

The restoration of the removed panels, which are smaller and have more self-contained designs than those of Bay 23, was a delicate task. From the available evidence it seems to have gone through several stages. Further panels seem to have been removed at first[153] — to conform the bay to the "shutter" format of the nave's standing saints — before the final decision[154] to attempt the reassembling of the bay.

The checkered history of the window, its format of small narrative panels, and the considerable variations in style which are in evidence make it the most difficult and complicated puzzle in the church. Fortunately the ca. 1905 restorers produced a work of reconstruction which, considering the task, is altogether admirable (Fig. 14). The window will be described, therefore, in the form in which it can now be seen with comments on the reconstruction included *en passant.* A corrected reconstruction will then be offered (Fig. 15).

As it is reconstructed (Fig. 14), the window reads from bottom to top, left lancet first, a familiar format in the nave clerestory. The lower rows of both lancets (Pls. 62, 63) form the exception to the rule, the six lights at present containing a pair of later prophets (one in each lancet), a pair of standing figures of Peter and Paul with attributes (right lancet), a donor panel (left lancet) and the introductory scene of the Calling of Peter (left lancet). It seems fairly obvious that such an assortment does not reflect the original state (see Fig. 11).

The two later prophets[155] can be dismissed from the original scheme. The

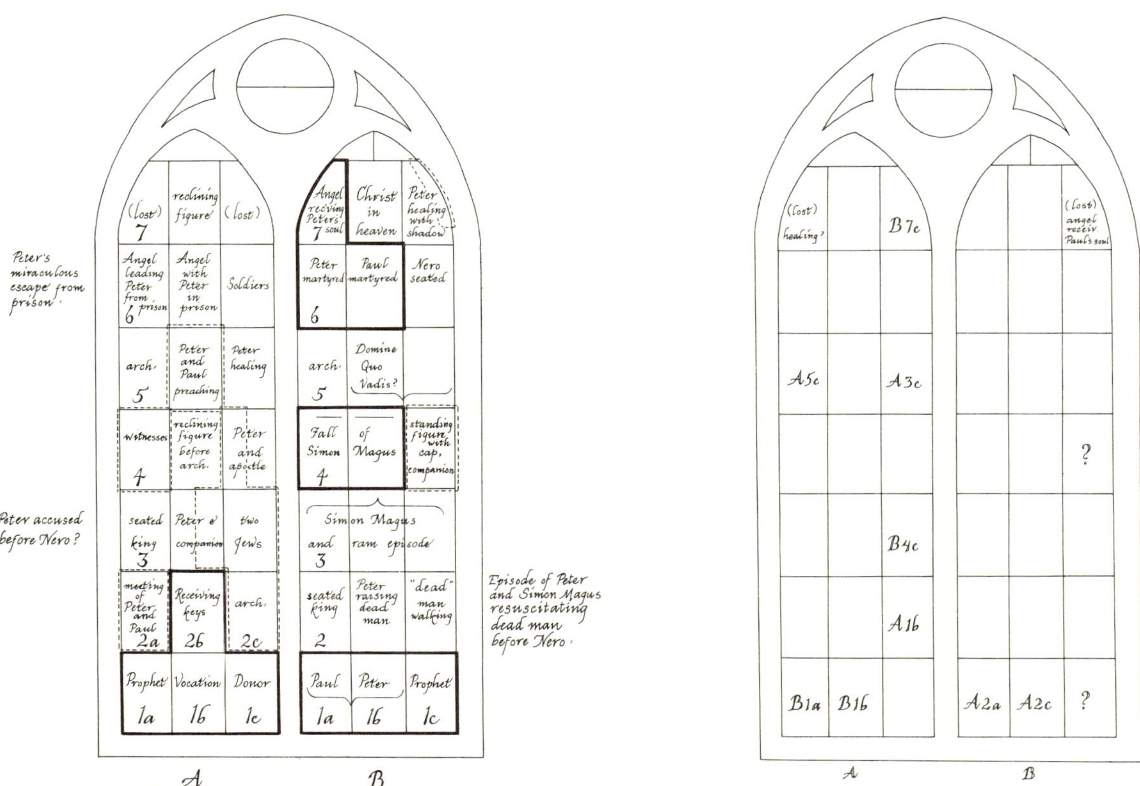

Figure 14 Bay 22 — present reconstruction. (Drawing by Kevin McIntyre)

Figure 15 Bay 22 — suggested reconstruction. (Drawing by Kevin McIntyre)

panels' provenance is unknown. They show traces of silver stain, a technique in general use in Europe by the second quarter of the fourteenth century but totally absent from Saint-Père otherwise. They also have foliate grounds of vigorous Germanic design,[156] quite unlike the elegant *damasquiné* grounds common in fourteenth-century Normandy (Evreux, Saint-Ouen de Rouen). A French example comparable to Saint-Père can be found in the central medallion of the west rose of Lyon (Agnus Dei), late fourteenth century. Note also the panel of flying drapery behind each prophet. Because they maintain the window's arch format and because at least one of them was among the panels retained in the window during the eighteenth and nineteenth centuries,[157] it seems likely that the two prophet panels were incorporated into the bay at an early date in its history, before 1400.

On the other hand, the pair of panels showing Sts. Peter and Paul holding attributes (Pl. 62) was probably part of the window from its conception.[158] They are stylistically the earliest panels of the bay. It is likely that they were designed for a lower location in the church, as part of a hypothesized series expanded ca. 1305 to suit the enormous space of Bay 22. Like these two panels, the other early panels seem to have been designed in matching pairs (Figs. 11, 14): cf, the two panels of Simon Magus' fall (Pl. VI); the martyrdoms of Sts. Peter and Paul; the vocation of Peter and giving of the keys (Pl. 63). If the truth lies here, then it was the original format of the series of matching panels which subsequently dictated the seven-row pattern of the Peter window in the clerestory, at the time of their re-use there (and subsequently of the Joachim-Anne lancet of Bay 19 [Pl. 51], designed to match). After that time the unsuitability of the seven-row format for the more elevated location was recognized.

The donor panel (Pl. 63) has also traveled before coming to rest in its present location. It shows a kneeling abbot with crozier and inscription. In 1672 Dom Aubert noticed it in *"une vitre de la nef de l'eglise de septentrion,"*[159] and a drawing made for Roger de Gaignières (1642–1715) (Pl. 65) labels it *"Vitre dans la nef de l'Eglise . . ."*[160] It can be assumed that both are referring to Bay 22. The inscription as recorded by the Gaignières artist between 1692 and 1704 reads:[161]

IE HAN .
ABB E•DE•
CEA NS•I
FIT FAI=
RE• C
ECI
LAN•M• CCC.V.

By the nineteenth century the donor panel had traveled to the hemicycle, where Guilhermy found it in *"la galerie du chevet"*[162] and Ferdinand de Lasteyrie (Pl. 64) with customary precision pinpointed it: *"Ce vitrail est situé au pourtour du choeur, un peu à gauche, en arrière du sanctuaire."*[163] Presumably it was in one of the four locations in the ambulatory where Brunet found the displaced fragments in 1906. The mutilated inscription then read:

Guilhermy: IEHAN
DE MANTE
A . . . . PERE

De Lasteyrie:[164] IE HAN
DEM ANTE
PAR LA
GR̄CE
DE ⁝IS^{h} [Jesus]ABE
DE S ⁝PERE

In the present restoration it reads (Pl. 63):

IE HAN
DEM ANTE
PAR LA GRCE
DE DIE U
ABE
DE SAINT PERE

Jehan Ier de Mantes was abbot of Saint-Père from 1306 until his death in 1310, a period of great activity in the stained-glass workshop. He was a known benefactor of the abbey, presenting it with a great bell in 1308.[165] His predecessor in office, Abbot Hervé, died the Monday after Passion Sunday (i.e., two weeks before Easter) in 1306. As the source of the document is a seventeenth-century copy, it is unclear whether the date is n.s. or o.s.[166] In either case the nave clerestory of St. Peter was probably the gift of Abbot Jehan in his first years of office. If the date is n.s., the window would assume importance as an immediate donation to commemorate Jehan de Mantes' election. As the earliest in style, it would further assume importance as the instigator of the series of narrative windows in the nave.

The issue is just how much confidence may be placed in the inscription in the Gaignières drawing (Pl. 65), the last line of which gives the date LAN.M.CCC.V.[167] Unfortunately the date, the seventh line of the Gaignières inscription, bears no resemblance whatsoever to the garbled remains of the seventh line half-cemented into the masonry during the nineteenth century and thus reported by de Lasteyrie (Pl. 64). Furthermore, the entire Gaignières inscription follows the basic wording of a late-fifteenth-century inscription (now lost) which Gaignières also had copied, undoubtedly from the aisle of the nave where it would have been much easier to see than that of the clerestory window (Pl. 66).[168] As its accuracy cannot be specifically discredited, however, the possibility must be allowed that Abbot Jehan de Mantes could have given the window upon his election in the spring of 1306.[169]

In any case the emergence of Abbot Jehan as donor of the first nave window, a pastiche of earlier panels hastily augmented to fit the clerestory, pushes into the period following his donation the gifts of the Canons Laurent Voisin and Nicolas de Maison-Maugis and of the Countess Béatrix de Montfort-l'Amaury, all of which fall in the first decade of the century (the latest predates 1315). The Abbot Jehan I assumes a significant role in the embellishment of the monastery church. The glazing of the nave — a unique vision — was probably largely his achievement.

The legend of Bay 22 begins in the lower left with the Vocation of Peter (Matthew IV:18ff.). The panel (Pl. 63, Fig. 14) is one of the earlier series which probably formed the nucleus for the clerestory window. In the Gaignières drawing (Pl. 65) a small but recognizable part of the Calling of Peter panel is shown directly above the donor panel, i.e., in the right light of the second row, probably its original location. Christ, with cruciferous halo, stands to the right beckoning a youthful Peter, who has put down his nets and thrown one leg over the side of the boat in the act of obeying. The design, which maintains an ancient formula for the episode,[170] very closely resembles several scenes of Christ calling the apostles in the Apostles window at Chartres (central apse, Bay 34).[171]

The three panels of the second row (Pl. 63) also seem to be out of the original order. The central light contains an early panel which matches the Calling of Peter, showing Peter receiving the keys from Christ (Matthew XVI:15–19). During the eighteenth and nineteenth centuries this panel was in the second row of the other lancet (see Pl. 60). The two protagonists stand next to one another, their hands grasping the key between them in the traditional pose.[172]

The two panels now framing the scene of Peter receiving the keys have canopies of a later style. The panel to the right contains architecture of a walled city bordered by verdant countryside (the outskirts of Rome?). In the left-hand panel are two haloed figures who embrace one another, both barefoot and holding books.[173] During the eighteenth–nineteenth centuries the panel was in the third row center position (Pl. 60); next to it was another panel of two figures, either disciples or Jews.[174] The subject is either the embrace of Peter and Paul at their first meeting in Rome, or their final embrace before being led to separate martyrdoms.

The details of Peter's apostolate in Rome are apocryphal. The meeting in Rome is related briefly in the Golden Legend:

> . . . Paul came to Rome, and laboured with Peter in the preaching of the word.

The final embrace is given in more detail:

> And when the moment of their separation came, Paul said to Peter: "Peace be with thee, cornerstone of the Church, shepherd of the lambs of Christ!" And Peter said to Paul: "Go in peace, preacher of truth and good, mediator of Salvation to the just!"[175]

An understandable confusion existed between the two scenes in art. They can usually be identified by their position in the narrative, the final meeting being slightly more common.[176] In its present location the panel has been assumed by the restorers to represent the saints' first meeting (cf. the Tours clerestory window).[177]

The third row of the left lancet now contains panels comprising a scene of Peter before an enthroned monarch (Pl. 59). The king is seated in state to the left; in the center panel Peter, haloed and holding the key, is accompanied by a halo-less figure holding a book; the right panel shows two figures in Jewish caps.[178] Peter was imprisoned by Theophilus of Antioch, by Herod, and by Nero; and scenes of the saint before a seated ruler are very common in cycles of his legend. The three panels now grouped together contain no overlapping design elements which would necessitate their being placed adjacently. It is possible that the panel of the Jews belongs elsewhere, perhaps as part of a scene of Peter preaching (see infra). The panel of the seated ruler and the panel of Peter and his companion form a logical pair. Whether they simply represent the apostle before a tyrant, however, or the more common scene of Peter (and Paul?) disputing with Simon Magus before Nero is impossible to say.

The episode of Simon Magus and Peter before Nero was one of the few of Peter's legend to evolve a special format during the thirteenth century: Nero is usually seated to the left; Simon Magus, in a hat, sometimes accompanied by an attendant, takes center stage; and Peter (sometimes with Paul) stands to the right.[179] If the subject of the panels of Row 3 is indeed this, the panel of the Jews (right) should be replaced by one of Simon Magus in a hat, possibly the strange panel now in the right lancet, Row 4, right. In support of the hypothesis are such factors as the importance of the scene in general, the stress on the Simon Magus episode at Saint-Père, and the existence of the peculiar, hatted-figure panel now in the other lancet. Factors to be weighed against the hypothesis are the frequency of general scenes of Peter before a crowned ruler and the fact that the eyes of the proposed "Simon Magus" appear to be looking up. Also, in the suggested arrangement, the intended Simon Magus would necessarily occupy the right rather than the customary central position. The reason is ground color. The ground of the seated ruler (left) is red. That of the Peter panel is curiously divided (as in a similar panel in Row 4), red behind the left figure and blue behind the other. The consistency of ground colors elsewhere in the window would indicate that any completing panel with a blue ground would have to be placed to the right. Color is discussed more generally later.

The fourth row represents a miracle of Peter healing, as do parts of the fifth and seventh rows as well as a misplaced panel now in the seventh row of the right lancet. The "miracle" panels are the most confused of the series, exhibiting several different styles and offering the meagerest of hints in design and iconographic detail as to their precise subject or original grouping. In the fourth row, as reconstructed in the window, St. Peter with an apostle (in the right panel) is blessing a figure who reclines, hands folded in prayer, before a background of fantastic architecture (center). To the left has been placed a panel of three witnesses, one of whom is praying. The elaborate traceried window in the architecture and the young saint accompanying Peter make the most likely identification of the scene Peter and John healing a cripple at the Beautiful Gate of the Temple (Acts III:1–22). These two panels are in the same location they occupied during the eighteenth and nineteenth centuries, while the left one was in the central light of the row directly above (cf. Pl. 60).[180]

In the following row the exact subject and original order are more obscure. The left panel contains city architecture. Peter and a bald and bearded Paul[181] occupy the central light, Peter making a gesture of benediction. The right-hand panel is out of place. It contains a haloed saint holding a book, who seems to be supporting (?) a standing figure accompanied by a praying attendant. Weathering has blanched the faces and mutilation has put the gestures out of focus. During the eighteenth and nineteenth centuries the panel was located in the central light of the top row (Pl. 60), very likely its original location. The curved panel which originally occupied the right position in that row (now misplaced in the same location of the right lancet, Pl. 68) matches it in style and may offer a clue to the subject.

The curved panel in question (Pl. 68, right) has been cropped to fit its present location, the top row of the right lancet being shorter than that of the left. Note the relative size of the tympana and the fact that St. Peter's feet have been cut off. The panel is not only a misfit in proportion but in subject matter, and unquestionably belongs to the left lancet.

It shows a St. Peter in better preservation but otherwise very similar to the wreck in the panel of Row 5. Before him is a small kneeling figure with two attendants, who is being blessed by Peter's hand. A "ray" connecting the hand with the supplicant reveals that a representation of the Healing of the Sick with Peter's shadow (Acts V:15) was intended, a very rare subject for the thirteenth century. Could the light-colored patch near Peter's hand in the mutilated panel also have been such a ray? It is no more than a guess.

The most likely panel to have accompanied the Peter and Paul of Row 5 (center) originally is the panel of the two Jews previously discussed in the description of the third row. The subject would then be "Peter and Paul preaching," one treated occasionally in Gothic windows.[182] Although the ground colors are the same, the decoration of the framing pilasters differs and the suggested grouping must remain hypothetical.

A word about background color, a problem of interest mainly in the left lancet (see Fig. 14). The grounds of the right lancet are red, with the exception of the supposed Simon Magus now in Row 4. In the bay as a whole about thirty panels have red grounds and six or fewer have blue (the ground in the architecture panels is difficult to identify). In three panels the ground is divided. These three all include Peter occupying one side of the composition: left lancet, third row center and fourth row right; right lancet, top row right. Was the arbitrarily-split ground intended to symbolize Peter's miraculous powers? It would be a naive but appropriate idea for the medium.

In any case, the few blue panels do not appear to have been designed at random, but instead form groups either within themselves or with the blue side of a divided panel. The projected grouping of "Peter and Paul preaching" (see supra) is a case in point. Another would be the meeting of Peter and Paul outside the city gate (left lancet, second row, left and right panels).

The sixth row of the left lancet shows Peter's release from prison by the Angel (Acts XII:3–11) (Pl. 67). In the center, Peter, in prison, is aroused by the angel. To the left the angel leads Peter out. In the right-hand panel is a multitude of soldiers in chain mail, the front row of them sitting down. The huge number of guards, very unusual in art, follows the text (Acts XII:4):

> And when he (Herod) had apprehended him, he put him in prison, and delivered him to four quaternions (i.e., sixteen) of soldiers, to keep him. . . .[183]

The Saint-Père artist has even augmented the sixteen.

The final row (Pl. 67) now has filler in the two outer lights framing a panel of the "healing" group, showing a figure reclining in the foreground. As the head is a restoration and the upper right part of the panel rather confused, the subject cannot be identified further.[184]

The left lancet, as reconstructed, dwells mainly on Peter's activity in Asia Minor as related in the Acts of the Apostles. The right lancet, on the other hand, is devoted to the largely apocryphal incidents of his ministry at Rome. The unflagging interest of the Middle Ages in these "apostolic romances," as well as their unique and unmistakable plots, make them easily recognizable. Iconographically speaking we are at last out of the woods.

The legend continues in the second row of the right lancet (Pl. 62) with three episodes in Peter's rivalry with the magician Simon Magus: their contest to resuscitate a dead youth (Row 2); Simon's false execution (Row 3); and Simon's fall (Row 4) (Pl. VI). The huge amount of space allotted to the scenes reflects the enormous popularity of this section of Peter's apocrypha during the medieval period. While the three incidents chosen for illustration at Saint-Père are not the only stories of Simon Magus which were illustrated in Gothic art, it is unusual to find such a number of them in the same work.

Row 2 presents the contest before Nero to resuscitate a dead youth, a subject treated in more detail at Bourges[185] and Lyon.[186] In the legend Simon, having promised to resuscitate the youth, can only make him move his head. Peter, in his turn, orders him to get up and walk, which he does. The Saint-Père panels concentrate on Peter's miracle. Simon Magus does not appear at all. Nero is seated to the left; the shrouded youth reclines in the center, before Peter. The eyes of the former corpse are open (in reference to Simon's partial resuscitation?). Peter points at him in command. In the right panel he obeys, walking with his litter on his shoulder.

Row 3 (Pl. 62) contains a rarer subject, Simon's false execution. According to the legend, Simon agreed to allow himself to be beheaded before Nero, at the last moment magically substituting a ram in his place. The executioner, who has already raised his sword over Simon's head, is turning in great surprise to look at a ram which seems to be butting him from the rear. The design overlaps the irons and unites the three panels into a coherent scene, the only such row in the window. Note the executioner's hand and sword in the upper corner of the left panel and the ram's body spilling over into the right panel.

The design is perhaps an early work of the artist of Bay 23, a master whose distinctive talent lay in telescoping dramatic detail into vivid pictorial concentration. While not precisely verisimilitudinous, the Simon-ram design is vivid and probably was invented directly from a text such as the Golden Legend.[187]

Row 4 (Pl. VI) contains two panels of a much earlier style, presenting the popular tale of the Fall of Simon Magus. The third panel, to the right, may be out of place. It depicts two standing figures on a blue ground, one of them dressed in a cap and vair-lined cloak and striding forward with one hand raised. It was suggested earlier that the figure was Simon Magus and belonged with the seated ruler and Peter now in Row 3 of the left lancet.

The two panels of Simon's Fall have been designed across the irons, forming a unified scene. Peter and Paul are seen praying in two framing niches on either side of a central tower, from which Simon "set sail" to fly away from Rome. Simon is shown three times, first held up by two beast-like devils, then falling, and finally fallen to the ground. Of all the apocryphal stories of Peter, the episode of Simon's fall most attracted the medieval audience. It appears regularly in Gothic art from the twelfth through the sixteenth centuries. Its popularity in the thirteenth has been attested by Mâle: "Nos vitraux du XIIIe siècle, consacrés à Saint Pierre, ne manquent jamais de représenter la chute de Simon le magicien."[188] Although varying slightly, the scene generally maintained a format in which Simon appeared twice, flying and falling, a pattern probably ultimately derived from the lost mosaics of Old St. Peter's, Chapel of John VII (705–707).[189] Saint-Père is quite unusual in augmenting the number of Simons to three.

Another apocryphal episode, *Domine quo vadis?,* appears in two panels of Row 5 (Pl. 59). The third panel (left), containing fantastic architecture, may or may not have been designed for the spot. As related in the Golden Legend Peter, finally agreeing against his wishes to leave Rome, encounters Christ on the Appian Way and asks Him "Lord, whither goest thou?" Christ replies: "I go into Rome to be crucified." Peter, ashamed, returns to Rome to face his martyrdom.[190] No consensus had been reached during the thirteenth century as to the postures of Peter and Christ, sometimes shown both standing, sometimes with Christ emerging from above. At Saint-Père Peter kneels before Christ who stands with a cross-staff, in postures strongly resembling the traditional form of the *Noli me tangere.* Peter's words are inscribed between them:

DOMINE
Q.V . . .
S

As a wall or building was frequently indicated in the background of this scene, the present reconstruction of the row with an architectural panel is quite appropriate.[191]

The last two rows of the right lancet present the martyrdoms of Peter and Paul. The lights of Row 6 contain the beheading of Paul (left), the crucifixion of Peter (center) and a seated Nero (right). The top row (Pl. 68) includes, besides the misplaced panel discussed earlier, a seated Christ with book and orb (center) and an angel receiving the soul of St. Peter (left). Several of these panels remained in the window during the eighteenth and nineteenth centuries in the same location,[192] which is undoubtedly the correct one. The inclusion of the enthroned Nero at the martyrdoms was standard by the thirteenth century. The Nero panel and the two martyrdom panels, however, do not match in style. The former very probably was designed to complete the pair (the earliest designs in the window, ca. 1280's?) when the latter were moved into the clerestory at the beginning of the fourteenth century. The enthroned Christ and angels are also occasional participants at the martyrdoms.[193] It is more than likely that a matching angel, now lost, received Paul's soul where the misplaced right panel is now located.

The iconographic formulae for the martyrdoms themselves are of particular interest. By the thirteenth century representations of St. Paul's execution commonly included some reference of an apocryphal nature, either a blindfold over his eyes (referring to Plautilla's veil) or the severed head already on the ground (in reference to the miraculous fountains). The simple beheading shown at Saint-Père — it occurs both in Bay 22 in the nave and later in the hemicycle medallion in the tracery of Bay 2 (Pl. 4) — reflects the earlier tradition,[194] an example of which can be found in the Troyes Cathedral window of the 1240's.

St. Peter's crucifixion is even more of a curiosity. The apostle is shown in a long robe, upside down, being nailed to the cross by two executioners with hammers. One stands nailing the feet, while the other crouches on the opposite side and nails one hand; in a word, they are positioned asymmetrically. Unlike the crucifixion of St. Peter in the tracery of Bay 2 of the hemicycle (Pl. 4) (a regional Western variant also found at Poitiers, Tours, and Angers), the Bay 22 design, dating perhaps several decades earlier, repeats the standard Germanic design, a design hardly varied in Eastern Europe from Ottonian and even Carolingian times.[195]

The German asymmetrical pattern is found, also, in the windows of Troyes Cathedral dating in the 1240's, and at Auxerre, ambulatory window (ca. 1220–1234). Earlier in this study[196] I have tried to draw comparisons of a stylistic nature between trends in stained-glass design in Burgundy and Champagne and at Saint-Père, from the 1240's through ca. 1280, when the straight choir of Saint-Père was filled with old glass in a new layout. In the stylistic treatment of Bay 22,[197] the Peter window, I suggested that it contained some of the earliest narrative panels in the church (among them the Peter crucifixion), panels probably re-used here to get the campaign of nave-glazing underway. The date suggested, on stylistic grounds, for these "earlier" panels, was perhaps as early as ca. 1280. The discovery of a rare iconographic formula such as the asymmetrical, Germanic crucifixion of Peter, included in the early narrative panels of Saint-Père as well as in the suggested area of influence on Saint-Père during those years would seem to clinch the argument.

Equally appropriate is the evidence provided by the discovery of the local Angevin type of symmetrical nailed crucifixion in the Saint-Père hemicycle, Bay 2 (Pl. 4). Whereas those stylistic qualities peculiar to the Western school of glass were in the process of definition during the early campaign at Saint-Père (the choir, both re-used glass and glass designed ca. 1275), they realized their supreme moment in the Saint-Père hemicycle at the end of the century. Details of the iconography of Bays 22 and 2, then, hold the key to the wellsprings of the early and the mature styles at Saint-Père. For two designs which, after all, do not appear to be so very different, their genealogies are surprising.

What conclusions can be drawn from the complicated and muddled evidence concerning the sources of the iconography of the Peter window? Let us examine the early pairs of panels first (Figs. 11, 14), those probably designed in the last quarter of the thirteenth century for an unknown (lower?) location in the church. This group uses largely traditional iconographic forms: the standing Peter and Paul with attributes, the Receiving of the Keys, the Fall of Simon Magus and the Vocation are all fairly stable thirteenth-century designs. Of the early core of panels only the martyrdoms deviate from the French Gothic norm, and these evidently follow Troyes and Auxerre.

The panels designed to augment the early group for placement in the clerestory after 1305 are freer creations. Many appear to have been invented directly from a textual source of apocryphal stories. Even the canonical scenes, such as the Deliverance from Prison, exhibit specific details (in this case the number of soldiers) and a general lack of dramatic order which indicate reliance on texts rather than on art works. As the 1305 panels form the greater part of the window, it is their general air of hesitancy and imprecision which governs it and makes identifications and reconstructions so difficult. Add to this situation the unfortunate act of fate which chose the Peter window as one of the two to be dismantled in the late seventeenth century. It is surprising indeed that the bay is as beautiful of itself and as harmonious a part of the nave series as it is.

F. Bay 26: St. John the Baptist

The Baptist window (Pl. 76) is the most successful design of the nave's narrative group and a model of clarity and richness. It is organized in the more comfortable five-row format which quickly replaced the original seven-row design in the nave clerestory. The framing canopies of each row are shrunk to minimal size, allowing for taller, more massive — more legible — figures than in any other window of the group. The story unfolds in ten quiet tableaux employing only the essential personae, frequently apportioned one to a panel.

A pair of anonymous secular donors kneels in the lower left panel of the left lancet (Pl. 78), observers to the Lord's Baptism. Man and wife, they wear simple robes and caps of popular medieval type. No clue exists to their identity. They have immense significance nonetheless. As in the Virgin lancet, where an abbot witnesses the Annunciation, their participation in the Baptism is unknown in High Gothic practice. It was Franciscan piety, specifically that of the Pseudo-Bonaventura Meditations, which was to encourage the faithful to imagine themselves present[198] at great Biblical events. Although by no means does the Saint-Père artist slavishly illustrate Pseudo-Bonaventura, several other minutiae in the Baptist window hint at his precocious familiarity with that iconographic landmark, as we shall see.

The scenes of the Baptist's life run from bottom to top, right lancet first. They are:

Right lancet: Row 1 — Annunciation to Zacharias
Row 2 — Birth of the Baptist
Row 3 — Visitation (right panel)
— Naming of the Baptist (left and central panels)

Row 4 — Baptist rebuking Herod
Row 5 — Preaching in the Wilderness
Left lancet: Row 1 — Baptism of Christ with donors
Row 2 — Feast of Herod and Salome's Dance
Row 3 — Decapitation
Row 4 — Salome presents head to Herodias
Row 5 — Baptist bears witness (symbolic version)

Several scenes, i.e., the Visitation, Baptist rebuking Herod and the "Bearing Witness," are out of the regular order. In each case there is a discernible reason. The Visitation was delayed to allow the artist to spread the Baptist's Nativity across a full row of three panels. The Rebuking of Herod was undoubtedly displaced so that the donors in the bottom row could participate in a more suitable devotional scene, that of the Baptism of Christ. The symbolic version of the Baptist bearing witness to Christ is an eminently suitable conclusory scene.[199] Its use as such reflects the growing tendency in Gothic art to merge its elements with the devotional image of St. John, the disc of the *Agnus Dei* thereby becoming his attribute. Across the nave this lancet faces its complement, the *Agna Dei* (Saint Agnes). The placement of both at the west end of the church, traditionally the location of the baptismal font, is among the subtleties typical of the Saint-Père iconographer.

The Baptist window is strikingly similar to the Virgin lancet of Bay 19 (Pls. 51, 53, 54) not only in its participatory donors but in its concentration on a few dramatic scenes presented with economy and clarity. Decorative and narrative elements are minimal. As an example of the combination of beauty of design and the storytelling function — the artistic problem posed in all medallion and "legend" windows, but particularly important for those in the clerestory — the Baptist window is a model of its kind.

The legend commences with a standard representation of the Annunciation to Zacharias (Luke I:9ff.) in the first row of the right lancet (Pl. IX). The haloed Zacharias swings a censer (central panel) before an altar over which an angel appears holding a phylactery (right). Only the two witnesses in the right panel, extremely rare in Gothic art, mark the iconography as in any way unusual. Luke I:2 states that Zacharias's companions remained without the temple, and in art works where they are included they are customarily separated from the scene by architecture.[200] The Saint-Père artist has tried to indicate the change of situs by a shift in ground color, as he does also in the two scenes of Row 3. This fact plus the figures' gestures of surprise offer the explanation. The witnesses are not intended to be present at the Annunciation itself. They embody, instead, a brief reference to a detail of the story less popular in art, that of Zacharias returning speechless to his companions. The compromise is visually effective and in no way impairs the legibility of the basic design. It evidences, moreover, a meticulousness with textual detail which is evident in the window and in several other of the nave clerestories. The same technique of merging elements of two episodes into one scene appears notably in Bay 23 (St. Denis lancet).

The Baptist's Nativity (Luke I:57) of Row 2 shows St. Elizabeth reclining, a standing midwife at the foot of her bed (Pl. 77). An interesting apocryphal detail is included in the scene, perhaps for the very first time in French art: the Virgin herself is shown holding the newborn child.[201] The source could be Voragine's Golden Legend,[202] as well as Pseudo-Bonaventura; it is certainly Italian. Even before its inclusion in the Latin Meditations of Pseudo-Bonaventura in the late thirteenth century,[203] the story of the Virgin's presence at the Birth of the Baptist was current in Italy. The iconographic format of the Virgin standing and holding the infant Baptist was included in several Italian or Italian-inspired art works in the second half of the thirteenth century and is almost certainly of Italian origin.[204] The significance of the scene's necessary apocryphal detail — actually no more than the Virgin's halo — was not understood in the north before the fourteenth century,[205] and it may have been introduced there in its original form at Saint-Père.

Italy may have fostered the iconographic formula, but the textual source lies more deeply buried in the Eastern apocryphal legends, where the subject of Mary's "abiding visitation" first took root in apparent contradiction of St. Luke.[206] In the Homiliae Jacobus, eleventh-century Greek manuscript (Bibl. Vaticana, gr. 1162, fol. 159r), the Virgin, although not included in the actual Nativity, is shown conversing at length with Zacharias during her stay. In an Ottonian Latin manuscript dated before 1014 (Pericope of Henry II, Munich, Staatsbibl., Clm. 4452, Cim. 57, fol. 150r) she makes an appearance at the Birth but does not yet hold the child *à la manière italienne.* The legend was definitely not a new one at the time of its general diffusion from Italy ca. 1300. At Saint-Père, however, it was perhaps manifested for the first time in France.

Row 3 (Pl. 77) comprises the Visitation (delayed for purposes of design until after the Nativity) and the Naming of the Baptist. The artist has varied the grounds to distinguish the two scenes. The two women of the Visitation (Luke I:39ff.) embrace warmly, as they do in the Virgin lancet of Bay 19 (Pl. 53). The Naming of the Child (Luke I:63) also assumes a typical Gothic appearance, Zacharias sitting to the left, two women standing before him with the child. Zacharias is presented in the guise of a medieval scribe seated before his lectern with stylus and knife in hand. These writing implements so well known from evangelist illuminations were rarely supplied to the father of the Baptist,[207] although he sometimes sits before a lectern in France.

At the beginning of the fourteenth century, perhaps through the dissemination of Pseudo-Bonaventura, the scene of the Circumcision, rare in French Gothic art, was combined occasionally with the Naming.[208] While a mohel customarily performs the circumcision, in at least one fourteenth-century copy of the Meditations (Bibl. Nat., ms. ital. 115, fol. 15r) Zacharias himself holds the knife.[209] Could the Saint-Père artist, confronted by a new iconographic grouping, have translated the knife of the circumcision into a more familiar writing implement? It seems quite possible.

The scene which unfolds across Row 4 (Pl. 76) is the displaced episode of the Baptist rebuking Herod (Mark VI:18, Luke III:19). Herod,[210] enthroned to the right, and two of his courtiers standing to the left, flank the towering figure of the Baptist in hairy mantle, the familiar Gothic equivalent of the camel's-hair raiment mentioned in Matthew III:4 and Mark I:6. The king and courtiers carry gloves, one of the accoutrements in the Saint-Père windows of royal or noble status. The scene, although not among the most familiar of the Baptist's legend, can be found in the windows of Angers and the Sainte-Chapelle. It can with difficulty be distinguished from the episode of John's arrest, in which John is brought before Herod by guards.[211]

The correct order of the Public Life is resumed in the top row of the lancet, where John is shown preaching in the wilderness (Matthew III:1ff.; Mark I:4; Luke III:2; John I:19ff.). The scene is represented with great economy. John in hairy mantle (center) addresses two standing figures (left). Trees (right) and a brown ground-pattern of delicate floriate scrollwork indicate the wilderness setting.[212] The preaching scene is an iconographic composite which had evolved by the end of the thirteenth century from the rich narrative materials of the canonical texts.

The two Lilliputian trees flanking St. John in the center panel, tucked in almost as an afterthought, make this iconographic history clear. At the commencement of the thirteenth century little conformity existed in illustrations of wilderness episodes. In one of the scenes occasionally shown, "John alone in the wilderness," he is flanked by two trees.[213] The device was not always maintained in more specific wilderness scenes such as Preaching, Bearing Witness, the Ax at the foot of the Tree, "I am not the Christ," "I am the Voice," etc. The flanking trees did not entirely disappear, however, and remained in art as a symbol of John's life in the wilderness. A late trace of them is found in the familiar rustic pulpits from which John preaches in French fifteenth-century art.[214] The most common form of such pulpits is a horizontal bar between two trees which, of course, flank the Baptist as he preaches.

The left lancet of Bay 26 (Pl. 78) commences with the Baptism of Christ (Matthew III:13–16), observed by the pair of kneeling donors in the left panel.

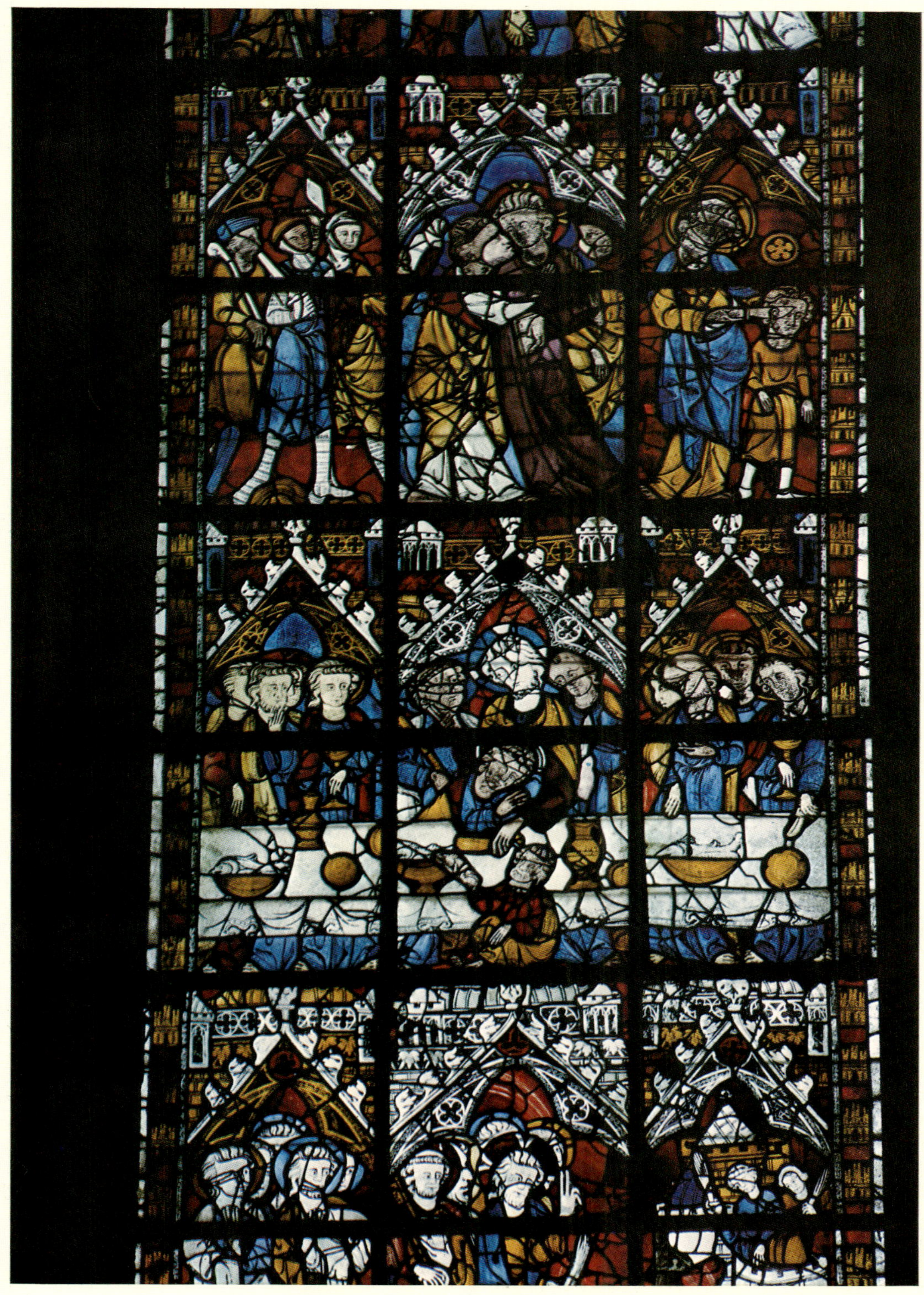

PLATE XI Nave: Bay 18. Passion window, Last Supper; Betrayal of Christ *(Edouard Fièvet)*

The Gothic format for the baptism by infusion, which remained absolutely fixed throughout the thirteenth century, is maintained. The Baptist and an angel holding garments flank Christ, who stands nude in the Jordan, the waters rising before Him in undulating horizontal waves. The only detail which varied in this scene for well over a hundred years was the dove of the Holy Spirit mentioned in the gospels and occasionally included in art. At Saint-Père — as in numerous thirteenth- and fourteenth-century examples[215] — the dove is absent.

Another episode about which the Gothic world reached nearly absolute iconographic conformity, the Feast of Herod (Mark VI:21–23), appears in the following row (Pl. 76). Herod, flanked by Herodias to the right and two courtiers to the left, sits to a long table laden with plates, pitchers and goblets. Before the table Salome performs an acrobatic maneuver bent backwards in a complete circle, her hands resting against the floor. Herodias is always present at the table in thirteenth-century French art, while Salome's pose varies but slightly in detail, never in its basically acrobatic nature, from its introduction in the twelfth century throughout the entire fourteenth century.[216] She appears as a medieval juggler of the type who entertained at fairs and feasts, and the acrobatic stunt she does actually came to be known as the Dance of Salome from its representation in art and mystery plays.[217]

The tragic sequel to the feast unfolds across the following rows. Row 3 shows the Beheading (Mark VI:27–28). As the martyrdom scene, the Beheading was extremely popular in art and appears in its traditional form twice at Saint-Père, in the series of martyrdom medallions in the hemicycle (Bay 3) (Pl. 6) as well as in the Baptist window. The saint (center) kneels before architecture representing his prison, an evangelical detail always observed in French Gothic art. The executioner (left) grasps him by the hair and raises his sword while Salome (right) waits holding a salver. Nearly identical examples are numerous in Gothic art.

Less rigid conformity was reached on the format of the succeeding scene of Row 4, Salome delivering the head to Herodias (Mark VI:28), although the episode was not uncommon. The scene was sometimes set at the feast table, sometimes reduced to the two women alone. Sometimes both stand and occasionally both mother and daughter grasp the bowl. The Saint-Père design shows Salome (center) presenting the head on a salver to Herodias enthroned (right), while behind the girl the executioner (left) sheathes his sword. The grouping of the two women was approximated at Saint-Julien-du-Sault, ca. 1250, but the executioner and his action are otherwise unfamiliar and probably were invented by the Saint-Père artist.[218]

The final scene of the window is one of the preaching episodes, the Bearing

Witness (John I:35–36), displaced until the end because it is used as a devotional image. The symbolic version of the text, in which St. John shows his disciples a disc with the *Agnus Dei,* rapidly grew in popularity in the thirteenth century and was maintained well into the fourteenth. It is a more fitting conclusory tableau than the burial scene occasionally found, and more suited to Saint-Père, where scenes after death were unpopular and where no standing figure of St. John appears in the saintly parades of the apse and nave. The Baptist's disc of the *Agnus Dei* had been metamorphosed into a universal emblem of the Death and Resurrection of Christ by the end of the thirteenth century, and as such appears on seals and coins of the reign of Philippe-le-Bel.[219] Its appropriation in the Baptist window as the climax of the legend is one more indication of the sensitivity and inventiveness of the Saint-Père iconographer. His Baptist legend thus partakes of the strong Christological focus of the north side of the nave.

The design of the Baptist window, one of the supreme achievements in Saint-Père, was the work of a thoughtful and talented artist. The iconography reveals that he was very much a man of his time. The window, particularly the second lancet, could stand as a canon of High Gothic practice for the legend. The several hints of apocryphal sources in the early scenes, on the other hand, reveal a receptivity to new forms. Bay 26 is still very much a French Gothic work. It includes none of the Infancy scenes which would be introduced in the fourteenth century by the Meditations of Pseudo-Bonaventura. But with the "haloed midwife," Zacharias's knife, and the "participatory donors," the first slight evidence of that very influential text in the north appears at Saint-Père.

NOTES

1. The daughter Béatrix, born between ca. 1265 and 1282, was elected abbess of Port-Royal ca. 1326 and died ca. 1328. Her tomb bears the arms of Dreux and Montfort. Père Anselme, *Histoire généalogique et chronologique de la maison royale de France* (Paris, 1726), I, p. 429.

2. The countess's death-date from Anselme, I, p. 428. See also: D'Armancourt, pp. 230–231 (#101) and pp. 313–315 (#192); André du Chesne, *Histoire généalogique de la maison royale de Dreux* (Paris, 1631), pp. 90ff. Although marshalling of arms was introduced generally in the later thirteenth century, it does not occur in the arms of this house until the mid- or late-fourteenth century.

3. Béatrix's two sons both fought in the Flemish wars (1296–1305). Robert died ca. 1303 and Jean II 1309. In 1311 she disposed of a château to a niece.

4. See discussion Chapter IV.

5. Edgar Hennecke, *New Testament Apocrypha,* ed. Schneemelcher (Philadelphia, 1963), I, p. 374ff.; James, *Apocryphal New Testament,* p. 39ff., cited hereafter as *ANT.* Although Anna is not mentioned in I:2, she is not infrequently included in art.

6. Chartres, Bay 16 of south choir (Delaporte and Houvet, I, pl. XLIV), the Joachim-Anna

window. The apparent rarity of the scene may derive in part from the fact that it is difficult to recognize, containing only two figures and no specific background or "props." Non-French examples: two Greek manuscripts of the *Homiliae Jacobus,* eleventh–twelfth century: a) Bibl. Nat. gr. 1208, fol. 21v; and b) Rome, Bibl. Vaticana, ms. gr. 1162, fol. 16v; *Drui Liet von der Maget,* a twelfth–thirteenth-century manuscript by Wernher von Tegernsee depicting all of the apocrypha of the Virgin (Berlin, Staatsbibl., germ. oct. 109, fol. 14r, lost since World War II); and, possibly, a Book of Hours of the use of Sarum, ca. 1240, illuminated by William de Brailes (Brit. Mus. Add. 49999, fol. 1v) (see Sidney Cockerell, *The Work of William de Brailes* [Cambridge, 1930], pp. 18ff.).

7. James, *ANT,* p. 39. Cf. Hennecke, p. 375.

8. In the photomontage in the *Archives photographiques,* the right panel (two shepherds and sheep) is interchanged with the one above (one shepherd and sheep). The panels are correctly mounted in the church.

9. Cf. the list of examples given in Mirella Levi D'Ancona, *The Iconography of the Immaculate Conception in the Middle Ages and Early Renaissance* (New York, 1957), p. 45, fn. 109.

10. Witnesses (unhaloed) do appear often in Italian trecento frescoes. Examples: Arena chapel at Padua, ca. 1303–1308; Santa Croce, Florence, Baroncelli chapel, 1322–1338; Rinaccini chapel, ca. 1365. It is more likely, however, that the Saint-Père panel is out of place. The framing panels may have been removed in the late seventeenth century, as were those of Bays 20, 21, 22, and 23. Both of the missing panels of Bay 19 are outer (framing) ones, as in those windows. The lost panel of Row 4 might have shown Joachim and Anna together, a grouping which appears in sequence between the Golden Gate and the Nativity of Mary in several French Gothic examples: (a) Chartres, Bay 16, south choir aisle (Delaporte and Houvet, I, pl. XLIV); (b) Auxerre (archivolts of left portal, west facade, second half of the thirteenth–fourteenth century). Perhaps Protev. IV:4 is intended: "And Ioacim rested the first day in his house."

11. James, *ANT,* p. 73. Pseudo-Matthew relates how Mary walked up fifteen steps without looking back. Protev. VIII:1 (James, p. 42, Hennecke, p. 378) simply states: "And her parents gat them down Marvelling, and praising the Lord God because the child was not turned away backward." The Saint-Père scene includes a stairway, but not of fifteen steps, probably because the panel is quite cramped.

12. Although in both of the basic sources of the legend, i.e., Protevangelium and Pseudo-Matthew, Joseph is chosen by a dove on his rod rather than a flowering rod, the latter is frequent in art. It may derive originally from the Life of Mary by Epiphanius the Monk, eighth century (*PG,* CXX, p. 195). It is probably a reference to Isaiah XI:1. See Grimouard de St-Laurent, "Etude sur l'iconographie de saint Joseph," *Revue de l'art chrétien,* 3e ser., I (XXXIII) (1883), pp. 357–358, 363–364.

13. At Chartres Cathedral, a draped altar is flanked by the Virgin and a female companion (left) and a suitor with rod and Joseph with flowering rod (right). The inclusion of both Joseph and the priest marks Saint-Père as later. No set format emerged for the scene in Gothic France. It was often excluded or only tokenly represented: i.e., a group of suitors carrying rods (Notre-Dame, Ste. Anne portal, archivolts); a priest and altar with flowering rods upon it (Le Mans, Virgin chapel, thirteenth-century window).

14. The trend is less apparent in ivories and manuscripts.

15. Königsfelden (second quarter of the fourteenth century) and Niederhaslach (Alsace), Florentius church (1390–1420) both include more scenes than these two, but in neither case as many or in as elaborate detail as at Saint-Père. See Michael Stettler, *Stained Glass of the Early Fourteenth Century from the Church of Koenigsfelden* (New York, 1949), p. 28.

16. James, *ANT,* pp. 212–213; Hennecke, p. 429; Jacopus de Voragine, *The Golden Legend,* trans. Granger Ryan and Helmut Ripperger (London, 1941), II, pp. 449ff. It is demonstrable

that English art retained a strong interest in the apocryphal scenes of the Death of the Virgin; such cycles often culminate with the Dormition rather than the Coronation. Examples occur in a number of media and well into the fourteenth century.

17. Examples in Gothic France include: a) Lyon Cathedral, apse pilasters, capital 6 (second half of the twelfth century); b) Laon, thirteenth-century apse window; c) Auxerre, archivolts of right portal, second half of the thirteenth century.

18. They are not included in the Chartres west window, ca. 1145, nor in the Ste. Anne portal of Notre-Dame (late-twelfth-century section). By the fourteenth century they are almost never found. The midwives are revived by the more earthy Flemings in the early fifteenth century (see Robert Campin's Dijon Nativity).

19. James, *ANT,* pp. 74 and 46–47; Hennecke, pp. 384ff.; Schiller, I, p. 64.

20. Many examples can be cited. Among the earliest: a) ivory throne of Maximianus, in Mus. Arcivescovile, Ravenna (sixth century); b) Syrian ivory book cover, sixth century, Brit. Mus. (illustrated in O. M. Dalton, *East Christian Art* [Oxford, 1925], pl. XXVI); c) sculptured altar-canopy from San Marco, Venice, front of left column (for illustration see Wilpert, II, fig. 319); d) Coptic ivory plaque from diptych, Bologna, Mus. Civico (seventh–eighth century) (illustrated in Goldschmidt, IV, pl. XLI [#125]).

21. a) destroyed mosaics from Old St. Peter's, Chapel of John VII (dated 705–707), preserved in Grimaldi drawings (see Raffaele Garrucci, *Storia dell' arte cristiana nei primi otto secoli della chiesa* [Prato, 1872–1881], IV [1877], pl. 279 [1] and 280 [2] and [3]); b) frescoes in cubiculum, Cem. Valentino, Rome (seventh–eighth century); c) fragments of fresco in right aisle, Santa Maria Antiqua, Rome (second half of the eighth–second half of the ninth century) (see Wladimir de Grüneisen, *Sainte Marie Antique* [Rome, 1911], pl. XXI [photo] and fig. 83 [drawing]); d) destroyed fresco of late tenth century, nave clerestory of San Sebastiano al Palatino, Rome (preserved in drawings) (see Wilpert, II, fig. 321).

22. Alberto de Capitani d'Arzago, *Gli affreschi di S. Maria di Castelseprio* (Milan, 1948), pls. XLVIII, L, LI, LII; Kurt Weitzmann, *The Fresco Cycle of S. Maria di Castelseprio* (Princeton, 1951), p. 55.

23. Illustrated in Schiller, I, fig. 160.

24. The crouching midwife does not occur in Greek manuscripts. (The New Testament-Psalter of the University of Chicago Library, Greg. 2400, ca. 1265, is a late exception.) She does not appear in the tenth–eleventh-century frescoes of Cappadocia, even in the Göreme and Qeledjlar chapels where the Bath of the Christchild is regularly included. She is almost never found in German illumination. The *Drui Liet von der Maget,* a twelfth–thirteenth manuscript by Wernher von Tegernsee (Berlin, Staatsbibl., Germ. oct. 109, esp. fols. 68v and 69v, lost since World War II) is an important exception, but seems to have had little influence on the mainstream of German Marian iconography.

25. a) Psalter, Brit. Mus., Lansdowne 420, fol. 7v (early-thirteenth century), the midwife offers the Virgin a bowl; b) Psalter, Pierpont Morgan, ms. 756, fol. 7r (thirteenth century), the midwife is nimbed; c) "Huth" psalter, Brit. Mus. Add. 38116, fol. 9v (after 1280), Salome grasps Virgin's left hand (*Catalogue of the Fifty Manuscripts and Printed Books Bequeathed to the British Museum by Aldred H. Huth* [London, 1912], pl. 2[a]); d) fresco in nave, St. Clement, Ashampstead (thirteenth century), Salome extends hand toward the crib; e) Laon apse window (thirteenth century), Salome approaches bed carrying Child. On the Chartres frieze, west portal (mid-twelfth century), and the Lyon Cathedral apse pilasters, capital 5 (second half of the twelfth century), the midwife extends her hands but no longer crouches, and the motivation of her gesture seems forgotten. Isolated examples can be found as late as the fourteenth century, although not in France.

26. She is exactly reversed, but what the significance of this would be in the glass medium is unclear.

27. The other possibilities would be that his source was textual, or was a Gothic object such as those listed in fn. 25, supra. However, the Saint-Père midwife is much closer to the Early Christian original type than to any of the other Gothic variants.

28. After Norman invasions of 857, 898 and 911, the abbey was restored and reformed under Bishops Aganon (926–941) and Rainfroi (941–955). A tenth-century inventory of its treasures exists (Chartres Bibl. ms. 31, 1-B) (see de Mély, "Les inventaires," IV [XXXVI], July 1886, pp. 307–313; and more uncritically, Abbé Poisson, "Inventaire de Saint-Père," *Annales archéologiques,* VII [1850], p. 190). The source for the abbey's early history is an eleventh-century cartulary, "Aganon vetus" (Chartres Bibl. ms. 1060 is a twelfth-century copy; see Guérard, introduction pp. 9–10).

29. On Saint-Père's relations with the Pope in the Gothic era, see Berger, pp. 12–13.

30. See de Mély, V (XXXVII), Jan. 1887, p. 64.

31. Much of the following section was presented at the Sixth Conference on Medieval Studies at Western Michigan University, 1971.

32. Poisson (*Chroniques,* p. 422) describes Bay 23 at this time: "les formes ont une large bande en verres blancs, ce qui rend les sujets incomplets." In the old photograph (Pl. 71), only one fragment (head of Denis pushed into furnace) appears to be a center, and not a border, panel. Its presence among the debris is not easily explained.

33. The photograph taken after the ca. 1905 restoration (Pl. 70) is more reliable than the photomontage (Pl. 69) made after the 1950's restorations, which omits several old panels (the two left tympanum panels, the left panel of Row 4 of the Clement window) and includes one of the new panels made ca. 1905 (the bottom right panel, right lancet).

34. Although St. Paul's name is not included in that of the abbey, his patronage is informally assumed along with that of St. Peter. See Chapter VIII, fn. 21.

35. On the pairing of Sts. Clement and Denis, see Chapter VI, fn. 9.

36. It is distinguished from the bishops' miters in the windows by a less angular silhouette and a small knob at the top.

37. The head of the monk in the central panel is a restoration.

38. See Roman representations of the Clement consecration by Peter: a) mutilated fresco in San Clemente, lower church, nave, ca. 1100, Clement in bishop's vestments is enthroned between Peter and some named Roman pope-saints (Cletus, Linus and others) (illustrated in Wilpert, IV, pl. 240 [top]); b) Rome, Bibliotheca Vaticana, ms. lat. 8541, Passional of first half of the fourteenth century, p. 59, Clement in tiara kneels before Peter and three men, two of whom are unhaloed bishops.

39. Paris, Bibl. Nat., Dept. des Manuscrits, *Vie et histoire de Saint Denys,* pref. by Henri Omont (Paris, 1905) (cited hereafter as Omont).

40. For Bibl. Nat. ms. fr. 2090–2092, refer to facsimile edition, Henry Martin, *Légende de Saint Denis* (Paris, 1908).

41. It is rare in art; the only example I know of is the thirteenth-century choir window of St. Kunibert (formerly St. Clement) in Cologne, where Trajan is included as well. The window is illustrated in Heinrich Oidtmann, *Die Rheinischen Glasmalereien vom 12. bis zum 16. Jahrhundert,* 1912, I, pl. VII and figs. 99 and 100.

42. It does not occur at St. Kunibert, Cologne, either (see note supra).

43. Illustrated in Wilpert, IV, pl. 240.

44. The device is common in Gothic art. A few of the kings and courtiers in the Saint-Père nave hold gloves. See Bay 26, right lancet, fourth row from bottom; Bay 22, right lancet, third row from bottom.

45. Clement's legend, of fourth century origin, was perpetuated in the Roman breviary; bibliography is given in *Butler's Lives of the Saints,* ed. Thurston and Attwater (New York, 1963), IV, pp. 406–407. See also Voragine, II, pp. 703ff.

46. The anchor is found almost as often as the millstone and seems to be more frequent in later examples. Examples of anchors: Chartres, relief of south porch; window in St. Kunibert, Cologne, thirteenth century (scene identification questionable); and fresco in the nuns' choir, convent church of Wienhausen, fourteenth century (illustrated in Oskar Beyer, *Norddeutsche Gotische Malerei* [Braunschweig, 1924], fig. 22).

47. It was described in the window by nineteenth-century authors: Poisson, p. 422; Bulteau, p. 296.

48. The most sizeable restoration is above the central horizontal iron, to the left, in the red ground.

49. Chartres, south porch, socle of St. Clement; window of St. Kunibert, Cologne.

50. The new design was made on the advice of the Canon Delaporte, according to M. Lorin.

51. Bourges Cathedral chevet, Lady of Lourdes chapel (first to north of axial chapel). Illustrated in Clement and Guitard, pl. XIV; top of window shown in Cahier-Martin, pl. XII. The window is heavily restored.

52. See Raymond Koechlin, *Les ivoires gothiques français* (Paris, 1926), II, pl. LXXIX and no. 345.

53. It has been pointed out (see Charles J. Liebman, Jr., *Etude sur la vie en prose de Saint Denis* [Geneva, N.Y., 1942], pp. i–vii et suiv.; Robert Bossuat, "Traditions populaires relatives au martyre et à la sépulture de saint Denis," *Le moyen âge,* LXII [1956], pp. 481–483) that the main text upon which it was based, the *Vita et Actus beati Dionysii* written at Saint-Denis starting in 1233, was a total reworking and pervasive elaboration of the saint's legend, with the purpose of establishing him firmly as patron both of the abbey and of the Capetian monarchy but more specifically of Blanche, who as regent for her minor son the future St. Louis, was fighting the barons at that moment to save the crown for him against heavy odds. It was thus a piece of political propaganda often used later on to train princes of the blood, and likely to be resurrected whenever the monarchy was under attack — as in 1314. The "modernizing" of the setting from Roman Lutetia to early fourteenth-century Paris is thus a logical (as well as charming) tactical maneuver.

54. The 1317 manuscript, a treasure object from the moment of its creation, was copied several times in the early fourteenth century. See discussion of Bibl. Nat. ms. lat. 5286 in William Hinkle, "The Iconography of the Four Panels by the Master of Saint Giles," *Journal of the Warburg-Courtauld Institutes,* XXVIII (1965), p. 113ff. Since the Saint-Père artist draws upon the 1250 manuscript as well and occasionally merges details from both, he most probably worked from the originals, in the scriptorium of Saint-Denis 1314–1317. Since I first presented this theory in 1971, Philippe Verdier has suggested a similar relationship between the same two manuscripts and two ivory diptychs, Cluny Museum (CL. 395a–d). He inexplicably dates them "third decade of 14th century" (I, p. 160) or "1320s" (II, p. 132), by which date the second manuscript would have left the monastery of Saint-Denis. See: Philippe Verdier, Peter Brieger, Marie Farquhar Montpetit, *Art and the Courts,* National Gallery of Canada (Ottawa, 1972).

55. His halo is original, however, as are all the others in the row.

56. The panel was presumably lost during the dismantling of border panels sometime after 1672. The existing restoration dates from the 1950's. In the restoration of ca. 1905 the light was filled with scraps of wide, early thirteenth-century border (see Pl. 70).

57. Among the manuscript subjects falling between that used in the first row Clement lancet and that of the second row Denis lancet are "Denis in Paris consecrating an altar" and "baptising in a font." In either case the identifying object — altar, font — could have occupied the lower right lost panel. Cf. Bibl. Nat. nouv. acq. fr. 1098, fol. 36; Bibl. Nat. ms. fr. 2091, fol. 100v.

58. The episode is included in early stained-glass cycles at Saint-Denis-de-Jouhet (see Albert

Mayeux, "Vitraux de Saint-Denis de Jouhet [Indre]," *Bulletin monumental,* LXXXII [1923], pp. 181–184) and Bourges, and also in the Tours choir clerestory. Tours dates after the 1250 manuscript but shows no influence of it at all. See Boissonot, pp. 21–22 and drawing, pl. II, in which the order of scenes has been rearranged to conform with the author's conception of the saint's legend, and differs from the order of scenes presently in the cathedral.

59. This format was probably introduced in this manuscript. The draped altar was abandoned during the fourteenth century (see the marble relief from Saint-Denis, second half of the fourteenth century, Louvre, Inv. R. F. no. 462, illustrated in Musée du Louvre, *Description raisonnée des sculptures du moyen âge, de la Renaissance et des temps modernes* [Paris, 1950], I, p. 131 and fig. 188).

60. In the 1250 manuscript the saint assumes a frontal, almost symmetrical, *orant* position.

61. The scene is ms. fr. 2091, fol. 111r. The listening figure is not reversed, but the gesture of the disciple varies.

62. It is rare in art, not included in the thirteenth-century windows previously mentioned nor in the later ivories.

63. See for example the ivory diptych in the Cluny Museum (Koechlin, II, pl. LXXIX).

64. The quiet, formal composition of Bourges, for example, shows St. Denis flanked by two animals within a crenellated brick edifice. At Saint-Denis-de-Jouhet the animals, a winged lion and a beast with flames emerging from its mouth, rush forth from a furnace.

65. The saint is seated nude to the left, out of doors, confronting wild beasts. In the 1317 manuscript this newer figure arrangement is adopted but placed oddly enough in the traditional interior setting.

66. The 1250 text refers specifically to lions:

Hic Dominum laudans orat, datus esca ferarum,
Et sanctis precibus feritas mansuescit earum;
Tanquam cognoscat nature lege patronum,
Supplicat ut poscat veniam sibi turba *leonum.*

The animals pictured, however, like the Saint-Père creatures, are distinctly short-haired canines. Réau (III, pt. 1, p. 376) reports that St. Denis was invoked against the bites of mad dogs, which were treated by touching them with his chains preserved at Saint-Denis-de-la-Chartre in Paris. Voragine (II, p. 620) states "savage beasts."

67. For example those of the 1317 manuscript, ms. fr. 2092, fol. 24v.

68. See the 1250 manuscript, fol. 41v; the 1317 manuscript, ms. fr. 2092, fol. 28r; also the fourteenth-century ivories.

69. Discussed by Mayeux (pp. 181–184), who states that the episode is absent from the Golden Legend. But see Voragine (II, p. 620): "Then he was cast into an oven, but the fire was extinguished."

70. Compare the 1250 manuscript, where the halo encircles the decapitated head. In depicting cephalophores there was little medieval consensus on the question of whether the halo goes with the head or remains with the neck and shoulders.

71. Mayeux (p. 183 and fn. 1) states that the cranium tradition is earlier, possibly introduced in the chronicles of Hilduin, 840 A.D., and Usuard, d. 876 (Martyrology of the usage of Saint-Germain-des-Prés). He maintains that one finds the whole head only at the very end of the twelfth century, and especially after the Golden Legend (which was translated into French at the beginning of the fourteenth century).

72. Another possible thirteenth-century example would be the mutilated statue (ca. 1260–1265) from Notre-Dame, south portal (deposited in 1950 in the Musée de l'oeuvre, Notre-Dame, from the Cluny Museum; illustrated in Geneviève Souchal, "Un reliquaire de la Sainte-Chapelle

. . .," *Revue des arts, la revue du Louvre et des musées de France,* X [1960], fig. 4, pp. 188–189 and fn. 39). The cephalophore with cranium at Chartres (south porch, relief on south side of pier 1) is probably not St. Denis but the local saint, Chéron.

73. Chartres Bibl. mun., ms. 519, fol. 219r; see Chapter VI, fn. 7.

74. See also the mutilated quatrefoil relief from Saint-Denis, mid-fourteenth-century (Louvre, Inv. N 15006, illustrated in Musée du Louvre, *Description raisonnée*, I, pp. 130ff. and fig. 187).

75. See Chapter VI at fn. 7.

76. Both lights are shown blocked with cartons in Pl. 80, a photograph probably taken at the time of the ca. 1905 restorations. The glass now filling the panels is of a style typical of the restorations of that time (see Pl. 79).

77. Catherine's heads in Rows 3 and 4 (center) are modern. Row 3 is illustrated at the top of Pl. 81.

78. Voragine, I, p. 110. The connection of Agnes and *agnus* occurs as early as Saint Augustine and in art at Ravenna, Sant' Apollinare Nuovo. Réau (III, pt. 1, p. 33) states succinctly that, for Voragine, Saint Agnes "est l'*Agna Dei,* la personnification féminine de l'*Agneau de Dieu*." See Chapter VI, fn. 8.

79. Voragine, I, p. 111. He does not clearly differentiate between this personal visit and a more formal confrontation, however.

80. For a scene of Agnes in her hair see the initial in the Belleville Breviary (Bibl. Nat. ms. lat. 10483–10484, ca. 1325) illustrated in Kathleen Morand, *Jean Pucelle* (Oxford, 1962), frontispiece and pl. VIId.

81. Examples of Agnes legend: a) fresco, nave of Santa Maria di Donna Regina, Naples, first half of the fourteenth century; b) enamel cup in the British Museum, late-fourteenth-century (illustrated in Brit. Mus., Dept. of British and Mediaeval Antiquities, *A Guide to the Mediaeval Room and to the Specimens of Mediaeval and Later Times in the Gold Ornament Room* [Oxford, 1907], fig. 171 and pp. 122, 236).

82. Minor figures do occasionally wear white or near-white in the bay, for instance the two angels of the tympana, occasional guards, and executioners. The friend standing behind the throttled Procopius in Row 3 wears a white tunic under a dark cloak lined in gold. (Pl. 82.)

83. Bulteau (p. 295) refers to two censing angels in the Catherine lancet in 1850: "enfin deux autres anges l'encensent." The diaper remained in the Agnes tympanum until World War II.

84. Bay 26, south apse (Delaporte and Houvet, I, pls. LXVIII–LXIX).

85. La Trinité, Fécamp (Seine-Maritime), ca. 1280. See Lafond, "Les Vitraux de l'abbaye de la Trinité de Fécamp," ch. XLVIII of *L'Abbaye benedictine de Fécamp, ouvrage scientifique du XIIIe centenaire* (Fécamp, 1961), III, pp. 99–101, notes pp. 254–255, and pl. opp. p. 100.

86. Nave, third window on north side, now dated by Hayward and Grodecki ca. 1190. For illustrations: *VF,* fig. 72 (top three medallions); Hayward and Grodecki, fig. p. 19.

87. Ritter, pl. I (first half of the thirteenth century).

88. In 1850, before the current restorations and rearrangements were made, Bulteau (p. 295) described the subjects of the lancet as: "la vierge d'Alexandrie dispute contre l'empereur Maximin [Row 1]; elle dispute contre les philosophes en presence de l'empereur [Row 2]; les philosophes convertis par la savante vierge sont jetés dans les flammes [Row 3]."

89. The head is original. There are large areas of restoration in the panel, notably in the lower right.

90. The only notable restoration is in the lower right light.

91. See Angers window. See also a Rhenish legendarium, Oxford, Keble Coll., fol. 273v

(second half of the thirteenth century), where the headless body sits with the head in its lap (illustrated in Hanns Swarzenski, pl. 67 [fig. 385]).

92. See Queen Mary Psalter, Brit. Mus., Roy. 2B, VII, fol. 284r (Sir George Warner, introd. *Queen Mary's Psalter* [London, 1912], pl. 278b); wax stamp of Thomas de Garton, 1329, London, Public Record Office WS. 19.

93. See also: a) east window, West Horseley church (Surrey), ca. 1210–1225 (Herbert Read, John Baker and Alfred Lammer, *English Stained Glass* [London, 1960], pl. X); b) Rouen, first half of the thirteenth century (Ritter, pl. 1); c) Chartres Cathedral, Bay 26.

94. The earliest I know of is in St. Kunibert, Cologne, north wall of transept, ca. 1220–1230.

95. Two examples can be cited: a) psalter, from Augsburg Cathedral library (Aug. Eccl. 200), now in Munich, Staatsbibl., Clm. 3900 (second half of the thirteenth century); fols. 1v–7r (see Swarzenski, *Lateinischen,* figs. 957–968); b) wing of tabernacle attributed to school of Abruzzi, fourteenth century, in Museo Aquilano, in Aquila degli Abruzzi (the torture by beating, absent at Saint-Père, is included here).

96. See discussion in Chapter I, at fn. 21.

97. See mid-twelfth-century sculptural friezes at Etampes and Chartres.

98. The body has been replaced by a stopgap which must be quite old, as it shows a considerable amount of weathering on the exterior. Such a figure is traditional in the scene. The feet are clearly visible.

99. Mâle, *"L'art religieux du XIIIe siècle en France,* 3rd ed. (Paris, 1910), p. 218, fn. 4. The detail of Christ Himself carrying a palm, while irregular in French art, was almost standard in the art of Germany throughout the Gothic period, as the most casual survey of stained glass or manuscript illumination will bear out.

100. Examples: (a) gospel book, Mount Athos, Mon. Iviron, 5, fol. 423r (illustrated in Andreas Xyngopoulos, *Illustrated Gospels from the Iviron Monastery on Mount Athos* [Athens, 1932], pl. 51); (b) gospel book, Etschmiadzin, Monastery library, 362 G, fol. 8r, dated 1057 (Frédéric Macler, *Miniatures arméniennes* [Paris, 1913], pl. XI, fig. 21); (c) gospel book, Venice, Lib. Congregazione Armena, no. 1917, fol. 128v, dated 1307 (Sirarpie Der Nersessian, *Manuscrits arméniens illustrés . . . de Venise* [Paris, 1936–1937], text pp. 125–126 and pl. XLIX, fig. 108).

101. Examples: (a) ivory relief, Metz group, ninth–tenth century (Victoria and Albert #257–1867, illustrated in: Schiller, II, fig. 33; (b) Sacramentary from Fulda, Göttingen Univ.-Bibl., Theol. lat. 231, fol. 54r, tenth–eleventh century; (c) Pericope of Henry II, Munich, Staatsbibl. Clm. 4452, Cim. 57, fol. 78r (Ottonian, before 1014) (illustrated in Georg Leidinger, *Miniaturen aus Handschriften der Kgl. Hof-und Staatsbibliothek in München* [Munich, 1912], V, pl. 16); (d) sheets from a psalter, London, ca. 1200, in Cambridge, Emmanuel College, III.3.21 (illustrated in Victoria and Albert Museum, *Exhibition of English Mediaeval Art* [London, 1930], pl. 26). It was a strong tradition in Swedish stained glass of the mid-thirteenth century (Aron Andersson et al, *Die Glasmalereien des Mittelalters in Skandinavien,* CVMA Skandinavien (Stockholm, 1964), pls. 9, 53, 37, 15 and 75).

102. Lecture, spring 1959, Columbia University. See also Schiller, II, pp. 19, 21.

103. For example: (a) lectionary, perhaps from Salzburg, in Fitzwilliam Museum, Cambridge, McClean 22, Ashburnham, fol. 18v (late twelfth century) (illustrated in Georg Swarzenski, *Die Salzburger Malerei* [Leipzig, 1908–1913], pl. LXXI [fig. 232]); (b) Lintolt gospel, Vienna Hofbibl., Cod. 1244, fol. 140v (G. Swarzenski, pl. LXXXI, fig. 271); (c) window in Barfüsserkirche, Erfurt, ca. 1230 (Hans Wentzel, *Meisterwerke der Glasmalerei* [Berlin, 1954], pl. 65).

104. Cambridge, Corpus Christi College, 286, fol. 125r (from St. Augustine's, Canterbury, probably written in Italy) (illustrated in Francis Wormald, *The Miniatures in the Gospels of St.*

Augustine [Cambridge, 1954], pl. IV). Wormald calls the object in Christ's hand a "scourge"; the palms carried by the crowd are a totally different, feathery design. See Schiller, II, p. 21.

105. See, for example: (a) Gospel Book, second half of the twelfth century, from S. Martial de Limoges (Pierpont Morgan 44, fol. 6r) (illustrated in Walter Cook, "The Earliest Painted Panels of Catalonia V," *Art Bulletin,* X [1927–1928], fig. 33, p. 173). Christ and the apostles have palms which look something like bananas; the onlookers have Gothic, foliate acanthus with short stems. (b) Twelfth–thirteenth-century enamel retable from Saint-Donat(?), Bruges, attributed to the school of Godefroid de Huy, in Brussels, Musée des Arts Décoratifs (zone 2). (c) De la Twyere Psalter, Yorkshire ca. 1320 (New York Public Library, Spencer coll. ms. 2) (illustrated in Karl Kup, *The Christmas Story in Medieval and Renaissance Manuscripts from the Spencer Collection* [New York, 1969], no. 49).

106. His gesture is a common one, occurring at Chartres (west window), Laon (second apse window, thirteenth-century), Bourges and Rouen (ca. 1230). On the fish at the Eucharist, see Schiller, II, pp. 31, 36.

107. The sop, in particular, enjoyed a long popularity in Gothic art. See Chartres west window (ca. 1145), Rouen (ca. 1230), Strasbourg, Niederhaslach (1390–1420).

108. Bourges, outer ambulatory window (illustrated in Marcel Aubert, pl. XVI).

109. Laon, apse window, ca. 1210 (illustrated in A. de Florival and E. Midoux, *Les Vitraux de la cathédrale de Laon* [Paris, 1882], pl. XIX), opp. ch. 4, p. 10). Judas reaches for a fish from the plate with one hand, holding his moneybag with the other. Christ pays no attention to him.

110. Bay 34, central apse, Apostles window (Delaporte and Houvet, II, pl. XCIV). Judas holds the sop and his moneybag; Christ pays no attention.

111. Such a familiar medieval bag can be found in the Sainte-Chapelle, Bay H (panel H73 — Judas delivers 30 silver pieces); and in the Catherine-Agnes window of Saint-Père, Bay 27 (bottom row of left lancet) (Pl. 79).

112. Brit. Mus., Cotton Nero C.IV, fol. 20r, a manuscript in parallel Latin and Norman French with distinctly English pen-illumination. Note also the Douce Psalter (Oxford, Bodleian, Douce 293) of the third quarter twelfth century. Christ, in the Last Supper, holds a different object in each hand. One is clearly a knife; the other is unclear. (Pl. XVII in Otto Pächt and J. J. G. Alexander, *Illuminated Manuscripts in the Bodleian Library* [Oxford, 1973], III.) The preface, p. vi, draws attention to "iconographic rarity, abnormality, or inventiveness as characteristic features of Insular medieval art."

113. In the Chartres west window, ca. 1145, both Peter and Malchus are depicted erect and full size, as they are in many twelfth-century Greek manuscripts (Delaporte and Houvet, I, pl. VIII). Emile Mâle, *L'art religieux du XIIe siècle en France,* 3rd ed. (Paris, 1928), pp. 98ff., discusses the various types, as does Schiller, II, pp. 54–55.

114. For example, alabaster relief, Yarnton church, fourteenth–fifteenth century.

115. Examples: (a) Beaucaire (Gard), Notre-Dame des Pommiers, frieze on south front, mid-twelfth century (illustrated in A. K. Porter, *Romanesque Sculpture of the Pilgrimage Roads* [Boston, 1923], IX, pl. 1292); (b) Saint-Gilles, frieze, central portal, right jamb (twelfth century) (illustrated in Géza de Francovich, *Benedetto Antelami* [Milan, 1952], pl. 57 [#112]). At both La Daurade and the Chartres west façade, however, Malchus has bent legs.

116. Example: lectionary, Brussels, Bibl. Royale, 9428, fol. 86r (ca. 1150?). The erect, dwarf-like Malchus is typical of eleventh-century Cappadocian frescoes, such as those at Göreme (Qaranleq Kilisse, Tchareqle Kilisse).

117. Brit. Mus., *Guide to the Mediaeval Room,* fig. 181; see also King, *Opus Anglicanum,* #56, pp. 32–33 and pl. 13.

118. Examples of a chalice: (a) Bourges, outer ambulatory window, ca. 1215 (*VF,* pl. VI); (b)

Reims, west front, gable of left portal; (c) Rouen ambulatory window, ca. 1230 (*VF,* fig. 27); (d) enamel triptych of St. Aignan, treasury of Chartres Cathedral, beginning of thirteenth century (illustrated in Taralon, *Trésors,* H. T. III [opp. p. 56]); (e) Lyon, apse window (Bégule, pl. III and fig. 28). Ecclesia holding a chalice is very old, while the broken attributes of Synagogue were introduced in the twelfth century. Schiller, II, pp. 110, 112.

119. Delaporte and Houvet, II, pl. CLV.

120. Illustrated in Ellen J. Beer, *Die Glasmalereien der Schweiz vom 12, bis zum Beginn des 14. Jahrhunderts, Corpus Vitrearum Medii Aevi,* Schweiz I (Basel, 1956), fig. 28a; Abbé Victor Leroquais, *Les Sacramentaires et les missals* (Paris, 1924), II, no. 296.

121. The manuscript was destroyed in World War II (see Delaporte, *Manuscrits enluminés,* pl. XIV and p. 87; Leroquais, *Sacramentaires,* II, no. 374). Another early fourteenth-century missal of the use of Saint-Père, unpublished, was also destroyed in the war (Chartres, Bibl. mun., ms. 519, Church and Synagogue on fol. 130v). On ms. 519 see Chapter VI, fn. 7. The figures in Chartres ms. 502 are reversed from the window and from those of the Compiègne missal. What the significance of such a reversal might be is unclear; other scenes at Saint-Père are occasionally reversed from their models (for example in Bay 23, the Denis lancet; the midwife of the Nativity, Bay 19).

122. Mâle, *XIII* (1958 ed.), II, p. 233, n. 4: "On a souvent affirmé . . . que la Résurrection de Jésus-Christ ne se rencontre pas dans l'art avant le XIIIe siècle; et en effet, à l'époque romane, ces représentations sont très rares. . . . Les artistes primitifs n'avaient pas osé représenter la mystérieuse sortie du tombeau, parce qu'elle n'est pas décrite dans l'Evangile. Ils se contentaient de représenter les Saintes Femmes au tombeau."

123. Late examples: (a) Lyon south rose (ca. 1250); (b) Sainte-Chapelle (ca. 1245) (Grodecki and Lafond, CVMA France I, p. 204, H38 and H45–46); (c) Tours, clerestory, ca. 1257–1270 (Boissonot, pl. VIII).

124. Early examples: (a) Bourges, outer ambulatory (Cahier and Martin, pl. V; Clement and Guitard, pl. VII); (b) Canterbury, medallion now in south choir aisle, triforium, ca. 1220 (Rackham, *Canterbury,* pl. 24a); (c) Reims, west front, archivolts of left portal; (d) Clermont-Ferrand, St. Anne chapel, third quarter of the thirteenth century (illustrated in du Ranquet, pl. opp. p. 196 [color drawing]).

125. G. Sanoner, "La vie de Jésus-Christ racontée par les imagiers du moyen âge sur les portes d'églises," *Revue de l'art chrétien,* LVII (Nov. 1907), p. 366, states that the Holy Women at the Tomb, and Christ Leaving the Tomb, being two forms of the same subject, are almost never found together. Rare examples do exist, however: (a) Tours, axial chapel, ca. 1250–1255 (Boissonot, pl. XVIII); (b) windows from Neue kirche, Strasbourg (now in the Cathedral, Lawrence chapel), fourteenth century; (c) ivory plaque, fourteenth–first half of the fifteenth century, where the two scenes are merged into one (Brit. Mus., illustrated in Koechlin, II, #857, pl. CLV).

126. Late examples in French art: (a) Rouen, tympanum of south facade; (b) Strasbourg, tympanum of central portal, west facade; (c) possibly, Bourges choir screen (Musée de Berry), the remnants of which are quite incomplete. The scene seems to have lasted in Italian art to a considerably later period: (a) fourteenth-century Umbrian manuscript of Vita Christi, Pierpont Morgan 643, fol. 14r; (b) Milanese ivory diptych, early fifteenth century, National Gallery, Washington (C-9, illustrated in Erwin O. Christensen, *Objects of Medieval Art* [National Gallery of Art Handbook no. 3, Washington, 1952], p. 27).

127. See: Chartres west capital-frieze, ca. 1145; Etampes frieze; Saint-Gilles capitals (mid-twelfth-century); Sainte-Chapelle, window H, panels H38 and H47.

128. William H. Forsyth, *The Entombment of Christ, French Sculptures of the Fifteenth and Sixteenth Centuries* (Cambridge, Mass., 1970), p. 9: "The Emperor Constantine Porphyrogenitos had

covered the rock (bench on which Christ's body lay) within the Holy Sepulcher with a marble facing to protect it, and the Russian pilgrim Daniel thus describes, in 1106–1107, the three holes through the marble: 'And now this holy bench is covered with marble plaques and one has cut in the side three little round windows and by these windows one sees this holy stone.' "

129. For example at Bourges, ambulatory window (Cahier and Martin, pl. V; Clement and Guitard, pl. VII).

130. The original round shape was also retained in some late examples. Forsyth, p. 9: "In some French fourteenth-century ivories these holes became elaborately decorative motifs resembling rose windows. Several monumental Entombments also have circular ornamentation on the sarcophagus of Christ (i.e., fifteenth–sixteenth centuries)."

131. Bendy (of six OR and AZ) within a border (GU) is, for example, Burgundy. For shields of the traditional, idealized rosette pattern, see: Window at Lyon (*VF*, fig. 87); Canterbury, Resurrection panel (Rackham, *Canterbury*, pl. 24a).

132. Twelfth-century example: La Daurade, 1115–1125 (Marie LaFargue, *Les Chapiteaux du cloître de Notre-Dame La Daurade* [Paris, 1940], pl. XIX, fig. 1). Late Gothic examples: (a) Mézières-en-Brenne (Indre), ca. 1340 (*VF*, fig. 129); (b) ivory plaque, fourteenth–fifteenth century, Brit. Mus. (Koechlin, II, #857, pl. CLV.)

133. Examples where the two scenes are found together: (a) Sainte-Chapelle, Bay H, panels H18 and H21, ca. 1245 (Grodecki and Lafond, CVMA France I, pp. 204–205 and pls. 50–52); (b) Tours, axial chapel (ca. 1250–1255) (Boissonot, pl. XVIII); (c) Notre-Dame choir screen, late-thirteenth–fourteenth century, a work which goes into the appearances after the Resurrection in great detail.

134. See Bay 26, the Birth of the Baptist. Another fourteenth-century Italian manuscript exists with the Road to Emmaüs without the Supper: the Vita Christi (Pierpont Morgan ms. 643, fol. 15r), a *retardataire* work by an Umbrian artist which also includes such archaisms as the Holy Women at the Tomb in place of the Resurrection, and a Pentecost with no Virgin present. It is unlikely that this manuscript could be related to Saint-Père; its archaisms probably came from an earlier model by much the same process as those in the Saint-Père window.

135. In direct contradiction to the opinion of Gert von der Osten, it is demonstrable that the "coercive" Doubting of Thomas is older in art than the more passive form of the scene. (See von der Osten, "Zur Ikonographie des unglaübigen Thomas, angesichts eines Gemäldes von Delacroix," *Wallraf-Richartz Jahrbuch,* XXVII [1965], pp. 384–385.) The "coercive" form occurs on a fifth century sarcophagus fragment from Ravenna (Santi Muratori, "La più antica rappresentazione della incredulità di San Tommaso," *Nuovo bullettino di archeologia cristiana* [1911], fig. p. 39); and on the ampullae of Monza and of Bobbio, ca. 600 (Brit. Mus., *A Guide to the Early Christian and Byzantine Antiquities,* 2nd ed. [London, 1921], p. 183, fig. 15); and on a Byzantine pressed-gold plaque dated before 700, Berlin Staatliche Mus. I. 6861, illustrated in Helmut Schlunk, *Kunst der Spätantike im Mittelmeerraum,* Ausstellung aus Anlass des 6. Internationalen Kongressen für Archëologie (Berlin, 1939), no. 55, pl. 11. Such early examples are all of Eastern Christian origin or influence. Although I am as yet unable to prove it, it is my feeling that the forceful gesture of Christ thrusting Thomas's finger into His wound may derive from Coptic texts. The Copts were Monophysites, as were the later Jacobites. The "coercive" gesture is retained in a Jacobite liturgical manuscript finished in 1220, Bibl. Vat. sir. 559, fol. 163v (see Guillaume de Jerphanion, introd., *Les miniatures du manuscrit syriaque n.559 de la bibliothèque vaticane* [Vatican City, 1940], pl. XXI, 44).

136. (a) Late thirteenth-century psalter, belonged to John Grandison, Bishop of Exeter 1327–1328 (Brit. Mus. Add. 21926, fol. 23r); (b) English cope in St. John Lateran, Rome (Christie, pl. CIII); (c) the Syon cope, Victoria and Albert Museum (Christie, pl. XCVIII); (d) fresco in south transept, Westminster Abbey, ca. 1300 (Peter Brieger, *English Art 1216–1307* [Oxford,

1957], pl. 81); (e) enamel triptych, first half fourteenth century, Victoria and Albert Museum (Salting Collection, M. 545–1910, illustrated in Mary Chamot, *English Mediaeval Enamels* [London, 1930], pl. 19, #29); (f) the lost Douai Psalter, ms. 171, fol. 13r, ca. 1322, illustrated on pl. XVI of Sydney C. Cockerell, *The Gorleston Psalter* (London, 1907).

137. It occurs in two thirteenth-century tympana in Strasbourg, on the church of St. Thomas and on the west central portal of the Cathedral. In the fourteenth century, German examples of the "coercive" type multiply and become more varied, the type probably disseminated by the *Biblia pauperum* (exs.: Constance, Mus. Rosgarten, ms. 31, p. 16; Munich, Staatsbibl., Clm. 19414, fol. 168v). For an extensive list of late examples from Germany and the Low Countries, see the von der Osten study referred to in fn. 135. In France, an early Renaissance example can be found in the windows of Saint-Germain-l'Auxerrois, Paris, ca. 1530: *VF,* fig. 195.

138. Although some French scholars claim this manuscript for the Ile-de-France, see Leopold Delisle in *Histoire littéraire de la France,* XXXI (Paris, 1893), p. 266: "Il pourrait bien être venu de l'Angleterre"; Henry Martin, *Les Joyaux de l'Arsenal, I, Psautier de Saint Louis et de Blanche de Castille* (Paris, n.d.), pp. 11–12: "ce qui donnerait à penser que le livre a été exécuté, soit pour une dame picarde habitant l'Angleterre, soit pour une Anglaise vivant en Picardie." In 1972, Professor Robert Branner indicated that he believed the psalter to have come from the Corbie area.

139. See fn. 135 supra.

140. For a late example see ivory plaque, Brit. Mus., fourteenth–fifteenth century (Ormonde Maddock Dalton, *Catalogue of the Ivory Carvings of the Christian Era . . . in . . . the British Museum* [London, 1909], pl. LXXI).

141. Examples in the stained-glass medium: (a) Le Mans panels, ca. 1145 (*VF,* p. 82); (b) panel, ca. 1175, found in use as a stopgap at Saint-Père (Popesco, ill. p. 50); (c) Poitiers, apse window of ca. 1190; (d) Canterbury, two panels of early thirteenth century (Rackham, *Canterbury,* pls. 24b and 30); (e) Laon chevet, central window, ca. 1210.

142. The traditions of including or excluding her, stemming ultimately from early Christian and Byzantine practice, coexisted in the West until the early thirteenth century. She is absent at Clermont-Ferrand, ca. 1190 (illustrated in Louis Grodecki, "Un Groupe de vitraux français du XIIe siècle," *Festschrift Hans R. Hahnloser* [Basel, 1961], pp. 289–298, fig. 3); Canterbury, ca. 1220 (Rackham, *Canterbury,* color pl. X); psalter of Paris, first half of the thirteenth century (Bibl. Nat. nouv. acq. lat. 1392, fol. 13r). A late and quite unusual example, with the apostles standing, is found in the Cathedral of Rouen, ca. 1330 or later (*VF,* fig. 135 and p. 166).

143. Examples: (a) Le Champs, ca. 1160 (Grodecki, *Hahnloser,* fig. 1); (b) Canterbury, ca. 1220; (c) psalter of Jully-sous-Ravières, Lyon, Bibl. de la ville 539, fol. 212v, first half of the thirteenth century (illustrated in V. Léroquois, *Le Psautier de Jully* (Lyon, 1923), pl. X).

144. Grodecki and Lafond, CVMA France I, p. 205.

145. Delaporte and Houvet, II, pl. XCIV.

146. Christ's arrest has no Judas-kiss; Christ pays no attention to Judas at the Last Supper.

147. For example, Liège psalter, after ca. 1250, Liège, Bibl. de l'Univ. 431, fol. 11v (Last Judgment is one of six border medallions).

148. Cf. rosace from Châteauroux, ancienne église des cordeliers, ca. 1235–1240 (Grodecki, *Vitraux de France,* pl. 12).

149. The absence of the Washing of the Feet, Transfiguration, Entombment, Deposition, etc. can more probably be explained by lack of space.

150. It is possible that the archaisms were transmitted by a source-object in a medium such as *opus anglicanum,* where earlier forms were occasionally embalmed; or that they derive from more than one source.

151. Cf. Evreux, ca. 1325 (*VF,* fig. 132).

152. Four lower windows in the choir (marked on Pl. 2) were filled with fragments: the two ambulatory lights framing the entry to the axial chapel, and windows in the north and south radiating chapels. See Chapter I, fn. 30; Chapter IV, fn. 28.

153. Panels described as present in the clerestory bay by mid-nineteenth-century observers, for example the Christ of *Domine quo vadis?* and the angel carrying Peter's soul, are absent in a photograph from the files of the restorer Charles Lorin (located in 1960 by his son François Lorin; Pl. 60). Cf. Bulteau (1850), p. 294; Poisson (1857), p. 420. The photograph shows the bay with panels in only the central strip of each lancet, the four framing strips all glazed in clear glass. The leading pattern of the inner blank strip of each lancet differs from that of the outer such strip and would seem to be the work of Charles Lorin in 1907 (in documents of Feb. 25 and July 4 he was specifically assigned the restoration of Bay 22, being "the 4th clerestory of the nave, north side"; and throughout this year the clerestory fragments remained in the ambulatory).

154. A *devis* of April 27, 1908, calling for a "revision" of certain clerestories of the nave, may refer to a decision to return the dismantled panels to them from the ambulatory. The fragments were removed from the ambulatory by 1908.

155. Parts of the grounds are restored, and the head of the prophet now in the right lancet is modern.

156. Foliate grounds appeared in German windows very early (see panel, ca. 1220, by Rhenish master Gerlachus, in Berlin, Kunstgewerbe Museum), and maintained their popularity throughout the Gothic period. German types are generally more vigorous and less delicate than French *damasquins*.

157. Pl. 60, the mysterious photograph found in Lorin's files (of 1907?) shows the "prophet facing left" in the center of the bottom row, left lancet, and before the head was restored. Poisson (1857) refers to this panel as "jumbled subject."

158. There is little restoration. Both panels were in the window during the eighteenth and nineteenth centuries (Poisson, p. 420 — "Peter and Paul"; Bulteau, p. 294 — "Peter talks to Paul"). The mystery photograph shows the Peter panel in place (Pl. 60).

159. Chartres, Bibl. ms. 1151, ch. 144.

160. Oxford, Bodleian, Ms. Gough Drawings — Gaignières 9, fol. 56. A mid-nineteenth-century copy (Bibl. Nat., Gaignières no. 3568) is illustrated in Guibert, pl. 91; it is described in Henri Bouchot, *Inventaire des dessins éxécutés pour Roger de Gaignières et conservés aux Départements des Estampes et des Manuscrits* (Paris, 1891), I, p. 470.

161. See Lecocq, "Monuments chartrains," III (1868), p. 239.

162. François de Guilhermy, Bibl. Nat. nouv. acq. fr. 6098, fol. 198v.

163. De Lasteyrie, pp. 219–220.

164. See Pl. 64, showing a lower line, evidently consisting of 12 letters and no stops, engaged half-way into the masonry. The meaning is lost. This line probably gave the date.

165. See Chapter I, fn. 19.

166. Dom Bernard Aubert, writing in 1672, reports the document in the abbey's archives (Aubert, ch. 144). Modern writers give the date alternatively as March 21, 1306 or 1307.

167. On the liberties taken by draughtsmen in the employ of Gaignières, see Suzanne Honoré-Duvergé, "Le prétendu vitrail de Charles le Mauvais à la cathédrale d'Evreux," *Bulletin monumental,* CI (1942), esp. pp. 58–61 and 64–66.

168. See Chapter I, text at fns. 31, 32, where the inscription is discussed.

169. Easter fell on April 3, in 1306. If the date of Hervé's death is n.s., it becomes March 20, 1306. Jehan's election as abbot would have had to fall between the two, i.e., very close upon his predecessor's death, to carry the date 1305 (o.s.). It is likely, however, that the community would have elected a new abbot before Easter.

170. See the early sixth-century mosaic from Sant' Apollinare Nuovo, Ravenna, in which Peter stands in the boat (illustrated in Mâle, *Saints compagnons,* p. 97 bottom).

171. Delaporte and Houvet, II, pl. XCIII.

172. Cf. Tours clerestory, ca. 1257–1270 (Bourassé and Manceau, pl. X).

173. The heads are restorations. They are weathered beyond recognition in contrast to the good condition of the lower part of the panel. The former state of mutilation can be seen in Pl. 60.

174. Bulteau (1850), p. 294, called them disciples; Poisson (1857), p. 420, called them Jews. Pl. 60 seems to have been made after their (undocumented) removal from the window.

175. June 29, St. Peter, in Voragine, I, pp. 333 and 337. Voragine states that his source was a letter of Pseudo-Dionysius to Timothy on the death of St. Paul. I have used Voragine to illustrate a text familiar to the Gothic period. The ultimate source of the apocryphal stories of Peter's ministry in Rome is the Acts of Peter, known by ca. 300; for a thorough discussion of the early texts see Hennecke, II, pp. 259ff., esp. pp. 271–272. These 'apostolic romances' achieved their accessible form in Latin in a compilation probably done in France in the sixth or seventh century, the Apostolic History by the Pseudo-Abdias; see James, *ANT,* pp. 438, 462.

176. See: Bourges, window of Lady of Lourdes chapel (Clement and Guitard, pl. XV); Rouen, sacristy, Paul window, thirteenth-century (Ritter, pl. XXIV–XXVI).

177. The first meeting of Peter and Paul is shown beside a doorway representing the gate of Rome. It comes after scenes of Peter with James the Less, and before scenes of the miracles, arrest, etc. in Rome (Bourassé and Manceau, pl. X).

178. The heads of Peter and the Jew on the right are old restorations.

179. Cf.: (a) Bourges, window in Lady of Lourdes chapel (Clement and Guitard, pl. XV); (b) Tours, choir clerestory (ca. 1257–1270) (Bourassé and Manceau, pl. X); (c) Catalan altar frontal, Brussels, Musée des Arts Décoratifs, beginning of the fourteenth century (illustrated in Chandler Post, *A History of Spanish Painting* [Cambridge, Mass., 1930], II, fig. 116).

180. Poisson, p. 420; Bulteau, p. 294. As in the previous case, one of the paired panels has been removed in Pl. 60, the mystery photograph which probably shows an aborted stage of the ca. 1905 restorations.

181. There is restoration in the drapery of both figures, particularly of Paul.

182. See: (a) Poitiers, southeast window of apse (Peter and another saint with a group of men, two in pointed caps, some with raised hands); (b) Lyon, window in Peter chapel (1181–1192) (Peter and a companion to right, two men to the left) (illustrated in Bégule, *Monographie de la Cathédrale de Lyon* [Lyon, 1880], pl. opp. p. 106).

183. Holy Bible, King James Version. Although the Douay-Rheims Version has "files" for "quaternions," the Vulgate specifies: "tradens quatuor quaternionibus militum."

184. The panel was not photographed in the 1950's, and is therefore missing from the photomontage at the *Archives photographiques.*

185. Bourges, Lady of Lourdes chapel. Two scenes: (a) Simon Magus, wearing a cap, bends over the youth reclining under a coverlet, and places a hand on his chin; Peter stands to the right; (b) Peter, holding a book, and Paul, praying, are beside the youth who, nude under his coverlet, sits up on his couch.

186. In four scenes (illustrated in Bégule, 1880, pl. opp. p. 106): (a) Simon Magus and attendant are beside a man in a shroud on a mattress; (b) the man in the shroud sits on his mattress, Peter grasping his arm; (c) Simon hides his head in shame while Peter quiets the companions who intend to stone him; (d) Simon retires, threatening Peter. See discussion in Mâle, *Saints compagnons,* p. 105.

187. Voragine, I, pp. 333–334. Examples in art are extremely rare. The only other one

known to me is a Catalan altar frontal of a date contemporary with the window, and has a much less expressionistic format. A seated Nero with armed guard watches as Simon appears twice, once standing and once kneeling with hair grasped by an executioner with upraised sword. There is no ram. The scene can be identified by the inscription: "His decapitatus simon jussu neri imperatoris." (Illustrated in Josep Gudiol, *Els Primitius [La Pintura Mig-eval Catalana,* Barcelona, 1929], II, fig. 165 and p. 338.)

188. Mâle, *Saints compagnons,* p. 105.

189. See Grimaldi drawings (ms. Vat. 6429), Codex Barberini lat. 2732, fol. 75v (illustrated in Wilpert, p. 399, fig. 136). Only one Simon Magus figure was shown in the scene in frescoes from the porticus of St. Peter's (Wilpert, p. 403 and fig. 137).

190. See: Acts of Peter, in James, *ANT*, p. 333; Voragine, I, p. 336. The ultimate source of the story is considered to be St. Ambrose, "Sermo contra Auxentium."

191. Cf.: (a) Angers, Bay 24, north choir; (b) Catalan altar frontal (Gudiol, fig. 165).

192. Poisson, p. 420; Bulteau, p. 294; and Pl. 60.

193. See: (a) Lyon, window of Peter chapel, 1181–1192, where Christ is enthroned between two censing angels (Bégule, 1911, fig. 14 — drawing); (b) Rouen, Paul window of sacristy, where two angels bear away Paul's soul (Ritter, pl. XXIV–XXVI); (c) Angers, Bay 24, north choir, where angels preside at Peter's crucifixion.

194. See discussion of tracery of Bay 2, Chapter IX. Bay 2 (hemicycle) postdates the scene of Paul's martyrdom in Bay 22, one of the re-used panels, by perhaps a decade.

195. The Stuttgart and Munich libraries contain many Romanesque manuscripts with nailed crucifixions of the asymmetrical format, one executioner nailing the feet and the other on the opposite side nailing the hand. See also the cover of the reliquary casket of Maurinus, ca. 1180, in St. Pantaleon, Cologne, where the pattern of Bay 22 of Saint-Père is exactly reversed (illustrated in Otto von Falke and Heinrich Frauberger, *Deutsche Schmelzarbeiten des Mittelalters und andere Kunstwerke der Kunst-historischen Ausstellung zu Düsseldorf,* 1902 [Frankfurt, 1904], pl. 48). For later examples see: (a) twelfth–thirteenth-century Alsatian lectionary from St. Peter in Schwarzwald (Karlsruhe, Landesbiblio. S. Peter 7, fol. 8v); (b) second half of the thirteenth century Legendarium from Regensburg, Dominican convent of the Holy Cross, in Keble College, Oxford, fol. 102r (illustrated in H. Swarzenski, *Lateinischen,* pl. 63 [#361]). The formula lasted well into the fourteenth century in the stained-glass medium. Example: (a) late thirteenth-century panel from Wimpfen im Tal (Landesmuseum Darmstadt) (illustrated in Hans Wentzel, *Die Glasmalereien in Schwaben von 1200–1350, Corpus Vitrearum Medii Aevi* Deutschland I [Berlin, 1958], pl. 550); (b) fourteenth-century window of Kappenberg Castle, possibly from church in Dausenau; (c) fourteenth-century window of St. Florentius, Niederhaslach (Bas-Rhin).

196. See Chapter II.

197. See Chapter IV, Bay 22.

198. For a slightly earlier example in a work of Franciscan orientation see the Psalter and Hours of Yolande de Soissons, ca. 1290(?), as discussed by Karen Gould, "Illumination and Sculpture in Thirteenth-Century Amiens: The Invention of the Body of Saint Firmin in the Psalter and Hours of Yolande of Soissons," *Art Bulletin,* LIX (June 1977), p. 165.

199. Thirteenth-century stained-glass cycles which include the "Bearing Witness" in its correct order (i.e., in the Public Life, usually between the Baptism of Christ and the Feast of Herod) are: (a) Chartres, Bay 117, south choir clerestory (Delaporte and Houvet, III, pls. CCXXII–CCXXIII); (b) Saint-Julien-de-Sault, Baptist window; (c) Sainte-Chapelle, Bay G.

200. For example, Lyon Cathedral, west front, central portal (zone 6), first half of the fourteenth century, where three men appear outside the temple.

201. Mâle lists Saint-Père as the earliest French example he knows of this detail (*Saints compagnons,* p. 13), and my research is in agreement.

202. Voragine, I, p. 323.

203. See Pseudo-Bonaventura, *Meditations on the Life of Christ,* trans. Isa Ragusa and ed. Rosalie Green (Princeton, 1961), pp. 24–25.

204. Examples: (a) St. John altar frontal (ca. 1260–1270), Siena Pinacoteca (attributed to Sienese school), from the suppressed Convento di Santa Petronilla, Siena; (b) late thirteenth-century panels (attributed variously to Ravennate school, Umbrian school, Deodato Orlandi), in Berlin, Staatliche Museum (I.1182); (c) mutilated fresco of second half of the thirteenth century, Stiftskirche, Seckau (Austria), from a destroyed baptismal chapel.

205. An extremely odd example is found in a miniature from an antiphonary dated 1290, executed for the Cistercian convent in Beaupré (Brussels, Bibl. Roy., II $3634^{1\text{-}2}$). All three of the attendants of Elizabeth are haloed. One sits with the baby on her lap, feeding him with an open-ended horn into which milk is being poured from a pitcher by another attendant, while the third fans the new mother. Clearly the Virgin's halo in some Italian art work has been misconstrued. The view of medieval infant care is delightful.

206. Luke I:56–58: "And Mary abode with her about three months. And she returned to her own house. Now Elizabeth's full time of being delivered was come: and she brought forth a son." Elizabeth was, however, in her sixth month at the time of Mary's Annunciation. Luke I:36: "And behold thy cousin Elizabeth, she also hath conceived a son in her old age: and this is the sixth month with her that is called barren."

207. Another example is a twelfth-century miniature (verso), probably from a psalter, Pierpont Morgan 724. In the window of Saint-Julien-de-Sault, ca. 1250, Zacharias has a lectern and stylus but no knife.

208. See, for example, gradual from Katherinenthal, fol. 179, ca. 1312 (coll. D. Perrins, Malvern) (illustrated in Wentzel, CVMA Deutschland I, fig. 11).

209. Ragusa-Green, pp. 25 and 407 (commentary on the scene's rarity).

210. Herod's crosslegged pose is not standard at Saint-Père although it had become established in French art by this period. On the crosslegged pose as symbol of a monarch or judge in the exercise of his official power, see: Henry Martin, "Les enseignements des miniatures: attitude royale," *Gazette des beaux-arts,* série 4, IX (1913), pp. 173–188. Martin's observation that the crosslegged pose is very rare in Italian art (p. 183) is some evidence against the use of an Italian model for this bay.

211. Angers, choir window 9 (there are no witnesses and the Baptist holds a cross-staff); Sainte-Chapelle, Bay G, panel G28 (Grodecki and Lafond, CVMA France I, p. 210) (no witnesses). Examples of John's arrest: (a) Lausanne, medallion (Beer, CVMA Schweiz I, col. pl. 6); (b) Lyon, west front, embrasures of central portal, right side, first half of the fourteenth century.

212. Only the ground behind the Baptist and the trees is brown foliate work. Behind the witnesses to the left, the ground is clear blue. In the row below (John Rebuking Herod), the ground behind the witnesses differs from that of the rest of the scene in the same manner.

213. Examples: (a) Bourges, window of Joan of Arc chapel (Martin and Cahier, text vol. p. 278 and Clement and Guitard, pl. XXI); (b) Rouen, window of St. John chapel (Baptist is seated) (Ritter, pls. I–IV).

214. Mâle, *Saints compagnons,* p. 25, states that all fifteenth-century examples of St. John preaching, to his knowledge, include such a pulpit. They probably derived from the *mise-en-scène* of medieval mystery plays.

215. See, for example: (a) Sainte-Chapelle, Bay 6, panel G52 (Grodecki and Lafond, CVMA France I, p. 210); (b) Angers, choir window 9; (c) Clermont-Ferrand, window of St. John chapel (Du Ranquet, pl. opp. p. 132).

216. She walks on hands and feet, as at Saint-Père, in: (a) Lyon apse window, first quarter of the thirteenth century (illustrated in Bégule, 1880, fig. 11, p. 114); (b) Sainte-Chapelle, Bay G,

panel G17 (Grodecki and Lafond, CVMA France I, pl. 56). In other examples she walks on her hands, knees bent in the air, and at Clermont-Ferrand she walks on her hands while carrying two swords (Du Ranquet, pl. opp. p. 132).

217. Réau, II, pt. 1, pp. 453–454, quotes Gautier d'Orléans, who warned his readers against shameless entertainers miming obscenely "in modum filiae Herodiadis."

218. A very close design including a figure behind Salome (an executioner?) occurs on a capital from La Daurade in the Toulouse Museum (late eleventh–early twelfth century).

219. Mâle, *Saints compagnons,* p. 50. For a full discussion of the Agnus Dei as symbol of Christ's Death see Schiller, II, pp. 117ff. The prayer was introduced into the Eastern liturgy in the sixth century; from the same century is the Maximianus throne, Ravenna, on which the Baptist holds the Agnus Dei disc as attribute.

Conclusion

THE six immense narrative bays of the nave of Saint-Père offer vast riches for iconographic study. No two windows offer precisely the same solutions, in source materials or treatment. In some, notably Bay 23 (St. Denis lancet), the use of specific manuscripts is imprinted clearly. In others (the Joachim/Anna lancet of Bay 19, the stories, of Catherine and Agnes) the artist probably followed an account like that of the Golden Legend. Bay 18 (the Passion window), a beautifully drawn window which is stylistically the latest of the church, shows indisputably that it was modeled on a source in the twelfth-century tradition, almost certainly foreign, probably in black-and-white: an English Romanesque psalter? Isolated details such as the crouching midwife in the Nativity (Bay 19) and the haloed midwife of the Baptist's Nativity (Bay 26) indicate other models, the former a venerable object brought from Rome, perhaps, and the latter — less centainly — an Italian art work of the late thirteenth century.

What is the lesson taught by such a minute study of a great narrative cycle? Most centrally, the evidence tells us that the designing of each great bay was a serious concern, a task for which the artist sought preparation in other works of art or texts which were made available to him. Nothing was done carelessly or approximately. The fact that models can be suggested for many scenes is indication enough of the precision of detail therein. Such care would normally be expected in works of art of high quality. It is something of a surprise, however, to find it in the works of a stylistic school such as that of the West of France, the basic traits of which were broadness, vigor, an unconcern with the niceties of elegant proportion wherever an effect could be produced by expressionistic means. One is left with a sense of respect for those medieval craftsmen who studied sources, texts, models, and then went ahead to design windows which dazzle us by their color, delight us with their variety and vigor, and awe us with their spirit.

The choice of subjects is instructive. There is a pattern, a definite program for the whole ensemble — one that was consistently maintained throughout a period of a half-century of glazing campaigns. The choir presents its orderly procession of prophets and patriarchs of the Old Testament. The hemicycle shows references to the central events of the New Testament (the Virgin and Child, i.e. the Incarnation, and the Crucifixion) framed by representatives of the Church on Earth (apostles, martyr-saints, prelate-saints). The nave presents an ordered view of the history of Christianity: from the Baptist, its great precursor; through the Christological and Mariological cycles; to the great saints, the latter chosen with sophisticated, never blatant, reference to the abbey church which houses them.

Several features are noteworthy about the ensemble. First of all, the completeness and consistency of the program is, as far as we are able to tell from the Gothic remains of glass elsewhere, unusual. It is the more unusual considering the span of time involved. Second, a nice, one might say tasteful, balance is observed between the great themes of Christianity and those particular to the abbey itself. A third point which strikes the observer is how little the program derives from themes and forms dictated by the cathedral. This fact is really not so surprising. Not only was Saint-Père glazed several generations after the cathedral was finished, but the latter had no great glass program to offer as iconographic model. Excepting the roses, it had no program at all, it seems, only a logically dictated and commonly observed stylistic format of large figures above and medallion scenes below. The patronage was, of course, different, as were the times. The cathedral windows, very many of them, were paid for by guilds and individuals, and put up in a tearing hurry. At Saint-Père we don't know what was (or perhaps was not) intended for the aisles, but the clerestories were planned, clearly, by a few strong personalities whose chief interest lay not in personal goals but in the adornment of a beautiful abbey church.

The cathedral chapter and the monks of the abbey were at war during most of the thirteenth century. By the end of that period they seem to have risen to a less petty and more Christian peace, possibly reflecting politically the royal interest in the abbey. Several of the canons gave sums to the abbey's final glazing program in the nave, at any rate. Beyond that, however, the outlines of social history are blurred. The most surprising omission in the Saint-Père glass is the absence of any reference to Fulbert, the sainted and legendary bishop of the cathedral whose tomb lay in the abbey church itself. Perhaps his name was included, along with St. Lubin (also a bishop of Chartres), among the inscriptions now lost from Bay 25.

Relics play almost no part in the choice of subjects. The abbey owned pieces of Sts. Ignatius, Philip, and Soline, and possibly of the true cross and St. Stephen.[1] None is the subject for a window (Philip takes his place quietly among the apostles). Of the named standing saints in the clerestory, none can be explained on the basis of the abbey's relics. St. Lubin of Bay 25 was a bishop of the cathedral; the other named bishop is St. Martin, one of the great saints of France. The name of St. Maur in Bay 29 may be a later addition, and at any rate merely underlines the abbey's Benedictine status.

One must conclude that, not only did the iconography of the cathedral glass and sculpture have no influence at Saint-Père, but neither did the cults of the abbey itself. The iconography points not inward but out to the abbey's larger relationships — with the crown and with the history of the Christian Church.

Another explanation seems more plausible, perhaps. The ultimate sources of Saint-Père are in Champagne and northern Burgundy. This is true in many aspects of style, such as the interest in combining color and grisaille, the use of large medallion frames for standing figures, etc. It is equally so, it would seem, in the iconographic program, at its origin at any rate. The idea of placing a Virgin and Child and a Crucifixion in the axial bay, flanked by apostles and prelate-saints, seems to have originated in Reims in the late twelfth century.[2] The program at Saint-Remi included the Virgin and Child in the axial bay of the clerestory, above a monumental Crucifixion directly beneath in the tribune, and flanked by apostles, prophets and archbishop-saints.[3] The Cathedral of Reims (both the early and later glazing campaigns?) included both a Virgin and Child and a Crucifixion in the axial clerestory, flanked by apostles and prelate-saints. Because of the fragmentary nature of the remains of the earlier campaign,[4] the program of Virgin and Child and Crucifixion side by side in axial clerestory bay can be dated with certainty only from the later Reims campaign initiated by Henri de Braisne, ca. 1235–1245.

Between Reims and Saint-Père are a few intermediaries, the chief in the West[5] being Le Mans (mid-thirteenth century), where the idea is rather over-enthusiastically elaborated and where, it is apparent, individual donors had some voice. Le Mans contains both Western and non-Western style glass. In the Le Mans clerestory, apostles, saints and bishop-saints, placed over a wild assortment of groups and individuals in the category of patrons, do flank an axial bay showing the Crucifixion and the Virgin and Child, both themes being embroidered with scenes above them of a Christ showing His Wounds and a Coronation of the Virgin by an angel. Scale and style are also in exuberant disorder.

At Saint-Père order is again restored. Guild donations and the like are again dispensed with. The position occupied, at Reims, by Henri de Braisne and the emblem of his see — and at Le Mans, by Bishop Geoffroy de Loudun and eight copies of his coat of arms — has been filled, at Saint-Père, by symbols not of an abbot but of the abbey itself. It stands represented by its own saint, Gilduin, whose miracles provided in a very real sense its very fabric; and by St. Louis, grandfather of the probable kingly patron, a statement of the abbey's eminence within the realm.

A study of style at Saint-Père yields as many rewards as that of subject matter. Its range is very great, from the blue-dominated, somber icons of the earliest period to the delicate whites and yellows of the Passion window — the tints of *jaune d'argent* even before the technique itself. Painters came and painters went, leaving their 'handwriting' as witness. The first prophets of the choir are painted in several styles, notably an old-fashioned heavily worked approach and one which is more curvilinear and descriptive of massing. The black triangles of choir draperies develop into the quick, angular clusters of short lines which impart a nervous immediacy to the added figures of Bays 14–15. At this point — ca. 1280 — a Norman appears in the workshop, producing the paired remnants now preserved for us in the Peter window and the inhabited canopywork and many of the tracery medallions of the hemicycle. The master expressionist is in charge of that program, the finest artist the Western school was to produce. His taste and daring set the tone for the even more distorted bay of the nave, Bay 23 (Clement and Denis). A more naive spirit left his handiwork in Bays 27 and 18, and among the great parade of abbots and bishops in the south nave. A classically trained painter worked the lovely shaded 'spoon-folds' in some of the hemicycle saints (for example, Bay 3, bottom left) and in the Virgin lancet — where he may have worked to the cartoons of one of the other great designers of Saint-Père, the brilliant narrator of the Baptist window. The latter paints like the designer of the telescoped stories of Bay 23 and may be the same artist at a simpler task. It has not seemed suitable or profitable in this study to attempt to distinguish the work of this team of craftsmen by assigning them names — the Passion Master, the Master of the Norman Medallions, etc. — since, in each of the abbey's glazing campaigns, they worked together in a complicated division of labor.

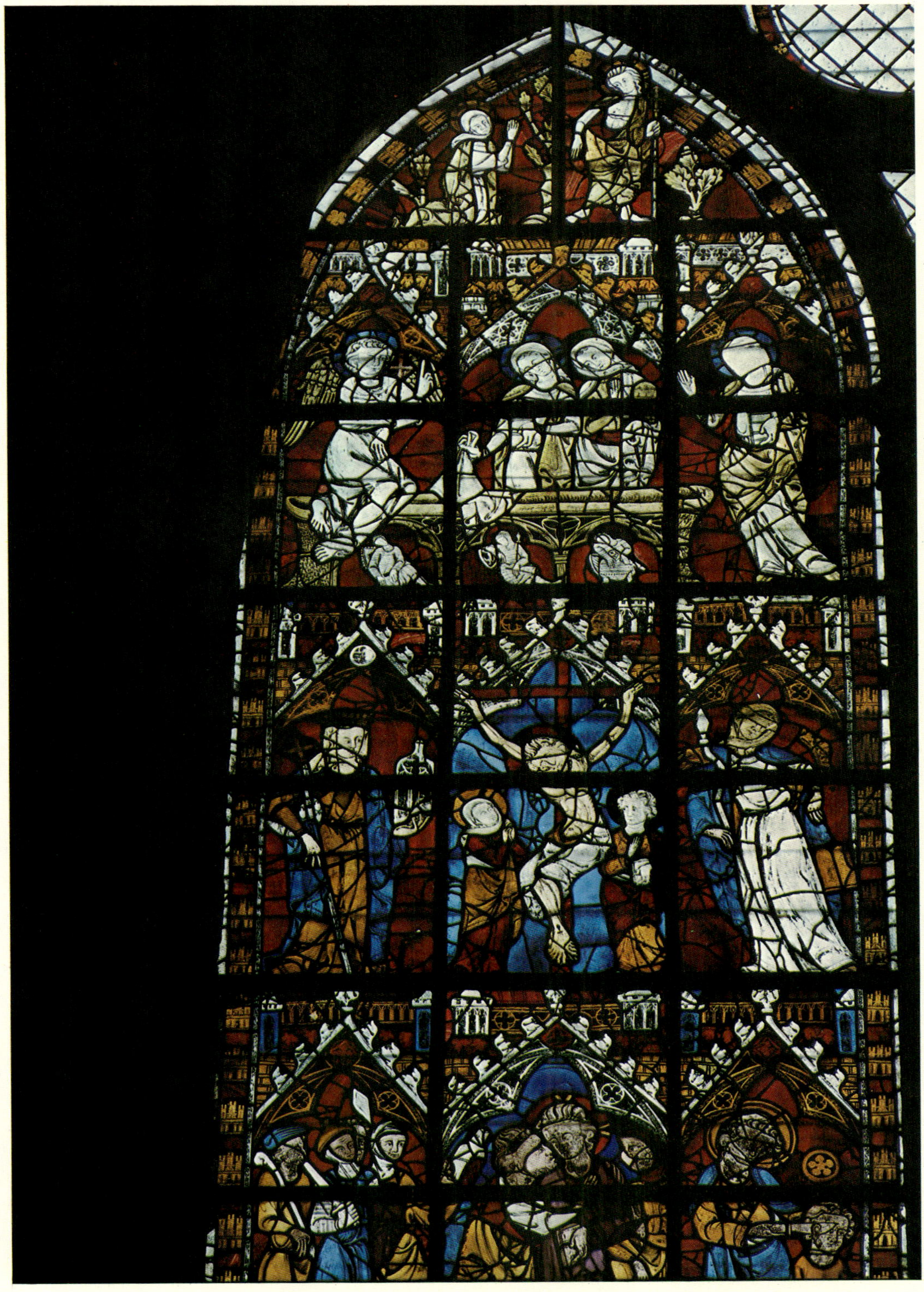

PLATE XII Nave: Bay 18. Passion window, Crucifixion, Three Marys at the Tomb. *(Edouard Fièvet)*

Their constant goal through all campaigns was to conform their artistic product to the whole. Thus it is that each campaign builds on those preceding. The added bays of the choir copy the large medallion figures used there, freshening and modernizing the forms with canopies and bases, courtly gestures and a more clear color. The hemicycle draws variations on the choir in its turn, refreshing the canopies while recapitulating the hierarchical postures and saturated color of the early patriarchs, as well as adding the marginalia of the tracery martyrdoms. The nave presents all of this in a tight, encyclopedic structure. Parts may be splendid or curious in turn but never are they more memorable than the whole.

What useful purpose is served by a detailed monograph of the stained glass of Saint-Père de Chartres? First of all, an examination of the documentation peels away a few layers of guidebook "myth" which has gradually accrued to this monument as to almost all remnants of the medieval world left to us. The picture of the abbey in its richest and most active period comes into sharper focus; the busy campaigns of building and glazing take on an air of greater reality.

A study of the style of these windows, not only internally but in comparison to other regional monuments, helps to rebuild an artistic heritage in the glass medium which had been lost sight of. The delineation of the Western school, a new world ripe for further exploration, is not only helpful to our understanding of provincial Gothic art; it provides one more facet to the composite which is French medieval art.

A study of the iconography of these windows can be equally valuable for this long view. A case in point would be the manuscript sources for the St. Denis lancet, Bay 23. One of the largely unexplored truisms of Gothic studies has been the assumption that a relationship exists between stained glass and manuscript illumination. The medallion form, and color harmonies, common to the *Bibles historiées* and to the thirteenth-century windows contemporary with them in the Ile-de-France, have often been noted; and an occasional manuscript, such as Pierpont Morgan ms. 44, has been identified tentatively as a glass-maker's model book.[6] The relationship between the two media was probably always a complex and multifaceted one. It is usually by no means easy, even in precise cases of similarity, to guess whether the more portable manuscript (obviously a transmitting agent) transmitted the model *to* the glazier, or transmitted his specific forms to a broader ambiance. Attempts to make connections of these types have been confined largely to the early period, when the vigor and success of the medallion form in window design would seem to give that medium preeminence; and to the very late period, when the complicated narratives of windows are sometimes clearly drawn, for example, from the *Biblia pauperum.*[7] The Saint-Père example helps bridge the gap.

The iconography of Saint-Père provides many more such ingredients to contribute to our general picture of the multiplicity and rich variation of medieval art. French Gothic art was not monolithic — that has been realized for a long time — but the exploration of its variety and range has only just begun. This is true not only of the medium of glass, but it is, perhaps, particularly true of that medium. Stained-glass studies are barely emerging from a long infancy.

In the Introduction to this study it was pointed out that the clerestory ensemble at Saint-Père is a rarity, a full set. One lesson which cannot help but impress is that of the programmatic homogeneity of this full set, ranging in date, as it does, over three-quarters of a century. Perhaps medieval artists were more conscious of the "whole" than we have thought. Perhaps it is time and troubles, not the originator's intent, which have touched medieval monuments with that air of the amalgam which is so often present. Why do the two towers of Chartres cathedral look different, the tourist asks? Didn't the artist care? Perhaps he did care very much, but ran out of money; perhaps he died. Scholars may realize the grand intent in the grandiose dreams of medieval artists, but it is an evanescent concept to document.

The Saint-Père ensemble not only makes use of older glass in new settings, but builds stylistically and iconographically upon itself until the very moment of its completion. Perhaps we are coming to realize that medieval art, which seems so often iconoclastic, so constantly changing, discarding, rejecting, did indeed relish and appreciate its own achievements.[8]

In the Introduction the hope was expressed that a close examination of Saint-Père would help illuminate a little-understood moment of transition in the stained-glass medium, between the recognized achievements of the early thirteenth century and those of a century later.[9] The energy and verve with which this transition was undertaken are certainly evident at the very least. Many more studies are needed — not only monographic and documentary in nature but of the experimental color harmonies, the new designs and layouts.[10] Saint-Père is probably not the only monument where an alternative band window was invented, ultimately to be discarded. One can hardly dream of the diversity awaiting scrutiny.

The study of these windows is finally, one hopes, of some intrinsic value. How they dazzle us, when we stand far below them, necks bent back, mouths open. Man has made something beautiful and it cannot be wrong to enjoy it.

NOTES

1. The relic of St. Ignatius (probably Ignatius Theophorus, Bishop of Antioch, d. 107 A.D.) is mentioned as the object of a dispute with the cathedral in 1233. That of St. Soline, a virgin

martyred in Chartres, was provided with a new reliquary in 1325. The relics of St. Stephen and St. Philip, mentioned in the 1399 inventory, were probably gifts to the abbey by the seigneurs de Puiset (the Chartrain house to which St. Gilduin was related) on return from crusade to seal a peace-pact made before they left. See de Mély, "Les inventaires," IV, pp. 316–317 and V, pp. 63–64 (quoting Souchet, *Histoire du diocèse et de la ville de Chartres* [Chartres, 1867–1876], II, p. 157: ". . . qu'en même temps que Louis, comte de Blois et de Chartres, était en Orient, un seigneur d'Ouarville en Chartrain rapporta des reliques de saint Philippe qu'il offrit à l'église de son bourg.")

Unfortunately the only inventory of the abbey which dates before the glazing campaigns (Chartres, Bibl. mun., ms. 31, 1-B, tenth century) lists no relics by name, simply 10 reliquaries ("filacteria [x]") (de Mély, IV, p. 313; Poisson, "Inventaire," p. 307).

2. I am indebted to Professor William M. Hinkle of Columbia University for suggesting the investigation of this idea. For the programs of the clerestory windows of Saint-Remi and of Reims Cathedral, see Appendices G and J of his study cited Chapter VI, fn. 1.

3. See *VF,* p. 108.

4. Of the earlier campaign, which seems to have been generally similar to that of Saint-Remi, the Virgin and Child lancet, as well as some of the flanking ones, remain. See Reinhardt, *Reims,* p. 186 and pl. 42.

5. According to Dr. Jane Hayward (communication of April 1969), the combination of Virgin and Child and Crucifixion in the axial bay was common in small, parish church programs in Western France by the early thirteenth century.

6. Jean Porcher, *Medieval French Miniatures* (New York, 1960?), pp. 44–45. The suggestion (somewhat more probable, but unprovable) is made occasionally that some of the figure studies of Villard d'Honnecourt's sketchbook (Bibl. Nat. fr. 19093) could have been intended for windows. For a review of hypothesized glass "projects" or cartoons, see Hans Wentzel, "Un projet de vitrail au XIVe siècle," *Revue de l'art,* X (1970), pp. 7–14; see also Dr. Jane Hayward's remarks in *Bulletin of the Metropolitan Museum of Art,* XXX #3 (December 1971/January 1972), p. 99, figs. 2–3. I have discussed briefly evidence of the use of a pattern-sheet or model-book in "Apostle from Sées," pp. 499–500.

7. Von Witzleben, *Stained Glass in French Cathedrals* frequently discusses models from the *Biblia pauperum,* engravings, etc., in her sections on fourteenth- to sixteenth-century glass.

8. For an impressive study of this question see Madeline Harrison Caviness, " 'De convenientia et cohaerentia antiqui et novi operis:' Medieval Conservation, Restoration, Pastiche and Forgery," *Intuition und Kunstwissenschaft, Festschrift für Hanns Swarzenski* (Berlin, 1973), pp. 205–221.

9. In addition to the essay by Gruber (see Introduction, fn. 3) and the monument-oriented studies by Lafond ("Normandie," "XIVe siècle"), stained glass of the transitional period has been discussed briefly by Philippe Verdier in *Art and the Courts,* pp. 108–112. See also the exhibition catalog produced under the direction of Dorothy Gillerman, *Transformations of the Court Style, Gothic Art in Europe 1270 to 1330,* Rhode Island School of Design (Providence, 1977), pp. 100–109 (essay by Margaret Patricia Haneberg and Ann Hartley Sievers).

10. See for example Becksmann, *Die Architektonische Rahmung.*

Selected Bibliography

Selected Bibliography

The following bibliography has been selected on the basis of specific concern with the problems of Saint-Père and/or frequency of reference in the footnotes. The choices of both omission and inclusion were necessarily arbitrary in many cases. Additional references will be found in the text, especially to comparative materials, to works cited chiefly for illustrations, and to archival materials, mainly in Chartres (Arch. d'Eure-et-Loir) and in the Commission des Monuments Historiques in Paris.

The following abbreviations have been employed throughout the text:

CVMA — *Corpus Vitrearum Medii Aevi*
For titles in this series, see entries under the following authors: Andersson, Beer, Helbig, Grodecki and Lafond, Lafond, Wentzel.

VF — Marcel Aubert et al, *Le vitrail français* (Paris, 1958). Of primary interest:
Jean-Jacques Gruber, "Technique"
Louis Grodecki, "Des origines à la fin du XIIe siècle"
Louis Grodecki, "De 1200 à 1260"
Jean Lafond, "De 1380 à 1500"

Andersson, Aron, et al, *Die Glasmalereien des Mittelalters in Skandinavien, Corpus Vitrearum Medii Aevi Skandinavien* (Stockholm, 1964).

Anselme, Père, *Histoire genealogique et chronologique de la maison royale de France,* I (Paris, 1726).

Aubert, Dom Bernard, "Veritable inventaire de l'histoire de la royalle abbaye de Sainct-Pere-en-Vallee de Chartres, 1672," Chartres, Bibl. mun., ms. 1151 (unpaginated, charred in World War II). Eighteenth-century copy, from Gaignières collection: Paris, Bibl. Nat., ms. fr. 22474.

Arnold, Hugh, *Stained Glass of the Middle Ages in England and France,* 2nd ed. (London, 1939).

Beer, Ellen J., *Die Glasmalereien der Schweiz vom 12. bis zum Beginn des 14. Jahrhunderts, Corpus Vitrearum Medii Aevi* Schweiz I (Basel, 1956).

Becksmann, Rüdiger, *Die architektonische Rahmung des hochgotischen Bildfensters, Untersuchungen zur oberrheinischen Glasmalerei von 1250 bis 1350* (Berlin, 1967).

Bégule, Lucien, *Les vitraux du moyen âge . . . dans la région lyonnaise . . .* (Paris, 1911).

———. *Monographie de la cathédrale de Lyon* (Lyon, 1880).

Berger, Eugène, "Etude historique et archéologique sur l'abbaye de Saint-Père de Chartres," thesis, Ecole des Chartes, 1913 (summarized in *Positions des thèses,* 1913, pp. 9–18).

Bienvenüe, Paule, "Les Bâtiments conventuels de l'ancienne abbaye Saint-Père de Chartres, *Bulletin monumental,* CXVI (1958), pp. 7–27.

Biver, Comte Paul and Edmond Socard, "Le Vitrail civil au XIVe siècle," *Bulletin monumental,* LXXVII (1913), pp. 258–264.

Boissonnot, Chanoine H., *Les verrières de la cathédrale de Tours* (Paris, 1932).

Bouchot, Henri, *Inventaire des dessins exécutés pour Roger de Gaignières et conservés aux Départments des Estampes et des Manuscrits,* I (Paris, 1891).

Bourassé, Chanoine Jean-Jacques and F. G. M. Manceau, *Verrières du choeur de l'église métropolitaine de Tours* (Paris-Tours, 1849).

Branner, Robert, *St. Louis and the Court Style* (London, 1965).

———. "The Painted Medallions in the Sainte-Chapelle in Paris," (*Transactions of the American Philosophical Society,* n.s., LVIII, pt. 2), Philadelphia, 1968.

Brassinne, Joseph, *Le Psautier liégeois du XIIIe siècle* (Brussels, 1923).

Brossier-Géray, "Le Rouleau mortuaire de Guy Ier, Abbé de Saint-Père de Chartres, 1231," *Bulletin de la Société Dunoise,* III (1875–1880), pp. 228–240.

Bulteau, l'Abbé, *Description de la cathédrale de Chartres . . .* (Chartres, 1850).

Burlington Fine Arts Club, *Exhibition of Illuminated Manuscripts* (London, 1908).

Cahier, Charles and Arthur Marie Martin, *Monographie de la cathédrale de Bourges* (Paris, 1841–1844).

Christie, A.G.I., *English Medieval Embroidery* (Oxford, 1938).

Clement, Silvain and A. Guitard, *Vitraux de Bourges* (Bourges, 1900).

Clerval, A., *Guide chartrain* (Chartres, 4th ed., n.d. and 5th ed., 1927).

d'Armancourt, Comte, "Chartres. Notes héraldiques et généalogiques," *Société archéologique d'Eure-et-Loir, Le Cinquantenaire,* I (1906), pp. 126–416.

Delaporte, Chanoine Yves, *Les Manuscrits enluminés de la Bibliothèque de Chartres* (Chartres, 1929).

Delaporte, Chanoine Yves and Etienne Houvet, *Les Vitraux de la Cathédrale de Chartres* (Chartres, 1926), text vol. and 3 vols. plates.

de Lasteyrie, Ferdinand, *Histoire de la peinture sur verre* (Paris, 1857).

de Mély, F., "Les Inventaires de l'abbaye de Saint-Père-en-Vallée," *Revue de l'art chrétien,* 4th ser., IV (XXXVI), July 1886, pp. 306–317; V (XXXVII), Jan. 1887, pp. 63–72.

du Chesne, André, *Histoire genealogique de la maison royale de Dreux* (Paris, 1631).

Durand, Paul, "Eglise de Saint-Père à Chartres; explication de la nouvelle décoration exécutée dans la chapelle de la Sainte-Vierge," *Société archéologique d'Eure-et-Loir, Mémoires,* III (1863), pp. 298–320.

du Ranquet, Henri, *Les Vitraux de la Cathédrale de Clermont-Ferrand* (Clermont-Ferrand, 1932).

Geijer, Agnes, *Textile Treasures of Uppsala Cathedral* (Stockholm, 1964).

Gillerman, Dorothy et al, *Transformations of the Court Style, Gothic Art in Europe 1270 to 1330,* Rhode Island School of Design (Providence, 1977).

Grodecki, Louis, *Vitraux de France du XIe au XVIe siècle* (Catalog of exposition *Vitraux de France,* Musée des Arts Décoratifs, 1953) (Paris, 1953).

———. *Vitraux des églises de France* (Paris, 1947).

Grodecki, Louis, and Jean Lafond, "Les Vitraux de Notre-Dame et de la Sainte-Chapelle de Paris," *Corpus Vitrearum Medii Aevi,* France I (Paris, 1959).

Gruber, Jean-Jacques, "Quelques aspects de l'art et de la technique du vitrail en France (Dernier tiers du XIIIe siècle, premier tiers du XIVe)," in l'Université de Paris, Faculté des lettres, *Travaux des étudiants du Groupe d'Histoire de l'art* (Paris, 1927–1928), pp. 71–94.

Guérard, Benjamin, *Cartulaire de l'abbaye de Saint-Père de Chartres* (Collection de documents inédits sur l'histoire de France, Première série, Histoire politique, Collection des cartulaires de France, tomes 1–2), 2 vols. (Paris, 1840).

Guibert, Joseph, *Les Dessins d'archéologie de Roger de Gaignières* (Paris, n.d.), Series II, Vitraux, Planches 1 à 100 (Ambroise-Etival).

Guilhermy, Baron François de, "Notes sur diverses localités de la France. Chalons-sur-Marne — Clermont-Ferrand," 1856–1858, Bibl. Nat. nouv. acq. fr. 6098, esp. fols. 197–199r.

Hayward, Jane, "The Choir Windows of Saint-Serge and their Glazing Atelier," *Gesta,* XV (1976), pp. 255–264.

Hayward, Jane and Louis Grodecki, "Les vitraux de la cathédrale d'Angers," *Bulletin monumental,* CXXIV (1966), pp. 7–67.

Helbig, Jean, *Les vitraux médiévaux conservés en Belgique 1200–1500, Corpus Vitrearum Medii Aevi* Belgique I (Brussels, 1961).

Héliot, Pierre and Georges Jouven, "L'église Saint-Pierre de Chartres et l'architecture du moyen âge," *Bulletin archéologique du Comité des travaux historiques et scientifiques,* nouv. sér., VI (1970), pp. 117–177.

Hennecke, Edgar, *New Testament Apocrypha,* ed. W. Schneemelcher (Philadelphia, 1963).

Hinkle, William M., "The Iconography of the Four Panels by the Master of Saint Giles," *Journal of the Warburg-Courtauld Institutes,* XXVIII (1965), esp. pp. 112ff.

James, Montague Rhodes, trans., *The Apocryphal New Testament* (Oxford, 1953) corrected ed.

Jossier, l'Abbé O.-F., *Monographie des vitraux de Saint-Urbain de Troyes* (Troyes, 1912).

Jusselin, Maurice, "Les Peintres-verriers à Chartres au XVIe siècle," *Société archéologique d'Eure-et-Loir, Mémoires,* XVI (1931), pp. 153–254.

———. "Un Donateur pour les verrières de Saint-Père de Chartres au début du XIVe siècle," *Bulletin monumental,* LXXXIX (1930), pp. 540–541.

King, Donald, *Opus Anglicanum,* Victoria and Albert Museum (London, 1963).

Lafond, Jean, "La Famille Pinaigrier et le vitrail parisien au XVIe et au XVIIe siècles," *Bulletin de la Société de l'histoire de l'art français* (1957), pp. 63–75.

———. "Le Vitrail du XIVe siècle en France," in Louise Lefrançois-Pillion, *L'art du XIVe siècle en France* (Paris, 1954), pp. 187–238.

———. "Le Vitrail en Normandie de 1250 à 1300," *Bulletin monumental,* CXI (1953), pp. 317–358.

———. "Les Vitraux de l'abbaye de la Trinité de Fécamp," ch. XLVIII of *Fécamp, l'abbaye bénédictine, ouvrage scientifique du treizième centenaire, 658–1958,* III (Fécamp, 1961), pp. 97–120, 253–264 and Addenda p. 105.

———. "Les Vitraux de la cathédrale de Sées," *Congrès archéologique,* CXI (1953), pp. 59–83.

———. "Les Vitraux de la cathédrale Saint-Etienne d'Auxerre," *Congrès archéologique,* CXVI (1958), pp. 60–67.

———. "Les Vitraux de la cathédrale Saint-Pierre de Troyes," *Congrès archéologique,* CXIII (1955), pp. 29–62.

———. *Les Vitraux de l'église Saint-Ouen de Rouen, Corpus Vitrearum Medii Aevi* France IV (Paris, 1970).

Lecocq, Ad., "Dissertation historique et archéologique sur la question: "Où est l'emplacement du tombeau de Fulbert, évêque de Chartres, au XIe siècle?", *Société archéologique d'Eure-et-Loir, Mémoires,* V (1877), esp. pp. 310–321.

———. "Monuments chartrains de la collection Gaignières," *Société archéologique d'Eure-et-Loir, Procès-verbaux,* III (1868), pp. 238–243.

Ledit, Chanoine Charles J., "Le Samit de Troyes" and Marguerite Dubuisson, "La Chape pontificale de Montiéramey," *Zodiaque,* LXVII (Jan. 1966), pp. 2–14 and pls.

Lillich, Meredith Parsons, "The Band Window: A Theory of Origins and Development, *Gesta,* IX (1970), pp. 26–33.

———. "The Choir Clerestory Windows of La Trinité at Vendôme: Dating and Patronage," *Journal of the Society of Architectural Historians,* XXXIV (1975), pp. 238–250.

———. "Découverte d'un vitrail perdu de Saint-Père de Chartres," *Société archéologique d'Eure-et-Loir, Mémoires* (année 108, no. 13, 1964), pp. 264–268.

———. "Les donateurs de quelques vitraux de la nef de Saint-Père de Chartres," *Bulletin des Sociétés archéologiques d'Eure-et-Loir, Mémoires,* XLVI (1972), pp. 287–302.

———. "An Early Image of Saint Louis," *Gazette des beaux-arts,* LXXV (1970), pp. 251–256.

———, ed. *Medieval Art in Upstate New York,* Everson Museum of Art (Syracuse, New York, 1974).

———. "A Redating of the Thirteenth Century Grisaille Windows of Chartres Cathedral," *Gesta,* XI (1972), pp. 11–18.

———. "A Stained Glass Apostle from Sées Cathedral (Normandy) in the Victoria and Albert Museum," *Burlington Magazine,* CXIX (1977), pp. 497–501 and pl. opp. p. 470.

———. "Three Essays on French Thirteenth Century Grisaille Glass," *Journal of Glass Studies,* XV (1973), pp. 69–78.

———. "Les Vitraux de la nef de Saint-Père de Chartres: Analyse stylistique," *Bulletin des Sociétés archéologiques d'Eure-et-Loir, Mémoires,* XXV (1971), pp. 207–237.

———. "Les vitraux de Saint-Pierre de Chartres," *Les monuments historiques de la France,* no. 1 (1977), pp. 52–57.

Lorin, Charles, "Les Vitraux de moyen âge, ceux de Chartres en particulier," *Société archéologique d'Eure-et-Loir, Le Cinquantenaire,* I (1906), esp. p. 465.

———. "Médaillon du XIIe siècle dans l'église Saint-Pierre de Chartres," *Société archéologique d'Eure-et-Loir, Le Cinquantenaire,* I (1906), pp. 508–514.

Mâle, Emile, "Histoire et légende de l'apôtre saint André dans l'art," *Revue des deux-mondes* (October 1951), pp. 412–420.

———. *Les Saints compagnons du Christ* (Paris, 1958).

Martin, Henry, *Légende de Saint Denis* (Paris, 1908).

Merlet, Lucien and E. Bellier de la Chavignerie, "Documents sur des travaux exécutés à Notre-Dame de Chartres et dans d'autres églises du pays chartrain pendant le seizième siècle," *Archives de l'art français,* VII (1855–1856), esp. pp. 384–390.

Merlet, René, "Visite des monuments de Chartres, Saint-Père-en-Vallée," *Congrès archéologique,* LXVII (1900), pp. 51–52.

Michon, Louis-Marie, "L'Abbaye de Saint-Père de Chartres, étude archéologique sur l'église abbatiale et les bâtiments monastiques," thesis, Ecole des Chartes, 1922 (summarized in *Positions des thèses,* 1922, pp. 95–103).

Montfaucon, Dom Bernard de, *Les Monumens de la monarchie françoise,* II (Paris, 1730).

Muley, Dom Charles, copy of the abbey archives made for King Louis XIV, 1772–1775, Chartres, Bibl. mun., ms. 1136. (Included in Guérard.)

Oliver, Judith, "The 'Lambert-le-Bègue' Psalters: A Study in Thirteenth Century Mosan Illumination," dissertation, Columbia University, 1976.

Paris, Bibl. Nat., Dept. des Manuscrits, *Vie et histoire de Saint Denys,* pref. by Henri Omont (Paris, 1905).

Pasquier, l'Abbé Victor, *L'Eglise et l'abbaye de Saint-Pierre de Chartres, notice historique et guide* (Chartres, 1921).

Poisson, l'Abbé Jean-Charles-Benjamin, *Chroniques de l'abbaye royale de Saint-Père-en-Vallée* (Chartres, 1857).

———. "Inventaire de Saint-Père," *Annales archéologiques,* VII (1850), p. 190.

Popesco, Paul, "Les panneaux de vitrail du XIIe siècle de l'église Saint-Pierre de Chartres, ancienne abbatiale," *Revue de l'art,* X (1970), pp. 47–56.

Pseudo-Bonaventura, *Meditations on the Life of Christ,* Isa Ragusa, trans., and Rosalie Green, ed. (Princeton, 1961).

Ritter, Georges, *Les Vitraux de la cathédrale de Rouen* (Cognac, 1926).

Sauvel, Tony, "Le crucifiement de Saint Pierre," *Bulletin monumental,* XCVII (1938), pp. 337–352.

Schiller, Gertrud, *Iconography of Christian Art,* I–II (Greenwich, Conn., 1971–1972).

Sommers, Georgia Wright, "The Tomb of Saint Louis," *Journal of the Warburg-Courtauld Institutes,* XXXIV (1971), pp. 65–82.

Verdier, Philippe, *Art and the Courts, France and England from 1259 to 1328,* National Gallery of Canada (Ottawa, 1972).

Viollet-le-Duc, Eugène, *Dictionnaire raisonné de l'architecture française du XIe au XVIe siècle,* IX (Paris, 1868), pp. 373–462 ("Vitrail.")

Voragine, Jacopus de, *The Golden Legend,* trans. Granger Ryan and Helmut Ripperger (London, 1941).

Wentzel, Hans, *Die Glasmalereien in Schwaben von 1200–1350, Corpus Vitrearum Medii Aevi* Deutschland I (Berlin, 1958).

General Index

A separate Index of Monuments and Works of Art will be found following this General Index.

Index of Monuments & Works of Art

The Stained Glass of Saint-Père de Chartres

---

was composed in Baskerville and Bulmer types, and printed by offset lithography on Mohawk Superfine, soft white. Color plates, from photographic transparencies, were printed on Warren's Lustro Offset Enamel Dull. Composition by Connecticut Printers; printing by The Meriden Gravure Company; binding by the Tapley-Rutter Company.

WESLEYAN UNIVERSITY PRESS

Middletown, Connecticut

MCMLXXVIII